The Blue Queen

By Scott F. Nielsen

I would like to dedicate this book to all of the victims of the MKUltra program or any of the other shady shit that the CIA did, and is perhaps still doing. Unfortunately, CIA director Richard Helms destroyed virtually all MKUltra files in 1973. Many believe that to this day, there are still offshoots of the MKUltra program in existence.

Chapter 1

Sometime in 1997

He was sitting in a bar, he wasn't sure where, but somewhere outside of the United States. He had no idea how he got here. It was dark in the place, but there were several lights in the corners spinning around the room, and floodlights trained on the dancers. The dancers were all tiny and Asian. The Philippines.

What was the name of the bar? It had been a long time, but he had definitely been here before. He was here with Viggie and John. Abe had suggested the place. It still wasn't coming to him. The bar was also the name of the band; there were several of those in Olongapo City. Credence? The Who? The Rolling Stone. That was it.

He wasn't used to his memory failing him. It always happened for a few hours after...after...it was useless, he couldn't remember. Normally, he remembered everything, no matter how insignificant. He was sure it would return, it would just take some time.

The last thing he remembered was talking to Murphy. He was a little foggy. Like someone hit him in the head a little too hard. The mental haze, as well as the memory loss were courtesy of Murphy. The spinning lights weren't helping.

Just then he noticed her. One of the dancers was walking towards him. She had a huge smile on her face. He was instantly on guard. He hated it when it happened this way. He couldn't return quietly, on his own terms, Murphy put him in a potentially dangerous situation without a second thought. Not having his memory was also problematic.

It was coming back in small drips. P.I., the Rolling Stone, Viggie, John, the lights.

The woman was no threat, he knew that. She was wearing a bikini, and a pretty skimpy one at that. No place for concealed weapons.

When she smiled her dimples appeared in an appealing way. She looked like Jenna. Who was Jenna? From back in Bremerton...no, further back, Ann Arbor. It came back to him slowly. Jenna was his wife. Was he still married to her?

There was a familiar song in the background.

If you're down and confused
And you can't remember
Who you're talkin' to
Concentration slips away'
Cuz your baby is so far away
Well there's a rose in a fisted glove
And the eagle flies with the dove
And if you can't be with the one you love
Honey love the one you're with
Love the one you're with
Love the one you're with
Love the one you're with

He knew he had heard this before, but he couldn't remember when. It went with this bar, and everything else that was here. It was a small piece of the puzzle that he was putting together.

Don't be angry, don't be sad
Don't sit cryin'
about the good times you had

As the woman approached, he didn't think too much about it. After all, he was in P.I. and that's what they do. He was sitting in a booth, and she slid in right beside him.

"Erik!" she said. "I can't believe! You come back me!"

Should I know her? She seems to know me, she knows my name. He looked her over. She was definitely attractive. She had a thin streak of light blue in her hair, and the rest was jet black. Like Jenna. But Jenna's was grey. It was hereditary, from her father's side. The lights had changed to red, green, and white. He caught a brief glimpse of a red, green, and white taxi with a heavyset Italian man at the wheel.

Suddenly he was on his Harley, with Jenna riding on the back, her head on his shoulder.

"I missed you, Erik." she said.

"Are you ok?" he asked.

They were approaching an apartment building with the red, green, and white Christmas lights still on. They passed a

Cadillac with 4 men sitting in it. It all came back to him. Jenna was dead. She had set him up, and paid with her life. A flash of the carnage on Pacific Ave. appeared. He was lucky to get out alive.

The woman from the bar was looking at him expectantly.

There's a girl right next to you
And she's just waiting
for something to do

"I'm sorry, sometimes I have issues with my memory. It will come back. I'm sure we know each other, but I can't recall." he said.

"Oh, sure you can, Erik! You spent the whole fucking week with her last time." It was Abe. He and John were here after all. But wasn't he out of the Navy now? He couldn't remember. What was he doing here? Abe was dead, he remembered that, but he didn't know how he knew.

"You no remember Elvie?" said the girl. "Really?"

He looked at her again. Another flash hit him. He was standing in front of a jewelry shop display in Manila. There were several gaudy engagement rings and a few necklaces. One necklace stood out, on a silver chain with a black pearl mounted on a tiny half shell.

Now he was looking at her again, and that same pearl was nestled between her breasts. It came back to him now.

He met her on his first trip to P.I., and they had a wild week. But there was something else...he couldn't remember.

"Of course, Elvie, I bought you that necklace in Manila." he said.

"*YES!* You still have mine?" she asked.

He looked at the stage, trying to buy some time. He saw a flash of her dancing; she had a cowry shell necklace on a leather strap.

"The shell...the cowry shell." he said.

"Yes! You remember!" she said.

"You know, Erik, if you don't do it, I probably will." said Viggie. "After all, what happens here doesn't really happen. This is our place to be ourselves and relax. She looks spectacular. Why do they always gravitate to you?"

“There’s nothing to worry about anyway, Abe, Jenna’s dead, remember?” he said. “I’m no longer a married man.”

“That’s right, that whole thing was *your* fault, wasn’t it?” he asked.

“I don’t remember.” he said.

It sounded weak, but it was the truth.

“You no married now?” asked Elvie hopefully.

“Now you’ve done it.” said Abe. “What have I told you about talking about marriage in front of them? No good can come of it.”

Another woman entered the bar. Every single male head in the place turned and followed her path, even the ones with two girls on their laps.

Erik noticed a redheaded man with a goatee and an eyepatch a few tables away from him. There was a beautiful woman sitting with him, looking a little uncomfortable. He felt that he should know who these people are, but he didn’t.

Another flash.

“Espece de connard, You Americans! You think you own the world! You’re so arrogant! You play such a horrible hand and suck out on the river and you think you know how to play the game! You just cost me almost 2500 Francs! Va te faire encouler! You better watch yourself, pretty boy, as long as you’re in Monte Carlo!”

Pierre DuBois. He killed him seven, almost eight years ago. What was he doing here? And who was the girl?

The woman was coming straight to his table. Did he know her too? He hoped so.

“Let’s go.” she said. “Murphy needs us.”

“No, he stay.” said Elvie. “You *my* man.”

She had a cute little pout, which caused her dimples to appear in spite of her mood.

The other woman unbuttoned her overcoat and exposed a very large handgun.

“Sweetheart, I could take you apart without the benefit of this.” she said. “I don’t even need a knife. Whatever you think is happening here, I can assure you that it’s not.”

She reached in her pocket and produced a huge roll of 100 peso notes. She peeled off 7 or 8 and threw them at Elvie.

“There’s your bar fine, *NOW SCRAM!*” she said. Elvie scuttled away, picking up the bills as she went, but looked determined to return at first opportunity.

Viggie shrugged his shoulders.

“I tried.” he said. “We’re all in on it, you know. Do you really think I have the kind of pull with the Merchants to get you orders that quickly? That was Murphy.”

“Stop.” said the woman. “He doesn’t need this.”

“No, he’s right.” said John. “The cat’s out of the bag. He knows everything.”

I actually know nothing, thought Erik.

Just then, DuBois started laughing uncontrollably. The woman sitting with him...Dana, Donna, Diane...he couldn’t remember. Something with a ‘D’. She looked very troubled.

The beautiful woman in one swift motion drew her hand cannon and put one between Pierre’s eyes.

“Some people don’t have the sense to stay dead.” she said. “I suppose your amnesia includes me too?”

“I want to remember.” said Erik.

“He needs to know everything.” said Abe. “That’s what I was trying to do. We’re all in on it.”

“Do you remember what I said about staying dead?” she asked.

She was staring daggers through Viggie.

He held up his hands.

“Sorry, I’m just trying to help.” he said. “He’s going to find out eventually.”

“He doesn’t need your kind of help.” she said.

“What about me?” asked the woman sitting next to DuBois. “Where do I fit in?”

“Aren’t you dead too?” she asked. “You were the last time I checked.”

“That wasn’t confirmed.” she said.

“Claudette made the ID. You’re toast.” she said.

“And you know why she did that.” she said. “You know I’m alive.”

“And we both know that you need to stay dead.” she said. “Do I need to tell Murphy about this?”

She looked away.

“That’s what I thought.” she said.

"All you really need to know, the *only thing* you need know to set yourself free is 'The red kna..."

Viggie didn't get the rest out before a bullet parted his skull.

"Should have stayed dead too." she quipped.

"Are you going to come easy, or do we have to do it the other way?" she asked. "Forget about her, she's dead."

It finally came back to him. Lexie Tenenzapf. And the girl was Danielle.

"It is you!" he said. "You were there the night I killed DuBois. I knew it!"

"She can't confirm that." said Lexie. "We need to go. Murphy is waiting."

Danielle was looking at him in misery. Lexie was right, all of the evidence said that she was dead.

"Erik! Erik! Wake up!" she said. "It's not too late, you just need to wake up."

"That's enough!" said Lexie.

She turned and put a bullet between Danielle's eyes. As she slumped to the floor, he woke up.

He looked to the other side of the bed at Taylor, she was fast asleep.

This wasn't the first time. The deeper he got, the weirder the dreams. Why did she shoot Abe? It made sense in a strange way, he really was dead. Or was he?

What was that thing he was trying to say when he got it? The red...what? He didn't know why it seemed important, it just did. Certainly meaningless, like everything else.

What about Danielle? Lexie shot her too. Did that mean she was dead too? Of course she is, Claudette confirmed it. But she called him. Didn't say much, but enough to confirm she was alive.

"And you *know* why she did that, I'm alive." said Danielle.

Another flash.

Was she still alive?

Taylor began stirring a little.

"What are you doing up?" she asked.

"Another dream." he said.

"Where you couldn't remember?" she asked "What a joke."

“I was in the Philippines this time. John and Abe were there. And this girl I spent some time with over there. And DuBois! Fucking DuBois! What was he doing there?” he said.

“Was she there?” asked Taylor.

“Lexie? Sure, she makes an appearance in almost all of these.” he said.

“I don’t care about her. Was *she* there?” she asked.

“Babe, it’s just a dream.” he said. “I have no control over it. Why do you care so much?”

“You know why. It’s her. *You loved her*.” she said. “You’re holding onto that fucking cameo like it’s the crown jewels. On your keychain, so she’s always with you. She was the one. I’m just sloppy seconds.”

“She’s dead.” he said. “What does it matter? You know why I keep the cameo, it’s all I have left.”

“You said yourself that you had your doubts.” she said. “You swore that you saw her at the cottage after you killed DuBois. It makes sense that she could still be alive. Remember that liaison officer you were so suspicious about? That’s just the kind of thing that Murphy would do. And one day you just bump into her at the casino in Monte Carlo, and I lose.”

He had told her way too much, obviously. He would have to watch that in the future. It was disturbing how jealous she was of Danielle. It was wearing on his nerves and driving a huge wedge between them.

“So she’s working for Murphy now? Do you know how ridiculous you sound? For all I know, Murphy has been fucking with me for years.” he said. “Remember that ‘summer camp’ I told you about? I’m pretty sure the first time he used the MK Ultra shit on me. He mentioned it. I’ve done some research. The only problem is, all of the information is gone. Burned to ashes by the CIA, and not only that, the narrative is that it never happened. Yet it still happens to this day. Do you think the CIA would let anyone find it?”

“I just need to know that if she ever pops up somewhere, you’ll still be mine.” she said.

“It’s not going to happen.” he said.

“Say you’ll be mine.” she said.

“I’m yours, always.” he said.

“Thank you.” she said.

She knew how she sounded. Her father would have said she was hysterical. She couldn't help being worried, though. His work. Could he even call it work? It was dangerous, and it frequently put beautiful women in front of him. And Danielle. He could say what he wants, but if she *is* alive...I can't compete. Worse yet, I can't even compete with a ghost now.

"Hey." he said.

I'm never *that* girl. I'll be lucky if he doesn't dump her. Time to backpedal.

"I'm sorry, Erik, I don't know what came over me." she said.

"I love you. You have nothing to worry about." he said. "I can't control my dreams. She's almost certainly going to make an occasional appearance."

"And what about the other stuff? The club?" she asked.

"It fills my need for brotherhood." he said. "You know that. I've always had that...until now. I don't stay on one ship long enough to connect with anyone. What's this about?"

"I'm embarrassed." she said. "You're right, I do sound ridiculous. Even hysterical. And over what? A silly dream? Your riding buddies?"

"Did you go back to the 70s for that word?" he asked. "That's what my dad used to say to my mom. 'Dorte, you're being hysterical!' Except in Danish."

"It's exactly what my father would say about me right now." she said.

"I know this isn't you, Taylor." he said. "You know better. *It was just a dream.* I don't mind allowing you a little hysteria, but please stay in the world of reality. I know one thing. I'll be hearing from Murphy soon. He always calls when this happens. He's not a big believer in dreams."

"Neither am I." she said. "But it could mean something if you hear from him after."

"Not every time...but you know I have these dreams on a pretty consistent basis." he said. "Maybe that's why it seems like I hear from him after. Because I always have them and he's always calling me."

"Let him try. He'll never get past me." she said.

"You know as well as I do that he doesn't need your permission. If you try to get in the way, he'll just go around you." he said. "You forget who we're talking about. If he wants to talk to me, he will. There's no stopping him. Besides, it's my job."

"Your job is to be a sailor in the Merchant Marines." she said.

She really was sounding bitchy and demanding. There had been a lot of that lately. It was getting old.

"You're mixing that up again." he said. "*That's my cover.* The only reason I'm with them is so Murphy can maneuver me around. You know that. I thought we were good with this."

Taylor knew that she had lost. This is Erik. I can have him like this or not at all. Would he even care if he lost her? She had to wonder. But he keeps coming back, and tells me he loves me. That was a major breakthrough. She said it for 6 months before she even got a "me too".

"I'm sorry, Erik." she said. "Please grant me a do over for this day. I don't know what's wrong with me. It doesn't help that my period started yesterday."

He pantomimed erasing a blackboard.

"There. All gone." he said. "I must caution you that I don't grant do overs lightly. You have amnesty for the rest of the day, but if you ask for another tomorrow, we're going to have a problem."

He was going to let her off the hook, but he wished he had a built in excuse for bad behavior like being on the rag.

"Trust me, I won't abuse it." she said. "Give me an hour and I'll be right as rain. What does that mean, anyway, right as rain?"

"My guess is that it doesn't mean anything. There are literally hundreds of idioms that start with 'right as'." he said. "It probably caught on due to the pleasant sounding alliteration."

"You never cease to amaze me, Erik Stryker." she said. "You truly know everything about nothing, down to the most trivial detail."

"Triviality is my specialty." he said. "I know just enough to dazzle my friends with my expertise on nothing."

"You're too modest." she said. "You occasionally decipher things that can loosely be defined as something."

"You're going to be late for class." he said.

"I know. You're really okay?" she said. "About what I said earlier?"

"I don't recall that conversation." he said.

"You're the best." she said. "I need to get ready."

"Don't let me stop you." he said.

She left in what seemed to be a better mood, but he honestly couldn't tell anymore. This new clinginess was disturbing. Maybe she's just going through a phase. In another week, she'll be right as rain.

The phone rang, as if on schedule.

"Anthony. What can I do for you?" he said.

"Strange. I don't speak a word, yet you know it's me." he said.

"Are your ears burning, Murph?" he said. "We were just talking about you."

"You and Taylor? How is Miss Bremerton?" he asked.

"I'll pretend you care and tell you that she's feeling needy of late." he said. "And how's Miss...oh...right...you don't have one."

"Keeps things simple, my friend." he said. "When would I have time? How are things with the club?"

"Why? Do you think you have what it takes to be a Centurion?" he asked.

"Probably not." he said. "But I could have all of you killed with one phone call. But back to reality. What's going on?"

"They voted me in as Sergeant-at-Arms at the last church." he said. "There's some chatter about guns, they may be making the trip over."

"I'm so proud of you, Erik." he said. "You're moving up in the world."

"I take it you know what I had to do to get here?" he asked.

"Surely nothing you haven't done before." he said. "If they only knew."

"It isn't like he was a choir boy." he said. "Whether I came along or not, his days were numbered. Cost of doing business. They like to do it that way. An initiation kill that helps the club."

"A solid business model." he said. "Let me know who's coming over as soon as you know."

"Sure." he said.

"Probably either way, you'll be making the trip." he said. "We can't risk you doing it stateside. Too many people know you here. Besides, we want all of them. We may have to kill you. That would be the safest way."

"All the way? With *everyone*? Even Taylor?" he asked.

"It has to be convincing." he said. "What did you say? Needy? Maybe this is good timing."

"It would destroy her." he said. "Please don't make me do that. There has to be another way."

"I do this with operatives all the time, Erik." he said.

"It's usually best. The mission may require it. We all know what that means."

"Let's look for another way." he said. "I'm willing to sacrifice a little safety not to crush Taylor."

"The mission." he said. "Keep me posted. We have eyes in Belfast as well."

"You have eyes everywhere." he said.

"I'm serious, Stryker. If we have to do it my way, that's how it's going to be." he said. "Remember our conversation about serious relationships?"

"How could I forget?" he said. "It was after you used that MK shit on me for the first time...I think. Try explaining that one to Miss Bremerton."

"Think of a situation where you didn't have to explain it to anybody. Wouldn't that be ideal? I have a job to do, Erik." he said. "I will use any tools at my disposal to complete it. I like you. But that's not ever going to stop me from doing what I need to do. Besides, you never know who might show up. There may come a day that you leave Taylor for someone new...or old. Who knows? I'll be in touch."

The line went dead.

It was obvious that Murphy expected him to end things with Taylor.

"Keeps it simple my friend."

He grabbed his boots and sat down. Huckleberry, the cat immediately sat down directly in front of him in an attempt to prevent him from putting on his boots. He figured that if he can stop Erik from putting on his boots, he can stop him from leaving.

"Sorry, little man, I have to go." he said. "As a human, there are things I have to do. You don't know how good you have it."

He gently nudged Huck out of the way and put his boots on.

He grabbed his cut. It had the word "Centurions" on the top rocker, "Washington" on the bottom rocker, and a picture of a Roman Centurion head facing upwards, with a red vertical crest splitting the bronze helmet, bronze neck and face protectors, the eyes hidden by a bronze visor, and a stoic look on the Centurion's face. The letters MC were in the lower right hand corner of the cut.

He went out and got on his bike. It felt good to be able to do that. The reason he was with the Centurions was Murphy. He was undercover. It wasn't much of a stretch. His natural personality was pretty close to outlaw biker, although he was nicer than most. At least he used to be. That was part of the deception. He had to prove himself all the time, and he never failed. He was in deep. The line was constantly blurred as to which side he was on.

Taylor thought what he wanted her to think. Yes, he had gotten better at *that*. It would have had to change or end. In the beginning, he couldn't get anything past her, but you keep doing the same thing long enough, you get good at it. He had her convinced that he was involved for the brotherhood with a twist of wild oats.

She knew nothing about his dealings with the MC, none of the violence, criminal behavior, or the women. She knew nothing of any of it.

After the way it was when they first met, he was astonished that he could keep it from her. Now, there were huge swatches of his life that she knew nothing about. She just thought that the club were his riding buddies. All the tatts just enthusiasm I guess.

Did she know more? If she did, she hid it well. He figured there was no way she would put up with it if she knew the whole truth. Hell, she was still upset about Danielle, and for all she knew, the woman was dead. He tried not to think about how stupid she would have to be to not know that at least *something* wasn't right. She was by no means stupid. So she must know. Maybe not. If she knew, she wouldn't be able to hold the impending tirade in.

It seemed to him that they were growing apart. What would he do about Murphy's suggestion (or more accurately potential demand)?

If they did kill him, he would have to prepare her in advance. Would he have to break up with her? Move away? Or do it the easy way and just disappear? If Murphy did it, it would be convincing. She would really think (know) that he was dead. There wouldn't be any letting her in on it. He would never be able to come back.

What a fucking mess. Maybe Murph was right, maybe it is time. We had a good run. Nothing too low, but she had become a little...well needy. Dependent. Clingy. Things seemed to be going in the wrong direction. He couldn't fault her, this is what chicks do. It just wasn't working for him.

He could have taken the ferry over, but as he often did, he took the 101 to the southern edge of the sound, and then took the 5 north, past Olympia, through Tacoma and into Seattle.

The clubhouse didn't look like what it was. It was a small building with a big parking lot near the water, and when you entered it looked like a bar. There were, of course, other rooms in the building, like the meeting room with the huge table with a centurion, identical to the cut, carved in the middle of it where they held church. John had the gavel for the past 14 years, and before him, his father Will. He was killed in a bar fight in 1983.

It wasn't a dynasty, it just takes a different kind of person to be a biker. Some may have felt that the gavel was John's birthright. Some felt safer with the son of a good leader, and felt that John must have inherited Will's better qualities. Some were superstitious, some didn't want to lead. The main thing was that they all agreed.

That, of course, wasn't always the case. There was plenty of internal strife, power struggles, and jealousy. If you wanted something, you had better be prepared to fight (sometimes to the death) to get it. As Sergeant-at-Arms, it sometimes fell on Erik to settle disputes. That was never a problem. His brothers knew that if necessary, *he* would settle it, with the serious potential for people getting hurt. When Erik fought, it tended to be all the way. He had sent many to long term hospital stays. Most weren't members, but membership didn't get you a pass if he thought you were wrong. It would be inappropriate to say that they were scared of him, however, nobody ever argued with him.

All it took was one time, while Erik was still making his bones. Erik knew what he needed to do to prove himself. While his opponent was talking, Erik showed him that the time for talking was over. He grabbed the guy's (Jerry's) head and proceeded to pummel it into the bar repeatedly. He didn't stop when Jerry was unconscious. He kept going until he they pulled him off. Jerry was in intensive care for six weeks. The guys in the club were awestruck. It sent a pretty strong message.

He didn't need to do that stuff too often, but now and then, people would forget, or just want to test him. He always answered the bell, and the fights were never close. Lately, he had a hard time controlling it. He seemed to put someone in the hospital once every two weeks or so. Jerry apologized when he got out of the hospital, but by then, Erik was over it. It was odd that Jerry apologized to him under the circumstances. It created an awkward moment for everyone involved. The following day, they found Jerry's cut and a gun that was club property at the back door. There was a note.

"My brothers, I apologize for everything. This isn't the life for me."

Erik wasn't trying to get rid of him, he just said something inappropriate, and he felt that Jerry needed his face beaten in. All was forgiven after he got out of the hospital, but he didn't want to stay. Fights among brothers were a common occurrence. He had a hard time calling this one a fight though.

He approached the parking lot and rode in front of the spot he wanted to park, then backed in with his feet. He entered the clubhouse, and surveyed the situation. As usual it was dark, with a few well-placed lights, a few members sitting around, playing cards, a prospect tending bar, and a few women. One in particular caught his eye. A true beauty. She was wearing blue jeans, and a Nirvana tee shirt cut off at the midriff. She had long dark hair, with streaks of blond here and there. She looked familiar. Really familiar. She saw him and approached.

"Are you the guy?" she asked.

"What guy?" he asked.

"The badass who beat up my brother?" she said. "You might have to answer for that."

"I fight a lot." he said. "Can you be more specific?"

"He was a Centurion. Name of Jerry." she said. "Did you do that?"
"*Was* a Centurion is right." he said. "He walked away like a pussy. So he sends his sister? I have to admit, you look tougher."
"You have no idea." she said. "Can we go somewhere and talk? I don't want to embarrass you."
The others were hanging on every word at this point. Who is this bitch? Is it really Jerry's sister?
"Anything you have to say you can say here and now." he said. "You look tough, but after all, you're from the same gene pool as Jerry."
She wound up to punch him, but he caught her hand and quickly twisted it behind her back.
"You telegraph. That's your problem." he said. "I knew you were going to try to hit me before you did. Anyone in the crib?"
The prospect looked at him nervously.
"Brendan was using it because he was fighting with his old lady, but he hasn't been in there since Thursday." he said.
"Good, leave us alone." he said.
He led her into the interior of the building, and everyone went back to what they were doing, no one even wanting to give the slightest hint that they cared about him and this woman.
He walked her into the crib.
"You can let go now." she said.
"Relax, it has to look real." he said. "Sometimes there are people back here."
"What? You going to hit me in the face next?" she said.
"You should have seen what I did to your brother." he said. "What brings you to my world, Lexie?"

Chapter 2

"So Brendan has an old lady?" she asked.

"Why would you care?" he asked. "Most of us do, at least officially."

"Does that include you, Stryker?" she asked. "You still stuck on Taylor?"

"She's still around." he said, noncommittally. "Did they run out of Arabs? What brings you to the Pacific Northwest?"

"The Arabs are procreating like rabbits, so there's no shortage." she said. "I got in a little scrape with my people, that's why I got sent here. Brendan was supposed to be my assignment, that's why I care. Apparently he has a high ranking uncle in the Irish Republican Army."

"So what? You think you come in here, bang him good a few times, then he rolls on his uncle?" he asked. "You have a lot to learn about biker culture. Old ladies aren't in the loop. They're there for other reasons."

"That's not what concerns me. Do you really think he doesn't know that Brendan has an old lady?" she said. "I can still get what I need from him. Besides, under the circumstances, he wants two of us here."

"I'm sure he does know. Who knows why he sent you here? Did you see them out there?" he said. "I don't need you. I got this."

"The mission." she said.

"You sound just like him." he said. "I just talked to him today. Why didn't he mention that you were coming?"

It dawned on him that Murphy might have been hinting at that very thing when he said "There may come a day that you leave Taylor entirely for someone new...or old."

"Who knows?" she said. "I've given up trying to figure Anthony Murphy out. Honestly, I don't need to get next to Brendan at all. You're in a better position to get information from him. He just wants me here. It will probably make sense when the time comes."

"You might have a hard time understanding him anyway." he said. "He has a pretty thick brogue."

"Aye, but you forget, boyo." she said. "I speak 7 languages fluently, and Irish is only English with a wee bit Celt mixed in. I'll be fine, laddie."

She winked at him.

He had no idea where that came from. She had mimicked the brogue perfectly. She could have been Brendan's sister.

"Amazing." he said. "The Nirvana shirt is a nice touch. Part of your cover?"

"Hey! I've liked Nirvana for years." she said. "But when in Rome..."

She peeled off her shirt and started unbuttoning her jeans. She still looked great, even better than before. Maybe Murphy *was* right.

"You're on, Stryker." she said. "Make me scream, and remember, it needs to sound believable. I want to walk back in there satisfied. They'll be able to tell if it's fake."

Could he have sent her out here just to get rid of Taylor? It wasn't out of the realm of possibility. He had heard of more twisted things.

"You seem pretty confident." he said.

"I always have been." she said. "Besides, if I don't leave here either fucked or dead, your boys lose respect for you."

Any resistance he may have been planning flew away like a sparrow. She was right. He couldn't walk back out there without one of those two things happening, and he couldn't kill her. Maybe the quasi-fight he had with Taylor clouded his judgement, but he didn't think so. This felt right. Things between them were bad for a while now. And it was never anything but great between him and Lexie. Of course they weren't together for long...

"You misunderstand. Just because I say you seem confident, doesn't mean I'm not going to do it." he said. "After all, I'm only human. And I'm a guy, which allows, almost demands that I throw caution to the wind in this situation. How long has it been?"

He started taking his clothes off.

"Too long since I've been fucked the right way." she said.

No warning. Lexie. Naked in front of him. He had tried to be faithful to Taylor...mostly. In this case, he had to. The mission. He wasn't complaining.

Being an outlaw biker put him in these situations frequently, as did his work for Murphy. He told her that she could, that there would need to be special rules when he was on the road (probably should have included at home after he became a Centurion). He gave his blessing, she just never took advantage. He felt a slight pang of guilt knowing that she had never done it. He had lost track of how many times it had been for him.

As he laid down, Lexie straddled him. She was looking deep into his eyes. He thought he saw something there. Something...something that told him that everything was all right.

This is what you're supposed to be doing. I'm yours, always. It wasn't that he needed to hear it, but it felt pretty good. Didn't hear it, but he heard it.

He had thought about her quite a bit after their assignment together. Even after he got home and was with Taylor for a while.

Yes, he had to admit, he even thought of her after Danielle. That call...she was alive. And scared to talk to him. Of course, Murphy was involved, no doubt.

And Veronika, who was arguably the most beautiful woman that he had ever encountered. He had a brief, torrid affair with her before he had to end it...permanently. Veronika was the target, a Russian spook who had unfortunately, come too close to some potentially harmful intelligence. Murphy couldn't allow her to live.

Erik did the right thing on his own, but he knew that Murphy would activate the MK Ultra if he didn't. That one was tough. It became work, simply because he had developed feelings for the target.

They had a long talk about it afterwards, and he reminded Erik of his responsibility to make the tough choices. He also reminded him that he would intervene with the MK Ultra if necessary. The mind control, other than taking his will away, had some short term physical side effects. He felt lethargic, and he lost memory briefly.

He looked at Lexie. This was one of the good things to come out of his involvement with Murphy.

She was smiling, still looking deep into his eyes.

“Who would have thought this would be happening today?” she said.

“I wasn’t planning on it.” he said. “Lexie…”

She put her finger to his lips.

“Hush. There will be time for that later.” she said.

They made love for more than an hour, and he made sure they could hear it in the bar. When they walked out, there were a lot of blank stares.

“So who’s this, then?” asked Brendan.

“Jerry’s sister, Lexie.” he said. “Lexie, Brendan.”

He gave Erik a quizzical look.

“You mean the Jerry who din’t make it? Spent time ‘n the sick bay, then came back an’ ‘pologized to you for baytin’ up t’bar wit his face?” he said. “Then disappeared, leavin’ his cut at t’ back door. *That* Jerry?”

“The very same.” said Erik.

“Aye! It seems ya have more balls than yer long lost brother, luv!” he said. “Why would ya return to t’ scene o’ the savage baytin’? And why are ya wit t’ miscreant who nearly killed ‘im, like?”

“After Erik explained it to me.” she said. “Well, somehow after hearing his story, I thought it was okay. As a matter of fact, we’re good friends now.”

“I can see that, lassie. We could hear ‘t too.” he said. “Us here in t’ bar, those in t’ parkin’ lot, an’ half the ships at sea! Erik, Explain yerself, son!”

“Well, Brendan, you know, sometimes I have this effect on women.” he said. “It’s a gift.”

“Some gift! Where was *I* when they were passin’ that aut?” he said.

“My guess is that you were in line for brass knuckles when they were passing out the charm.” he said.

“How’s yer brother, lassie?” he asked

“He’s living in Minnesota. Selling insurance.” she said. “Apparently this wasn’t the life for him.”

“Aye, it’s not fer all.” he said. “It takes a special kin’ o’ lad to live this life. But t’ rewards are keen. And the freedom, like. Aye, Erik?”

“Aye.” he agreed. “There’s no other way for me.”

"Prospect! Drinks!" said Brendan. "Let's celebrate! Bushmills Black for me, Bacardi and coke for Erik, and what can we get for you, luv?"

"I'll have what you're having." she said. "But drown it with soda."

"Hold the Coke." said Erik

Brendan looked at her with a little disdain.

"Bushmills needs to stand alone to be truly appreciated, like." he said. "Are you sure about that, lassie?"

"I'm a lightweight." she said. "If we weren't celebrating, I probably wouldn't drink at all."

"It's fine Irish whisky!" he said. "One shot!"

"She said no." Erik said quietly.

Brendan knew that when Erik got quiet it was time to back off. It was the first sign. If he pushed it, he might be the one in intensive care.

"More fer me!" he said.

Just then a beautiful long haired redhead walked in.

"Jenny!" cried Brendan. "Where have you been keepin' yerself, luv?"

"Hi Brendan," she said. "What are you up to?"

He went over to the table she went to, and sat down.

"I thought you didn't drink." he said.

"When the situation requires it I do." she said. "I think this situation qualifies."

"I see." he said.

"Has he ever talked to you about killing me off?" he asked. "You know what I'm talking about, right?"

"Of course." she said. "I've seen him do it with others. Sometimes it's the only way."

"He mentioned it to me today." he said. "Where are you staying?"

"The Fairmont Olympic." she said. "It's not far. On University."

"Swanky." he said. "Right on the water."

"Well, it's no 'Beijing Juba', but I can rough it for a while." she said.

He started laughing.

"That place was great!" he said. "The boy who went into town for food. That dinner was pretty sketchy, but we got real bacon and eggs the following day."

"That was one of the best times of my life." she said. "I love being with you, Erik."

"Me too." he said.

Just then a song came on the jukebox. It was by Bob Seger, A musician who was from Erik's hometown back in Michigan. Every time he heard it he wanted to ride.

Took a look down a westbound road,
Right away I made my choice
Headed out to my big two-wheeler,
I was tired of my own voice
Took a bead on the northern plains
and just rolled that power on

Twelve hours out of Mackinaw City
stopped in a bar to have a brew
Met a girl and we had a few drinks
and I told her what I'd decided to do
She looked out the window a long moment
then she looked into my eyes
She didn't have to say a thing,
I knew what she was thinkin'

"Lexie..." he said.

She put her finger to his lips.

"Shhh. Later." she said.

Roll, roll me away,
won't you roll me away tonight?
I too am lost, I feel double-crossed
and I'm sick of what's wrong and what's right
We never even said a word,
we just walked out and got on that bike
And we rolled
And we rolled clean out of sight
Somewhere along a high road
The air began to turn cold
She said she missed her home
I headed on alone

Stood alone on a mountain top,
starin' out at the Great Divide
I could go east, I could go west,
it was all up to me to decide
Just then I saw a young hawk flyin'
and my soul began to rise
And pretty soon
My heart was singin'

Roll, roll me away,
I'm gonna roll me away tonight
Gotta keep rollin, gotta keep ridin',
keep searchin' till I find what's right
And as the sunset faded
I spoke to the faintest first starlight
And I said next time
Next time
We'll get it right

"Let's get out of here." said Erik.

"*BRENDAN!*" he yelled.

He looked up from what looked like a very intense make out session with Jenny.

"Aye?" he said.

"I'm out." he said. "I'll see you tomorrow...unless...maybe you shouldn't count on me for a few days."

"Aye, brother." he said. "Don't do nothin I wouldn't do. Leaves ya open to almost anythin'. Ya be here fer Liam?"

"When's that happening?' he asked.

"Friday eve, ya have a few days." he said.

"Wouldn't miss it." he said. "Johnny and everyone, eh?"

"Everyone of importance, brother."

"Cheers." he said. "I'll be back in plenty of time."

"I know ya will, lad." he said. "We need you. You take it easy on that little lass, eh?""

"Speak for yourself, laddie, I'm lookin' for more o' what I got this afternawn!" she said. "It's been a wee bit tow long, like!"

Brendan looked at her in shock.

Erik figured this could go one of two ways. Brendan had a good sense of humor, so he figured it would be okay.

"Aye! This one speaks Catholic, son!" he said. "Bring 'er along fer translation when I get too ossified!"

"That would be a full time job, brother." he said. "It's probably a safe bet she'll be around for a while. So drink up, laddie. She can tell me what you mean."

"Aye. Keep the shiny side up, brother!" he said.

"I know you ride better when drunk, but maybe you stay here tonight?" he said.

"Aye, Deirdre has already seen me to the curb so I hafta." he said. "Maybe young Jenny here can provide a wee bit of solace."

"It would be my pleasure." she said.

She took him by the arm and started steering him to the crib.

They walked out and got on Erik's bike. He started it with a loud roar. He put it in gear, and took off.

He got on the 405 north, and took it to 522 northeast to the 2. From there he headed east into the Cascades. Neither of them spoke. They didn't have to. It was perfect.

The sun was setting behind them, and it was starting to get dark. About a half mile ahead there was a hotel with a small diner attached to it.

Her arms were around him tight, and she had her head on his shoulder.

"I missed you Erik." she said.

It was eerie. The exact same words that Jenna spoke to him all of those years ago, yet he decided to give the same response.

"You okay?" he asked.

"Yeah, I just fucked some shit up back home." she said.

"Any way I can help?" he asked.

"No, there isn't anything us mere mortals can do." she said.

"I'm glad you're here." he said. "You hungry?"

"Starved." she said.

He pulled in to the diner. She was shivering a little so he gave her his cut.

"That's a vital part of my cover." he said. "You don't know what I had to do to get it."

"Thank you." she said. "I could make an educated guess."

"I'm sure you would be right on." he said.

They entered the diner and sat down at a booth. The waitress came up, and her nametag declared that she was Danielle.

"Could I get a coffee, cream and sugar, and a slice of that apple pie?" he asked.

"Sure, darlin', and what can I get you ma'am?"

"The same."

She disappeared behind the counter.

"So you're "darlin'" and I'm "ma'am'." she said.

"So it would seem." he said.

"They just throw themselves at you wherever you go, don't they?" she asked.

"What can I say?" he said. "I made sure to get some charm before I got in line for the brass knuckles."

She chuckled a little.

"What you have is beyond charm. Did you catch her nametag?" she asked.

"It wasn't lost on me." he said. "I thought we weren't talking about her."

"I'm not, believe me, I'm not trying to talk about *her*, it's just weird." she said.

"I'm sure there are plenty of Danielles out there." he said. "Right Danielle?"

"Absolutely, darlin'." she said.

"We were just talking about a mutual friend named Danielle." she said.

"Centurion, eh?" she asked.

"Yeah." he said.

"Used to know a dude named Larry belonged to your club." she said. "One day he just disappeared."

Erik knew who she was talking about. The guy stole money from the club. After they jumped him out, they caught him in town with club ink...lots of it. He was supposed to have it covered as a condition of them letting him live. He had a choice, the knife or the flame to remove it. He took the flame.

The VP, Kirk didn't like him even when he was a member, and when they got the torch going, he took it to the next level. After they burned off half of his face Larry was begging to die. Everyone knew that they had gone too far, yet they couldn't stop, and they knew they were going to kill him in the end. Kirk made sure he stayed alive for the next 3 hours. He found more interesting areas to burn.

They were, of course, only supposed to burn off the ink, but it didn't go that way. Everyone was still pissed that he stole from the club. Afterwards, at church, they made a rule that such a thing should never happen again. It was a close vote, 6-5.

"I remember Larry." he said. "Were you close?"

"He was a prick who used my sister for a punching bag." she said.

"Without going into detail, I'll just say he got what he deserved." he said.

Almost certainly more than he deserved, Erik thought.

"Glad to hear it, darlin'." she said. "You think he'll ever have the balls to darken her door again?"

"Not likely." he said. "In fact I can guarantee it."

He winked at her.

"Oh my God, what did he do?" she asked.

"Less than he did to your sister." he said. "If it wasn't us, he was already on that road."

"Makes you think." she said.

She delivered the coffee and pie.

Lexie looked at him puzzled.

"Closure." he said. "Believe it or not, we're loved in the community. We do some civic stuff, as any other 'club' would do. She knew Larry. That's all I need to trust her. We did her sister a huge favor, and she knows that. I won't tell her the gory details of how he suffered. All she knows is that we handled it. He begged for death for 3 hours before we gave it to him."

"Keep it from her, but I must insist that you tell *me*." she said.

"I'm not proud of it." he said. "And I can't tell you. Club policy. Someone went too far. We took steps so it won't happen again. I think they may have used lard for this crust, and your coffee has cream in it. Have you changed?"

"Yes." she said. "I'm not depriving myself anymore."

"What about the religious aspect?" he asked.

"Fuck that." she said. "I can do what I want."

"You really have changed." he said.

"It's not as drastic as it sounds, let's just say that I have some fundamental differences with some people I was working with." she said. "I still support the cause, just...some people! I've decided to let my free flag fly, Stryker, you should be happy for me."

"If you're happy, I'm happy." he said. "It's just hard to believe that you had a personality conflict with *anyone*."

"You see the *old* Lexie might have taken offense." she said. "The new Lexie gets the joke."

"You really *have* changed." he said. "You must allow me to take you out for a 2 inch thick ribeye."

"That sounds great!" she said. "Club policy? No way around that?"

"What can I say? I'm part of something bigger than myself." he said.

"You've changed too." she said quietly. "So what's *really* going on? With her?"

She wasn't sure if she should bring it up, but she had to know. After all, she had changed. She had become more like him.

"Honestly, I don't know." he said. "If it was going great, today never would have happened. She's become unusually needy. And irrationally jealous. She got jealous of this dream I had."

"Dream?" she asked.

"Yeah, I was in the Philippines, at this bar that I went to with some shipmates. This girl I spent some time with over there-Elvie was in it, my buddies Abe and John, DuBois, Danielle, and you." he said. "She didn't give a shit about you or Elvie, but she zeroed in on Danielle. You said Murphy was waiting for us, and we had to go. You ended up shooting almost everyone before it was over. You shot DuBois, and told him he should have stayed dead. Abe was trying to tell me something, something about...the red...I don't know. You shot him before he could finish, and told him to stay dead too. In the end, there was a debate between you and Danielle whether she was dead or not, so you killed her too."

He had thought about telling her about the call he got from Danielle after he got home, but decided against it. He was pretty sure she knew that Danielle was still alive (Was she? That was a long time ago), and he knew that she didn't want to discuss it.

“So...she’s worried about Danielle, and I fuck your brains out the following day.” she said. “Ironic. She was worried about the wrong one. She *does know* that Danielle is dead, doesn’t she?”

“Of course.” he said. “She has this conspiracy theory in her head that she’s still alive, and somehow determined to reclaim me. Like I said, it’s irrational. A dream. Things haven’t been good for a while. And fucking Murphy picked up on it. He doesn’t like her anyway, he made some crack today about me leaving her for someone else.”

“You don’t think?” she asked.

“I wouldn’t put it past him, but no.” he said. “It would be proof that he’s really in my head...I have to confess, I’ve thought about you quite a bit since we last saw each other. I couldn’t see him ever using the job for something like this. He’s too professional.”

“Really?” she asked. “I’m rattling around up there?”

“Life has gone on, but you’ve always been there.” he said.

That seems noncommittal, she thought. But that might be all I get from the great Erik Stryker. Always aloof. But making progress.

“We could keep going east until we hit another ocean, or we could stop here for now.” he said. “What do you think?”

“Been a while since I’ve seen the Atlantic.” she said.

“Let’s go.” he said.

“You would, wouldn’t you?” she said.

“You wouldn’t?” he asked. “I thought you were letting your free flag fly...”

“Whether we stay here or not, we’ll be hearing from you know who in the morning.” she said. “Besides, you have to be back for the thing with Liam.”

“Foiled by the responsibilities of being an outlaw biker!” he said.

Danielle was on her way back.

“Just the check, love.” he said.

“It’s on the house.” she said. “The least I can do.”

“Thanks.” he said.

He knew better than to argue.

“You two kids be good.” she said.

“Have a lovely night.” said Lexie.

“Thanks, darlin’.” she said.

"See that? I made it from ma'am to darlin'." she said.

"You're a true woman of the people." he said.

He secretly put a hundred dollar bill under the plate.

"So we're staying?" he asked. "I know a few spots around here that are pretty cool."

"Where are we?" she asked.

"The Cascade Mountains." he said.

"Wow. Nature." she said.

"The desert was nature too." he said.

"No, the desert was a wasteland." she said. "I'm very happy to be here. Civilization. What were you trying to say to me earlier? Back at the clubhouse? When I stopped you?"

"What I was saying was more of a feeling. Does that make sense?" he asked. "Something you have a hard time putting into words, but you know what the feeling is. The way I feel about you...it runs deep. Deeper than I knew. I'm sure someday I'll find a way to express it better."

"You're doing fine." she said. "I feel the same way. Let's stay here tonight. You can take me on a mountain adventure tomorrow."

They went in and got a room.

"Do you think he'll be able to find us?" he asked.

"We should expect a call bright and early." she said.

"How does he do it?" he asked.

"Remember when we were in Mombasa? After we just met?" she asked. "We went to dinner at Yul's on the beach? Remember how I told you to just assume that he knows everything? Well he still does. If anything he's gotten better with the newer technology."

He thought about it. Not the part about Murph knowing everything, which was a rhetorical question. He remembered that place, and everything about that day.

"So...if we were back at Yul's today, would you take the ice cream?" he asked.

"How can you remember...oh, right." she said. "I probably would, but I might try to pretend I was strong for you."

"You don't have to pretend. You are the strongest woman I've ever met." he said.

"At that point, I was still trying to impress you." she said.

"And you're not anymore?" he asked.

"You know, because we just met. I was really nervous. But once I got to know you..." she said. "You made it easy."

"Nervous?" he asked. "Over me? I was just trying to figure you out. You really surprised me out there on that sandbar. I wasn't expecting *that*! You were nervous? Really?"

"What can I say?" she said. "I *was* nervous. The thing I did on the sandbar was just me knowing that I had to try. I was grateful that you were receptive."

"But you had to know..." he said. "You said that few had refused you. My guess is that nobody ever did."

"I was pretty sure." she said. "But I knew that if anyone was ever going to put me in my place, it would be someone like you. I bet you weren't nervous at all."

"I rarely am." he said. "But I was trying to impress you too. I've never stopped."

"Me either." she said. "You mind if I take a walk? Clear my head a little?"

"Of course. I'd tell you to be careful, but you're tougher than a lot of dudes I know." he said.

"What would really happen? I mean where are we?" she asked.

"Nehalem." he said.

"You take lots of chicks up here?" she asked.

"Once or twice." he said. "But never any like you."

"Nice save, Stryker." she said. "I won't be long."

"I'll get a fire going." he said.

"Pretty romantic, finding a motel with a fireplace." she said. "I'll pretend I'm the first."

"No matter where you are in line, you're the best." he said. "I mean that."

"Taylor been here with you?" she asked.

She immediately regretted saying *that*. What was she thinking? She wanted to know how she compared, that's what she was thinking, but there was certainly a better way than this!

"She's the only other one." he said quietly.

She didn't know what to say. She knew what it sounded like, but it probably had a different meaning. Sometimes Erik was hard to figure out.

She didn't feel quite as insecure as she used to about Taylor, though. But he *did* mention that things weren't going well.

Sometimes when guys fight with their girlfriend, the eye starts to wander. But Erik didn't seem the type.

Something to think about. Maybe I'll know where I stand by this time next year. That wasn't fair, he had been with Taylor for a long time. It was a big decision. She didn't want to be the reason, but she would protect her interests by whatever means necessary. It would be his call. Unless Murphy...he couldn't. It made no sense.

"I'll be right back." she said.

She held up his cigarette pack.

"May I?" she asked.

"Sure." he said. "I got some of that Humboldt homegrown for when you get back. Best weed in the states. Probably not as good as that Lebanese we had while we were cruising down the Nile, but it's good."

"I lost my connection." she said. "The guy in Tel Aviv. Disappeared. I haven't had any good weed in months."

"That's unfortunate." he said. "You'll like this stuff."

She walked out.

She intentionally walked past the diner, and the payphone outside. That would be too obvious. She remembered seeing a service station about a mile west of them. There was a payphone there.

She told herself that she was doing nothing wrong. There were plenty of times during their mission that *he* talked to Murphy. She didn't know if he ever snuck out in the middle of the night to do it, but that's what Murph wanted. He wanted to get a "feel" of where Erik was at. All she could report was that he still seemed to have the world by the balls. But Anthony certainly knew that.

What's really going on? is he testing me? She hadn't had any experience with this type of mission. There was no sand. How could she help?

"How could you not?"

It was Erik's voice in her head. This is great, she thought. Now I'm hearing voices. She got to the service station and went to the phone both. She punched in the numbers.

"Collect from Domino." she said.

Murphy appeared on the line.

"Ms. Tenenzapf." he said. "How are things?"

"Things are great, Anthony." she said. "I'm not complaining, but I'm wondering what I'm doing here."

"You could say you're watching the watcher." he said. "How is he? Has he changed?"

"Well, he's an outlaw biker, but other than that, about the same." she said.

"Was he receptive to seeing you?" he asked.

"You could say that." she said. "He fucked me within a half hour, so there's that. He seems to be having a little trouble at home."

"That doesn't surprise me." he said. "There was only so long that Taylor could have kept him interested before he got restless. How deep is he in the club?"

"You know, deep." she said. "He gave me a vague description of how they killed an ex member. Made the guy suffer for 3 hours before they ended it. I pressed for details, and he pleaded "club policy" and clammed up. It was some medieval shit though. He's...changed. Using the words "more open" to describe Erik didn't used to make sense, but he may have turned the corner. I'm glad you sent me here."

"You couldn't stay in the sandbox. It seemed like a good place to send you, your role will become apparent." he said. "You can get an idea of what civilization is like again."

"Well, we're not exactly there at the moment." she said. "We're in..."

"The Cascades." he said.

"Right. I'll bet you a dollar you don't know what town..."

"Hmmm...a challenge." he said. "Diablo."

"There's actually a town called Diablo?" she asked.

"Guess that means you're not there then, I owe you a dollar." he said.

"Nehalem." she said.

"I should have known." he said.

"How many times has he been here?" she asked.

She felt a bit guilty cheating this way, but she wanted to know.

"Once or twice." he said.

"What about Diablo?" she asked.

"Several times a year." he said. "But that's only because they have a charter there."

“If you’re still planning on doing that thing, you probably don’t have to.” she said. “He’ll go on his own. He just needs time.”

“We may not have time.” he said. “Where are you staying?”

“The Starlight Resort. Only motel in town.” she said. “But let us sleep in a little. I’m going to wear him out when I get back.”

“Didn’t really need to know that.” he said. “So we’ll say around noonish?”

“Sounds good.” she said.

The line went dead.

Chapter 3

He knew she was calling him. There was no other reason for her to "go for a walk" in the middle of the night. He watched her walk past the diner, and head west, where she undoubtedly saw the service station on the way in. Clear her head. He knew that the events back at the clubhouse did more to clear her head than a ten mile hike.

He wondered why she was here. Murphy knew he didn't need her. Although this was a mission, an assignment, inside it was him. The club...that was him. He was exactly the part he was playing. As smart as Anthony was, he had to recognize that. Maybe that was what this is. He's worried I won't be there when the time comes. Honestly, he didn't know if he would either.

Murphy allowed him a condition under the circumstances. Probably because it was the only way he would do it. Unless he pulled the MK, then he would have no control over his actions. Erik gets him the IRA, the club doesn't get hurt. Simple. Of course, it would be optimal if none of it pointed towards him, but it seemed that Murph was already planning for that eventuality with his plan to kill him. He didn't know who he would miss the most Taylor, or the club. If he was being honest, he would say the club right now.

Things weren't good at home. She wasn't the same. Neither was he. The things she wanted, he didn't. The things he wanted...well, right now he just wanted to be left alone.

They had these problems before Lexie showed up, but Lexie showing up out of the blue didn't help. He knew that he couldn't trust his feelings for Lexie right now, but it felt good. She just felt so...right. She was so different from Taylor, and he knew that was part of it.

She was just getting back, she was wearing his cut. It seemed that she liked it, maybe she liked being the bad girl. Like she wasn't already.

"Cold out there?" he asked.

"Actually not really." she said. "But I can tell we're in the mountains."

"You like that coat, eh?" he said.

"I feel like one of the cool kids." she said.

"You look like one too." he said.

He got up to get a cigarette.
"Stop." she said.
He stopped and put his hands up, in mock surrender.
His back was still to her, and she walked over to him. She slowly traced the tattoo on his back. It was remarkable. A mirror image of his cut, it had a rocker with "Centurions" at the top, "a rocker with "Washington" on the bottom, and a perfect likeness of the Centurion between. The letters MC were in the lower right, just like the cut. How did she not notice this earlier?
"How did I not see this before?" she said. "So you're in pretty deep, eh?"
"It's just a tattoo." he said.
"Just a tattoo." she said quietly.
"This is who I am." he said. "It's who I've always been. I just didn't know it. When Murph suggested it, I already knew some of the guys."
"Are you happy?" she asked.
"I never knew I could be this happy." he said. "They're my family."
"Then I'm happy." she said. "Can you turn it off if you have to?"
"I don't want to." he said. "When Murphy first suggested this, it didn't sound so bad. Then I got to know the guys better, joined the club. Things are different. It's hard to explain to someone who's never experienced it."
"You think I haven't?" she asked. "I know it's apples and oranges, but my team back in Tel Aviv...well, they're my family. If he asked me to go against them, I don't think I could do it. So I'll ask you again, can you turn it off if you have to?"
"I don't know." he said. "He's given me assurances that the club won't get hurt. He's never flat out lied to me. They're my main concern."
"I get that." she said. "You could be in trouble. He can still..."
"Believe me, I know." he said. "It's the worst thing for someone like me. I don't like not being in control. If he shared that with me when we first talked, I might not be here."
"Who are you kidding?" she said.
"I know, I know." he said. "Should I be grateful that he got to know me before he started controlling my mind?"

"Could have gone the other way..." she quipped.

"Right." he said. "Does he have that on you? You know? Can he...?"

"I don't think so." she said. "I guess there's no real way to be sure."

"Unless you know he's done it." he said. "Like me."

"Should you call home? Let her know what's up?" she asked.

"Not ready for that conversation yet." he said.

"I don't want you getting in trouble on my account." she said.

"Does it look like I'm worried about getting in trouble?" he asked.

"Honestly, no, not at all." she said. "Do you have some kind of arrangement?"

"We've had one for quite some time now that she's never taken advantage of." he said.

"Like what?" she asked.

"It started with my job on the ship. We agreed that while I'm gone, we can sleep with other people." he said. "Lots of married guys in the Navy have this type of arrangement. Then when I became James Bond, we folded that job in too. After I joined the club, it was never official, but there are lots of times when the opportunity presents itself, and I have to look good in front of my boys..."

"Incredible." she said. "You're not James Bond, by the way. You've really got her whipped don't you? And she's never? How do you know?"

"Trust me, I know." he said. "She can't keep a secret to save her life. I've asked her friends, the ones who are friendly with me. It's just not happening."

"The ones who are friendly with you, eh?" she said. "You banging them too?"

He looked at the floor momentarily.

"REALLY?" she asked, "You're banging her friends too?"

"No." he said sheepishly. "Close once or twice, but I never closed the deal. A lot of them have made it known that they would be willing."

"Should she be grateful for that?" she asked.

"It's not all me." he said. "She's changed. She used to be so easy. Now she's...well not easy. I'm doing my best to just hang on."

"Didn't you tell me that she had you figured out?" she asked. "That you couldn't get anything past her?"

"Not so much anymore." he said. "That was something that either had to change or end. After a while I was the one who had her figured out. I can get away with almost anything now."

"I can see that. But, how about a little restraint?" she said. "You're probably getting more action than when you were single."

"It's just not there anymore." he said. "Most of it is that we're growing apart. And you're right, women do tend to throw themselves at me."

He chuckled a little.

"Joke all you want, Stryker, but there's something to that." she said. "If it's like that with her, you should end it."

He knew she was right, but he didn't want to talk about it right now, much less do it. It was by far his least favorite social obligation. He had literally behaved badly in hopes that the woman would break up with him so he wouldn't have to be the one do it.

"You know, even with our arrangement I always call." he said. "I hope you understand why I can't tonight. This is different."

"Different how?" she asked.

"I'm sure you know, but I'll tell you." he said. "It's different because of you. You're not just another woman. You have a deeper meaning. Much deeper. To me, and probably to her, even though she's more worried about Danielle. I'm thinking a face to face is the least I can do."

"You're right." she said. "Would I sound stupid if I said I had no idea? That you felt that way about me?"

"You? Who was, and I quote, 'really nervous' on our first date? Not really a date, I guess, but still. And then made love to me on the sandbar?" he said. "I can see why you might not believe it. But let's be realistic. There's no way you can't know after tonight."

He pulled out a hefty joint.

"Would you care to partake?" he asked.

"I'd love to." she said.

He fired it up, and passed it to her.

She took a long drag and held it in.

"How was your walk?" he asked.

"You know, don't you?" she said.

"It's okay." he said. "I know how he is. He'll probably be keeping secrets from you tomorrow."

"We could always make an agreement." she said. "Tell each other everything."

"I thought about that." he said. "But there is sure to be a time when one of us really would be better off not knowing. In that case, we shouldn't tell. But if we make an agreement, we'll feel obligated to tell, and it will put us in a quagmire. How about if we tell what we can, and leave the rest? If it's something that would be dangerous to know, we'll use our best judgement."

"That sounds good." she said. "I actually felt guilty coming back. I don't want to keep secrets from you."

"And I'll only keep the secrets that I have to." he said. "You know, like the club."

"I don't know how to tell you this, but you're going to spill everything to me one day." she said. "Just wait. You don't think you will, but you will. Club business, or whatever, you'll sing like a canary."

He looked at her. It wasn't that he thought he would, but she was so sure. He was probably high. She was definitely high, no doubt about it.

"Do you always have delusions of grandeur when you're stoned?" he asked.

"Do you think me knowing your little secrets is grandeur to me?" she asked. "You were right about this weed, by the way, it's amazing. I've been delusional about a lot of things in my life, Stryker, but not this. You'll tell me."

"You seem pretty confident." he said.

"Always have been." she said.

She moved over to the bed and gently pushed him onto his back and climbed on top of him.

"I feel deeper than what I've let on too, you know." she said.

"I know." he said. "I've known for a long time. Even when we were apart."

"Really?" she asked.

"Really." he said.

"Is there more to you than I know, Stryker?" she asked.

"Probably less." he said. "I think that's enough conversation for now."

"It certainly is." she said. "I had something entirely different in mind."

She reached down and unbuckled his belt.

***

Around 11:30 am the phone started ringing. Erik rolled over and tried to focus on it.

"Hello?" he said.

"Mr. Stryker. How are things?" he asked.

"Well, an old friend dropped in out of the blue yesterday, and a heads up would have been nice, but I'll probably live through it." he said.

Lexi got up and went to the shower.

"Sometimes spontaneity is better, Erik." he said. "It appears more natural to the untrained eye. We wouldn't want your brothers figuring things out, would we?"

"There are a lot of ways you could have done that and let me know." he said. "I'm not worried about my brothers. But Jerry's sister? That was what you came up with? All the spontaneity in the world can't make that sound natural. "

"All good relationships start with a good story. She may be your next old lady. Are you displeased that Ms. Tenenzapf is there?" he said.

"Of course not, but I'm wondering why." he said. "Do you think I need help?"

"You're not the one I'm worried about." he said. "Lexie has had a bit of a hard time lately. She needs support. Realistically, there's not much she can do to help. She's seen some bad shit. She's vulnerable. I need you to support her. And who knows? She'll probably find a way to contribute."

"The word vulnerable and Lexie don't belong together." he said. "I hope it's okay if I fuck her, because we've been doing that."

"I was counting on it, Erik." he said. "She just needs some time away from the desert. Time away from some of her people."

"She mentioned that. What happened?" he said.

"I can't tell you that, Mr. Stryker. Club policy." he said.

"You know there are rules to this life." he said. "That's one of them. You don't get to know everything. If you want me to help her, I should know what's going on."

"She needs to tell you herself." he said. "If it comes from me, it won't work. Any news on the Irish?"

"Liam Gallagher is going to be in town on Friday." he said. "As far as I know, it's just logistics. It will probably be from B.C. somewhere."

"It's good that you're in the north. Doubtful that the IRA would be willing to work with Mexicans." he said. "How are things on the homefront?"

"Is that what you asked her about last night?" he asked.

"Among other things." he said.

"Not great, Anthony." he said. "I feel more and more like I'm living a lie."

"Lexie have anything to do with that?" he asked.

"Well, it didn't help, her popping up suddenly, but we were having problems before that. Why the interest in my love life, Anthony?" he asked.

"I don't think it's any secret how I feel about her." he said. "She distracts you. I just want to know the status, nothing more."

"You wouldn't do something like send Lexie here to try to advance your agenda, would you, Anthony?" he asked. "Maybe lure me away from Taylor? Get me back with the program?"

"The obvious answer is yes, I would use all of the tools at my disposal to advance my agenda, Erik." he said. "*All of them*. But in this case, it was just a happy coincidence. Lexie needs some camaraderie with someone who understands her. There isn't another person in this world who I trust more than you for that."

"Okay." he said. "I'll call Friday after the meet."

"If I really wanted Taylor gone, she would be gone." he said. "What's more, you would be the one to do it. Just like you should right now. It would probably feel better if you do it on your own."

"I know." he said. "But I need to do it my own way."

Lexie was getting out of the shower.

"Fair enough." he said. "Can I speak with the warrior princess?"

Erik handed the phone to her as he walked to the shower.

"Hello?" she said.

"Hello. He knows about last night?" he said.

"It's hard to get anything past him." she said

"He tells me that he's having trouble at home." he said.

"Try saying that without the smirk." she said.

"Relax, Lexie." he said. "We're on the same side here. It's been over for a while, he's just figuring it out now. Do you want them to stay together?"

"Of course not." she said. "This feels a little like you're playing with his life though."

"If I were playing with him, it would look much different, I can assure you, Ms. Tenenzapf." he said.

"I don't want to think about that." she said. "He really is in deep. Do you know about the tattoo?"

"Which one?" he asked.

"The big one." she said. "On his back."

"Oh, the cut. Lots of those guys do that." he said. "He's undercover as an outlaw biker. He needs to fit in. When it's time, I have a guy for that. They're doing amazing things with lasers. It will be like he never had it."

"He's not undercover, Anthony. This is who he is." she said. "I'm going to try to bring him back, but it won't be easy."

"Don't worry too much about it." he said. "If push comes to shove, I can bring him back."

"So much for not cheating." she said.

"We all cheat." he said. "I indulged you last night when you asked how often he comes to Nehalem. I hope that information was useful."

"It was." she admitted. "I'm going to do my best to make sure you don't have to use your hole card."

"It really is best that way." he said. "There are times when I wish I didn't have it."

"What did you tell him? About me? Why I'm here?" she asked.

"The truth, without details." he said. "But you may become a vital part of this mission yet, Lexie."

"I need to get a handle on him first." she said.

"Trust me, you already do." he said. "Talk to some of the old ladies. Sometimes they say more than they should. Especially if you're with someone as high up as Erik is in the club. Don't force it, but use that finesse I know you have."

"Right." she said. "Anything else?"

"He may need an extra nudge where Taylor is concerned." he said. "Try to do it so he thinks that the concern is about him."

"The concern is about him." she said.

"But we both have reasons to want it to fail." he said. "Make sure that doesn't come through. The best way would be to make it his idea."

"Do you think I'm stupid?" she asked.

"No, but sometimes you have a hard time with your emotions. If it looks like you're pushing him, he will resist." he said.

"I know that." she said. "He knows he has to end it. He wants to do it face to face."

"That could be a delaying tactic." he said. "Make sure he stays on course."

She hadn't thought of that. Does he want this?

"Okay." she said. "Anything else?"

"The club is meeting with Liam Gallagher on Friday." he said. "They'll hold church, and it would be a good time to meet some of the other women."

"Church?" she asked.

"Biker talk for a meeting. It's where all of the decisions are made." he said. "Liam will be excluded, but he'll be there. There will undoubtedly be a vote on the Irish guns. The mission hinges on the outcome. Meet some of the women, but be careful, these biker bitches are catty."

"I can take care of myself." she said.

"It's not you I'm worried about." he said "Play nice."

The line went dead.

Erik was just getting out of the shower.

"So what do you want to do?" he asked.

"I don't know." she said. "Show me around. But I don't want to take a trip down memory lane. We can do something you didn't do with her."

"You know we're in Nehalem, don't you?" he said. "There isn't that much to do that hasn't been done before."

"There must be some virgin territory." she said.

"I've got it." he said. "It's a ways away, but there's no way she would ever do this, but you'll love it."

"Let's go." she said.

They got on his bike and headed northeast. They went about 30 miles, steadily climbing all of the way. He turned down a narrow dirt path that she didn't see coming. They came to a clearing and stopped.

He started taking off his clothes.

"I'm going for a swim, would you care to join me?" he said.

Not waiting for a response, he started heading into the forest. She quickly started following, shedding her clothes as she went. She caught up to him, and saw that he was standing on a huge rock on the edge of an opening in the ground.

"Do you trust me?" he asked.

"Of course, what are you doing?" she said.

"If you trust me, follow me." he said.

With that he dove into the hole.

"Erik?" she said.

She went and looked into the hole, but didn't see the bottom.

She heard a splash.

"ERIK?" she cried.

Still nothing. She did hear a splash, so that meant there was water at the bottom. It went a long way down, and she still didn't see it.

"If you trust me, follow me."

His words sounded in her head. Was this a test?

"She would never do this, but you'll love it."

I better go, she thought. Here goes nothing. She dove. It seemed like an eternity before she finally hit the water.

There was little splash because she parted the water so gracefully, and she swore she went 30 feet underwater. She surfaced and saw Erik sitting on what looked like a giant swing.

"What the hell was that?" she asked.

He laughed.

"It's a natural rock formation." he said. "The magma filled up the crater, but it kept burning through the earth. Just a narrow hole. I say narrow, but you can see that it's about 30 yards wide. The ice from the mountains melts every year and fills it. It's never been less than 60 feet deep."

“How far is the drop?” she asked.

“It depends on the water level.” he said. “Who knows? A long way.”

“Hop on.” he said. “We’ll go back up.”

She got on the board, and he started pulling on a rope which made them start rising.

“There’s a pulley at the top.” he said.

“Mr. Stryker, you are truly full of surprises.” she said. “Do you ever take other chicks up here?”

“You’re the first.” he said.

“I like that.” she said.

“You should stop worrying about other chicks.” he said.

“Are you really going to do it? With Taylor?” she asked.

“I think I am.” he said.

“You know Murph thinks maybe I should be your old lady.” she said. “What do you think about that?”

“Maybe.” he said. “They all know Taylor, and everybody likes her.”

“Right.” she said.

They got to the top, and got off the lift.

“If it all comes to pass, I’d be happy to have you as an old lady.” he said. “So would that just be for the mission...or?”

“You figure it out, Stryker.” she said. “And when you know, let me know.”

Then she dove into the hole without another word.

***

They were on their way back to Seattle. She had been strangely quiet since all of the “old lady” talk. So maybe it isn’t strange, he thought. She wants to know where she stands. Maybe I could tell her if I only knew where I stand.

He was pretty sure it was over with Taylor, but she had a way of making him lose his edge. He could be completely ready to do it, but just a look from her...a soft smile, a gentle touch...he could fall to pieces. There was no way that Lexie could ever know that. It would be crucial to keep them separated.

“I can drop you at the hotel, I’ll go home and get a change of clothes and meet you back here.” he said.

"You sure you're coming back?" she asked.
"She won't be home now, she has school." he said. "Quick in and out."
"You're going to have to face her sometime." she said.
"I know, I'll do it later." he said.
"What are you scared of?" she asked.
"I'm not scared." he said. "It's complicated."
"I've found that when people say it's complicated, it's usually pretty simple." she said. "Why don't we do this? You deal with her, then you come back and get me. Don't come back until it's over."
She was forcing the issue. Worse than that, she was right. He needed to deal with this.
"Okay. She won't be home for about an hour." he said. "I'll talk to her, then I'll come back for you."
"I'll get some sleep." she said. "Something tells me I'm going to need it."
"What room?" he asked.
"815." she said. "Don't be long..."
"I won't." he said.
"I want to be your old lady." she said.
"You can start right away." he said.
"I think it would be best if the previous holder of that title has moved on before I assume the duties." she said.
"I'll do it." he said.
"Thank you." she said.

***

When he got home, she was waiting for him. She was sitting on the couch between two suitcases. Both cats were in their travel carriers, DeeDee was howling, while Huck remained calm.
"Who is she?" she asked.
"Who is who?" he asked.
"Are you really going to play dumb?" she said. "Marsha called me. She was at the club. She saw and heard everything. You didn't even call last night!"

Marsha was there? He didn't see her. Of course he was pretty distracted. A lot of people involved with the club were scared of him. Marsha wasn't one of them.

"It was nobody." he said. "Does it really matter?"

"She said that the woman said she was Jerry's sister." she said. "But we both know that's not true, don't we?"

"I don't know what you're talking about." he said. "Who do you think it is?"

"Are you going to act like you don't know?" she asked. "Danielle, your long lost love. She's here, isn't she?"

He couldn't believe it. She thought it was Danielle. He knew that she was alive, but as far as he knew, nobody else did but Murphy...and probably Lexie.

"How many times do I have to tell you?" he said. "Danielle's dead. You're chasing a ghost."

It really was getting old, this obsession with Danielle.

"Fine." she said. "If you don't want to be honest, there's nothing I can say. You stay here, it's your place anyway. I'm going to Casey's."

With that, she grabbed the cat carriers and headed out. He picked up the suitcases and followed her.

This was actually going better than expected. She was doing it. But was it over? Almost certainly not, it was too easy. He loaded the suitcases into the hatchback.

"We should talk some time." he said. "After you've had a chance to calm down."

"AFTER I'VE HAD A CHANCE TO CALM DOWN?!" she said. "Are you making this my fault? You fuck your long lost love at the clubhouse, and put on such a performance that everyone in the house is still talking about it, *AND THIS IS MY FAULT?!"*

"Sorry." he said.

"You may have them all fooled, but not me. We both know that that wasn't Jerry's sister. I will know who it really is." she said.

She got in the car and sped off. Is it over? He wondered.

Not likely.

He thought about Lexie. Was that what he wanted? He was starting to feel like he did at the end of his latest mission.

Maybe he didn't want a relationship at all. They're mine fields, with an ever changing map.

He had to admit that a lot of this was his own fault, but she had to admit that it had become boring. There used to be a flame, now there was barely a spark. Whenever it got like this, he had the same answer. They had been together too long. He didn't know why, he just didn't have much interest in anything long term, relationships, jobs, whatever. Taylor was special though. She was the first thing after Jenna died, and whether he admitted it or not, that meant something.

He came home to end it, and it's over. Mission accomplished. Even if he knew that it wasn't over for her, which meant she wouldn't let it be over for him, oh hell.

I can't let her dictate my life. It's not like we both have to agree. It's over, and that's all there is to it. He still couldn't convince himself.

He headed for the ferry. On the ride over, he looked over the side at the jellyfish. Every year, they come here. I wonder why?

He pulled up to the Fairmont Olympic. It really was swanky. It was surely costing Murphy a ton. But it wasn't like he was paying for it. He had that black ops budget, so secret the President doesn't even know about it. Business must be good, because he's never cared about money.

He got to room 815 and knocked. She looked through the peephole and unlocked the door.

"This place really is nice, but I think I would prefer the Beijing Juba." he said.

"I stay there whenever I'm in Sudan." she said.

"When was the last time?" he asked.

"I'd rather not talk about that." she said.

He thought about what Murph said. He had to at least try.

"You have to talk about it sometime." he said.

"Not ready for that conversation yet." she said.

"Well, when you are, I'm here for you." he said.

"How did it go?" she asked.

"Pretty easy." he said. "She did all the heavy lifting."

"What does that mean?" she asked.

"Well, I walked in to her sitting on the couch with a suitcase on either side." he said. "She thinks you're Danielle. I tried for the thousandth time to tell her that Danielle is dead, but she wouldn't listen."

"How does she know about it?" she asked.

"Marsha. She was at the club when it happened, and she called." he said. "She doesn't know who you are, but she knows you're not Jerry's sister."

"No shit." she said. "I don't know what he was thinking when he came up with that."

"He made some crack about how all good relationships start with a good story." he said. "I think he's trying a little too hard."

"What do you mean?" she asked.

"Isn't it obvious?" he said. "He wants us to get together. He probably figures if that happens, we'll keep each other in line, and his job will be easier."

"I don't think so." she said.

"Why not?" he asked.

"There was a time..." she said. "It doesn't matter."

She always figured he was the one who kept them apart back in Europe. He knew that she wanted Erik. And then to bring that bitch into it, just to rub her nose in it! It seemed like he was actively against them being together back then.

A lot had changed since then. She had changed. That time with Erik...looking back, she was embarrassed how she chased after him. She had never done that before, except with Herschel.

She knew how she felt, her main objective this time was to make sure that he didn't. Not that she didn't want him to know that she wanted him, she just didn't want to look as desperate as the last time.

"What were you going to say?" he asked.

"It's just that Anthony Murphy has a whole lot more to worry about than getting Erik and Lexie together." she said.

"You may be right, but I'm not convinced." he said. "You want to go get a drink?"

"Sure." she said.

He took off his cut and set it on the bed.

"You're not taking it?" she said.

"Tell the truth, you're just into me because I'm a Centurion." he said.

“You got me.” she said. “If you’re not going to wear your jacket, we may as well not go.”

“We’re going to a biker bar.” he said. “No colors allowed. I promise I’ll let you wear it later.”

“Well in that case...” she said. “Maybe that’s all I’ll wear.”

“Let’s get out of here.” he said.

Chapter 4

They got down to the parking lot and got on the bike. He went past the club and south for about 5 miles.

There was a huge neon sign declaring that the place was "The Red Knight." There were several other bikes in the lot.

They walked in, and the music was loud. It was Pearl Jam, a local band that made it big, as so many Seattle bands had.

At home
Drawing pictures
Of mountain tops
With him on top
Lemon yellow sun
Arms raised in a V
And the dead lay in pools of maroon below

They sat down near the pool tables. Erik could hear some guys who were playing pool talking about Jerry.

"Yeah, get this." he said. "His sister shows up, acting like she's going to take him out, then ends up fucking him! A story like that just has to be true!"

Erik got up and started walking over there.

"Erik, let it go." said Lexie. "It's not worth it."

He kept walking.

"You got something to say about Jerry, say it to me, punk." he said.

Daddy didn't give attention
Oh, to the fact that mommy didn't care
King Jeremy the Wicked
Ruled his world
Jeremy spoke in class today

The guy sized him up, and not knowing Erik, he swung the cue at him. Absent the element of surprise, Erik grabbed the cue, tore it from his hands, broke it in half and pinned the mouth to the wall while he took the other one out with the heavy end.

Clearly I remember
Pickin' on the boy
Seemed a harmless little fuck
But we unleashed a lion
Gnashed his teeth
And bit the recess lady's breast

How could I forget?
And he hit me with a surprise left
My jaw left hurting
Dropped wide open
Just like the day
Oh, like the day I heard

"Jerry was a Centurion." he said. "No matter what else he was, he was a brother."

Daddy didn't give affection, no!
And the boy was something that mommy wouldn't wear
King Jeremy the Wicked
Ruled his world

He bounced the guy off the wall, and his momentum carried him towards the pool table, Erik grabbed his hair on the way down and guided his face into the sharp edge.

"Do not talk about things you don't know about." Erik said, slamming his face into the pool table to emphasize every word.

A shot rang out.

"Right now, motherfucker, drop it and kick it over here." she said. "I only clipped your ear to get your attention. The next one's going to be a few inches further inside, I can promise you that."

It was, of course, Lexie, talking to the other guy who had produced a gun.

Meanwhile, Johnny was trying to extricate Erik from the proceedings. The guy's face looked like oatmeal with way too much strawberry in it, a mushy pulp with lots of bone spurs.

He kicked the gun to Lexie, and she calmly picked it up, disassembled it into 4 different parts and scattered them around the bar without breaking eye contact.

Erik looked at her.

"We need to go, now." said Johnny.

They backed out the door, on the alert for any retaliation. A lot of the guys in the bar knew Erik, so he was pretty sure nobody "saw anything."

He still had his CIA get out of jail free card in any case. Most of the time he just did the time to avoid suspicion.

"Clubhouse, now." said Johnny.

Yes, it looked like he fucked up again.

They got to the clubhouse, and Lexie looked at him like she didn't know what to do.

"It's okay." he said. "Johnny is the president. He worries when I get in scrapes. It'll be okay."

"What should I do?" she asked.

"We're just going to the back for a few minutes to talk." he said. "Stay out here, meet some people. I'll be right back."

"What the hell was that?" she asked. "Back there. That was a little excessive."

"Just standing up for my brother." he said.

"You mean the brother that you almost killed?" she said. "That was pretty brutal. I've never seen you like that. I've never seen anyone like that."

"It looked worse than it was. It's my job to keep people in line, I'm Sergeant-at-Arms. He'll be fine. And where did that come from?" he said. "I had no idea you were armed."

"When have you ever known me to not be armed?" she asked.

"Good point." he said. "I'll be right back."

"Do I need to worry about you, Stryker?" she said. "That was a bit of an overreaction. You could have killed that guy. And over what? Talking about another guy you almost killed. This isn't like you."

"How would you know what I'm like?" he asked.

"Oh, I don't know. Life and death situations, having your back, you having mine." she said. "When we do something like what we did, it speeds up the 'getting to know you' process. I think it's a safe bet that I know what your normal behavior is like."

"I'm sorry." he said. "I don't know why I get so violent sometimes. I wish I did. You're right, it's not me."

"We'll talk about it later." she said.

***

"Who's the girl?" he asked.

"I did some freelance work a few years ago in the desert." he said. "You know mercenary stuff. Lexie was my partner. She's tougher than half the guys in the club."

"Did she really aim for that kid's ear, or was that luck?" he asked.

"If she hit him in the ear, that's what she was trying to do." he said. "She's better than me with a gun."

"Jesus Christ, Stryker, what am I going to do with you?" he asked. "Anyone pisses you off, you beat the living shit out of them. Do you know someone? Are you protected? There have been at least a few times that you should have gone away and you didn't."

"I've had a colorful life, John." he said. "I've met lots of people. I tend to make a strong impression either way. Sometimes it helps, sometimes it hurts. To answer your question, I'm not working for anyone except the Merchant Marines, and some occasional freelance work."

"As a soldier of fortune..." he said. "And she is too. What are you going to do about Taylor?"

"I'm pretty sure that situation has taken care of itself." he said.

"You're a complicated man, Erik." he said. "You travel the world, sometimes as a soldier, sometimes as a sailor, everyone's scared of you, and you pull down some of the finest tail I've ever seen, yet you don't know that you have a problem with Taylor. Do me a favor? She's a sweet kid. Don't let Lexie kill her."

"You say that like I have a choice." he said. "I'm pretty sure Taylor isn't in any danger. That's not Lexie's style. Can we keep her as Jerry's sister for now? I know how ridiculous that sounds, but those people out there will believe almost anything if you and I both say it's true."

"Best I can do is no comment." he said. "What are you worried about? No one would dare disagree."

"Thanks, John." he said. "I better get out there, make sure she's not sticking bamboo needles into anybody."

"You're funny." he said.

"That's why you love me." he said.

"The reason I love you, Stryker, is that you're good for the club. But you give me cause to worry sometimes." he said. "We'll figure out something for your mystery woman."

"Thanks." he said.

He headed back out to the bar. He was surprised to see Lexie talking with a few of the women. He walked over and sat down.

"Hey." he said.

"Everything okay?" she asked.

"Yeah, no, it's no problem." he said "We just needed to talk. Club business, you know. How are things out here?"

"Fine. I'm just getting to know some of your friends." she said. "They're wondering what's going on with Taylor."

Oh shit. Here we go.

"I'm pretty sure it's over." he said.

"You don't know?" she asked.

"The way we left things...it's complicated." he said.

"Hmmm...complicated again, eh?" she said. "Remember what I said about that? You say it's complicated, I say it's simple."

"You weren't there." he said. "She wouldn't let me get a word in, then she just sped off."

"So it's over?" she asked.

"It's over." he said.

"Good." she said. "I was just telling the girls here about how we met. Remember that job we did together?"

His heart skipped a beat. What the hell was she doing? It sounded a lot like she was telling them about the mission.

"How could I forget?" he said.

"Yeah, he was living in Baton Rouge, and he came into New Orleans looking for work as...well, for now we'll just say a problem solver." she said. "You ladies can use your imagination. We were both looking for work, and we thought only one of us was going to get the job. He hired us both and we worked together. What was that guy's name Erik?"

What was she doing? He had already gotten John to do the Jerry's sister thing! At least she made something up, and she wasn't telling the real truth.

"Anthony. Anthony Murphy." he said.

"Right you are!" she said. "I moved out here a few months ago, and I had heard he was around, so I went to the local biker bar and heard someone talking about Jerry. I thought it would be perfect lead in, since Erik surely wouldn't have wanted me talking about the "work" we did in NoLa."

"Of course." he said.

"So really?" asked Jessica. "You and Taylor? You're such a cute couple."

"We've been growing apart for some time now. Honestly, it has nothing to do with Lexie, this is just a happy coincidence." he said. "I wouldn't expect to see her around here."

Just then, an incredibly attractive, confident looking blond woman walked in, and turned more than a few heads.

"You spoke too soon." said Allie.

Taylor had just walked in the door. Lexie sized her up to see how she compared. The thing she noticed right away was that she was a natural beauty. She had long blond hair, her eyes were the color of faded blue jeans, and everything else was where it was supposed to be. It didn't happen too often that she thought about another woman's beauty, because she looked so good herself, but she took notice.

Taylor quickly scanned the room and zeroed in on Erik.

She walked right over.

"Hey, Tay, how's it going?" asked Emily.

"Not great, Em." she said. "You must be Danielle."

She was trying her best to be intimidating, but Lexie didn't respond the way she wanted her to.

"Danielle's dead." she said. "What makes you think that bitch would have the nerve to come out here, anyway?"

"Taylor, Lexie." he said. "Lexie, Taylor."

Here we go, he thought.

"I don't know why you thought it was the sweet one." said Lexie.

Taylor had heard a lot about Lexie. For some reason, she never considered her a threat. She knew what it looked like when a guy was in love. It was how Erik looked when he thought about Danielle. He always seemed indifferent about Lexie. So why was he leaving her for Lexie?

"I have to say, I didn't see this coming." she said. "He was so stuck on her."

"You don't need to tell me, it was the same way when we were together down in New Orleans." she said, hoping Taylor would catch on. "He thought about her every day."

"That time in...New Orleans...that could have been the beginning of the end for us." she said. "But we had a few good years after that."

"Of course you did. He loves you, and he always will." she said. "But you've both changed. Those two people are gone. That's why it's not working."

Erik was watching with great interest. Lexie was somehow saying all of the right things, without being offensive. He thought about bringing her along for his next breakup, but that would probably be with her.

"You created such a bond with him, in such a short time." she said. "And I was worried about the other one."

"It had quite a bit to do with what we were doing." she said. "In those situations you get close fast."

"What were you doing?" asked Emily.

"That doesn't matter." said Taylor. "They worked together very closely for a little over a week. There are things that we shouldn't talk about. I have to go."

She ran away crying.

"Under the circumstances, we probably should too." said Lexie.

"Right." he said. "Tell Frank, Mike, and Charlie that we said hey."

"Sure." they all said in unison.

"Will we be seeing more of you, Lexie?" asked Emily.

"Try to keep me away." she said.

"We all love Taylor, but we can't hold that against you. You seem nice." said Jessica.

Got them fooled, she thought.

"It's an awkward situation for everyone." she said. "But Erik and I have known each other for a long time. Almost as long as him and Taylor."

About half as long, he thought. But she was right...the circumstances made them closer much more quickly.

"You seem...to lead an exciting life." said Emily. "All that stuff about New Orleans...NoLa. Any way I can ever get you to spill?"

"You can try." she said.

"Don't get your hopes up." said Erik. "She's like a vault. I can only confirm your suspicion that she leads an exciting life."

"Right." she said. "You guys have a great night."

***

They got on the bike and headed back to the hotel. As they were in the elevator he looked at her in amazement.

"That was some pretty fancy footwork back there." he said. "I had no idea that you were such a diplomat."

"You haven't seen every side of me." she said. "I have decent people skills when the situation requires it. I told her a mixture of the truth and what she wanted to hear. Just so you know, it's not over."

"Really?" he said. "After that performance? Even I believed it."

"You didn't believe it before?" she said.

"Well...you know...it just seemed too easy." he said.

"It was." she said. "That's why it's not over. She needs to take at least one more run at you."

"Really?" he asked. "She can't just ride off into the sunset?"

"No way." she said. "You were together too long. Not tonight, maybe not even tomorrow, but she's going to make another attempt."

"You can come and stay with me." he said. "If she shows up, you can talk her down."

She thought about it. It was what she wanted, but not under those circumstances. It did appear that Taylor was calling the shots with this break up, the problem was that she didn't know it was a break up yet. He was just going along for the ride, remaining neutral. It would require more than that on his part to be successful.

"I'm staying here." she said quietly. "What you witnessed at the club is probably the extent of my diplomacy. As you know, I tend to settle disputes with a gun. You need to do it. It won't work if you don't."

"Okay." he said. "Should I call her?"

"That sends the wrong message. It gives her hope." she said. "You need to wait for her to come to you. Then explain it to her. Like you would to a 2 year old. Make sure that she understands. Maybe then we could talk about different living arrangements."

She grabbed his cut and went into the bathroom. She shed her clothes and put it on. She looked at herself in the mirror. Not bad. Seeing herself in the biker jacket made her wonder where she was going. There's no denying that this is a huge part of his life. She walked back out.

"Nice. I guess this means we have to do it at your place." he said.

"For the time being." she said. "Here or Nehalem."

"Oh, there are plenty of other places we could go..." he said.

She sat down next to him.

"She will be over soon, Erik." she said. "You need to do this. You'll feel much better after it's over."

"I always do after a difficult situation." he said.

"So tell me about your anger issues." she said. "That was a little scary."

He was hoping that this situation would lead to the obvious conclusion, but she wants to talk. Coming out of the bathroom in just his cut wasn't conducive to that. Here we go.

"I don't know what it is." he said. "I never used to be this way. To a lesser extent everyone in the club does it."

"Is that lesser extent more than what yours used to be?" she asked.

"Well, you know me." he said. "I'll always answer the bell when I'm in the field, but other than that, I'm peaceful. I used to be peaceful. I guess seeing it on a daily basis...I went out to prove myself early on, and never looked back. I'm sure that's why they made me Sergeant-at-Arms, but I just kept going."

"How's Johnny feel about that?" she asked.

"How could you know that?" he asked.

"It doesn't take a genius. You get called to the principal's office immediately after you make a bloody mess of someone's face." she said. "They know you're tough. Tougher than everyone. It's time to reel it in. Don't worry, they'll still be scared of you."

"Are you?" he asked. "Scared of me?"

"Have you ever known me to be scared?" she asked.

"You were a little scared back in Cairo when you fucked up that timer for the C-4." he said.

"That wasn't fear, it was embarrassment." she said. "I still can't believe I did that. I'm not scared of you, Stryker, to answer your question. But I don't like what you've become. Think about it, that's all I ask. That animal at the 'Red Knight' isn't the guy I fell in love with."

"You fell in love with me?" he asked.

"You're kidding, right?" she said. "I was a lovesick puppy dog."

"You seem to have grown out of that." he said.

"Is that a problem?" she asked.

"No, I like the new you." he said.

She really didn't want to do it, but she needed to show that she was strong. She took the cut off and put on a robe.

"You should go." she said.

"Really?" he asked.

"It's best." she said. "Until you take care of things."

"And I can't call her?" he asked.

"That's the worst thing you could do." she said. "Do you want it to be harder? Wait her out."

"Okay." he said. "I lo...like you a lot."

"I like you a lot too, Erik." she said. "I'll see you tomorrow."

He got on his bike and headed home. It was disappointing that she shut him out, but he understood. Did he really just almost tell her he loved her? Did he? Or was he trying to get laid? He was pretty sure he loved her, but it would be out of character for him to say it.

Tomorrow Liam will be here. There will almost certainly be a vote on the guns. He figured that Murph wanted him to vote for it to put things in motion, but the way he looked at it, if it was close and he voted against it, he could keep them out of danger. Even someone with Murph's resources wouldn't be able to find out what happened in that room with the vote. He knew that Johnny wanted it, it was his retirement plan. It meant around $50,000 every two weeks or so. Everybody could get well.

There was some opposition, though, and not without cause. Running guns was dangerous. Some didn't want to get in bed with the IRA, which was also understandable. The club had dabbled in crime, as all motorcycle clubs do, but not on this level. What would the Irish want next? If they said yes to this, they might expect them to do more. Much more. No, if it's close, I'll vote it down. Murphy will never know, for that matter nobody outside the club will. Not even Lexie.

Not that he didn't trust her, but he didn't know if he could really trust her. The information on the vote could be useful, particularly if she got in a jam with Murphy. He wanted to trust her, but she didn't need to know about this.

***

"It's not the Red Knight, it's the Red Knave." said Abe.

"I remember those stupid Knight and Knave puzzles from camp." said Erik. "That camp they sent me to."

"No, you don't remember anything about that camp." said Murphy. "But now you remember everything."

A spotlight covered Murphy with a red light as he spoke.

"His name is Mike, and this is Dave; one is a Knight, the other a Knave. The Knight tells the truth, while the Knave always lies;
You won't tell by looking in their eyes. You're allowed one question of either man; try to find the Knight if you can."

"You couldn't come up with anything harder than that?" asked Lexie. "I'm disappointed, Anthony."

"I remember the name of the bar is the Red Knight not the Red Knave. It's a biker bar, so I should know!" he said.

"Not the bar, you idiot." said Abe, exasperated. "The whole key is the Red Knave. At least it's a start. Then it goes to the fat chicks, and we all know you love to drink and sometimes you dance and chase chubby chicks when you're drunk. It's so simple."

"What the fuck are you talking about?" asked Erik.

"You're wasting your time." said Murphy. "He'll never get it. Even if you say the whole thing he won't. He's programmed."

"Wait, what?" asked Erik.

"Nothing for you to worry about." he said. "Petty Officer Vignolo is a troublemaker. Always has been."

"I just want you to be happy joyous and free, Erik." he said. "This suit wants you in chains. Which would you rather?"

"Aye, we can't trust 'im." he said. "He's workin' with the Feds. Seen it a thousand times, I 'ave."

It was Liam Gallagher. Where did he come from?

"You better watch out." she said. "I saw him give a guy brain damage at the Red Knave. It's okay, baby, if you want to call it the Red Knave, that's fine with me."

It was Lexie. Or was it Taylor? They were sitting next to each other, and he couldn't tell which one said it.

"It was her." said Taylor. "It always has been, except when Danielle was around. I guess she really is dead, huh? You know I've never seen you get violent. To me you're just a pussycat."

"Never seen me either, eh?" said Lexie. "I settle all of my disputes with a gun."

She pulled out a gun and shot Taylor in the head.

"See honey?" she said. "Now you don't have to do it. Much simpler than a messy breakup, don't you agree? You're next, Irish."

***"I could cry salty tears:
Where have I been all these years: Little wow tell me now:
How long has this been going on?"***

It was "l'amour brille," they were playing here. Wait, what? Where was he?

***There were chills up my spine, and some thrills I can't define, Listen sweet, I repeat,
How long has this been going on?"***

It was the same singer with denim shorts and a tank top ripped and secured loosely by safety pins. The same purple light bathed her, her hair was the same, everything was the same. It was like that first night with Danielle...or was it the night he was there with Lexie, when he killed DuBois? Was he really back at the Sun Casino in Monte Carlo? It looked just like it.

***"Kiss me once, then once more, what a dunce I was before.
What a break, For Heaven's sake,
How long has this been going on?"***

"Too damn long for me, that's for sure." said Lexie. "Could it get any more boring? Oh, right, this is your song with little miss perfect. She's dead, you know. So is that freak of a singer."

She aimed and shot the singer in her left eye.

"No I'm not!" said Danielle. "He knows it too. I called him!"

"You can't confirm that." she said. "Officially you're gone. You shouldn't have called him either. You really should have just stayed dead."

She put a bullet in the back of her head.

"You should have stayed dead too, Abe, you're trying to ruin everything." she said. "He can't know that shit."

She took aim and put one in his temple

"Don't you see he's with the Feds? And you thought he was loyal. How did you let this happen?" said Gallagher. "He's ruined us!"

"I know I said you were next, Irish, but some people jumped the line." she said. "Here ya go. You were looking a wee bit squeamish, anyway, don't you know."

She took aim and put one between Liam's eyes.

"Erik, how could you?" asked Johnny.

"It's okay, he promised the club won't get hurt." he said.

"And you believed him?" he said. "What about the Irish Kings? Do you think there won't be any retaliation?"

"Anthony, help me out here." he said. "Fix it!"

"I guess we're just going to have to kill you." he said. "Lexie?"

"My pleasure." she said.

She took aim and pulled the trigger.

He opened his eyes slowly and saw Huck about 3 inches from his nose.

Fucking weird dream. Why is Lexie always the bad guy? The Red Knave. That came up quite a bit. What does it mean? The Red Knight also came up, but it seemed to be a bridge to the other thing. This time, Taylor was in it. Lexie killed her. Does that mean it's over? Probably not.

"What are you doing here buddy?" he asked. "I thought you went with Mumma. Wait, you did go with her."

He smelled eggs and bacon cooking, and coffee. She was here. And she brought his cat.

He slowly walked down the stairs.

"Is your daddy up?" she said to the cat.

"Yeah, I'm up, what are you doing here?" he asked.

"We need to talk this through, Erik." she said. "I'm not giving up on you."

"It's not like we're launching nuclear missiles, we don't both have to turn the key." he said. "I'm done."

"I know you don't mean that, Erik." she said. "Just hear me out. If you still feel the same way after I'm through, I'll accept it. Huckleberry stays with you either way, he's your boy."

"Realistically, he'd be better off with you." he said. "Think about my lifestyle."

"It's okay, I'll look after him when you're away." she said. "You need him, and he needs you."

He doesn't need me, the cat will be fine with anyone who put a food bowl in front of it. He likes me, and I like him, but that's about the extent of it. He figured that this was a way for her to keep in contact if the worst happened. He wasn't going to start with that argument, he had so many other things to tell her that seemed more important.

He had kept drinking after he got home, and he had a hell of a hangover. He needed to keep this short and sweet, because he needed a few more hours.

"You're lucky." he said. "I am in the midst of one of the worst hangovers of my life. I'll keep it simple. We're done. Huck goes back with you. End of story."

"You're leaving me for her?" she asked.

I'm not leaving you for anyone." he said. "I'm just leaving."

"I know you fucked her at least once." she said. "And now, just by coincidence, you want to end it. Nothing to do with that gorgeous amazon woman that shows up out of nowhere."

"The average amazon woman was five feet, six inches tall, and Lexie is close to six feet." he said. "Murphy sent her. I have no control over that. And I'm not leaving you for her. I need to move on, that's all there is to it. It's not complicated."

"This is not the time to show off your knowledge of nothing." she said. "Although I did think they were taller."

"Yeah, Right?" he said. "Everybody does."

"We're not here to talk about amazon women." she said.

"But that's what you said Lexie is." he said. "Are we not talking about her?"

He told her point blank that it was over, but she wasn't listening. He had crawled out of the hangover at least enough to fuck with her a little. Probably counterproductive, but if she's not going to listen to reason, I may as well be entertained.

"I think that we just established that Lexie is six fucking inches taller than the average amazon woman." she said. "Why, Erik? What did I do? Is it because of my jealousy of Danielle? Talk to me."

"It isn't anything you did." he said. "It's not you, it's me. I just can't go on this way. We've been together for a long time. Sometimes, over the course of time, things change, and one person doesn't feel the same way anymore. I'm that person. Lexie was right, I'll always love you, but this is over."

Simple like talking to a two year old, right?

"Don't bring her into this." she said. "It's bad enough that she chased you all the way out here, but don't use her words against me."

"Listen carefully. Murphy sent her here." he said. "I didn't ask for this, yet here she is. I had sex with her at the clubhouse because it could have been dangerous for both of us if I didn't. The guys in the club wouldn't have bought it. Murphy didn't give us a very good cover."

He, of course, didn't tell her about the other times they had sex.

"Dangerous?" she said. "How? They're your riding buddies. Why would they care?"

Now would be a good time for her to know a little more about the club, but if he told her now, she would think it was fake.

"You don't know much about us. That's not by accident." he said. "If you knew everything you would be shocked."

And might want to break up with me, he thought. Hey!

"I'm a big girl." she said. "You can tell me anything. I can take it."

"You see, you say that, but..." he said. "The club started out as a mission. Haven't you noticed that I haven't had any assignments lately? The Centurions are a job."

"You're working stateside?" she asked. "I thought that was the FBI."

"Murphy goes where he's needed. Where ever he wants, really. The FBI doesn't know about him." he said. "The President doesn't even know, and believe me, he doesn't want to know."

"So the Centurions are the mission? You're going to bust your buddies?" she asked.

"It's not that simple." he said. "I've been given assurances that the club won't be hurt. What I've told you about the club...is essentially what I thought you wanted to hear. You would have a hard time accepting what they really are...what I really am."

"It doesn't have to be that way." she said. "You're a good person. It's that fucking Murphy that's turning you into something you're not. I can help you."

"He's not turning me into something I'm not." he said. "I've always been this way. I live in a world that you could never understand. That's part of the reason I'm doing this. To protect you. There are things that could happen...it's just best that you're not around me."

"You're scaring me, Erik." she said.

"Good. You *should* be scared." he said. "I can't bring you along for this ride. It's not for you. And I'm not asking, this is how it's going to be."

"But it is for her?" she asked. "She gets to come along for the ride?"

"Lexie is a complicated woman." he said. "But I can safely say that she is more prepared for what is going to happen than literally anyone else in the world. This is what she does. This is what I do. It's something you could never do."

That bond was hard to compete with. Maybe she needed to go on a killing spree with him sometime.

She swore that she would never do this. From the time she learned about it, it just fell into the category of playing God. This was a desperate situation, and it was exactly the situation to use it. To protect him. Bad things happened because of this, it was time something good came from it.

"Erik, I want you to listen carefully to me." she said. "The Red Knave dances with fat girls when he's drunk."

"What the hell are you talking about?" he asked.

She repeated herself, careful to fully annunciate every word. She looked at him expectantly.

"I'm sorry, I got nothing." he said.

What the hell happened? She knew that they were the right words; she had practiced them a million times! Ever since that night she listened in on his call with Murphy. He spoke those words, and Erik went into a waking trance. His sole reason for living seemed to be to do whatever Murphy asked him to after he said those words. Why doesn't it work for me?

"Listen, I have a thing with the club later on, and I need to sleep for a while longer." he said. "Please take Huck with you. If you need me to explain this to you again, I will, but I have a big meeting, and I need my sleep."

"This isn't over." she said.

"Yes, that would make far too much sense." he said. "Goodbye."

He climbed the stairs, not bothering to look back to see if she was leaving. He climbed into bed, and was asleep within a minute.

Chapter 5

He woke up again around 4. Huck was still there, in fact, he was the one to wake him up. He didn't mind. He really did love the cat; it just wasn't practical for him to stay here. He would have a hard time keeping a plant alive, as flighty as his life was, much less a cat.

"Well, I guess it's you and me for the moment, little buddy." he said. "At least I hope."

He had just thought that it was possible that she was still here. If she was, he would surely have heard her by now. She wasn't exactly a quiet person.

He got up and got in the shower. He would head over to the hotel and see what Lexie was up to.

Was it over? He was making progress, but she had told him point blank that it wasn't over. Those were her exact words. Did he need to reveal more about the club? More about him? He would have to be careful. She was unstable, there was no other way to describe it. If he told her too much, she could use it against him. She didn't need to know all that anyway, but maybe just enough to scare her off.

"I gotta go do some things, Hucker, I'll be back when I get back." he said.

He got on his bike and headed for Seattle. It was a nice day. Most days here were overcast and a little cool, which suited Erik just fine, but the sun was actually trying to make an appearance.

He got to the hotel and went up to 815. He knocked on the door, and saw a shadow appear over the peephole and heard the locks tumble open.

He went inside and sat down. Lexie was in the bathroom doing her face. He didn't figure that there was much work there, because she started out with an incredible template.

"So what's going on?" she asked.

"She showed up first thing in the morning, and cooked breakfast for me." he said.

"Is she a good cook?" she asked.

"Not bad, but I didn't eat." he said. "I had a bad hangover, so I did my best to get rid of her as quickly as possible. She still doesn't think it's over, but it's not because of anything I did. I was tough, you would have been proud."

"So she's not giving up yet?" she asked.

"Unfortunately not." he said. "She did do something a little weird though."

"Oh?" she said.

"She said this thing. It seems like she expected some kind of reaction from me." he said. "I had another weird dream where it came up too. She said 'The Red Knave dances with fat girls when he's drunk.' Does that mean anything to you?"

She froze at the words. How did she know?

"That's an odd thing to say." she said. "Tell me about the dream."

He told her about the dream.

"Why do I always have to be the bad guy?" she asked.

"I know, right?" he said.

"Murphy wants us to call." she said.

She picked up the phone and dialed the number.

"Collect from Domino." she said.

"You remember what we were talking about the other day?" she said. "Things we might not need to know? With Murphy?"

"Say no more." he said. "I'll go get some ice."

"Thanks." she said.

She reached out and gave him a big kiss.

"Ms. Tenenzapf. You're in country for 3 days, and your prints are already being run." he said.

"There was an incident." she said. "I had no choice. He was in trouble."

"Trouble that he couldn't handle?" he asked.

"He was distracted. He was busy pummeling someone's face into a pool table." she said. "The other guy had a gun, I had to do it."

"I think I can safely say that this isn't typical behavior for him." he said.

"No shit!" she said. "Didn't I tell you he was in deep? I'm worried about him."

"Perhaps that's why you're there after all, Lexie." he said. "You called me."

"She knows his go phrase!" she said.

"Actually she knows what it used to be." he said. "Do you think I wouldn't know that it had been compromised? We changed it. Did she actually try to use it on him?"

"They're going through a tough breakup." she said. "I'm sure it was a last resort."

"I may have underestimated her." he said.

"We all did." she said. "We met at the club yesterday."

"How did that go?" he asked.

"Surprisingly well." she said. "You would have been proud. I didn't touch her. I made a few friends while he was talking to the president in the back."

"Good. Was this before or after the incident at the Red Knight?" he asked. "The Irony of that name is killing me."

"After." she said. "Who ran my prints?"

"Seattle PD." he said. "Nothing to worry about, I have a 'do not touch' order on you, but whenever they run your prints or do any kind of check on you, I'm going to know. I wish you would be more careful. We don't want people even knowing that you exist."

"Okay, I'll try to be good." she said. "So he's got a new code?"

"Of course." he said. "You should have known there was a new code when you found out about it. It was compromised. This is something we take seriously. I don't want to use it, so I damn sure don't want anyone else to."

Erik was back at the door. He mouthed asking if it was okay, and she nodded.

"You want to talk to him?" she asked.

"Absolutely." he said.

She handed him the phone.

"Would you please ask Miss Tenenzapf to leave?" he asked.

"Uh, yeah, sure, I guess." he said.

He covered the phone.

"He wants you to leave." he said.

"Oh...okay." she said, and headed out the door.

"I didn't want you to feel like she was the only one I have secrets with." he said.

"Oh, no, yeah, I didn't feel that way." he said.

"You know why she wanted you to leave, don't you?" he asked.

"It was that Red Knave thing." he said. "She had a reaction after I said it. Then suddenly she needed to call you. My guess is that's what used to be my trigger."

"Why used to be?" he asked.

"Because it didn't trigger me when Taylor said it. She was really confused." he said. "You must have changed it."

"You're very perceptive, Mr. Stryker." he said. "How is the vote going to shake out tonight?"

"I don't have a crystal ball, Anthony, but it could go either way." he said. "I don't think there's any secret to how you want it to go."

"It would be preferable if the guns were approved, but there are some rumblings of a backup plan with the Irish. Can I count on you?" he said.

"I really can't divulge that information, Anthony. Club policy." he said.

"Of course. Club policy. Either way, you're here until the end. I need to let you know that if certain scenarios happen, I'll probably have to 'kill' you."

"Like you 'killed' Danielle?" he asked.

"Now there's a blast from the past." he said. "What brings her to mind?"

"I've never stopped thinking about her." he said. "You will at least admit that she was working for you?"

"I can neither confirm nor deny." he said. "Do yourself a favor? Focus on what's in front of you? Don't go chasing ghosts. She's gone."

The line went dead.

Lexie returned, peeking her head in to make sure he was off the phone.

"If it was about the Red Knave thing, you didn't need to send me away." he said.

"Really?" she asked.

"I had it figured out already." he said. "Your reaction confirmed it. He changed the code, obviously."

"How did you know?" she asked.

He shrugged his shoulders.

"Murph thinks I'm perceptive." he said. "I really put it all together when she tried to use it on me. She can be a big blubbering pile of tells. She really expected some earth shattering reaction from me, and when it didn't happen, she was so disappointed. The weirdness of what she said, combined with her reaction was all I needed. I watched you closely when I told you. You're better than her, but you still have a tell."

"Really? And what is that?" she asked.

"Wouldn't you like to know?" he said. "No, if I tell you, not only will you be aware of it, you could use it against me. You know, use the tell on purpose to mislead me. No, I'm sorry, I can't tell you."

"I'll be damned." she said. "Are we going to church?"

"Look who's fitting in!" he said. "I'm going to church, but you can wait with the other old ladies."

"Other?" she said. "Whose old lady am I?"

"Well, it's not official, because Taylor claims it's not over, but I was hoping you would be mine." he said.

"Is it over for you?" she asked.

"Definitely." he said.

"Good enough for me." she said. "You don't both have to agree. But we keep it on the down-low until it's official."

"Fair enough." he said. "Let's get out of here."

***

They walked into the club, and it was crowded. It always was for church. Brendan was sitting at the edge of the bar, looking like he was waiting for them.

"Aye, lassie, how are ya?" he said.

"Ah, bollocks, I'm doin' just fine, but I need a wee bit o' that Bushmills Black, hold ta' soda!" she said.

"Prospect!" You heard the cailín! Bushmills Black, posthaste!" he said.

"Aye, tanks. We'll have some craic in here tonight!" she said. "Just need to mek sure dis gobshite don't let me see t' bottom!"

Jessica and Emily were there, and they just stared blankly at Lexie as she put on her little performance.

"That was remarkable!" said Jessica. "How did you do that?"

"I spent some time in Belfast on assignment." she said. "If you spend any time at all there, you can't help but pick it up."

Brendan looked at her in amazement.

"What kind of assignment was that, luv?" he asked.

"I could tell ya, but then I'd have to kill ya." she said.
"Come and sit with us." she said.
"I'd love to." she said.
"Ya need ta watch out fer this one, Rikky boy!" he said. "She been 'round t' block a few times, like!"
"Don't I know it." he said.
"Now that yer here, we can get the party started." he said. "Liam and Johnny and Kirk waitin' out back."
"Aye." he said.
Lexie impressed him yet again, the way the brogue rolled right off her tongue.
They got back to the table, and sat down. This is where the vote would take place later on. Johnny, Kirk, and Liam were already there. Kirk was the VP.
"Liam, Erik." he said. "Erik, Liam."
Erik stretched to shake his hand.
"I need to ask ya somethin', son." he said.
"Anything." said Erik.
"Do you work fer the Federal Government?" he asked.
"No, Never." he said.
"Technically he was telling the truth. By definition, black ops didn't exist to the federal government.
"John boy tells me you've done some freelance mercenary work in the desert." he said. "What's that all about?"
"Well, sir, I can't tell you too much about that." he said. "My employer wouldn't approve. I can assure you that I don't work for the crown."
"Do you think you're funny, boy?" he said.
"No, sir, I just wanted you to know that we're on the same side." he said. "For lack of a better word I can say I'm helping people to be free. The thing about the crown...I don't know much about the IRA, but I know you don't like those bastards. You know? The British."
"Aye, son, we don't." he said. "Don't like the Protestants much either. You're not one of those, are ye'?"
"I was raised Catholic." he said.
They didn't need to know the last time he'd seen the inside of a Church. Hell, most of them probably hadn't seen it too recently either.

"Catholic, eh? That's the right answer. A soldier o' fortune and a freedom fighter, eh? We've noticed that you don' seem to do as much time as ye should. What's that about?" he asked.

"I've done plenty of time." he said. "My best friend growing up, Carl, is a lawyer, and a good one. We went to St. Francis together. He's gotten me out of plenty of scrapes."

"Aye, it's good to have such friends." he said. "We got friends too, don't ya know? Our guys are good. They went through your life with a fine toothed comb. They found nothing. Still I had my suspicions. After talking to you here, I trust ya, and there isn't a reason to suspect ya. Let's talk about how we're going to get these guns to ya."

"It's usually pretty quiet on the Northern border." said Johnny.

"We're going to be really careful." said Liam. "There's a little town called Rossland pretty close to the Idaho border. I know it's a long way, but we've been watching it fer a while, an' it's safe. We bring the guns over there, then you drive 'em through the mountains back to Seattle. We have a buyer who will take delivery of 50 crates every two weeks. For the foreseeable future. We could make a lot of money, gents."

"I wasn't really worried about your side of the border." said Erik. "Speaking of the Federal Government, we should be the ones worried about that. You'll never come over, at least not when the guns are involved. Have you looked at our side at all?"

"There aren't any guarantees in life, boyo, but I can tell you that if there was activity in the states, we would know about it." he said.

"I hope you're right." he said.

"We'll have to vote on it." said Johnny. "I think you know my feelings."

Johnny hadn't hidden his feelings on this at all. Everyone in the club knew how he felt. There was opposition. It was entirely possible that Erik would be part of that opposition. It would have been a great plan, but he had inside information. He didn't trust Murphy not to hurt the club either.

Everyone left but him and John.

"Can I count on you?" asked Johnny.

"I'll tell the truth, John, I'm skeptical." he said. "The money's great, but guns are a whole different animal. Different charges, different time, and it's more dangerous. I know people who fucked around with guns and got clipped just because of who they were dealing with. It's a whole different world."

"I don't think it's anything we can't handle." he said. "The club is solid. Nobody's going in with their eyes closed."

"See, you say that, but..." he said. "Most of the guys don't know what's involved. The risks. They're only thinking about the money, not the possibility that they won't be able to spend it."

"There are no guarantees." he said. "I can tell you one thing though. If we pass this thing up, we'll never see it again."

"That could be a good thing." he said. "Look, Johnny, I understand where you're coming from, believe me. This is major. We could all get well. They could also lock us up. Liam's talking about the Federal Government, they don't care too much about the shit we're doing now. Bring in the kind of weight we'll have with the guns, that's gonna change. We'll be on the radar. A big huge fucking blip. I don't want to be the one to put anyone in that position. Whatever the club's decision is, you know that I'll fully support it, and do my very best to make sure it succeeds. But I will vote my conscience."

"You know that you carry a few votes, don't you?" he said.

"Of course. I can't help that. Everyone is free to vote as they wish." he said. "I'll always do what's best for the club."

"As will I." he said. "Even if we disagree on what that is."

"The beauty of democracy." he said. "I know what this means to you, John. But there are 9 other members that I have to think about."

"Just give it some thought." he said. "That's all I ask. This could be a good thing for all of us."

"I've thought of little else since it came up." he said.

If you don't count Lexie blowing into town unexpectedly and me breaking up with Taylor, he thought, my mind is clear as a bell.

John had said his piece. The rest was up to Erik.

"You still think you have that thing with Taylor figured out?" he asked.

"I'll admit that last we talked it was wishful thinking." he said. "I've come back down to earth, and I'll just say I'm making progress."

"Slow and steady." he said. "Don't let this new filly cloud your judgement. It'll be worse if you have to do it again."

"I don't even want to do it the first time." he said. "Lexie isn't exactly a new filly, by the way, I've known her for 8 years."

"You'll have to tell me all about it someday, son." he said.

"The same applies to you as Liam." he said. "My employer...I can't talk about it. Let's just put it this way. You don't want to get on his bad side."

"Freedom fighter, eh?" he said.

"I'll admit that I embellished that a little." he said. "Considering my audience, freedom fighter sounded better than the truth."

"Aye, laddie." he said. "That's the extent of my Irish. We'll work out whether there's any wiggle room there later."

"There's not." he said. "And there never will be."

He was looking John directly in the eye. John didn't scare. He knew better than to push, though.

"Okay, son." he said. "Just do me a favor? You vote against me, don't make a speech? Don't give them anything to think about?"

"Just a yea or nay." he said. "They have all the information they need."

"Thanks, Erik." he said. "Vote's in 20 minutes."

***

He got back out to the bar to find Lexie sitting with Jessica and Emily.

"Tráeme una cerveza de jengibre, y trae a estas dos damas un par de más cervezas?" said Lexie.

She was talking to the prospect, Miguel, who was Puerto Rican.

"Si senorita." he said.

He walked away quickly.

"She's amazing, Erik!" said Emily. "Where did you find her?"

"I don't know who found who." he said. "What do you think, Lexie?"

"If I remember right, Stryker, It was me waiting for you on that pier in Mombasa. Guess that means I found you." she quipped.

"So it would seem." he said. "By the way, ladies, that was nothing. After we first met, she talked to the waiter in Swahili at this place called 'Yul's on the beach' in Kenya. She was, of course, trying to impress me."

"I was not!" she said.

"Need I remind you of a conversation we had very recently?" he asked "About you being nervous?"

"Oh, my God, I should never have told you about that!" she said.

"I think it's cute." he said. "Then you went all bad ass on me."

Miguel returned with the drinks.

"Gracias." she said.

"Bring me a coffee, Miggy." he said. "Oh and Miggy? English only in here."

""Yes, sir. Coming right up." he said.

"Swahili?" said Jessica. "What a life you've led!"

"There are large swaths that I can't tell you about." she said.

"So what?" she said. "Mombasa? Kenya? I don't need everything, just give me what you can."

"Okay." she said. "Maybe we can work something out. In a fictional location, fictional job sort of way."

"You too, Slick!" she said, punching Erik in the arm. "I had no idea."

"That's the way it should be." he said. "Lexie seems to have forgotten who we work for."

"I haven't forgotten." she said. "Remember the large swaths I just talked about? We'll keep it clean. We're not working for him at the moment, at any rate."

"But we both know that he could call at any time." he said.

She looked at Jessica, shrugged her shoulders and held up her hands in surrender.

"We don't want to get you in trouble." she said.

"And he's the last person you would want to be in trouble with." said Erik. "Lexie gets in trouble, we *all* do."

"Don't worry, I'll find something I can tell you, and I'll even run it by golden boy here to make sure it's safe." she said.

"No, I trust you." he said. "Believe me, ladies, there is plenty of exciting stuff that she can talk about."

"That's all I'm asking for." she said. "For a girl who grew up on the Sound all her life, it won't take much to get my juices flowing."

"Vote!" yelled Kirk.

"Gotta go, ladies." he said. "It's so nice to see you all getting along."

"Are you kidding?" asked Emily. "She's the most interesting person we've met in years."

"This might take a while." he said. "I'll be back a soon as I can."

"Sure, babe." she said. "Take all the time you need."

She pulled him in for a long kiss. Everyone knew about Taylor but she wanted there to be no mistake as to who he belonged to now. It wasn't lost on the girls.

"So...Africa?" she asked.

"Just for part of that trip." she said. "By the way, ladies, official disclaimer, none of this actually happened. I'm just a great storyteller. From there we went down the Nile to Egypt."

She knew that under the circumstances, she could probably tell a lot of the story. The job was dead for more than 5 years. She would carefully word any details she gave so that they could never put it all together. She had done this before. Erik hadn't been working for Murphy long enough to know what he could and couldn't do. And her new friends would love it.

"Egypt?" said Emily. "The farthest I've ever been is to B.C. That's only out of the country because we're so far north."

"Well, we we're on this boat." she said. "Have you ever seen a pontoon boat?"

"Yeah!" she said. "My cousin has one."

"It was like that, but not as nice." she said. "It's just me and Erik, and we don't know each other that well, but we've become...close. I usually don't do that, you know? Give it up right away? I usually don't have to, but I told myself that if I didn't try, I would regret it."

"Really?" she asked. "Did he put up much of a fight?"

She started laughing.

"Are you kidding?" she said. "Do you remember who we're talking about? But I was seriously worried at the time that he would say no. Most don't, but if anybody was ever going to say no, it would be someone like Erik. Maybe say something about professionalism or something."

"Professionalism?" she asked.

"Maybe I shouldn't have said that. The point is that we were on a job." she said. "I've met people who don't mix business and pleasure."

"I would ask, but you probably can't tell me." she said.

"You're very perceptive, Jessica." she said. "Both of you are. We're going to get along fine."

"So what happened next?" she asked.

"Okay, what *can* I tell you? Oh, there were these natives on the shore who attacked us." she said.

"What happened?" asked Emily.

"Let's just say it had been a while since they'd seen a white woman." she said. "They were shooting poison darts at us. I exchanged words in their native tongue, Erik doesn't understand any of it by the way, and I convinced them that I needed to go in the cabin before I can surrender."

"And?" she asked.

"I came out with a shotgun and shot the leader in the head, then I put one in the guy standing next to him." she said. "After that, they all scattered. I knew that I had bought us some time, because this particular tribe has an extensive death ritual that they would perform for everyone, that was even more elaborate for the leader, who I had just killed."

"Wow. So you've killed someone?" asked Jessica.

"Remember when I said none of this ever happened?" she said. "To answer your question, yes, I've killed, I popped my cherry when I was 16." she said. "But since none of this ever happened, and the non-existent job I'm telling you about certainly wouldn't involve killing people, we'll keep this as fiction."

"When I was 16, I was popping a different kind of cherry." said Emily.

"You see there, Em?" she said. "You have me beat in that department. But I did have the opportunity to make up for lost time."

"So what happened next?" Jessica asked.

"We get to Cairo, and we're posing as man and wife at this swanky hotel. I needed to do something for the non-existent job, so I leave Erik at the hotel. I come back, and this floozy is all over him. And I'm not talking subtle. I walk into the card room, and she has taken his hand and placed it on her tit." she said. "Erik, of course doesn't see a problem there. He claims that he didn't even know that he'd been feeling her up. Says he's trying to blend in. I'm falling in love with Erik, an unprecedented event for me, by the way, with the exception of one other guy. I hit the skank with a left hook, she hits the deck. Erik's still acting like it's no big deal. We are, of course, actually *trying* to blend in, and decking the tramp doesn't exactly qualify."

"So what did they say?" asked Emily.

"Luckily, nobody saw it. It was dark in there." she said. "Later we had another part of this no-existent job to do. We head out to this warehouse. By now I'm not myself. I'm falling in love with Stryker. He has me so whipped that I make a mistake at the warehouse. To this day I still can't figure out why I did what I did. I wasn't thinking straight. I fucked it up. I wasn't even supposed to be there. Erik was supposed to go to the warehouse alone, but I wormed my way in. I could tell you why I went against orders and went along anyway, but it would involve a different story about the only other guy I fell this hard for. I set the timer on the c-4 for 4 minutes. As it turns out, the c-4 would have gone up anyway. I tell Erik that I set the timer. Setting that timer cost us 2 minutes of escape time. As we're running away, the building blows up, throws us about 20 feet in the air, and I twist my ankle. We get back to the hotel and there's a bottle of Vicodin sent up by the boss. The following morning, he tells me I'm going to Europe with Erik, and Mur...our boss chews me out inviting myself along to the warehouse, and for setting the timers. Meanwhile, Stryker gets a hefty bonus for killing one of the bosses in Egypt. He found the guy by accident, and shot him before he even knew who it was. That's why I call him golden boy sometimes. Everything always seems to work out for him."

"So you blew up the warehouse and got hurt by the blast?" she asked. "What happened next?"

"He found some Blond Lebanese hash while he was taking out a couple of guards. They were smoking when he got them. We're on the way back to the hotel in the rover, and there's this empty soda can rolling around on the floor. Get this. He makes a pipe out of it, so we can smoke the hash." she said.

"I've done that." said Jessica." "You create a dent, and punch holes in the bottom part of the can and inhale through the part you drink out of."

"My formative years were...different. I never learned how to make a pipe out of an empty can." she said. "Or how to open a bottle with a lighter."

"I can do that too." said Emily.

"How did your boss know that you twisted your ankle?" asked Jessica.

"My boss knows everything." she said. "It's just simpler to think about it like that. He has resources that you can't imagine. He has spies everywhere. If it's possible for him to know, he knows. If it seems impossible for him to know, he knows. If you know there's no way he knows, he knows. It's really annoying."

"Wow...up the Nile, through Egypt, then on to Europe. How did you get involved in this?"

Same as Erik, he found me." she said. "We both have a certain skill set that most people don't."

"And what's that?" she asked.

Well...I could tell you, but then I'd have to kill you." she said.

They both stared blankly back at her.

"Oh, come on, it's a joke." she said. "You've never heard that one? Someone asks a spy something he's not supposed to tell, and he says, 'I can tell you, but then I have to kill you.' You know? So the secret doesn't get out?"

"Right, I get it." said Emily. "So you're a spy?"

"This never happened. Non-existent job." she said. "If it was real, I would say that Erik and I do work that other people are unwilling, unable, or just too scared to do. For the greater good."

"Okay." she said. "Do you work with Erik a lot?"

"Only that one time." she said. "I know it sounds a little corny, but it really was the best week of my life. That week...we got so close. It just felt so right. Neither of us are assigned to anything now, so I came to look him up."

"And rekindle things?" she said. "I really can't blame you."
"That wasn't the reason, I just wanted to see how he was." she said. "But now that I'm here..."

"All those exciting places, and now you're in Seattle." she said. "It must be a bit of a letdown."

"Please." she said. "You should see the places I usually work. Compared to that, Seattle is paradise. I'm usually stuck in a wasteland, with nothing but sand and hostile enemies."

"So what happened in Europe?" asked Emily.

"I've already told you too much." she said. "Another time, I promise. Tell me about Seattle. Tell me about your formative years."

***

"So first we drive almost all the way to Idaho, through the mountains, then we just turn around and come back?" asked Pat.

"It's not as bad as it sounds." he said. "I've already talked to Theo in Diablo, and they're willing to pick it up from the checkpoint across the border from Rossland. They're willing to take it from there to Diablo. They'll do it for 5%, $2,500. Under the circumstances, it's a good deal for both of us. He's still got a piece of that trucking company."

"The $2,500 comes from our end?" asked Mike.

"It's a drop in the bucket!" he said. "We still net $47,500."

"$2500 is a lot to me." he said.

"Look at the big picture. This is happening every 2 weeks." he said. "We'll be rich!"

"Or in prison." he said.

"This is getting us nowhere. Let's have a vote." said John. "I vote yea."

Kirk spoke up.

"Yea."

He knew that Kirk would back John no matter what. He said no speeches, but he didn't say anything about when he would vote. By voting early, he would probably pick up some of those votes John was talking about.

"No." he said.

"Aye." said Brendan.

"Nay." said Pat.
"Nay." said Frank
"Nay." said Charlie.
"Yea." said Bill.
"Yea." said Nick.
"Nay." said Mike.

"It was up to Daniel, who had been on the fence the entire time. Nobody had any idea what he was thinking.

"I'm sorry, it's just too dangerous." he said. "No."

"GOD DAMN IT!" screamed John.

Daniel jumped back as if the force of his words knocked him over.

"Do you all not know what this means? Do you know what we just turned down?" he asked.

"A lot of money, and a good chance of going to prison." said Erik. "And not the kind of time we're used to. We'll regroup and think of something else. This wasn't right.""

John was shaking his head.

"The club has spoken." he said. "No fucking guns."

He slammed the gavel down.

Chapter 6

"So it got voted down?" he asked.

"Yeah, close vote." he said. "6-5. It could have gone either way. You should have seen Daniel, he made the deciding vote. John was very disappointed."

"Daniel didn't cast the deciding vote, you did." he said. "You knew just the right things to say, and you knew that Daniel would vote with you regardless."

"You think you have it all figured out, don't you, Anthony?" he said.

"Tell me I'm wrong." he said.

He was bluffing. There was no way he knew how Erik voted, much less what he said to his brothers. But he seemed confident. Confident like it was an established fact. Talking about it like they were only rehashing what they already knew.

"You're very perceptive, Anthony." he said.

"So you voted against it?" he said.

"I can neither confirm or deny." he said.

"That's what I thought." he said. "The Irish haven't been sitting on their hands. They knew that this was a possibility all along. They're working with someone else now."

"Who." he asked.

"Do I need to tell you how much easier this would have been if the Centurions would have taken the deal?" he asked.

"Do I need to tell you that I'll always do what's best for my club?" he asked.

"Satan's Saints." he said.

"The Saints? You've got to be kidding!" he said. "Does Johnny know?"

"Nobody knows." he said. "I don't need to tell you the importance of keeping it that way, do I? It changes things. With Brendan's ties to the IRA, I would guess it won't be long before the club knows."

Why would they choose one of our rivals?" he asked.

"Simple business. You weren't willing to work with them, and the Saints were." he said. "They needed to move the guns, get the money, kill more people, move the guns, get more money, kill more people and support the cause. The Irish Kings are hardcore."

"This isn't going to go over well." he said.

"No shit. You thought John was pissed before, wait until he hears this." he said. "It will soften the blow a little when The Saints get picked up by ATF."

"Like you had planned for the Centurions?" he asked.

"That was a sticky situation, which I suppose we both ought to be grateful that we're out of." he said. "I still need you to take the Irish out. All of them. The whole Canada thing is problematic, so we can't arrest them. They're better off dead anyway. They need to go. All of them, even the ones who never leave Ireland."

"So I guess I'm about to be deployed with the Merchant's then?" he asked.

"Either that, or we kill you, I haven't decided." he said. "Have you heard from Taylor?"

"Not since yesterday when she showed up at my apartment." he said. "She's going down swinging."

"How's Lexie doing?" he asked.

"She's doing well." he said. "Making friends believe it or not. With women."

"That *is* progress." he said. "Do you like working with her?"

"I don't know that you can actually call what we've been doing work." he said. "But the time that I did work with her, she was solid."

"Good." he said. "She's going across with you. You'll pose as newlyweds."

"Really?" he said. "Is that necessary?"

"Would you rather not?" he asked.

"No, it's not that, it's just that I can handle this alone." he said.

"That's what everyone thinks." he said. "A little help is never a bad thing. I picked the two of you based on your ability to be discreet. I could have it done quick and loud the other way, but we want to send a different message. That their never safe, and they won't see it coming. Things are great, then suddenly they're not. You know what I mean."

"I get it now." he said. "Makes sense."

"If she's reaching out to people of her own gender, you probably had something to do with that." he said. "She's becoming human again. Having her in on this thing is just what she needs."

"What happened to her? Seriously?" he asked. "You act like she's going through a crisis."

"Nothing that she can't handle, but it helps her more than you could know to be back in civilization with people who care about her." he said.

"You can't tell me?" he asked.

"If it was you, you wouldn't want me to tell, and I respect that." he said. "You're right, I can't tell you, but she can...and will in time."

"Okay." he said.

"The club can't know what you know until they hear it from someone else." he said "For your own safety."

"No shit. I'm not stupid, Murph. I know." he said.

"I didn't mean it the way you took it. I know that you know. It's just something that if I say it, I feel better. I would never want anything to happen to you." he said. "Have Lexie call me when you see her."

The line went dead.

So, I'm going over there. And taking Lexie. And we're newlyweds. He wondered again why Murph was trying to set them up.

He needed a little alone time, so he headed back to Bremerton. He would call Lexie later. She was still talking with Jessica and Emily.

He went around the southern edge of the Sound instead of taking the ferry. It helped to ride.

The last time, it took a while to get over her. Actually, he never did. That's where the "living a lie" part came in. As much as he loved Taylor, and he really did, Lexie had something that she didn't. He couldn't define it, but it was there nonetheless.

He pulled up to the building and saw Taylor's car. He almost turned around and went back to Seattle. Maybe he could get this over with tonight, he thought.

He walked in, and she was sitting on the couch scratching Huck between the ears.

"I'm sorry." she said. "I need to tell you something."

She looked different. More confident.

"What is it?" he asked.

"I really don't know how to say it." she said. "I find it a little hard to believe myself. I'm going to New York."

"New York?" he asked. "Why?"

"Well, you know that I did a little modeling when I was younger. Out of the blue, I get a call from this guy who has seen some of my headshots. He says he wants to hire me, and he's not taking no for an answer." she said. "The name of the agency is AMM. He's in Seattle to see me. I had never heard of it, but I called Victor at Whitecaps, and he said it's legit. He gives me a $20,000 signing bonus and he wants me to go to this extended orientation in New York, then it's off to Paris in a couple weeks!"

It was a little much to believe, but this kind of thing happens all the time. What could he say? The guy had given her a $20,000 signing bonus, and people don't do that if they're not serious. He knew she had the goods, she looked great. He could easily see her being a model. She had the temperament, that's for sure. That probably wasn't fair, all the models he had seen seemed to think that everyone owed them something because they were beautiful. Taylor was a little needy sometimes, but it wasn't like that. He was truly happy for her.

"That's great." he said. "I think I'm as shocked as you."

"I know, right?" she said. "I know we've had some problems lately, and I'm going away..."

"So am I." he said. "I heard from Murphy today."

"I thought you were working stateside." she said. "With the club."

"That's part of it." he said. "They got out of that deal, by the way, so I don't have to worry about Murph busting them. I need to go deal with the elements on the other side, you know, overseas."

"I never know what to say to you when you talk about it." she said. "Anyway, we're both going away, that might make it easier."

"I don't want to give up on you, Erik. Why don't we say we're just on break until we figure it out?" she said. "I love you."

"I love you, too." he said. "That's never been the problem. Your life just got as exciting as mine. We can play it by ear, but it's possible that we might end up with other people."

"You mean her?" she asked.

"I don't know, maybe." he said. "It's good that we're getting a break. So we can really figure things out."

"Yeah, I know. But it feels like we're splitting." she said.

"Well, you're a world traveler, I'm a world traveler, who knows?" he asked. "Maybe we'll run into each other somewhere in Europe. You still have my phone number and address, so you know how to get a hold of me. If you want me to contact you, you'll have to get me your information."

"Where are you going?" she asked.

"Ireland." he said.

"Okay." she said. "I'll take Huck back to Casey's if you want."

"Leave him here. Is it okay if I leave him with her when I'm gone?" he asked. "Then come pick him up when I get back?"

"I'm sure it is." she said. "That was the plan before all this happened. I'm leaving Dee with her until I'm settled."

"Why don't we do that then?" he said. "I hate to admit it, but you're right. I would miss him a lot. I'll let Casey know."

"Okay." she said. "I'm leaving in two hours. Shall I call when I get there?"

"If you want." he said. "You're going to make it, baby."

She went over and gave him a hug. She didn't want to let go. He understood.

"It's okay." he said. "Go live your dream. Forget about me."

"I could never forget you, Erik." she said.

She was crying. It was the last thing she wanted. He pretended not to notice. Suddenly she put her lips on his. She kissed him passionately. He didn't know what to do, so he just went with it. After all, she was leaving.

"I'll be in touch." she said.

She released him and walked away.

***

"Where did you go last night?" she asked.

"Home." he said. "You seemed to be having fun with the girls. I needed some alone time, but when I got home, she was there."

"Really?" she said. "What was that about?"

"It wasn't like that." he said quietly. "She's going to New York."

"Really?" she asked. "Why?"

"She got a modeling gig." he said. "Some guy saw some of her old headshots, and decided he couldn't live without her."

"No shit?" she said. "Taylor is a model?"

"Is that so hard to believe?" he asked.

"Not at all, she's a natural beauty." she said. "You know I've been asked to model."

"What, for the cover of 'Soldier of Fortune'? he asked.

"You never let one slip past, do you, Stryker?" she said.

"When you tee 'em up like that? I just can't resist taking a swing. You have to admit it's funny. It doesn't surprise me at all that you've had offers." he said. "You've got the looks in spades."

"So I guess it's over." she said.

"She doesn't exactly see it that way, but she took the job, and the money." he said. "He gave her a $20,000 signing bonus. She's framing it as a break. I told her that it's possible that I could find someone else, or maybe she will. She is, of course, not ready for that."

"Really?" she asked. "Do you have anyone in mind?"

"I'll have to think about it." he said. "I think we were talking just the other day about you becoming my new old lady, which reminds me, you need to call Murphy."

"Why would one thing remind you of the other." she asked.

"Call Murphy and find out." he said. "Should I leave the room?"

"Should you leave the room? Mr. 'I figured it out before we even talked.'" she said. "I'm sure there's nothing he needs to tell me that you don't already know."

"Well, last time you asked me to leave." he said. "So I want to respect your privacy."

"You having fun? Having a good time with this?" she asked.

"Of course." he said.

She didn't show it, but she was relieved that Taylor was gone, regardless of her calling it a "break." Maybe she will actually find someone else. Sometimes Erik needed...a little help. Out of sight, out of mind. Modeling? How did that happen? She must have done some work in the past. Erik said the guy saw some old headshots. Does this mean we have to see her on billboards and magazine ads?

"Collect from Domino." she said.

"Ms. Tenenzapf!" he said. "I hear you're a social butterfly these days."

"I've made some friends." she said.

"That's good." he said. "So this is the latest, Erik already knows. The Irish have made a deal with another outlaw biker club called the Satan's Saints. John is pissed that the vote didn't go his way, probably more so when he discovers that the Saints got the deal. I'm sure he'll feel better after I give the Saints to ATF. Nobody else knows about the Saints, by the way, so don't say anything. The club will find out soon enough."

"I'm not stupid, Anthony." she said.

"I know, Lexie, it's just something I have to say." he said. "We still need to deal with the Irish Kings. That's where you and Erik come in. You're going to Belfast, posing as newlyweds. Do you think you can pull that off?"

"I think I probably can." she said.

"Good." he said. "You have to take all of them out. Even the 'good' ones', even the priests. We need to be done with them...or at least slow them down for a few years. Will that be a problem?"

"I can't see how it would be." she said.

She put her hand over the phone.

"You okay with killing priests?" she asked.

He knew that this would come up. He had always heard that some of the IRA members, particularly higher ranking ones, were Catholic priests.

"I'll do whatever we need to do." he said.

He really didn't like the idea, but he knew that these men weren't like regular priests. They were vicious killers who eliminated anyone who got in the way of the cause. They wouldn't be like Father Leary back at St. Francis who never hurt a soul.

"Okay." he said. "I suggest that the two of you go over to the clubhouse and celebrate, now that Taylor is gone."

She heard the dial tone.

How did he always know everything? Did the man never sleep?

"He knows about Taylor." she said.

"Does that surprise you?" he asked.

"But why would he be watching her?" she asked. "It doesn't make sense."

"I've stopped trying to make sense of Anthony Murphy." he said.

She started thinking about her life again. She had been doing that quite a bit lately. Wondering where she was going, was her life what it was supposed to be, that kind of thing.

Back home...it was a mess. She was pretty sure Murphy fucked her, but she couldn't prove it. All she could do is wait it out and hope for the best. She had almost told Stryker a couple of times, but she couldn't bring herself to speak the words.

It would surely be something that he wouldn't understand. Or maybe he would. Nothing ever seemed to get to him. She took it back-nothing ever used to bother him. She thought of the scene at that bar, The Red Knight, where he almost killed that guy just for talking. He said it looked worse than it was, but who did he think he was talking to? She knew. The poor guy could be a vegetable for the rest of his life.

"He thinks we should go to the club." she said. "You know, celebrate? Because Taylor is gone?"

"We probably should, but the reception could be a little frosty." he said.

"Why?" she asked.

"Almost for sure the news about the Saints has made it there by now." he said. "After all, Brendan has strong ties to the IRA. I voted against the guns, probably brought a few people with me. There are people there who really wanted that deal. It was a club decision, but there can sometimes be friction between brothers."

"Right." she said. "You voted that way because you didn't trust Murphy. No guns, No possibility of arrest."

"They don't know that. I was lucky to get a few to come along." he said. "When we talked about it, Murph said something like it was a sticky situation that we were both fortunate to be out of. To me that means he was going to do it. You know him, any means necessary, all the tools in the chest."

"Believe me, I've heard that one more than a few times." she said. "The bad part is that he's serious. He really will. He doesn't care who gets hurt if the job gets done."

"The only thing that really bothers me is the MK." he said. "And this. If the Centurions would have been busted, that would have been worse."

"You're lucky. There are plenty of people that he has that option with that have no idea." she said. "That's how it's supposed to work. You're not supposed to know."

"Taylor helped me figure it out." he said. "Maybe that's how she got the code."

"I have no idea how she got it." she said. "All I know is that Anthony knew right away. She waited a long time to try it. In reality, she had less than a day."

"You want to go?" he asked. "To the club? Let me take what's coming to me before I get to say I told you so?"

"May as well get it over with." she said.

"Good." he said. "I guess you can finally see my apartment after."

"That should be interesting." she said.

"It will be fun." he said. "And if you want to move your things over, I can't think of any reason not to."

"Let me see the place first." she said.

***

They walked into the club, and there weren't too many people there. Those that were there were quiet. They must know, he thought. Jessica, Emily and Allie were sitting at a table. They waved at Lexie.

"I'm going to join them." she said.

"Okay." he said. "I'll go talk to John."

"I don't know if you heard, but the Saints got the contract with the Irish." he said.

"I didn't, but it makes sense." he said. "I hope now more than ever that I can say I told you so. Double rum and coke, Miggy."

"Don't hold your breath." he said. "That was by far, the most lucrative contract we were ever offered."

"Also the most dangerous." he said. "You know I never want to go against you, but this time I felt it was best for the club."

"Best for the club! Do you know how much money we just threw away?" he said. "I'm an old man, Erik, and I need to retire soon. This was my opportunity."

Miggy brought him his drink.

"There will be others." he said. "Maybe not exactly on your time line, maybe a little more work, but I can guarantee they won't be as dangerous. Do you want to spend your golden years behind bars?"

"You fucked me." he said. "It's that simple. Now we start from scratch."

"I'm sorry you feel that way, brother." he said. "Let's just see how it plays out with the Saints. You may be thanking me."

"Doubtful." he said. "I see you're here with that mystery woman again. What's up with that?"

"Well, the cat's out of the bag that she's not Jerry's sister if that's what you mean." he said. "She spilled it herself. Not about the work in the desert, but a different job here, in country."

"Thought that was the FBI." he said.

"I'll tell you again that I'm not working for the government." he said. "The guy I work for goes wherever he's needed, really wherever he wants. He doesn't answer to anybody."

"Someday, you'll tell me about it." he said. "Maybe on my deathbed."

"Someday never comes." he said.

"How's Taylor? How's she taking this?" he asked.

"She's off to New York." he said. "She got a modeling gig. She was actually in here the other night, while Lexie was here. Considering the principals, it didn't go bad at all."

"Modeling gig, eh?" he said. "Good for her. Has she ever done any modeling before?"

"When she was younger." he said. "The guy saw some old headshots and came to Seattle to make her an offer. Gave her a $20,000 signing bonus."

"Wow. Maybe you picked the wrong one." he said.

"It's not like that." he said. "I make good money, and she still doesn't want it to be over. Lexie...well, she has something that Taylor doesn't. I can't explain it."

He looked closely at Stryker. How in the hell does he do it? He already has the best looking woman in Washington State, another rolls into town who looks just as good, maybe even better, and to him it's just another day. He's willing to part with Taylor, which no red blooded American man could justify, and it doesn't even bother him.

"I want you to explain to me, son, how it is that you do what you do." he said. "Forget all of the mercenary shit, I just want to know how you handle the women."

"I just talk to them like they're people, I guess." he said. "I don't treat them any differently. Sometimes if you don't do what they want it makes them want you more."

"I know that part." he said. "But how do you do it with Taylor? Lexie? Most guys would be on their best behavior. You don't seem to give a shit."

"I guess it's all part of my charm." he said.

"My deathbed. I want you there." he said.

"Sure thing, if I'm still around." he said.

"You'll probably outlive us all, kid." he said.

Just then Brendan came in. He didn't look happy.

"I hope yer happy with yerself." he said.

"It could be the best thing." he said. "We still don't know what's going to happen."

"I know I'm a disgrace to me family." he said. "Me da won' even talk t' me."

"I did what I thought was best." he said.

Brendan came up and pushed him. John tried to get between them.

"What you thought was best!" he said. "You wouldn't know what was best if it hit you on the noggin, ya gobshite."

He reached around John and poked Erik again.

"Is this really how you want to settle this?" asked Erik.

"What, mebbe yer cailín can shoot me in the ear." he said.

He squirted around John, and was on Erik's back. Erik turned around so he was facing away, and slammed him into the bar. This jarred him loose, and he came up swinging. Erik caught his hand, twisted it behind his back, and began slamming his head into the wall. It would seem that Brendan was unconscious, because he wasn't resisting. Erik never slowed down and was mercilessly pummeling his head.

John wrapped his arms around both of Erik's and wrestled him away.

"THAT'S ENOUGH!" he screamed. "What the fuck is wrong with you?"

Erik came to his senses horrified.

"I'm sorry..." he said. "I don't know what..."

He quickly exited the club and got on his bike. He started heading for the mountains.

***

"Is he going to be okay?" asked Lexie.

"Brendan is tough as nails." said John. "Kirk called, they think he might have a concussion. We'll know more tomorrow. Do you know what's gotten into him?"

"I was hoping you could tell me." she said. "He's different. I've never seen him so violent. It's part of the reason I'm here, to try to bring him back."

"Did you get sent here by your mysterious boss?" he asked. "The one Erik won't tell me about?"

"Yeah. It's not just Erik...it's, well never mind." she said. "I'm here to help."

"I don't suppose you can tell me anything about your clandestine work?" he asked.

"No, I can't." she said. "I'm sure he explained that to you."

"Yeah. I don't like not knowing things." he said. "Call it a personal defect. I'll get over it though."

"You have to know that he didn't really want to hurt Brendan." she said.

"Actually I don't know that." he said. "But it's the nature of the beast. Sometimes these things cause infighting. It's normal. Everybody here understands that."

"I don't know how long you've known him, but I can tell you that this isn't normal behavior." she said. "I hold a little sway with him, if you know him at all, you know it's very little, but I'm trying to help him."

"So what's up with you?" he asked. "How is he going to help you?"

"What?" she asked.

"You're good, but you're not that good, sister." he said. "You don't think I noticed that little hitch? When you said 'it's not just Erik'? You got sent here to get well too."

"I can't talk about that." she said. "I haven't even told Stryker."

"You should unburden yourself." he said. "You'll feel better. Think of me as a priest."

"I'm Jewish." she said.

"Well then think of me as whatever you use." he said. "I still have room for more secrets."

He was probably right, and maybe it would be easier with someone she didn't really know. She looked around the room. The girls were still sitting where they were before, looking a little nervous. Most of the rest of the place wasn't necessarily empty, but quiet. She reckoned that it wasn't like this too often. Erik had scared the life out of them.

"You got somewhere we can talk?" she said.

"We can go back to church." he said.

"Let me say goodbye to the girls, I'll be right back." she said.

She went over to the table and said her goodbyes, and did her best to smooth over the horror that they had just witnessed.

"Okay, let's go." she said. "This can't get back to Stryker. I need to tell him myself."

"Why do you call him Stryker?" he asked.

"It was what I called him in the beginning." she said. "I guess I'm just nostalgic."

They got back to the table and sat down.

"That's where my VP sits." he said. "That means you have to tell the truth."

"I'm not planning on lying." she said. "This might be something you could find on your own anyway, if you knew where to look."

"Go ahead." he said.

"It all happened when I was in the army. Not the U.S. Army, the Israeli Army." she said. "Didn't have much of a childhood, for all practical purposes I was a soldier at 13. This was in the desert. I'm sure I don't need to tell you who we were fighting."

"I can figure it out." he said.

"I got involved with my Commanding Officer. A guy named Herschel. Was a lot like Stryker...I mean Erik. Turns out someone else was there before me. Melissa, who was, of course, still banging him at every opportunity." she said. "She was a shit soldier. A liability. One of the things Herschel had in common with Stryker is that he didn't see it as a problem that he occasionally banged his ex."

"That's probably still true, honey, just so you know." he said.

"I'm going into this thing with my eyes open, don't worry about that." she said. "Anyway, there's this mission to go blow up a warehouse that I wanted in on, but he picks Mel and this other guy Adam."

"So you're pissed that she gets to go, and you don't." he said.

"Exactly. Believe me, John, I tried everything to get him to change his mind." she said. "The day comes, and they're all up before dawn, and so am I. I follow them, discreetly, so I'm a ways back from them. The warehouse comes into view, and they're there. I hear a fire fight for about 10 minutes, then the place goes up. After the building explodes I start running towards it. Then I see a tiny figure running towards me. It is, of course, Mel. I ask her where he is, Herschel, you know?"

Okay," he said.

"She goes into this song and dance about how they held them off as long as they could, then it was too much. Then it was too much! She actually said that. She tells me that Adam didn't make it, and Herschel was in the building when it blew." she said. "I point out that if she had done her fucking job and held them off for a few more minutes, Herschel would still be alive."

"Maybe she couldn't." he said, "Maybe the shit was too much."

"She was such a shitty soldier, that's entirely possible. But at this point, I'm in no mood to listen to reason." she said. "She did take one in her shoulder, but it was her left shoulder. No excuse."

"I see." he said.

"I tell her to kneel. I have my Glock pointed at her for emphasis. She gives me a little static for a few more seconds, then kneels." she said. "I stand behind her and tell her if she admits she's a coward, I might let her live. She blabbers for a few more minutes, I'm sick of listening, so I put one in the back of her head. She never had a chance. There was no way I was ever going to let that bitch live."

"Okay." he said.

"If I could have killed her more than once, I surely would have." she said. "I throw her over my shoulder and carried her towards the building. I knew that there was a gas pump there, because I was there earlier on recon. I douse her with gasoline and light her up. Sat there as she was crackling away for a while thinking about life."

"Did you have marshmallows?" he asked.

"Hey! You're funny. Just like Stryker." she said.

"That's some medieval shit." he said.

"I figure nobody will find out because of what was left of her body." she said. "Several years later, this year in fact, the bullet was discovered and linked to me. I know it was Mur...my boss, since he had threatened me with it before. Still haven't figured out what I did to piss him off. Anyways, Mel, or more accurately her father, has friends in high places, including Mossad, and the General in charge of the entire region. So I had to get out of the sandbox. The boss sends me here to help him with his anger issues, and for him to help me with my guilt."

"Wow. That's a hell of a story." he said.

"I'm not proud of it, but I would be in danger around those people right now." she said.

He looked at her in amazement. This one was beautiful, but there was something else there. Maybe that unidentifiable thing Stryker was talking about earlier. She was tough, but inside she was a good person. He still couldn't believe that she was aiming at that guy's ear at the Red Knight.

"Something tells me you're going to be all right, kiddo." he said. "You're right, though. You need some distance from those people for a while."

I'm hoping maybe a few years..." she said. "Haven't been away from there since I was a kid. It's been a while since I've been in civilization. It's nice."

"So how did your boss know about this?" he asked.

"It's always best to assume with him that he knows everything." she said. "He usually does. He has resources that would put the CIA to shame."

"Interesting." he asked. "Tell me more about him."

"Do you really think I can do that?" she asked.

"I have to try." he said.

"I can't tell you anything, and I never will." she said.

"Maybe you can join Erik at my deathbed." he said.

"What?" she asked.

"Sorry, inside joke." he said.

"You're right, John, this did help." she said.

“Now you have to tell him.” he said. “You know? Stryker?”

“That’s not going to be easy.” she said. “Thanks for this. I need to get going.”

“I’m glad we had this chance to talk.” he said. “I like to know the people my guys are involved with.”

“Do you approve?” she asked.

“You’ve led a checkered life, but then so has he, so have most of us.” he said. “Not that you need my blessing, but you have it. When you talk to him, make sure he knows it’s okay to come back.”

“I think he knows that, but I’ll tell him.” she said. “Ciao, baby.”

“See you, Lexie.” he said. “I’m not big on languages, but I know what ciao means.”

“I know a few.” she said. “I’ll talk to Erik.”

“Thanks.” he said.

Chapter 7

By the time he slowed down, he was going through a little town called Moyie Springs on a tributary of the Kootenay River, near the Montana border in Idaho.

He still couldn't figure out where that came from, back at the club. Brendan was a brother, and a good friend, and if John hadn't stopped him...why did he take it that far? Lexie was right, he had some anger issues that were relatively new.

He could pretty easily trace it back to when he joined the club. He felt that he needed to prove himself. They didn't know that he was a hired killer. He made sure that they knew that he could handle things. His time as a prospect was short. If he was being honest, he would have to admit that some of the members being scared of him accelerated his time. Some were still scared of him. Is this what I want? People to be scared of me? When is it enough?

He could change, but he couldn't reel it in too much. If he did that, he would have the opposite problem. In his world, it was far better to be feared then to be thought weak. But hadn't he proved himself? Developed a reputation? That had to count for something. No, after everything that had happened, he didn't need to worry about looking weak.

So what now? He didn't know if he should go back or not. He didn't know if he could live with himself if he didn't. He was relatively sure they would forgive him, after all, Brendan started it. How bad did he fuck him up? Johnny stopped it pretty quickly, but he got some heavy licks in there before that happened. He knew Brendan was tough. He'd seen him live through worse.

He saw a small diner on the right, so he pulled in there and went inside. The place was empty, so he sat down at a booth.

The waitress came up and gave him a menu.

"Can I get you something to drink, hon?" she said.

"Just coffee." he said.

"Comin' right up." she said, and went behind the counter and poured a cup.

He looked at the menu.

The waitress reappeared with his coffee.

"What can I get you, hon?" she asked.

"How 'bout two eggs over easy with toast, hash browns, and bacon. Burn the hash browns." he said.

"Sure, doll." she said.

He poured a generous amount of cream and sugar into the coffee and stirred it.

A couple of bikers pulled into the lot, and they walked in. He didn't even have to look at their colors. Saints. They noticed him right away. One of them walked up, followed closely by the other.

"You're a long way from home." he said.

"Apparently, not far enough." he said. "Last I knew, your club is from Seattle."

"So's yours." he said. "What brings you to the beautiful state of Idaho?"

"I'm just out for a ride." he said. "I don't need to ask you. But you're still a ways away from that."

"Aye. But the top of Idaho is skinny, so it's not as far as you might think. We're waiting on a package." he said. "Could have been yours."

"Is that the extent of your Irish? The boys from Belfast will be disappointed. You can have it." he said. "We don't need that."

"Don't need it?" he said. "How could you pass on something like that? Are you all a bunch of pussies?"

The waitress had gone to the back room, quickly followed by the cook, locking the door behind them.

Erik looked at them. The bigger one was much bigger, almost certainly accounting for the other's bravery. While still looking in his eyes he grabbed the coffee cup and smashed it into his face, and simultaneously elbowed the other in the jaw. After that he focused on the bigger one exclusively. He pinned him to the ground and battered his face with his fists. The other guy just stared at the scene petrified. Erik thought briefly about snapping his neck, but then thought about how things had been going lately. He would restrain himself to a good ass beating this time, he had been subdued and unconscious for at least the last fifteen blows.

He looked to the other guy.

"Speaking of pussies, you can't escape this fucking thing unscathed." he said.

He grabbed him, twisted his arm behind his back, and started punching his face with his other hand. Fuck it, the wall's right there, I may as well use it, he thought. He started pounding the kid's face against the wall until teeth started hitting the floor. Shit, fucked up again, he thought. But this time it was a Saint, and not one of my own crew. Progress, not perfection.

He pulled out his notepad and wrote a short note.

"Sorry for the trouble. For any damages, or whatever."

He put it on the counter with five one hundred dollar bills.

Then he got on his bike and rode. It was a tough decision, east or west. In the end he headed back west.

As he was going through Nehalem he stopped at the diner. Danielle was there.

"By yourself this time, darlin'?" she asked.

"Just out for a ride. How are you?" he asked.

"Same as always." she said. "What can I get you?"

"Same as always, cup of joe and a slice of pie." he said.

"You know, what you did last time...that wasn't necessary, but appreciated all the same." she said.

"I'm sure I don't know what you're talking about." he said.

"Stop. I saw you." she said. "You're nowhere near as slick as you think."

"Some would argue that I'm slicker than I think." he said. "But then they don't know how slick I think I am."

"By the way, you have me at a disadvantage." she said. "You know my name, and I don't know yours."

"Erik." he said.

"Where's the babe?" she asked.

"Back in Seattle." he said.

"You know I get off in an hour." she said. "I got a room at the hotel, I live there."

He looked her over. She was very attractive. And Lexie did shut him out that night. But that was for good reason. But still...I probably shouldn't. It went against everything inside of him not to. One character flaw at a time, he thought. I acted out on those fucking Saints, so apparently that area still needs work. I fix that, maybe then I can start banging random chicks again.

"Another time, darlin'." he said. "I'm going through some heavy shit right now."

"Could be just the cure." she said.

She might be right, but more likely, it would cause more problems. I have enough guilt to deal with now, he thought.

"Really, I'm flattered." he said. "And normally I would absolutely love to. But I'm working through some guilt issues right now, and that would just add to it."

"Okay." she said. "Just so you know, if you ever change your mind, I'm always here."

"Thanks, hon." he said.

She went off to get his coffee.

She came back with his coffee and pie.

"This one really is on the house." she said. "I'll be insulted if you try to slip me money again."

"Well, the last thing I want to do is insult a pretty lady." he said. "Thanks."

The least he could do was to compliment her after shutting her down.

She left him alone.

He drank his coffee and ate his pie. He wondered what it was like to live somewhere as simple as this.

He got up and reached for his wallet and stopped. He felt guilty not leaving anything. But not guilty enough to fuck her.

"Until next time, Danielle." he said.

"Always a pleasure, darlin'." she said.

He left the diner and went to the payphone. He called the Fairmont Olympic.

"Room 815, please." he said.

Lexie answered the phone.

"Hello?" she said.

"It's me." he said.

"Where are you?" she asked.

"Nehalem." he said.

"Alone?" she asked.

"Yeah, I'm just passing through." he said. "I was heading east. Almost made it to Montana before I turned around."

"Why were you heading east?" she asked.

"It's what I always do when I'm lost." he said. "I don't know what happened back there."

"We'll figure it out. Johnny wants you to come back. *I* want you back." she said. "He says sometimes fighting is to be expected in these situations."

"But Brendan is my brother. I love him." he said. "How could I do that?"

"We'll figure all that out." she said. "I can help you. Just come home."

"Got into a little scrape in Montana." he said. "A couple of Saints."

"Are you okay?" she asked.

"Not a scratch. Them not so much. One should be seeing a dentist sometime in the near future." he said. "I lost control again. I finally stopped when I thought of Brendan. Or maybe it was when his teeth started hitting the floor."

"It's going to be okay, baby." she said. "We'll get through this. Come home."

"How is he? Brendan?" he asked.

"Mild concussion. He'll be out of the hospital tomorrow." she said. "Johnny told me that it's totally okay for you to come back, the club will welcome you. Everyone understands, these things happen."

"Okay." he said. "I'll call you when I get back. I'm going home."

"Do you need to be alone?" she asked.

"All I know is that I want to be in my own bed. I would wager that if you want to come over, you will be more than welcome." he said. "I'll go deal with the club tomorrow."

"I love you, Erik." she said. "Call me when you're home."

"I will." he said.

He hung up the phone, and got on his bike and headed west.

***

"I'm worried about him." she said. "It was one of his brothers. He told me he loves the guy."

"I'm sure the guys in the club told you that a little fighting is expected when deciding a major issue." he said. "He'll be okay. Minor concussion. He'll be back at the club drinking Bushmill's Black tomorrow."

"How do you know it will be okay?" she asked. "How could you possibly know? And how, for God's sake, do you know Brendan's beverage of choice?"

"When I got involved with this, I did research on biker culture." he said. "You know I have extensive resources, so I learned it all. I planned for every eventuality. I know about Brendan, because of his IRA ties. I know more about him than any other club member besides Erik."

She was getting paranoid. It started when they "found" the bullet. But he had taken care of her since. Maybe this was the plan all along. Find the bullet, create an excuse to move her, send her to Stryker. But why? It was just paranoia, she was pretty sure of that.

There were times she even questioned whether he was involved in the discovery of the bullet. It was possible that he had nothing to do with it. Still...she didn't even have the nerve to question him about it. He couldn't pretend it never happened, because it was the reason she was here.

"I'm sorry." she said. "I'm just a little nervous. I still haven't heard from him."

"Nehalem is a long way from Bremerton." he said. "I'm sure he's fine."

"When are we going over?" she asked.

"He doesn't want me to kill him, so we'll have to wait a while." he said. "We'll line it up with a 'deployment' with the Merchants, but some time needs to pass between the Saints bust and all of the Irish disappearing. For the time being, you should settle in to the Pacific Northwest."

"I like it here." she said. "I never thought I would say that. I can see why he made this his home."

"What about you?" he asked.

"At least for a while." she said. "I don't know about forever."

"There are no plans for that, but it's something to think about." he said.

"I was going to do that anyway." she said.

The light on the phone started flashing.

"I need to let you go, Anthony, I have another call." she said. "It might be him."

"Okay." he said. "I'll be in touch."

"Hello?" she said.

“It’s me.” he said.

“Are you home?” she asked.

“Yes,” he said.

“I’m coming over, what’s your address?” she said.

He thought about saying no, but he knew that she wouldn’t take it for an answer. He wouldn’t put it past her to find out his address from Murphy, and he was pretty sure he would give it up.

“Spyglass Hill.” he said. “646 Highland Ave, the driver should know it. Near the Manette Bridge. Third door, ring the buzzer.”

“I’m on my way.” she said.

She packed a small bag, called a cab and waited in the lobby. He was there about 15 minutes later. She got in.

“Spyglass Hill, Bremerton.” she said. “Do you know where that is?”

“Sure. The last ferry left an hour ago, we’ll have to go around the southern edge of the Sound.” he said.

“I don’t care, just get me there.” she said.

“So how’s it going?” he asked.

“I’m fine.” she said. “I don’t want to be rude, but I’m not much in the mood for conversation.”

“That’s okay.” he said.

He couldn’t help but notice how beautiful she was. She probably had guys hitting on her all of the time. She shut him down right away.

“I’m sorry.” she said. “I just have a lot going on right now. How are you?”

“I’m fine.” he said. “I understand if you don’t want to talk, really. I was just trying to be polite.”

“And now I’m trying not to be a bitch.” she said. “Where I come from...people are different. I didn’t mean any offense.”

“None taken.” he said. “Not from around here?”

“Not even this country.” she said. “And I’m not from some cushy European destination country either.”

“Okay.” he said.

He thought about where she might be from. She wasn’t Asian...maybe Africa?

“Israel. I’m a soldier.” she said. “I could hear the gears grinding in your brain.”

"Thanks. I hear Israel isn't so bad." he said.

"Not where I'm from. Well...it's probably not bad if you're not a soldier." she said.

"What brings you here?" he asked.

"Things went a little sideways back home." she said. "And there's this guy..."

"You're far too beautiful for there not to be a guy involved." he said. "But how did you end up here? You're a long way from home."

"This is where the guy is." she said.

"Right." he said.

"You ever hear of the Centurions?" she asked.

"The bike club? Sure. My cousin was with them for a while." he said. "Moved to a different charter in Diablo."

"My guy is a Centurion." she said. "There was some shit that went down at the clubhouse. He got in a fight with another member. Fucked him up pretty bad. He's a little worried about coming back, but I talked to the president, and he said it would be fine."

"Johnny?" he asked. "How is he?"

"You know him?" she asked.

"We go way back." he said.

"He's a little pissed about a recent vote, but other than that okay." she said. "Do you know Erik Stryker?"

That's the guy? She's with Erik Stryker?

"Did I touch a nerve?" she asked.

"No, nothing like that." he said. "I don't know Erik, but his reputation is well known. Is that your guy?"

"Yes. He wasn't like that before." she said. "Before, well he says it all started when he joined the club. I'm trying to bring him back to what he used to be."

He had never heard that Erik was anything but a vicious thug. Why did the good looking women always fall for the assholes?

"Well, good luck with that." he said.

For the rest of the trip, he only spoke when she spoke to him.

They pulled up to the building, and the meter read $37.50. She handed him a hundred dollar bill.

"Keep it." she said. "He really hasn't always been like this. Soon he won't be anymore."

"Thanks." he said. "I didn't mean anything by what I said. It's just I know some people that he's hurt."

"I'm sure that's a long list." she said. "Have a safe trip back."

"Thanks again." he said. "The average person doesn't tip $62.50."

"I'm far from the average person." she said. "Cheers."

She got out of the car and walked up to the door. She ran her fingers lightly along the buzzer selection until she found one that said "Stryker/Whitman, 543". Taylor Whitman, now I have a last name, not that I needed a reminder. She stretched out and stood up straight, and forgot about Whitman. After all, she had just left, and he had been out wandering, so there was no time to change the fucking name on the buzzer. She pressed the button.

"Come on up." he said.

There was a loud buzzer that signaled that the door was open. She walked in and got on the elevator.

When she got to his apartment, the door was ajar, so she walked in. It was pretty nice, and surprisingly clean.

"Haven't had a chance to mess it up since she left?" she asked.

"You're funny, Tenenzapf." he said.

"Just doesn't roll off the tongue like Stryker, does it?" she said.

"Few things do." he said.

"I thought you said you didn't get hurt." she said.

She took his hands in hers, and there were several small cuts on them.

"I forgot." he said. "I thought you meant did I get beat up. These are from the big one's teeth."

"The ones that landed on the floor?" she asked.

"No, the other one. The big one was on his back, so he may have swallowed a few." he said. "I smashed the little one's face against the wall. I stopped when I heard his teeth clinking on the floor. He was, of course, unconscious at the time."

"Let's get you cleaned up." she said. "Hydrogen peroxide?"

"In the medicine cabinet." he said.

She went into the bathroom and opened it. She found the hydrogen peroxide, triple antibiotic ointment, and bandages.

"You didn't think to take care of this before I got here?" she asked.

"I had other things on my mind, still do." he said.

Just like a guy, she thought. And yet, somehow they always heal.

"Let's go to the sink." she said.

He held his hands over the sink while she rinsed them. The peroxide bubbled fiercely as it covered the cuts. After it stopped, she carefully dried his hands. She applied the triple antibiotic and bandaged his hands.

"There." she said. "So what was the fight about?"

"Rival bikers don't need a reason." he said. "They said something about us being pussies for not taking the deal with the Irish, and that's all it took."

"They never saw it coming, eh?" she said.

"I'm sure they allowed for the possibility." he said. "I took the big one out first, and the little one didn't have the sense to run away."

"You probably did them a favor, albeit at a substantial cost, of course." she said. "If they're out of commission, they don't get busted."

"Maybe." he said. "It all depends on when Murph calls the ATF. He might not do that right away."

"He says he's not going to kill you, so the timeline is extended. We'll probably be here a while before we go over." she said. "That okay with you?"

"It suits me fine." he said. "I was never down to get killed anyway."

"And it gives me more time in the beautiful Pacific Northwest." she said.

"You like it here?" he asked.

"Yes." she said. "More than I ever thought I would."

She walked over to his door window, and went out on the balcony. There was a spectacular view of Puget Sound with the gleaming city of Seattle on the other side. In the distance she saw the Cascade Mountains. She knew the Olympic Mountains were on the peninsula behind them. This place was truly breath taking. The water, the mountains, and a major city nestled in between.

"It's beautiful, isn't it?" he asked.

"It's spectacular." she said.

"I need to tell you something, Stryker." she said.

"Go ahead." he said.

"I told you about Herschel, right?" she asked.

"Yeah." he said.

"And the thing. You know, what happened at the warehouse?" she said.

"That was a dark story." he said. "I like the part where you whacked Mel."

How could he...that's right he doesn't forget. It will definitely makes it easier that I don't have to tell it again. She had always been ashamed that she let her emotions control her that day. She hated to admit it, but the right thing to do would have been for her to save Mel, not kill her. Whether the bitch deserved it or not, she killed her for personal reasons.

"They found the bullet, and traced it to me." she said. "I had no choice but to leave the desert. Mossad and the regional General know about it. It's a minefield of friends of Mel. Murphy thought it would be good for me to come here, and it has been. Over the course of time, I have realized that I did the wrong thing there. I still hate that bitch. But I let my feelings get in the way of the greater good."

"The greater good is overrated. I think you did the right thing, if for no other reason than that she was a liability." he said. "She didn't do her job, and Herschel paid with his life. How many more unnecessary deaths would it take for it to be justified? I think one is too many. You did it, others thought it. There's nothing for you to be ashamed of."

"Is this the old Erik, or biker Erik talking?" she asked.

"It's the same person." he said quietly. "I still hold the same core values I've had for my entire life. Well, maybe not my entire life, but since I did my first kill."

"Stryker the biker." she said. "What are we going to do with you?"

"My guess is that I start by reeling it in a little." he said. "You know? Stop after they're unconscious at least."

"That would be progress." she said. "So you don't see any problem with what I did?"

"No. What you did was what you had to do. The way your mind works, you had no choice." he said. "You should have no regrets. I wouldn't be surprised if Anthony had something to do with the discovery."

She hadn't remembered telling him about Murphy's threats. She knew that she didn't, because back then she was always trying to look as good as she could to him. But he was smart. He had a way of figuring things out.

"Whether he did or didn't, here I am." she said. "I should have dug the bullet out at the time, which is my fault."

"That's the only thing you did wrong, then." he said. "You'll be okay. Probably more serious than beating up a brother, but time might fix it."

"If it doesn't, maybe I'll need to come back to civilization permanently." she said.

"Would that be so bad?" he asked.

"No, this isn't so bad." she said. "I still believe in what we're doing over there, but there have been times when I got...a little too intense, including the episode at the warehouse. It's good to get away. I want to go back, but if I can't it's not a disaster."

"Don't worry about what you did at the warehouse." he said. "It's in the past, and you were right."

He flicked his cigarette, and it landed about 5 feet from the water.

"That's impressive." she said. "Do you ever hit the water?"

"A few times." he said.

She flicked hers, and it landed on the double yellow line on the road.

"That sucked." she said.

"Not bad. I've had a lot more practice than you." he said. "What's her face didn't want me smoking inside. I'll admit to a little wind assistance on a couple of them."

"Well, now you can do what you want." she said.

"I think I'll keep the smoking outside thing, at least." he said. "Probably not an awful idea. I'll smoke less."

"I think it's a good idea too." she said. "Not that I'm making rules."

"Neither did she." he said. "It was a request that I honored...most of the time. This is my place."

"Didn't stop her from putting her name on the buzzer." she said.

"She lived here." he said.

"I know, don't mind me." she said. "There are bound to be reminders."

They went back in and sat on the couch. A black and white cat appeared in the stairwell, and boldly walked right up to Lexie and jumped on her lap. He was purring loudly and rubbing his face against her.

"Well, you're friendly!" she said. "I think he likes me."

"He likes everyone. Not that you're like everyone." he said. "This is Huck...Huckleberry is his full name. He is, hands down, the coolest cat in the entire world. Jenna had a cat who could fetch, but Huck's still cooler."

"Your ex-wife." she said. "What made you think of her?"

"I was thinking of her cat, Nikki, not her." he said.

"What do you do with him while you're gone?" she asked.

"Taylor used to watch him, but now I'll leave him with one of her friends, Casey." he said. "She has Taylor's cat for now too, now that she's off to see the world."

"Is this one of her friends you were friendly with?" she asked.

"Friendly yes. Did I try to bang her? No." he said. "They're far too close."

"So you have some scruples." she said.

"A few." he said.

"You helped me with mine, let me try to help you with yours." she said. "It might be more complicated. You made mine sound easy."

"My anger issues?" he asked.

"Exactly." she said. "When you get in a fight, try to think before you cause brain damage." she said. "I know it's hard in the heat of the moment. Maybe a good time would be when you realize they're unconscious. Like you said before. You could at least start there."

"That's what I was thinking." he said, "Problem is, sometimes I can't stop. I know I should, but I keep going."

"It's a start." she said. "When they're unconscious, it's over. Remember it. Next we'll try stopping when they stop resisting. This is normal, Stryker."

"You don't have to talk to me like I'm a child." he said.

"Frankly, you've been acting like a child." she said. "It has to stop. If I'm going to keep you in check, you gotta take me everywhere."

"I think I can live with that." he said. "If I need some alone time, I'll go riding."

Maybe back to in Nehalem, to take Danielle for a test drive, he thought. It sounded a lot like she was telling him what to do, and he didn't like that.

"I fit just fine on the back of that bike." she said. "We both know that you can get in trouble just going for a ride. It just happened with the Saints."

"But then I wouldn't be alone." he said. "It would defeat the purpose."

"Do you want help?" she asked.

"Of course." he said.

"Then it has to be my way, at least at first." she said. "You okay with that? Because I can just let you keep going the way you are if you want."

"Okay." he said. "But we might be spending a lot of time on the bike."

"That's fine, I love the bike." she said. "You had a chance to change those sheets yet?"

"This morning." he said. "You want to stay over?"

"That's why I packed a bag." she said. "Let's go upstairs."

"Okay." he said.

"Are you okay...you know...for other activities?" she asked.

"So much for spontaneity." he said. "I'll just tell you now for future reference. I could be on my deathbed, with a really weak pulse, and I'd still be up for it. Especially with you. There's never any need to ask, just let your body do the talking."

"Good to know." she said. "What are you waiting for? Upstairs before the night's too old."

"If only there was a Rod Stewart comeback that didn't sound gay..." he said.

"Not quite as easy as Guns'n'Roses, is it? Let's go, Stryker, you're on." she said.

"I'm always on." he said.

***

They walked into the club, and it seemed more animated than the last time. People must have gotten over the shock of what happened. Or maybe they realized that it had to happen.

There were a lot of personalities there, and most had no problem at all sharing their opinion whether it was popular or not. There were bound to be fights.

He knew he had to say something.

"Can I have everybody's attention for a minute?" he shouted.

It was almost instantly quiet enough to hear a pin drop.

"Some of you were here the other night when a fight took place between Brendan and I. I want to apologize for my behavior. Brendan is a brother, and I love him. I want to be a better person. That's all." he said.

"We never lost respect for you, Erik." said John. "Just save that shit for other people."

Everyone laughed.

"Reminds me of a story I have to tell you." said Erik.

Everyone went back to what they were doing.

"That was a classy move." said John. "It took a lot of guts."

"I don't know why I did that." he said.

"I do." he said.

Jessica and Allie walked in and waved at Lexie.

"I'll leave you boys to it, then." said Lexie. "I got my eyes on you."

She pointed to her eyes, then back at his a couple times.

"Right back at you, babe." he said.

"What's that all about?" he asked.

"She's trying to help me." he said. "Probably the secondary reason she's here."

"I know." he said.

"You know?" he asked.

"We talked a little the other night." he said. "Has she talked to you about anything lately?"

"As a matter of fact, she did. Last night." he said. "I'm guessing you already know what that is."

"Don't be too hard on her, son." he said. "She needed to unburden herself. Made me swear not to say anything until she told you. People trust me. Or maybe she thought it would be easier to tell someone she doesn't know too well."

“I’m glad she did if it was eating at her.” he said. “I think my assessment may have surprised her a little.”

“Oh? And what was your assessment?” he asked.

“That she did the right thing, no matter what the higher ups had to say about it.” he said. “Mel was a liability. She didn’t do her job, and Herschel paid with his life. I’ve been in the military. There’s no way that the General and Mossad didn’t know that Mel was weak, no matter how close they were to her father. I told her she shouldn’t have any regrets.”

“I didn’t exactly put it that way, but she knows that I support her.” he said. “I really like her. You did good for yourself, kid. You’re right, she has a little something most women don’t.”

“I’m glad you approve.” he said.

Chapter 8

Brendan was making his way into the club. He had a large bandage on his head.

He walked up to Brendan and opened his arms. They shared a heartfelt hug.

"You hit like a girl." Brendan whispered in his ear.

"I'm sorry, brother." he said.

"None of that." he said. "I ignored the cahdinal rule, like. Don't poke the bear. Got what was comin' to me, I did."

"Still, you're my brother, and I shouldn't have done it." he said. "If it makes you feel any better, a couple of Saints got it worse in Idaho. There I was, minding my own business..."

"Oh? Do tell, Rikky boy!" he said.

"Well, after what happened here, I got on my bike and headed east, as I always do when I'm feeling fucked up." he said. "Before I know it, I'm going through this little town called Moyie Springs, near the Montana border. I stop at a diner to get something to eat. Here come these two Saints, walk into the diner, and first thing they notice is little old me. They come up talking shit, so I clobber the big one with the coffee mug, and elbow the little one in the face. We all know that you deal with the big one first, if for no other reason than to scare the others. Meanwhile the staff makes a beeline for the back room and locks the door. I pin the big one to the floor and pound his face with my fists for a while. He's unconscious. I look up, and the other poor bastard hasn't had the sense to run. I grab him and start pounding his face with my fist. Well, the wall is right there, and it's about half the work, so I start smashing his face into it. I hear his teeth clinking on the linoleum, and I figure I went too far, yet again. I leave them some money and get back on my bike. Honestly, I could have gone east or west, but I knew I couldn't leave the club. Besides, Lexie is here a stranger in a strange land, even though I know she would have found me in less than a day.

"Wow. That's quite a tale, laddie!" he said. "What happened to Taylor?"

"She's in New York, she got a modeling gig." he said.

"Ya leave for one day..." he said.

"I'm glad you're okay, brother." he said. "I'm going to try and reel it in a little."

"Don' reel't in too much, laddie." he said. "We need ya like ya are."

"I'm just going to try to stop causing brain damage...to start." he said.

"I'm here t' tell ya, son, you'll have t' do better than that with me." he said. "I only have a few brain cells left up there, so you'd hafta look hard, like."

Lexie and the girls walked up.

"Aye, it's m' Irish lassie!" he said. "Drinks all 'round! What'll ya have, luv?"

"Bushmills Black! An' none o' that soda shite!" she said.

"Prospect! You heard the cailín! Bushmills Black!" he said. "Neat."

"I'm sorry about your father." said Erik.

"Aye, we got it all straightened, we did." he said. "Had t' 'splain the workins of the club. Me da and I are fine now."

"We'll let you boys talk." said Lexie.

They moved to a table.

Erik knew that in all likelihood, he would have to kill Brendan's uncle, and his father. Probably lots of his friends too. This part sucked.

"What about Liam?" he asked.

"He'da like t' keep it 'n the family, like, but he understands." he said. "They have the Saints runnin' 'em now, we'll see how that works aut."

"I'm really sorry, brother, I voted the way I had to." he said.

"Aye. Ya did you did what you hadta." he said. "T' dosh will be missed, that's sure. Ya could be right, it might come wit' a wee bit more than that."

"Should I call Lexie over for translation?" he asked.

"Dosh means..." he said.

"Money, I know." he said. "Sometimes you go too fast for me."

"Aye, apologies, boyo." he said. "I feel too comfortable wit' ya."

"That's not a bad thing." he said.

"Yer family to me, son." he said. "Even tho' ya likta cave me head in."

"Sorry about that." he said.
"Aye. We move on now, eh?" he said.
"Thanks." he said.
"Atallatall, yer grand, boyo." he said.
"I heard from the Merchants, I might be going away again soon."
Aye, a fine job." he said. "Where do ya think yer goin' this time?"
"Wherever they say." he said. "Probably Southeast Asia."
"An' what 'bout Lexie?" he asked.
"She's going to visit her uncle in New York." he said.
"Could be a recipe for fireworks, Taylor bein' there an' all." he said.
"It's a big city." he said. "She'll probably be in Paris long before I leave."
"Paris, eh?" he said. "She'll become worldly like you."
"I guess." he said.
"You'll have opportunities when yer deployed." he said. "Will ya stay true t' this one?"
"Well, Taylor and I had an arrangement. It was for both of us. Anything goes while I'm away." he said. "She never took advantage, but I've lost count."
"A feek like that, and she lets ya bang other broads?" he said.
"And I let her, let's not forget." he said. "It's not my fault that she didn't take advantage."
"I can tell ya, boyo, it wasn't for lack of opportunity, that's sure." he said. "Ya think ya can work out somthin' like that wit' this one?"
"It will be tricky." he said. "With the right kind of finesse..."
"You know sometimes I say youth is wasted on the young, but not wit you, Rikky boy!" he said. "Yer really flyin' it. Good luck wit that conversation!"
"I have hopes that it can be done." he said.
"Tell me true. What's up wit' Taylor? That cailín still wants you, eh?"
"How did you know?" he asked.
"I got eyes, lad." he said. "I saw her in here the other night. You're really the lucky one, eh? Two pretty lasses fightin' over ya?"

"She's looking at it as a break." he said. "I'm doing my best to disabuse her of that notion."

Lexie perked up.

"Let's hope she gets the message." she said. "It's good to see you two talking."

"How in the hell did you hear that?" he asked.

She smiled and started nodding, then pointed at her eyes, then back at his.

"Aye, ya made the right choice, lad." he said. "Taylor was a real feek, but this one might be dangerous."

"She's a feek? What 'bout this?" she said.

She ran her hand vertically across her face and down her body.

"Aye, you got a point. luv." he said. "It's close, but ya got 'er by a nose."

"You makin' fun o' me nose?" she asked.

"It's a racin' term, luv." he said. "It means ya win."

She looked back at him.

"Got me eye on you too." she said.

"The worldly lass is markin' her territory." he whispered. "I'm whisperin' because she could be earwiging with those bionic ears."

"No shit." he whispered. "There has been a steady increase in public displays of affection. You're right, she's dangerous. Of course nothing I can't handle."

"What are you two whispering about?" she asked. "Do I need to come over there?"

"Just man talk." he said. "Stay with the cailíns, we'll be fine."

"Pickin up some Irish, are ye, boyo?" she asked.

"How can I help it?" he asked.

She came over and gave him a big kiss.

"You know I'm just having fun, right?" she said.

"I think I liked you better when you were nervous." he said.

"The new Lexie will grow on you." she said.

"She already has." he said. "I love you."

She stared back at him with a blank look. Did he really just say what I think he did? She wasn't expecting this for at least a few more months.

"I-I love you too, Erik." she said.

"Does that buy me a little less suspicion?" he said.

"I don't mean it like that. I-I...I'm going to turn into a blubbering idiot." she said. "I trust you. I'm yours, and I hope you're mine. I'll try not to talk about it again, it's just that she was such a big part of you."

"And you're not?" he asked.

"Am I?" she asked.

"If you don't know..." he said. "You shared things with me that she never could, never will. I feel like we've lived a lifetime together. That's why I love you."

"I'm going to go back before I fuck this up." she said. "I love you."

"I'm glad you like it here, that you've found friends." he said.

"Me too." she said.

She walked back to the table.

"Ready for that conversation about the arrangements, like?" he asked. "I think she might be receptive."

"Might be a little tougher than I thought...especially now." he said.

"Ya think?" he said.

***

"He told me he loves me." she said. "I wasn't expecting that for months."

"That's great!" Allie said. "Was there ever any doubt?"

"You never know until they say it. Out of the blue!" she said. "He says he feels like he's known me his whole life."

"Well, with all the things you've been through, it's not surprising." she said. "Do you know how long it took him to say it to Taylor?"

"I'm guessing somewhere around what I thought my timeline was." she said.

"Close to a year." she said.

"That sounds about right." she said. "He's not a guy who says things like that easily. I can't believe he said it to me."

"So you never told us the rest of that story." she said. "You know, the non-existent job, going down the Nile. I think you were just getting ready to go to Europe."

"Okay. So we take this train from Cairo to Alexandria." she said. "Before I tell you the next part, you need to promise me that none of this gets back to Erik. I'm serious. He can't know. It would fuck him up too much."

"Okay." said Jessica.

"Okay, you can count on us." said Allie.

"I'm pretty sure he already knows, because he's smart like that, but I'm serious, nothing." she said.

They both nodded.

"So we get to Alexandria, and get on a ship to go across the Mediterranean." she said. "We get about halfway there, and there's a call for me. It's this bitch that Stryker has been pining over for the past 7 years. He thinks she's dead...or maybe he knows she's alive, you can never tell with him."

"Someone he met before? On another mission?" she asked.

"He met her while he was in the Navy. Before he started working for the non-existent boss." she said. "Our boss managed to bring her on board, though I have no idea why. Hell, maybe she was there before me. She's handling the logistics. Erik can't see her for obvious reasons. She and I have a history, she almost got me killed a few years before, and also fucked a guy I was seeing while I was there, so I'm not happy to hear from her. She tells me about this hotel she got us in Monte Carlo."

"How did she almost get you killed?" she asked.

"That's another story, honey, let me finish this one first." she said. "I call the boss and bitch about it. Tell him I won't work with her. He brings up a past transgression that he would make public if I don't play along. Believe me, ladies, I didn't want to do it. What the boss had on me was too strong, though, so I had to comply. He gave me another $30,000 to take some of the sting out of it."

"An extra $30,000?" she asked. "That's more than I make in a year."

"It's a lot to me too." she said. "But at the time I would have given it up not to deal with her. I'm trying to look at the bright side. I have more time with Erik, even though she'll be lurking in the shadows. So we get to the hotel, it's really nice by the way, not as nice as the one in Cairo, but still pretty classy. In the closet there's a shimmering blue evening gown for me and a tuxedo for Erik. Apparently we're going out on the town."

"I call the boss, and he says we're going to the Sun Casino, which by the way, is a place that holds special meaning for him and Dan...the other woman. We're supposed to go there and await further instruction. He also tells me that the only reason I'm there is to deal with that bitch, and do my best to keep Stryker happy."

"Why do you call him Stryker sometimes?" asked Allie.

"When we first met...back in Africa, that's what I called him a lot. I thought it sounded cool." she said. "Now, it just brings back fond memories...like I can call him Stryker, but no one else can."

"I see." she said. "You really have it bad for him don't you?"

"There was only one other...Herschel, that I've ever felt this strongly about." she said. "But that's a whole other story, which is one that I really can't tell. It would be too painful."

Part of the truth, she thought. The "too painful" thing was the best she could come up with on the fly.

"You're amazing." said Jessica. "The things you've done, the places you've gone. I can't imagine."

"Well, Jess, I can tell you it's not all unicorns and lollipops." she said. "I'm only telling you the good parts. I wouldn't subject you to the bad. Anyway, we get to the casino, me in my evening gown, which I looked great in, by the way, and Erik in his tuxedo. First thing he does is order a vodka martini, 'shaken not stirred'. He had to have his James Bond moment. He asks if we know who we're looking for. I'm thinking it better not be her. I wouldn't put it past her to crawl out of the woodwork in spite of the consequences, which the boss has assured me are more than enough to keep her in check."

"Did she show up?" asked Allie.

"Not then, but she did something incredibly stupid later that night." she said. "Erik tells me that Mu...the boss suggested that we see a show, since he's barred from the poker room. If he were to show up there, it could possibly set us back weeks if a certain person is there. Erik has no idea why he's not supposed to go there, by the way, but I do. I know pretty much everything except for a few logistical details."

"Why do you know and he doesn't?" she asked.

"The short answer is that they're fucking with Stryker. There are a lot of moving parts to this thing. If even one thing goes wrong, we lose the element of surprise. Remember for a moment that this is all fictional. Erik is supposed to kill the guy that he thinks killed little miss perfect. It's not that they couldn't have done it without him, but it's sort of a trial run for Stryker. If the boss wanted it done, he could have done it long ago. They want to test Erik, so obviously, he can't know everything. Believe me, it's tough for me not to tell him too. Have you ever been in love?"

"Of course." they said in unison.

"Like you said before, I got it bad, still do. The difference now is that he doesn't know how much anymore." she said. "Y'all need to keep that under your hat too."

"Do you think we're stupid?" asked Allie.

"No, just something I have to say." she said. "So we get to the show, which I'm sure the boss had a hand in, and it's the same band, same singer, same song, even the same lighting as the time he was there with her. Erik is in a daze. It's like he's going back in time. He probably thinks if he looks over it's gonna be her instead of me. The singer is singing cheesy song from the 40s or 50s, 'How long has this been going on'."

"I know that! I saw it on an episode of Alfred Hitchcock Hour." said Jessica. Then she started singing.

"I could cry salty tears; where have I been all these years; little wow, tell me now, how long has this been going on?"

Lexie clapped, and Jess stood up and took a bow.

"That was amazing!" said Lexie. "You really belted it out! Have you ever thought about singing professionally?"

"I've been in a few bands, but nothing serious." she said.

"You're really good. You took me right back to that night in Monte Carlo." she said. "So now Erik is in a haze over this turn of events, and I'm sitting there like an idiot. Then this French guy comes up and taps him on the shoulder. 'It's time.' he says. Erik gets up, essentially sleepwalking, I try to follow, but the French guy blocks me. Tells me it's just Stryker, boss's orders. I'm fuming, because I know the boss set the whole thing up, the casino, the show, the band, everything. I try to follow, but they get in a car."

"Why did your boss do that?" asked Jess.

"Who the fuck knows? I'm worried that Erik is going to be distracted by this choreographed trip down memory lane, so he might mess up the job." she said. "The guy he's after is dangerous, already thinks Erik is dead, and wouldn't hesitate to make it true if he sees him first. The other fucked up thing is that he's at this little cottage that she used to own. The first place they were together. Turns out the bad guy bought the place and has been banging her for the last six months. Part of her assignment."

"Has he ever...you know...made you do that?" asked Allie.

"He doesn't have the balls." she said. "There isn't enough leverage in the world to make me do that. Women who do that...I guess they serve a purpose, but to me they're just tramps."

"I couldn't do it either." she said.

"So he goes out to the cottage, it goes off without a hitch, and he decides to go for a swim. On the shore he sees a silhouette, which he claims looks just like this fucking cameo she gave him way back when, which looks 'exactly like her' to him." she said. "He runs out of the water and chases after her, but she takes off on a motorcycle. He knows it's her. Can't prove it, but he knows. He won't admit it, but to this day he still believes she's alive."

"Wow. So romantic." she said. "Do you think he still thinks about her?"

"I'd be a fool to think he doesn't." she said. "While we were going down the Nile, he told me he thought about her every day. And I know she's still alive. I almost cried right there in front of him."

"That's tough." said Allie.

"Tell me. I was the one who brought it up." she said.

"Is she...still alive?" she asked.

"I don't know. I don't get to Europe a whole lot." she said. "Let's hope he never gets sent to France."

"So was that it?" asked Jess.

"After it was over Stryker and I spent a few days in Rome." she said. "Now *that* was romantic. We saw the Colosseum, the Vatican, and we tossed coins at the Trevi Fountain and made wishes."

"That sounds romantic. Did your wish come true?" she asked.

"Took a while, but maybe." she said.

"What took a while?"

It was Erik. He had snuck up on them. Lexie was too lost in the story to notice.

"I was telling them about our trip to Rome." she said. "I said that it took a while for my wish to come true from the Trevi Fountain."

"Has it?" he asked.

"Maybe." she said. "Too soon to tell. What about yours?"

She instantly regretted asking.

"What I wished for is all but impossible." he said. "Since then, I've moved on."

"Really?" she asked.

"I would wish for something different today." he said.

"And I would see your wish granted." she said.

"Wow. The two of you." said Jessica. "What a fantastic story."

"How much did you tell them?" he asked.

"Only the really raunchy parts, since that's what girls want to hear." she said.

They all laughed.

"Sorry I missed that." he said.

"I know that you remember every detail." she said. "So do I."

"We're not still talking about just the raunchy parts, are we?" he asked.

"I'm talking about all of it." she said. "I wouldn't change a thing."

"Neither would I." he said.

"I'm getting chills." said Allie.

"You ready to get out of here?" he asked.

"Yeah, I need to get you home." she said. "Quickly. It could be an emergency."

"We can go back to the crib if it's that urgent." he said.

"Tempting, but I think I can wait." she said. "But we're leaving now."

"You ladies have a lovely night." he said.

She wrapped her arms around him and started steering him towards the door.

"Who knew?" said Jess.
"I love Tay like a sister, but those two belong together." said Allie.

***

He was in a nightclub, or maybe somewhere like Le Circus in Monte Carlo. Definitely a small venue. There was a very attractive long haired brunette wearing a wife beater tank top shirt and short cutoff jeans. The waitress told him she was Amy Winehouse, but he had never heard of her before. Blue light engulfed her. She was swaying back and forth in front of the microphone, there was a small band playing slow music behind her. She had more tattoos than him, but they looked good on her. "This goes out to..." she said. "Well you all know who it goes out to, I don't want to talk about it." She had a British accent. She looked like she had had a rough life. She started singing.

For you I was a flame
Love is a losing game
Five story fire as you came
Love is a losing game

One I wish I never played
Oh what a mess we made
And now the final frame
Love is a losing game

She had a very unique voice. Contralto, he remembered from music appreciation in high school. The lowest female vocal range. She sounded like a torch singer, and the love she sang about was very meaningful.

Played out by the band
Love is a losing hand
More than I could stand
Love is a losing hand

He couldn't take his eyes off her. He could tell that she meant every word she was singing, in fact, she had lived it.

Self-professed... profound
Till the chips were down
Know you're a gambling man
Love is a losing hand

In spite of himself, he felt bad for her. This was a woman who had suffered, had been hurt by...love.

Though I battle blind
Love is a fate resigned
Memories mar my mind
Love is a fate resigned
Over futile odds
And laughed at by the gods
And now the final frame
Love is a losing game

"She's right you know." he said. "It's a losing game. Also a waste of time."

It was Murphy.

"Taylor was no good for you. She was too needy." he said. "That was love, but it was one sided. You're much better off with Lexie. She'll let you be free."

"Putting aside how ridiculous it is that you're trying to tell me about love, what makes you think I want to be with Lexie?" he asked. "What makes you think I want to be with anyone?"

"You love me, you said it." said Lexie. "I have witnesses. Brendan?"

"Aye, there's no denyin' it. boyo." he said. "I was right there when ye said it, like."

"A moment of weakness." he said. "Don't tell me that you've never said it when you didn't mean it."

"Aye, but only wit' floozies." he said. "She don' qualify."

"So you don't love me?" she asked.

How did I get myself in this mess, he thought. I didn't know she was here.

"Of course I do." he said. "Murphy's trying to trick me. Make me say things I don't mean. I love you, Lexie, really I do."

"How long did that take?" she said. "It took me six months just to get a 'me too'."

It was Taylor. What was she doing here?

"Don't worry about me, she's the bad guy this time." said Lexie.

"But she's so sweet." said John. "She could never be the bad guy."

"Keep thinkin' that, Prez." said Taylor. "You make it too easy."

She took out a gun and shot him in the head.

"Told you." said Lexie. "I'm the sweet one. I love you, baby."

"What about those two over there?" asked Taylor.

A few rows back he saw the two Saints he beat up, heavily bandaged.

"We didn't do anything." said the big one. "Just minding our own business."

"You lie!" said Erik. "You came up to me. Looking for trouble, and you got it."

"Don't worry about them, baby, I'll finish them off. They were almost dead anyway." said Taylor. "Take care of the big one first, right, baby?"

She pointed the gun at him and shot him in the gut, then turned to the little one and put one in his head.

"Just kidding, dude, you don't get to live. I just wanted you to think you did." she said.

She aimed the gun and shot the big one in the forehead.

"How am I doing, sweetheart?" she asked. "Am I doing it right? Even if I'm not, I'm getting results."

"Aye, boyo, I think me nephew had it wrong." said Liam. "This is the dangerous one."

"Do I need to shoot you too?" she asked.

"No, lassie, 't would be futile." he said. "I'm already dead. It's that amadan yer fightin' over did it, like. Back home in Ireland. Least I get buried 'n me homeland."

"Well, she doesn't have any problem killing dead people." she said. "Why can't I?"

"Aye, the rules 'r different fer you, luv." he said. "She's earned it."

“That means she can’t kill me!” said Danielle.

“Shut up bitch, we all know you’re alive.” she said.

“I do have to take Brendan out, though. He’s the only witness to him saying he loved her.”

She took aim and dropped Brendan.

“Right, oh, and we established that you’re not dead.” she said.

She shot Danielle between the eyes.

“Now for the rest of the competition.” she said. “Then you’ll love me again by default.”

She aimed at Lexie.

“I can’t let you do that.” said Murphy.

“Why not?” she said.

“Because she’s too valuable. Besides, he’s supposed to end up with her.” he said.

“YES!” said Lexie.

“You I want to kill most of all.” she said. “You were the one that got him into this.”

“Yes, but you can’t.” he said. “You know why. In fact, you have to do everything I say. You’ve had your fun, but it’s over now. Time to be quiet.”

She sat down and looked the other way.

“Called it.” said Liam. “He’s with the Feds.”

“She can’t kill you, but I can.” said Lexie.

She took out her gun and shot him in the head.

“Take that, ya closet loyalist.” she said. “Bet ya actually wan’ ‘im to be with the Feds now, ya gobshite.”

“All I ask is that you think about it, Erik.” said Murphy. “It’s not complicated.”

“Maybe not to you, since you’ve never had a woman.” he said. “Why do you care, anyway?”

“If it affects you, it affects me.” he said. “And for the record, I have had a woman before.”

Lexie started laughing.

“You haven’t had pussy since pussy had you, and we all know it.” she said.

She pointed the gun at him.

“Who are you kidding?” he asked. “You can’t do it either. Nobody can.”

She shrugged her shoulders.

"Didn't say anything about killing her."

She shot Taylor in the head.

"She's gone, why did you have to do that?" he asked.

"You know nothing, Stryker." she said.

She smiled and turned the gun on him and pulled the trigger. She hit him in the shoulder. He looked at the singer again. It wasn't the original singer, it was Taylor.

She started singing. The words to the song resonated with her too. Had he done that to her?

She started singing.

For you I was a flame
Love is a losing game
Five story fire as you came
Love is a losing game

One I wish I never played
Oh what a mess we made
And now the final frame
Love is a losing game

"You want something to think about, think about that." said Taylor. "I'm the victim here."

The blue light faded to black and he woke up.

Chapter 9

Lexie wasn't next to him, but he could hear her talking to Huck downstairs.

He walked down.

"Let me know if he answers you back." he said. "He never says anything. Taylor's cat never shut up."

"There's nothing wrong with being quiet." she said. "Some people never shut up. And apparently some cats."

"Everything was a crisis with her...the cat, not Taylor, well Taylor had her moments too. The cat would whine, and Taylor would humor her. I did the opposite. I ignored her, and just like a woman, she would jump in my lap."

"Just like a woman? What does that mean?" she asked.

"The typical woman, you don't pay attention to her, she'll do something to make sure you do." he said.

"Oh, really?" she said. "Is that how it works?"

"It's a 'man thing' that only a privileged few of us know." he said. "I've probably already told you too much. I could get kicked out of the union for this."

"The man union?" she asked.

"I really have said too much." he said. "If this gets out, there could be a serious problem down at headquarters."

"Well, your secret's safe with me." she said. "You been using your little tricks on me?"

"If you remember correctly, I said the typical woman." he said. "You're anything but typical. If it wasn't a 'man thing' you might even be able to join."

"Should I be honored?" she asked. "To be considered for your little club?"

"You mistake what I said." he said. "You could never be considered because you're a woman. But I'm sure you have your own club."

"Not really." she said. "Women are too catty. We could never share secrets like you do. We find something good, we guard it with our lives."

"Like me?" he asked.

"You are something that could never be owned, Stryker." she said. "I need to let you be free. For it to work, you would have to fall in love with me. Then I just pray I don't fuck it up."

"Strange choice of words." he said, absently. "Murphy said the exact same thing."

"When did you talk to him?" she asked.

"No, I didn't, I had another strange dream." he said.

"Tell me about it." she said. "Want some coffee?"

"Sure." he said.

He told her about the dream.

"Was it a real song?" she asked.

"No, but it should be. I remember every word." he said.

"How could you do that? It was a dream." she said.

"Remember that thing I told you about?" he said.

"Really? Dreams too? It must be a real mess up there." she said.

"Actually it's not. It's like a library. Or more accurately like pulling up files from a computer." he said. "Very organized. All I need to do is think of it, and the file is there."

"Wow. That's amazing." she said. "I had no idea.

"That's a hell of a dream, Stryker." she said. "Why don't I have those?"

"I don't know." he said. "I've always had an active dream life."

"What do you think it means?" she asked.

"You tell me." he said. "It probably has to do with all the shit that's happened lately. I feel like this one is trying to make me feel bad for Taylor."

"Do you?" she asked.

"Let me think...she just got her dream job and a $20,000 bonus." he said. "I think she'll be okay."

"She didn't want to let go." she said.

"I told her it was okay. Forget about me and go live her dream." he said. "The rest is up to her."

"You think she'll do that?" she asked.

"If it was me, I wouldn't have time to think about my ex." he said. "She probably hasn't had time to think about it. Maybe I'm a distant memory for her now. She hasn't called."

"There could be a lot of reasons for that." she said. "You're probably right, she's busy. But don't think she's forgotten about you."

"It's strange that she hasn't called." he said. "It's not like her."

"It isn't." she said. "Not that I know her, but from what I know, it seems like she would have by now, no matter how busy she is."

"You've heard enough to know." he said. "I don't really care if she calls, I just hope she's okay."

"Do you know where she's staying?" she asked.

"She said The Plaza." he said. "Good money in modeling, I guess."

"No shit, $20,000 bonus on spec, it must be good." she said.

"She's probably okay." he said.

She didn't believe she was going to do this, but she didn't want him thinking about her.

"Do you want to try to call?" she asked.

"I'm pretty sure that would be sending the wrong message." he said. "She said she would call when she gets there. She didn't, so she probably just hasn't had a chance. I'll wait."

"I don't like it, but if you want to call, I understand." she said. "I'm not like that. Give it a few days. If she doesn't call, I might make you."

"Okay. If I do, it will just be to make sure she's okay." he said. "She's never really been away from here."

"New York City is an exciting place." she said. "Maybe she's overwhelmed. She's there with the modeling company, and they have a vested interest. They won't let anything happen to her."

"I'm sure you're right." he said.

"You ever use that thing?" she said, pointing at the computer in the corner.

"Actually, yeah, all the time." he said. "It was a replacement for her old one, which was obsolete. It was for both of us, but I'm the only one who uses it."

"What do you use it for?" she asked.

"I get a little writing bug every now and then." he said.

"Really?" she asked. "Anything good?"

"A few books. Nothing published, or even suitable for public consumption." he said. "It helps to put it on paper, well floppy disc."

"Can I read some of it?" she asked.

"I don't think so." he said. "I would have to look it over first."

"Okay." she said. "Let me know. I would be very interested in seeing your work."

"I don't know if I would call it work." he said. "Some of it's personal. You would have to read it at the computer, I can't imagine how much paper it would eat up. I never intended for anyone to read it."

"Well, let me know." she said. "I'm not going to ask you to do anything you don't want to. The dream was right about one thing, I know better than to try to tie you down. You're a person who needs to be free, and I respect that. Could you do me a favor, though?"

"Sure, what?" he asked.

"Print me a copy of that song? From your dream?" she asked.

"Yeah, I guess." he said. "Why?"

"Just trying to figure out what's going on up there." she said. "Is that okay?"

"Yeah, no, it's fine." he said. "I have very few secrets."

"Thanks." she said.

"You feel like getting some breakfast?" he asked. "I know this great place by the water."

"You don't know how to cook?" she asked.

"I'm actually a better cook than most people." he said. "I just don't feel like doing it now."

"Okay, that sounds good." she said. "Is it a diner?"

"Of course." he said. "You don't like diners?"

"No, I love them." she said. "Not too many back in the desert."

"Do you miss it?" he asked.

"A little." she said. "But I'm getting used to civilization."

"Good." he said. "I'm glad you're here. I didn't know if I was ever going to see you again."

"Me either." she said. "I'm glad I'm here too. And I'm glad I'm in your dreams, even if I'm the bad guy sometimes. But don't ever mistake me for sweet."

He started laughing.

"You have your own way of being sweet." he said. "My guess is most people don't get you. I do."

"I know." she said. "One of the many things I love about you."

"Let's get out of here." he said.

***

They got to the club, and it was the usual crowd. Lexie went and sat down with Jessica and Emily, and Erik went to the bar to talk to Brendan.

"You hear anything about the Irish and the Saints?" asked Erik.

"Nuthin' goin' on yet." He said. "Logistical problems. They're rethinking takin' it o'er at Rossland. Thinkin' of goin' further east to Erickson."

"That means they'll pick up in Idaho." he said. "That's crossing state lines. Probably not too much more serious considering what they'll be carrying. That would surely be the least of their problems."

"Liam's really olagonin' we didn't get the deal done here." He said. "Says the Saints are hard t' work with."

"I'm not surprised." he said. "The thing that really surprises me is that they went to them at all."

"Didn't have a choice." he said. "They need t' move'em. The pipeline is gettin' backed up, and t' clients 'n Seattle want their guns."

"I still think we did the right thing." he said. "I have a bad feeling about this."

"How's yer cailín?" he asked.

"She's fine." he said. "I had this weird dream last night, somehow the subject came up that I might not love her, and she called you as a witness, and you backed her up, said you were there when I said it."

"Always there t' help a damsel 'n distress." he said.

"That one is rarely in distress." he said.

"So is it true?" he asked. "Don' ya love 'er?"

"I think I do." He said. "We've been through a lot together."

"So've you an' Taylor." he said. "What's goin' on there?"

"Haven't heard from her." he said. "She's in New York."

"Don' ya think that's strange?" he asked.

"A little." He said. "Lexie and I talked about it. I'll probably call if I don't hear from her in the next few days."

"Aye. I'm surprised she din't call when she got there." he said.

"Me too." he said. "She's probably just busy, you know, first time in the big city."

"I hope yer right." he said.

***

"How's it going Lex?" asked Emily.

"Doing good, how are you?" she said.

"Fine." she said. "You staying with him now?"

"I still have my room at the Olympic, but I haven't been there lately."

"You must be doing okay, that place ain't cheap." she said.

"No it isn't." she said. "I have some money put away. When I work for the non-existent boss, I do pretty well. Even if it's only once or twice a year."

"I know, Allie told me." she said. "$30,000 bonus? Sign me up."

"I love this song." said Jessica.

They were playing "All Apologies" by Nirvana.

"I love Nirvana." said Lexie. "That reminds me, I have something for you."

"Really?" she asked. "How cool."

She went in her purse and pulled out a folded up piece of paper. She had written down a copy for herself.

"Know anyone who could put this to music?" she asked.

Jessica studied it. It was really good.

"Did you write this?" she asked.

"Oh, hell no." she said. "My creativity lies in other areas."

"Lemme see." said Emily.

She handed it over.

"Who did?" she asked.

"Well...nobody really." she said. "Erik heard it in a dream."

"Heard it in a dream?" she asked. "And he remembered it?"

"That's really good." said Emily.

"He remembers everything. I mean everything." she said. "It's this weird rainman thing that he's had his whole life. Completely photographic memory. I didn't know it applied to dreams until this morning."

“Everything?” she asked.
“Everything.” she said.
“His head must be a jumbled mess.” she said.
“See, that’s what I thought.” she said. “He says it’s organized like a computer, that all he needs to do is think of something, and his brain retrieves the file instantly, so it’s right there, down to the smallest detail.”
“Wow. That’s strange. Wish I would have had that in high school.” she said.
“So what do you think?” she asked.
“It’s beautiful. So sad. ‘Love is a losing game’.” she said. “I know this guy Jason, he’s a great musician, and he knows how to write music. Do we have anything to go on?”
“I tried, but Stryker is musically illiterate.” she said. “Slow and soulful was all I could get out of him. You know? Like a torch song?”
“Yeah, I know.” she said. “Jason is a renaissance man as far as music goes, I’m sure he can work with that genre. He’s really good.”
“That’s great.” she said. “Maybe we keep this to ourselves for the moment. It’s not like he wrote it, but he writes other stuff, and he’s a little skittish about sharing.”
“What else does he write?” she asked.
“Haven’t had a chance to see anything.” she said. “I asked him, and he said ‘I don’t think so’. Said he would have to look at it first.”
“That’s strange.” she said. “Most people who write want to be read.”
“He’s not your average person.” she said “Says some of it is personal.”
“That would only make me want to read it more.” she said.
“Not going down that road.” she said. “I wouldn’t want to read it if he doesn’t want me to.”
“But he let you have the song?” she asked.
“That’s different.” she said. “It’s from a dream. He printed it right up for me.”
“I always thought he was so simple...not stupid, of course, but easy to be with.” she said. “It seems that there’s more to him than I thought.”
“You have no idea.” she said. “What about Mike?”

"Not complicated, yet not simple...still talking about the not stupid kind of simple, of course." she said. "We've had our ups and downs, but I love him."

"We should all go out some time." she said. "You know, the three of us and our men."

"I'm sure Charlie would be up for it." said Emily.

"All I need to do is say Erik is coming to get Mike to come along." said Jessica.

"Let's plan that, next week or two." she said. "Maybe not a biker bar...somewhere more off the beaten path."

"Wouldn't that be a change." said Emily.

Erik walked up.

"How are you ladies doing?" he asked.

"Great." said Jess. "You know every time I talk to her, I learn something new about you."

"All good, I hope." he said.

"Nothing but five stars." she said.

"Out of how many?" he asked.

"Five, you dope, she loves you." she said.

Should I? It would mean a lot to her if I say it in front of her friends. More witnesses for Taylor to kill.

"I love her too." he said.

"That's so sweet." said Emily. "Charlie says it, but not often enough."

"For most guys, just saying it is progress." said Lexie. "Don't be too hard on him."

"Oh, I'm not." she said. "It would just be nice if he said it in front of other people."

"From everything I've heard, this is a relatively new thing for Stryker." she said. "It's appreciated, and I love him with all of my heart."

"What can I say?" he said. "You bring it out in me."

"We were thinking sometime in the next week or two, maybe we could all go out together." she said. "You know, I guess we could call it a triple date, us, and Jess and Em, and Mike and Charlie."

"Sure, that sounds like fun." he said.

"Maybe not a biker bar?" she said.

"I'm sure we could act like civilized people for one night." he said.

“Cool.” she said. “Ideas by the next time we see each other, girls. I don’t know anything around here.”

“Definitely.” said Em.

“You ready to go?” he asked. “Or you could stay, and get a cab.”

“I better go with you.” she said. “I’m tired.”

She was still trying to keep him out of trouble, and if he went off alone, who knows what might happen.

“Hopefully not too tired.” he said.

“Remember what you told me the other night? About letting my body do the talking?” she asked. “The same goes for me. I’m never too tired for that.”

Jess and Em looked at each other and giggled a little.

“You guys are so cute!” said Jess.

“Are we coming back here tomorrow?” asked Lexie.

“I don’t know.” he said.

“Let me give both of you my number.” she said. “We’ll hook this triple date up.”

She pulled a notepad out of her purse and wrote it down.

“I’ll give you mine, too.” said Jess.

“Me too.” said Em.

“Okay, if I don’t see you, I’ll call.” said Lexie.

“You guys have a great night.” said Em.

***

“They’re talking about bringing them in through Erickson.” he said. “That means they’ll pick the guns up in Idaho. Liam’s upset that we couldn’t get the deal done. Says the Saints are hard to work with. Of course no family connection either.”

“He’s right.” he said. “I knew they would have problems with the Saints. Doesn’t surprise me at all. They’re far more careless than the Centurions. If only you could have gotten the deal done.”

If only I could trust you, he thought.

“It’ll probably set them back at least a week.” he said. “The Irish don’t like it at all. Talking about the pipeline getting backed up, need to get the guns to Seattle, everything’s taking too long.”

“Have you considered that Brendan isn’t being completely honest with you?” he asked.

"That was the first thing I thought about." he said. "But he has no reason to lie."

"And you have no reason to beat his face in, yet here we are," he said.

"I'm working on that." he said.

"Any progress?" he asked.

"Well, I haven't put anyone in the hospital for four days now, so there's that." he said. "I've noticed that there's a certain behavior that I'm participating in that seems to bring out the worst in me."

"Oh?" he said. "And what's that?"

"I'm working on it." he said. "Lexie's helping."

"If you're not going to tell me, at least tell me she knows." he said.

"I need more information to make sure." he said. "You're just going to have to trust me."

"I don't trust anyone, kid." he said.

"Well neither do I." he said. "Probably a reason we didn't take the guns."

"You'll tell me when you're ready." he said. "Or maybe I'll tell you. Have you considered the fact that I might already know?"

"Not really." he said. "If you did, you would be rubbing it in my face right now."

"Is Ms. Tenenzapf around?" he asked.

"Hold on." he said.

He walked down the stairs and brought her the phone.

"He wants to talk to you." he said.

"Okay." she said.

"What's up?" she asked.

"I'll let Erik fill you in on the tactical stuff." he said.

"He already has." she said.

"Right." he said. "Mr. Stryker is on the verge of some self-awareness about his anger management issues, and I need you to find out what that is."

"He'll tell me when he's ready." she said.

"We need to deal with this Lexie, preferably sooner than later." he said. "It hasn't interfered with his work so far, but it tends to attract a lot of attention. So please. For me, for the mission, find out what you can."

“If he’s not ready, he won’t talk.” she said. “Just let me work with him a little.”

“Find out.” he said.

The line went dead.

“What was that about?” he asked. “Is he going through you?”

“He thinks that you’ve self-diagnosed your anger issues.” she said. “Is that true?”

“Maybe.” he said. “It’s just a theory.”

He knew that it wasn’t just a theory, he just didn’t want to admit it. Still, a little testing in the real world wouldn’t hurt.

“You wanna tell me?” she asked.

I’m not ready yet.” he said. “I could be wrong. Just let me figure this out.”

“Okay. No pressure.” she said. “But I want to help you.”

She wasn’t sure how far she could go with this laissez faire approach, considering the circumstances.

“He hasn’t told me, but my feeling is that the Saints get the first one without interference.” he said. “I would think that the second time through he’ll lower the boom.”

“What makes you think that?” she asked.

“I’ve done a few more missions since we had our little adventure.” he said. “Had a few James Bond moments. I know how he operates.”

“Yeah, I heard about Veronika.” she said. “Did you bang her too?”

“Why are you so concerned with who I fuck and who I don’t?” he asked.

“I was just wondering.” she said. “Trying to figure out how you operate.”

She had noticed that the conversation had taken a nasty turn. She couldn’t ever recall a time when he had been angry with her.

“You know damn well how I operate.” he said. “Probably the first thing you learned about me. I’m sure you’ve seen her pictures, take a wild guess.”

“James Bond indeed. Fuck her one day, kill her the next.” she said.

He grabbed his keys and his cut, and went outside, got on his bike and left. He had never hit a woman before, but she went too far. He figured it was best to just leave before it escalated any further.

He got on the 101 and headed for the 405. He didn't say it, but she had to know how hard that was for him. He never wanted to kill her. He had to. She was an enemy of the state, and that was his job. And for her to say something like that. Fuck her one day, kill her the next. It might have been funny under the right circumstances, but that was not the right spot for it. She needs to work on her delivery a little.

He looked at the speedometer, and he was going 123 MPH. Oh well, I have the 'get out of jail free' card, fuck it. I'm not slowing down. He was weaving in and out of cars, sometimes leaving only a few feet for error. They pull me over, the cop drives away pissed, and I get a slap on the wrist from Murphy.

Murphy! Had the nerve to try to enlist her to get information about him. And both of them wanting him to admit it. Admit what? He knew, but he wasn't going to say it, he wouldn't even think it. I can handle it. I'll find a way around it.

Before he knew it, he was getting off on the 522. He took that to the 2 and headed into the mountains. Wonder how far east I'll get this time, he thought. I'll at least stop at the rock formation and dive a few times. He was approaching Nehalem before he even thought about it. Danielle.

He looked down at his keychain and saw the cameo vibrating on the gas tank. No, he hadn't thought about that Danielle for a long time, in spite of what Taylor thought. A vision appeared to him in his mind of her.

"I'm still waiting for you, Erik. "I'm still alive. You have a..."

Then she was gone. What was that last part?

He stopped at the diner and went inside. There was a different waitress working named Sherry. He ordered a cup of coffee.

"Do you know the other waitress? Danielle?" he asked.

"She comes in at eight. Why?" she asked.

He looked down at his watch. It was 6:17.

"We're kind of friends." he said. "The last time I was here, she asked me back to her place...she said she stays at the hotel. Never mind. Probably not a great idea anyway."

"Okay." she said.

She went back behind the counter. He saw her pick up the phone, and have a somewhat animated conversation. She came back a few minutes later.

"Erik?" she asked.

"Right." he said.

"Room 136." she said. "Make sure she's here by eight."

"Sure thing, Sherry." he said. "Thanks."

He left a $20 bill next to the cup, and walked out.

Chapter 10

He made his way over to room 136, and knocked on the door.

She opened the door.

"Come in." she said. "I wish I would have known you were comin' I'm a mess."

"You look great." he said.

He could tell that she really wasn't expecting anyone, but still, she didn't look bad. Probably one of those lucky women that can roll out of bed, not work on her face for a half hour and still look good.

There was a bed, and a loveseat, and of course a fireplace, but it didn't look like she was using it. He sat down on the loveseat.

She sat down next to him, and put her hand on his leg. He looked at her, and she leaned in and started kissing him. He got into it for a minute, then it hit him. He pulled back from her.

"What's the matter, baby?" she asked.

"I'm really sorry, Danielle, I can't do this." he said. "It has nothing to do with you, it's just that I'm doing it for the wrong reasons."

"The babe on the bike?" she asked.

He nodded.

"She never needs to know." she said. "I can keep a secret. I promise you'll have a good time."

"I would know. I'm trying to be a different person." he said. "We got in a fight earlier, and I thought I was mad at her, but I'm actually mad at someone else."

"Who?" she asked.

"Myself." he said.

"I see." she said. "I can't blame you, she's a real looker."

"This is new behavior for me." he said. "The old Erik would have fucked you the first time you asked. You're quite a looker too, by the way."

"I'm really sorry that I caught the wrong end of your morality cycle." she said. "We really would have had some fun."

"Of that, I have no doubt." he said. "I'll keep your offer in mind, but today it's no."

“I hope that if we ever revisit it, I’m available.” she said. “If you come back through here with her, mum’s the word.”

“Thank you.” he said. “I should get going, I guess I’m going back to Seattle.”

“I’ll see you next time, Erik.” she said.

She gave him a soft kiss on the cheek. He could tell that she wanted more, but was able to exercise some restraint.

He walked out and went to the phone booth. He called his place, and there was no answer. He knew that she would answer if she was there. He tried the hotel.

“Room 815 please.” he said.

She answered the phone.

“Hello?” she said.

“It’s me.” he said.

“How far east did you get this time?” she asked.

“Nehalem.” he said.

“What stopped you?” she asked.

Obviously he couldn’t tell her that.

“I thought about things on my way out here.” he said. “I realized it’s not you, it’s not Murphy that I’m mad at.”

“You’re mad?” she said. “I just thought that was normal behavior to leave without a word. So what are you not mad at me about?”

“It’s not you...something I need to deal with.” he said. “That crack about Veronika didn’t help. That was when I just decided to get away before it escalated any further. I’m sorry.”

“You’ve never been mad at me before, Stryker.” she said.

“I wish I could say the same.” he said.

“When I got mad, it was mostly justified.” she said. “I’ll admit I acted like a child when we were over there.”

“All you’ve ever been is yourself, Lexie, I can’t fault you for that.” he said.

“I’m sorry for what I said.” she said.

“No, under the right circumstances, I would have thought it was funny.” he said. “Today wasn’t that time. I never wanted to kill her. It was the job, you know how that is. It’s just that with the other stuff swimming around in my head today, I was edgy. It’s not your fault, okay?”

“You don’t have to deal with this alone, Erik.” she said. “I’m here for you.”

"This I gotta do alone." he said.

He wasn't entirely sure he could do that, but he didn't see how she could help.

"I'm heading back." he said. "Do you want me to come over?"

"Just go home." she said. "Call me when you get up tomorrow, maybe we can work this out."

Maybe? What does that mean? She was still pissed.

"I might just stay out here tonight." he said, trying to regain the upper hand.

"Do whatever you want, Erik." she said. "Call me tomorrow."

That didn't work.

"Okay." he said.

He hung up the phone. It was somewhat of a new experience for him for a woman not to bend over backwards to appease him. Maybe Taylor in the beginning, Jenna got a little snippy now and then, but the way Lexie was framing this, she gave the impression that she didn't care either way. I might have to tell her just to get out of the doghouse.

He got on his bike and headed west.

He was going along the 2, about to pass by a bar near Skykomish that he had seen several times, but never stopped in. He knew after the day he had, he could use a drink. There were a bunch of pickup trucks and a few bikes there. The place was called "The Blackout Saloon." He took his cut off because it could be a potential problem if he wore it in. He locked it in his saddlebag, because the problem he would have if he lost it would be far worse than any trouble he would have inside. He walked in and sat at the bar. There were a few pool tables at one end that were open, and a dance floor at the other. It looked like a place where Danielle from the diner might hang out.

"Double 151 and Coke." he said.

"Comin' right up." said the bartender.

He put the drink in front of Erik.

Erik handed him a hundred dollar bill.

"This is yours." he said. "I don't want this glass empty. Run a tab for the drinks, keep the hundy, but keep it coming. Even if I go over to the pool table."

"Sure thing." he said. "Consider it bottomless."

He stuffed the bill in the front pocket of his jeans.

He checked the place out. There were a few good looking women. The crowd was pretty lively, everyone was happy, but it was the kind of place that could get unhappy quick. The bartender was true to his word, he seldom saw the bottom of the glass. He was about six or seven drinks in when he started thinking that he should have taken Danielle up on her offer. Why shouldn't he? He had no commitment with Lexie. Hell, she wasn't even home, and she told him to stay away from the hotel. He almost had an obligation at this point. He decided to go play a game of pool. There still wasn't anyone there, most people were dancing.

"Here, take these with you." said the bartender. "I don't get out from behind here too often."

There were a couple of doubles there.

"You keeping track of this?" he asked.

"Yeah." he said.

He looked at a piece of paper.

"$42.60 in drinks so far." he said.

Erik handed him another hundred.

"That should cover the rest of the night." he said. "If I go over a hundred, we should have a conversation."

"You go over a hundred, you won't be able to." he said.

"You obviously don't know me." he said.

He headed over to the pool table. Right after he broke, a woman came up and put a quarter on the table. She was about 5'4", had short red hair and big green eyes. She was wearing shorts and a Pearl Jam shirt.

"I got next." she said.

"Playing by yourself?" he asked. "Because if you are, there's two other tables open."

"No, I'm playing with you." she said.

He hadn't sunk anything on the break, so all of the balls were still on the table.

"Save your quarter." he said. "Roll me the rest of the balls."

She rolled them over and he re-racked them.

"Wanna break?" he asked.

"No, I'll just watch you." she said. "My name is Brenda, what's yours?"

"Erik, nice to meet you." he said.

He broke, and sunk the 14 ball.

"Do you know how to play?" he asked.

"Your stripes." she said. "I might need a little help with the shooting aspect, but I know the game."

He tried to sink the 11 ball but missed.

"Your shot." he said.

She went over to the wall and grabbed a cue that was slightly smaller than the rest of them.

"I hate it when this happens." she said. "I don't have a shot."

"Bank it." he said. "If you shoot it right here, it will bounce off and come back to the 4. It's so close to the pocket, it will be hard to miss."

"I'm not too good at that." she said. "Where should I shoot it again?"

"Right here." he said, pointing.

"Can you leave your finger there? So I have something to aim at?" she asked.

Was she for real? She was really playing dumb, but it was always possible that it wasn't an act. He had met some stupid girls before, and their saving grace was always that they were cute. That was one thing that Brenda had going for her. She reminded him of that girl Emily in Reno. Which reminded him of Ross Goodwin who he killed because he didn't know when to shut up.

"I would be happy to." he said.

He put his finger in the spot where he was pretty sure would help her make the shot. She shot the ball, missed the mark by a good three inches, and it went straight to the 4 and bumped it in.

She squealed really loud and did a little dance.

"Nice shot." he said.

"I love it when it works out, thanks for helping me." she said.

He drained the last of the second drink and looked up at the bartender who was motioning him over.

"Here's two more." he said.

"Thanks." he said.

"I might need your help again." she said.

He didn't point out that she had missed horribly the last time he helped her, yet still made the shot.

"Sure." he said.

"Come over here with me." she said. "Sometimes I have a little problem with depth perception."

"Okay." he said.

"Just lean over me, and see if I have this thing lined up right." she said.

What she was asking him to do would require him to put his arms around her, and line up some other body parts in an intimate way. He didn't have a problem with that at all. He had quite a bit to drink, and any sense of decorum he had was gone by now.

He got in position to line up her shot, and she backed into him and rubbed a little bit.

"Sorry." she said. "I'm a little drunk."

"Not a problem." he said. He was looking down the pool cue, which was lined up for at least for the moment, but he pretended that he was still working on it.

He never saw it coming. The heavy end of a pool cue smashed across the left side of his face. Just then the jukebox started playing "Welcome to the Jungle" by Guns 'n' Roses.

Welcome to the jungle
We've got fun 'n' games
We got everything you want
Honey, we know the names
We are the people that can find
Whatever you may need
If you got the money, honey,
We got your disease

He fell backwards against the wall, dazed, but pissed. He felt another pool cue in his left hand, and he came up swinging. His opponent was at least six inches taller than him. He had black hair, and a moustache that went to the bottom of his chin.

If you want it you're gonna bleed
But it's the price you pay
And you're a very sexy girl
That's very hard to please
You can taste the bright lights
But you won't get them for free

He connected with the pool cue, then broke it in half. The guy bounced back up, started to swing, but Erik caught it and ripped it out of his hand.

Feel my, my, my serpentine
I, I wanna hear you scream

He broke the other cue in half, so now he had both, and the other guy was unarmed. He started savagely beating his face with the cues, while Brenda screamed for help. Nobody wanted to get involved, they never did.

It gets worse here everyday
Ya learn ta live like an animal
In the jungle where we play

He reached down and grabbed both sides of his head and twisted. It snapped like a twig. Brenda looked on in horror. As he passed the bartender, he reached in his pocket and threw him another hundy. It was the least he could do.

In the jungle
Welcome to the jungle
Watch it bring you to your
Knees, knees
I'm gonna watch you bleed

He calmly unlocked his saddlebag and took out his cut. He put it on and got on his bike. Nobody had followed him out. He heard sirens in the distance. He started it up, put it in gear, and headed west, at the same breakneck speed he came out there at. He didn't slow down until he got to the 522.

***

He was in the elevator for what seemed like forever. He wondered absently why the bankers had to be so high up. He was going to S & N Financial on the 98th floor of the World

Trade Center. They called it S & N Financial, but Anthony knew that it was a front for something much bigger.

These were the people who really controlled everything. The man he was meeting was undoubtedly one of those mysterious Bilderberg people. He would have to be. This was the only guy that he answered to. His official employer was the CIA, but Leland paid him. He hadn't talked to anyone from the CIA in several years. Leland assigned the projects, and doled out the discipline. In a top secret way, of course. His CIA handlers didn't even know who Leland was, and didn't want to know. The stuff Murphy did was the stuff nobody ever talked about. Leland and his people made all the decisions. Big money controlled the government after all. Who knew? He was finally at the 98th floor, not that it mattered too much, S & N owned the top 15 floors. He knew the bank was a front, he didn't know who really pulled the strings. It was one of the few things Murphy didn't know.

As soon as he got off the elevator, he went through a metal detector. He already went through one on the ground floor, and he would go through at least one more before he met with Leland Andersen...if that's who he really is. It didn't matter to Anthony. He was used to all of the secrecy.

He walked through the automatic glass door, and entered a large office complex. There was a large desk in front of an attractive blond woman who looked like she was in her late 30s. Behind her was a large wall with the logo "S & N Financial" emblazoned across it.

"Hello, Janet." he said.

"Mr. Murphy." she said. "Here for Mr. Andersen?"

"Yes." he said.

"He's expecting you." she said. "Alicia?"

A younger woman appeared from behind the wall as if she had waited all day for this moment.

"Hello Alicia." he said.

"Mr. Murphy." she said. "So good to see you again. Right this way."

He followed a few paces behind here.

"My apologies, Mr. Murphy, one more time." she said.

He walked through the metal detector.

At exactly eleven AM, the light on the door to his office turned from red to green.

"Go right in, Mr. Murphy." she said.

"Thank you, Alicia." he said.

He paused for a brief moment outside, then opened the door.

"Close the door and have a seat, Anthony." he said.

His hair was a dark shade of grey, and he still had plenty of it. More, in fact, than Anthony. He had to be in his mid 70s at least, it was hard to tell. He had icy blue eyes, and he used them to intimidate people.

"What's going on in India?" he asked.

"There was a slight problem." he said. "Hartley was recognized."

"That's not good." he said. "I thought your people were professionals."

"It's his first mission." he said. "Someone else will be in country tomorrow, so we'll only be a day behind."

"That's unacceptable." he said. "I pay you a lot of money not to make mistakes."

He knew what was coming next. People always thought he had it so easy. Come talk to Leland one time, then tell me how good I have it.

"His replacement is Quinn." he said. "I don't expect anymore problems."

"Let's see that there aren't." he said. "Get rid of Hartley.
Have Quinn do it after the job is completed."

"Yes sir." he said.

People were expendable to a man like Andersen, and to a certain extent to him, but he tried not to be as cold as Leland.

"And Hong Kong?" he asked.

"Everything's on pace for the end of the month." he said.

"Excellent." he said. "And the Irish?"

"Working with another MC." he said. "They've moved the location further east. The new club is harder to work with. More careless. They're pissed that it's taking so long."

"Well, so am I." he said. "I thought you had someone inside. If you think your suitcase is the only one I fill up, you're mistaken. I have other people to answer to."

He has people to answer to. He answers to no one. He's more powerful than the President.

"Stryker did everything he could believe me." he said. "It was a club decision. Do you still want me to give them one free pass?"

"You better, but watch the run." he said. "Find a good spot for our boys in the ATF to intercept it. Did you bring the girl over? Tenenzapf?"

"Yes. She's going over with him to Ireland." he said. "That could take a while, it's a long list."

"I don't want to hear that, Mr. Murphy." he said. "It should be a quick strike."

"Shall I call in more people?" he asked.

"We can't do that, come on, Anthony, you know better." he said. "They'll see us coming. Do they work well together?"

"Fortunately yes." he said.

"Then get it done. I still can't do anything for Ms. Tenenzapf." he said. "Melissa Singer's father won't let it go. You may kill him if you like, but there are others. Did you really have to do that? Release the information?"

"It was a tactical decision, Leland." he said. "She was no good over there. Some personality problems. It was the best option."

"It seems to me that personal problems were what got her here in the first place." he said. "Maybe we should have sent her to India. Should I be worried about her too?"

"No, sir. She's one of my best. She's where she needs to be. Can anyone say they don't have any conflict with others?" he asked.

"Well I can't, but this is turning into a pattern." he said. "Is she stable?"

"I'm not worried in the least, and neither should you." he said. "Stryker has a stabilizing impact on her. She'll be fine."

"And Stryker. Didn't you say there might be an anger management issue with him?" he said. "How's he doing?"

"A certain amount of anger is an asset in this job, and he *is* undercover as an outlaw biker." he said. "Conversely, she has a stabilizing impact on him. He'll be okay. I do these things for a reason, Mr. Andersen."

"I hope you're right." he said. Anything else?"

"Have you thought any more about the French girl? Danielle? She's been inactive for 3 years now."

"When I said never, I meant never, Anthony." he said. "You can kill her for real if you like, but no. She has to stay away."

"Okay." he said. "Anything else?"

"The new girl? How's that working out?" he asked.

"She's been through the first phase, and we're on schedule." he said.

"Good. Keep me informed on India." he said. "I'm very disappointed. Let's have that suitcase."

He handed it over, and Leland moved the tumblers on the vault and opened it. He went to the shelf and methodically filled it with stacks of hundred dollar bills. He brought it back and put it on the desk. Anthony quickly counted it.

"It's all there, $ 1.5 million." he said.

"I expect results, Mr. Murphy." he said. "That will be all."

He pressed a button, and the door buzzed letting him out.

***

The phone was ringing, so he reached over, lifted it, and put it back in the cradle. He glanced at the clock, and it said 12:43 PM. The phone started ringing again immediately.

"Jesus fuck!" he said. "Take a hint!"

He did the same thing again with the same results.

"FUCK!" he screamed.

He answered the phone.

"What?" he said.

"Where have you been?" she asked. "I thought you were going to call me."

"I need some alone time, Lexie." he said. "You said you didn't care. Just stay where you're at. I'll call you when I get up."

"It's quarter to one." she said. "When were you planning on doing that?"

"Whenever I feel like it." he said.

"I know there's something wrong, Erik." she said. "Why won't you let me help?"

"Because you can't." he said.

"How do you know?" she asked.

God, how long is this conversation going to last?
"You just can't." he said.
"Do you want me to come over?" she asked.
"Do whatever you want, Lexie." he said, remembering what she said the day before.
He hung up the phone.
About an hour later he heard the door buzz.
"Oh, for fuck's sake!" he said.
He went downstairs, buzzed her in, opened the door, and went back to bed.
Moments later he heard her.
"Erik? Erik? Where is he, Huck?" she asked.
Like the dutiful little fuck he was, Huck bounded up the stairs, followed closely by Lexie.
"What the hell, Stryker?" she asked.
He rolled over slowly.
She immediately saw what had turned into a large purple shiner.
"How's the other guy look?" she asked.
"He didn't make it." he said. "Now, if you don't mind, I have a hangover to sleep off."
He rolled back over.
Didn't make it?
What do I do now? Won't do any good to try to talk to him. He's right, he needs to sleep this thing off. But I will get answers later. She took her clothes off and climbed into bed with him. Shall I test that boast about him always being ready? He sleeps naked, it'll be easy. Probably not the best idea I've had lately.
She spooned him and put her arm around him. He grabbed it and pulled it tighter.
She dozed for a few hours. When she looked at the clock it was 5:57 PM. Maybe now. I can't let him know, but I really missed him last night.
She reached between his legs, to test the waters. He rolled over on his back and turned to her.
"If that's all you wanted, we could have done it a long time ago." he said. "I meant what I said, death bed, with a weak pulse, whatever."
You were in bad shape when I got here, still are." she said. "I figured the last thing you wanted..."

He thought about the night. The close call with Danielle, that crazy chick Brenda at the bar, things were backing up down there.

"Did you ever think that it was exactly what I need?" he asked.

Exactly what he needs? Who is he kidding? That can't be true.

"You're a complicated guy, Stryker." she said.

"The time for talking is over." he said.

He rolled her over on her back and climbed on top. He had energy that he simply wasn't supposed to have in his condition. Maybe it isn't as bad as it looks. She looked down at him as he was thrusting vigorously, essentially doing all the work even though she was on top. The shiner seemed even bigger. What did they hit him with? And what about the other guy? Did he mean what I thought when he said "he didn't make it"? They kept going for what seemed like an hour and a half. She knew that he came at least 3 times. Finally he rolled over, exhausted.

"Where did that come from?" she asked.

"Just happy to see you." he said. "Didn't you have a good time?"

"I had a spectacular time, that's not the point." she said. "You were half dead earlier."

"Deathbed." he said.

She started cracking up.

"I guess I walked into that one." she said.

"I hope you're there." he said.

"At your deathbed? Don't talk like that." she said. "Even as a joke."

"I'm not joking. If I'm going to die, I want the last thing I see to be you." he said.

He had dropped a few such bombshells lately. Was he for real? Let's not get into it now. Another time. Maybe at his deathbed.

"Are you going to tell me what happened?" she asked.

He sat up and looked away from her.

"I got drunk." he said.

"You get drunk all of the time." she said.

"Remember when you told me that Murphy thought I had figured out my anger management issues?" he asked.

“Yeah.” she said.

“I figured it out a long time ago. Didn’t want to admit it.” he said. “Whenever I lose control, I’m always drunk.”

“Are you sure?” she asked. “You’re drunk a lot.”

“I know.” he said. “There was a time shortly after the vote. John and I got into it a little, well more than a little. Normally, he would have paid, president, or no. But I didn’t drink that day.”

“You ordered something from Miguel, I remember.” she said.

“Coffee. I wanted my head clear for the vote.” he said. “There have been other times too, that I didn’t drink with the same results. Make no mistake, what John said to me that day, he should be in the hospital.”

“What are you going to do?” she asked.

The answer was obvious, quit drinking, but she wasn’t going to be the one to say it. Should I tell Murphy?

“I don’t know.” he said. “I’m not great at moderation. In fact, I don’t think I’ve ever been in the same sentence with that word.”

What do I do? Is he suggesting he should quit? He has to say it, not me.

“Tell me what happened.” she said.

“I’m coming back from Nehalem, going through a little town called Skykomish. There’s this bar that I’ve seen a few times, and I need a drink to wash away the day. It’s called ‘The Blackout Saloon’. I go in there, take a seat at the bar, tip the bartender really good, and tell him I don’t want to see my glass empty.” he said. “The guy is good, and before I know it I’ve had six or seven doubles, and I’m feeling tipsy, soon to be hammered.”

“Uh huh.” she said.

“Everyone’s on the dance floor, I decide that I want to play pool. There are three pool tables open, so I go over there and rack them up. At this point, I need to stress that I’m minding my own business, not bothering anyone.” he said.

“Here it comes.” she said.

“Exactly. This cute redhead bops up and puts a quarter on the table. ‘I’m next’ she says.” he said.

“They just throw themselves at you.” she said.

“I can’t help that.” he said. “I point out the obvious, that there are two tables open. ‘I want to play with you’ she says.”

“And why wouldn’t she?” she asked.

“She asks for help with a bank shot. Wants me to put my finger at the place she should aim for. I put it at the right spot, she misses by a good three inches, but makes the shot anyway.” he said. “She squeals and does a little dance, and thanks me for my help.”

“Charming.” she said.

“Remember the part about me minding my own business? I wasn’t looking for any of this.” he said.

He was lying, but he had to make it sound good. He couldn’t let her know how he really felt about the cute redhead flirting with him. Technically, it was her fault anyway, for being such a bitch.

“Anyway, I go back to the bar for another drink, I come back, and she wants my help again. This time to help her line up a shot. I don’t know if you’ve ever done this, but...”

“I have, there’s no need to paint a picture.” she said

“She pushes back and rubs me a little with her butt.” he said. “Apologizes, says she’s a little drunk.”

“Do ya think?” she said.

“Next thing I know, I’m getting hit in the face with a pool cue. Got my attention real quick.” he said. “I fall back against the wall, and feel another pool cue in my left hand. I break it in half, and he comes at me again, and this time I’m the one who connects, in spite of him being completely aware that he’s about to get hit. He swings again, and I grab his cue, bust it in half, and start pounding his face with both of them. Brenda, the redhead screams for help, but nobody wants to get involved. By now, I’m getting tired, so I grab both sides of his head and snap his neck. Then I walked out got on the bike and left.”

“You weren’t wearing your cut, were you?” she asked.

“Hey, you’re becoming a real old lady.” he said. “No, I took it off before I went in. You never know what’s going to happen, obviously.”

“Then you came home?” she asked.

“Yeah.” he said.

“That little tramp got her boyfriend killed.” she said.

“See I don’t get that.” he said. “You call her a tramp, yet in the same situation, if you didn’t know me, you would have done the same thing.”

“Nobody does that.” she said. “She may as well have hopped on the table, spread her legs, and pulled her panties aside, if she was even wearing any.”

“Now that would have been interesting.” he said.

“Always with the quick comeback.” she said.

“I can’t help it.” he said. “We’re simpatico. I feed off of you.”

“What are you going to do?” she asked.

“I don’t know.” he said.

“If you need help from someone besides me, that’s totally cool.” she said. “After all, until recently I didn’t drink at all.”

“You mean like AA?” he asked.

Not necessarily, but maybe.” she said.

“I’ll try to deal with it myself.” he said. “Maybe try moderation. “Do me a favor? Don’t tell anyone else? Not even Murphy. Especially not him. I trusted you with this. I don’t think I made a mistake. Don’t prove me wrong.”

“Of course, baby.” she said. “We’ll get through this. Try slowing it down a little. That might be the right answer.”

She wasn’t sure that it would work, but she had even less confidence in him quitting.

Chapter 11

The phone was ringing.

"Do you want me to get it?" she asked.

"No. It might be Taylor." he said. "That wouldn't be a pleasant conversation."

For either of us, he thought.

He picked it up.

"Hello?" he said.

"Mr. Stryker. Been to Skykomish lately?" he said.

"You never ask a question you don't know the answer to, you tell me." he said.

"How often do you check your email?" he asked.

"I don't know, whenever you ask." he said. "Most people don't even know what that is."

"In the future, kid, that will be one of the main forms of communication. Buy Microsoft stock. They're the ones developing it." he said. "I was sent an article from the Skykomish Press about a tall, blond man who got in a tussle in a place called 'The Blackout Saloon.'" he said. Nasty picture of the victim. I'm guessing that you had the sense not to wear your cut in there. Problem is the guy's not breathing anymore."

"When has that ever been a problem?" he asked.

"You're attracting a lot of attention, Erik." he said. "That's why we need to get a handle on this fucking thing. Where are you at with that?"

"We're figuring it out." he said. "Lexie's helping me."

"Not good enough." he said. "I stood up for you. Lied for you, in fact. With a guy who runs the world. My boss. You need to get this thing under control. I'm not kidding. He'll have you killed."

He really didn't want to, but Murphy was forcing his hand. Besides, it was a lot to ask of her to keep his secret, especially with Murphy.

"It happens when I get drunk." he said. "Never used to. Things changed when I joined the club. We're trying to figure out the best option."

"Well, you're both smart." he said. "I think you'll find that the answer is very simple."

"It's not that simple." he said. "I don't think I can."

"Bill Wilson did it." he said.

"Who's that?" he asked.

"The founder of AA." he said. "And he didn't have the kind of help we do today. Back then, they thought alcoholism was a mental defect. He found a doctor who suffered from the same problem, and they discovered that by getting together with another alcoholic, combined with believing in a power greater than themselves, they could quit."

"I don't know Anthony." he said. "Won't that change me?"

"It will only make you stronger." he said. "There are plenty of people in recovery in our line of work."

"Do we share the same line of work?" he asked.

"Not exactly. You kill people, I have them killed." he said. "Same results, same guilt."

"Don't feel much of that anymore." he said.

"Neither do I." he said.

"You said there are others. Who else?" he asked.

"They call it Alcoholics Anonymous, but I'm not ashamed." he said. "I quit. And I was far worse than you."

"Really? You're always so together." he said. "I would have never guessed."

"Well, they don't brand us with an 'A' on our forehead, or make us wear a scarlet letter." he said. "We can even buy booze if we want. I haven't always been a dashing and debonair spook. There was a time when I slept in a dumpster."

"Really? How long has it been?" he asked. "Since you've drank?"

"Seventeen years." he said. "You can do this if you want to Erik. My way is the easiest. If you ever want to talk, I'm here. It has to be your decision. But you have to fix this thing one way of another."

"How did you stand up for me? Lie for me?" he asked.

"I told Mr. Big that you did everything you could to influence the vote. Didn't tell him which way you went, of course." he said. "He thinks that you did everything you could to pass the vote on the guns. I know why you didn't, and I was going to have to do something shitty if the Centurions would have got them. I'm glad it worked out this way. I didn't want to do that."

"Thanks." he said. "Is it going to cause any problems if I, well Lexie and I disappear for about a week?"

"I don't think so." he said. "What have you got planned?"

"Nothing, I just thought of it." he said. "It's been a long time since I've been home."

"That's an excellent idea, Erik." he said. "Get away for a while, get some perspective. Go check your email. I had it hooked up for a reason. Mainly a government thing now, but mark my words. Microsoft stock. Let me talk to her."

He handed her the phone and walked over to the computer.

He had fourteen emails. He's right, I should check this more often. He selected the latest one, He quickly read the article, then scrolled down to the picture. Even on the monochrome monitor it looked bad. He started looking over the other emails.

"He told you?" she asked.

"Yes." he said. "He can do this. I've done it."

"You?" she asked. "An alcoholic?"

"In another lifetime it seems, but yes, I still am. There's no cure." he said. "Don't get upset if he calls me in the middle of the night to talk, that's part of it."

"I'm glad he told you." he said. "He put me in an awkward position by telling me."

"He knows that, and I think that's why he told me." he said. "Did he tell you about his adventure last night?"

"Once he got past the part about the drinking he was in a talkative mood." she said. "Is he going to be okay?"

"Yes. But this has to be his decision." he said. "And don't be upset if it takes a while. Sometimes it's trial and error. Tell him to call me if he's having trouble, night or day. At least he's aware of the problem now."

"Thanks for your help, Anthony." she said. "I was a little out of my depth."

"Think nothing of it. I'm serious, night or day, I'm here for him." he said. "Have fun on your trip."

"Wait, wha..." she started to say, but the line was dead.

She walked over to the computer.

"What are you doing?" she asked.

"Checking my email." he said.

"What's that?" she asked.

"Apparently the wave of the future." he said. "Will you be okay if I try to call Taylor?"
"Sure, baby, I told you it's okay." she said.
"Just to see if she's okay." he said.
"Yeah, please." she said. "I don't want you to worry."
He called.
"Plaza Hotel, this is Tina, how may I direct your call?" she said.
"I'm looking for Taylor Whitman." he said. "She's with AMM modeling."
"Right." she said. "I think she's on location. They're on the sixteenth floor. Who shall I say is calling?"
"Erik." he said.
"Erik...?" she inquired.
Just Erik isn't enough?
"Erik Stryker." he said.
"One moment please." she said.
She put him on hold, which immediately went to classical music. He looked at Lexie.
"Well?" she asked.
"They said she's on location. She's going to try to find her." he said. "Just Erik wasn't good enough."
"It's a classy place." she said. "They want to make sure the clients are happy. What if they asked for a last name, and she didn't know?"
"Okay, that makes sense." he said.
She reappeared on the line.
"Mr. Stryker, she's not available at the moment, may I take a message?" she asked.
"Can I just have her room number, and I can try later?" he asked.
"She's on the sixteenth floor." she said.
"I know, you told me, what room?" he said.
"No, AMM rented the entire floor. We don't know who is in what room." she said. "May I take a message?"
"Sure, just tell her to call me." he said.
"Your number?" she asked.
"She ha..." he said "Never mind."
He gave her the number.
"So?" she asked.

"Probably not too likely that she's face down in the gutter somewhere." he said. "They're going to give her the message when she gets back from location or whatever."

"Okay." she said.

"You feel like going on a road trip?" he asked.

"Sure, where?" she asked.

"Michigan." he said. "You know, the one that looks like a hand?"

"I know where Michigan is." she said. "Why?"

"It's been a long time." he said. "Go see the parents. My brother may be able to help me with something too."

"What?" she asked.

She couldn't imagine him needing help from anyone.

He pointed his thumb up and made the international gesture for drinking.

"Oh...okay, that sounds like a great idea." she said. "Has she ever been there?"

"A few times. She's pretty well liked with my family." he said. "So I need you on your best behavior. No pressure."

"Right. Do I stand any chance?" she said.

"I told them I split with Taylor." he said. "Didn't say anything about you. Just be yourself, you'll be fine."

Here we go, she thought. Is this a test? No, he's going to get help, everything else is secondary. Good for him. She couldn't recall ever having to meet anyone's parents. Her lifestyle never required her to. Most of her boyfriends were fleeting, or in a wartime situation.

"The point is for you to get help, not for me to impress your parents." she said. "Still, I think I can pull it off."

"I'm sure you can." he said. "My dad will be easy. I don't think I've ever had a girlfriend that my mom liked from the start. Don't worry about that, everyone knows how she is. She has a problem thinking that anyone is good enough for me."

"Did she like Taylor?" she asked.

"Not right away." he said. "We'll spend a few days there, hopefully by the end, she'll warm up to you, but don't worry if she doesn't. Everyone else is cool."

"How long will it take to get there?" she asked.

"For a normal person, a little over a day if they go straight through." he said. "I am, of course, not normal. We can leave tomorrow morning, and I expect to have most of it behind us by around ten. Then we get up the next day and have a short trip."

"Okay." she said. "That's a long way on a bike."

"Is that something you can do?" he said. "If you can't I completely understand."

Here's probably your one and only chance to get out of this, she thought.

"No, I'll be fine." she said. "It will be fun."

"You know how to ride?" he asked. "I'm sure we could borrow one of Brendan's old lady's bikes."

"She doesn't even know me." she said. "How many does she have?"

"Four. Do you? Know how to ride?" he asked.

"Yes, but there's no way I'd be comfortable with that." she said. "I'll ride with you."

"Okay." he said. "But now that I know that, we should look into getting you one."

"Maybe after we complete the mission." she said.

The phone started ringing.

"Hello?" he said.

"Erik! It's so good to hear your voice!" she said. "How are you? Sorry I haven't called, I've been so busy."

"I'm fine." he said. "I was a little worried that I hadn't heard from you."

Lexie pointed to the stairs and started walking in that direction.

"I'm so sorry." she said. "I've been thinking about you, but the schedule is brutal. By the time I think about it, it's too late to call."

"You've forgotten my hours?" he said. "There's no such thing as too late."

"I'm really sorry, Erik." she said. "So how are things going with you?"

"Okay, I guess." he said. "I decided to go home for a few days."

"That's good. Make sure to tell everyone I said 'hi'." she said. "Have you thought any more about what we talked about? Taking a break?"

"Taylor, you would probably be better off just forgetting about me." he said. "You have so much to offer, and you just landed your dream job. You're part of the glitterati now. I'm just a sailor."

"You've never been 'just' anything, Erik." she said. "Give us a chance. We're so good together."

"There was a time, but we've been drifting apart for a while now." he said. "This is your time. Go live your dream."

"Is she going with you?" she asked.

"What difference does that make?" he asked.

"So she is." she said. "I really want you to be happy, Erik, and if that's what that means, I'm happy for you. But I'll always be here for you. Don't forget about me."

"When are you leaving for Paris?" he asked.

"In a few days." she said. "And you? Any idea when you're going to Ireland?"

"Things are taking a little longer here." he said. "Probably within a month."

He thought about telling her that Lexie would be coming along, but she didn't need to know that.

"I want you to write down a number." she said.

"Just give it to me, I don't need to write it down." he said.

"Right, I forgot. It's to my 'cell phone'." she said. "It's the latest technology, I can take it with me wherever I go. Sometimes the reception isn't good, and it will drop calls, but it's nice to have a phone with me anywhere I am. You wouldn't have had to talk to that bitch at the desk earlier."

"She seemed okay to me." he said.

"You have no idea." she said. "Do me a favor?"

"Sure, anything." he said.

"Call me when you get to Ann Arbor?" she said.

"Sure." he said.

She gave him the number.

"I miss you a lot." she said. "I love you, Erik."

"Me too." he said.

"We back to that?" she asked.

"Sorry, I forgot." he said. "I love you too, and you know it no matter what I say."

"Thanks." she said. "Call me when you get to Ann Arbor."

"Okay." he said.

He hung up the phone.

Lexie came down the stairs.

"So how is she?" she asked.

"She seems good." he said. "Says she has a tough schedule, that's why she hasn't called."

"Well, good." she said. "I'm going to go back to the hotel and pack a bag."

"Small." he said. "Like something that can fit in a saddlebag."

"Sure." she said. "I'll be back in a while."

"Do you want a ride?" he asked.

"Pretty sure I'll get enough of that tomorrow." she said. "But thanks."

She called a cab.

The security door buzzed.

Erik pressed the button.

"Who is it?" he asked.

"Delivery from Mr. Murphy." he said.

Erik buzzed him in.

Erik signed for the box and opened it. There were a couple of phones there, and a note from Murphy.

"Cell phones, the latest technology. So you can call me from the road. The one wrapped in blue is Erik's, sorry, Lex, no pink paper."

"Strange." he said. "Taylor was just saying she has one of these."

"Maybe she's in demand." she said. "Like they need to be able to talk to her wherever she is."

"Who knows?" he said. "Do you know that agency rented the entire sixteenth floor of the Plaza?"

She let out a low whistle.

"Those rooms are $2,500 per night minimum." she said. "What do you think? Maybe ten rooms per floor. 25 grand a night."

She heard the cab honking outside.

She went over and kissed him.

"I'll see you when I get back." she said.

***

The day after next they were in Ann Arbor. The first thing Erik did was find a hotel relatively close to his parent's house.

"Do you want to take a shower?" he asked.

"You're letting me go first?" she said. "You're the one covered in bugs."

"Go ahead, I'll make a few calls, let people know we're here." he said.

"Okay, I would love a shower." she said.

He looked at the cell phone. It looked like a regular phone. He remembered a few years back, Murphy had one that was as big as a brick, and just as heavy. Modern technology. If he was the type to invest, he probably would check out Microsoft stock. He dialed the number to the club.

"Hello?" he said.

It was Miggy.

"Hey Miggy, it's Erik. Is John or Kirk around?" he asked.

"Sure, hold on." he said.

A few minutes later, Kirk came to the phone.

"Hey, what's up?" he asked.

"I'm in Ann Arbor." he said. "Needed to get away for a few days, and it made sense to come and see the family."

"Okay." he said. "How was the ride?"

"Beautiful as always." he said. "Any news? From the Irish?"

"You seem more concerned now than you were when we were in the running for this thing." he said.

"Just trying to stay apprised." he said. "Will it be a problem if I stay here for a few days? I'll be back within a week and a half."

"No problem at all, brother." he said. "Say hi to mama and papa Stryker for us."

"Sure." he said. "Lexie went and got us some mobile phones. She always wants to have the latest thing. Take down this number, you can reach me any time."

"Hold on." he said. "Go ahead."

He gave him the number.

"I'll see you in about a week and a half then." he said.

"Keep the shiny side up, brother." he said.

Next he called his mom.

"Hey, I'm in town for a few days." he said.

"Just like you, Erik, never any warning." she said. "How am I supposed to make it nice for you if I don't know?"

"Just seeing you is enough." he said. "It was a spur of the moment thing. We're staying at the Holiday Inn."

"We? Who's with you?" she asked. "And after you got rid of Taylor. She was perfect for you."

"If you remember right, you hated her when you first met." he said. "She cried all night."

"I didn't do that!" she said. "I loved that girl like she was my own daughter! Who is this new one?"

"Her name is Lexie." he said. "We've known each other for a long time. Be nice."

"When are you coming over?" she asked.

"We just got here. I'm going to take a shower, then we're going to the greenhouse." he said. "Have you talked to Bjorn lately?"

"A few days ago." she said. "Why?"

"I'd like to get together with him." he said.

"Why don't I get everyone together for dinner tonight, then you can arrange it." she said. "And I'll set an extra place for Leslie."

"Lexie." he said. "Short for Alexandria. Can you remember that?"

"Of course I can, Lexie." she said. "When can we expect you?"

"Like six, six thirty." he said.

"Great. It's so exciting that you're back." she said. "How long are you staying?"

"Just a few days, ma." he said.

"You can't stay longer?" she asked.

"I have things to do back home." he said. "Lexie too."

"I'll try to be nice to Lexie." she said, making sure to annunciate her name correctly. "We'll see you at about six then."

"Okay, by ma." he said.

"Me too what?" she asked.

"My mother." he said "I have to make it seem like we can't stay, or she would have us living the rest of our lives here."

"How long are we staying?" she asked.

"A few days, maybe a week, but no longer." he said. "I'm going to get in the shower."

"Okay." she said.

***

They got to the greenhouse, and parked next to his father's Jaguar.

Lexie looked at the place.

"How big is it?" she asked.

"The actual store is relatively small, but there are three acres of greenhouses." he said.

"It's incredible." she said.

They went inside, and his father was behind the counter. He was about Erik's height, and had a lot of almost white hair. He came around and gave Erik a hug.

"I heard you were here." he said.

"Word travels fast." he said.

He looked at Lexie.

He spoke Danish.

"You break up with the sweet one, and you already have someone new?" he asked.

Erik responded in Danish.

"She got a modeling job. We were having problems anyway." he said. "You'll love Lexie, I've known her a long time."

"Your mother's not going to like it." he said.

"Has she ever?" he asked. "Speak English, this is rude. Lexie speaks seven languages, but I don't think Danish is among them."

"What's going on?" she asked.

"He was asking about Taylor." he said. "My father never misses an opportunity to show off his language skills. Am I really translating for you?"

"So it would seem." she said. "Just by my knowledge of languages, I can pick up bits and pieces, but I got none of that, except I heard my name, but who knows? Lexie could be something quite different in Danish. I thought you said you don't know any other languages."

“I really don’t count Danish.” he said. “The only people who speak it are me, my grandfather, my dad, and people who actually live in Denmark.”

“I’m impressed, Str...Erik.” she said.

“How rude of me.” he said. “Palle Stryker, I’m pleased to meet you.”

“Lexie Tenenzapf.” she said. “A pleasure.”

“Would you like a tour?” he asked.

“I would love one, Mr. Stryker.”

“If we are to be friends, Lexie, you must call me Palle.” he said. “No more Mr. Stryker.”

“At least he’s not calling you Leslie.” said Erik.

“What?” she asked.

“Never mind.” he said. “Let’s go have a look at this place.”

They walked through the swinging door that separated the main store from the greenhouses.

“What’s this? More tattoos?” he said.

Palle was still stuck on Danish. There were so few people that he could speak it with.

"Please, dad! With the Danish!" he said. "She doesn’t understand us. The tattoos are part of my lifestyle and you know that. Be grateful I don’t take my shirt off."

Lexie looked at him.

“Just a little commentary on the ink.” he said.

“I really do apologize dear, sometimes I don’t even know I’m doing it.” he said. “Danish is my first language.”

“That really is true, and it’s so rare that he finds someone who speaks it, he can’t help himself.” he said. “We’re not trying to exclude you.”

“No, I understand.” she said. “Mr. Str...Palle, do you have any books at home I can look at to try to learn?”

He perked up.

“I do, young lady.” he said. “The only one who took any interest is Erik. Do you remember?”

“How could I forget?” he said. “You were tougher than any of my teachers...to this day.”

“But you learned.” he said.

“How many kids do you have, Palle?” she asked.

"Four, but only two that still live near us." he said. "I'm impressed that you want to learn Danish. You speak seven languages?"

"How did...oh, right, the private Danish conversation." she said. "Yes, I do speak a few languages. I can follow along a little with you, but not enough to make sense of it. But now I want to learn."

"I like this girl." he said.

"You should keep your shirt on if he doesn't like the tatts." she said.

"I thought you didn't understand." he said.

"What?" she said.

"That's what I told him a few minutes ago in Danish." he said. "That he's lucky I don't take my shirt off."

"I honestly don't know Danish." she said. "Maybe by tomorrow morning."

"It will surely take longer than that." he said.

"She's smart, dad. Don't be surprised if she can hold down a conversation tomorrow." he said.

"That would be something." he said.

"No pressure." she said.

"I'm delighted that you're interested." he said. "Whatever the results."

"Your English is excellent." she said. "Most people who learn it as a second language, you can tell. I would never have known."

"Wait til he's had a few drinks." said Erik.

"I'm sure he'll be just as charming." she said.

"What? Are you working him to get to my mother?" he asked.

"Didn't you just say I'm smart?" she asked.

"My wife is a little tough." he said. "I'll put in a good word for you."

"Thank you." she said.

"Someday, this will all be yours, son." he said.

"What about Bjorn?" he asked. "Aren't you supposed to pass down the empire to the first born?"

"I don't know that I can trust him with it." he said.

"And you can trust me?" he asked. "He worked here for a long time. As vice president. I haven't even lived here since I left for the Navy."

"Did you know he's driving a cab?" he asked. "Like an immigrant!"

"Okay, dad I'm not even going to point out how ridiculous that sounds coming from you." he said. "Bjorn is the logical choice, and I'm sure he would be willing to give up his cab for you."

"We'll talk about it another time." he said.

Erik wasn't about to tell him that he made more money now than he could ever hope to make here.

"What's up with the rubber tree?" asked Lexie.

There was a huge rubber tree in the main greenhouse that was growing through the glass.

"You won't believe this, dear." he said. "Someone brought that tree in 1967 and said it wouldn't grow. We put it back there and forgot about it until it was several feet taller. It's never stopped growing. We've had to cut it back every year since."

"That's amazing." she said. "You sure about this, Erik? This place is really cool. It could be a decent gig."

Palle started laughing heartily.

"Dorte will love you, I'm sure." he said. "If she doesn't, I'll explain that you're on our side."

"Don't let that fool you." she said. "I'm always on Erik's side first."

"As you should be." he said.

They were going further and further back, and there was no end in sight.

"You should see it around Christmas." he said. "There are more poinsettias than you can count."

"I never had the pleasure of working here in the winter." said Erik. "I never even got to work up front. I was always in the back in the 120 degree heat in the summer."

"Yes, son, but I would never ask you to do anything I didn't do myself." he said. "That was my life for many years."

"Let me show you the roses." he said.

They went back further, and they were finally at the end. The last greenhouse had several benches about 50 yards long full of roses of different colors in various stages of development. Palle got very quiet, and a smile crossed his face. It seemed likely that he might shed a tear.

"This is his pride and joy." Erik said.

"It's beautiful." she said.

"We built this." he said. "From the ground up. And look at it now."

"It really is remarkable, dad." he said.

"This is why I want you, Erik." he said. "Right here. Bjorn never got his hands dirty. He couldn't do this. You can. You remember that summer?"

"It was tough work, but it was one of the best times of my life." he said.

"Him! A 16 year old kid! In charge of my roses." he said. "And it was one of the best crops I've ever had."

"But dad, now I can't even keep a houseplant alive." he said. "Give Bjorn a chance. I'm not coming back here."

He didn't want to put it so bluntly, but sometimes that was what was required when talking to his father.

"It's yours if you want it." he said. "I would be proud, and secure knowing that it's in good hands. I've said my piece."

But..." he said. "Never mind. Thanks, dad."

He thought about bringing up Bjorn again, but it was useless.

They started walking back to the front.

Erik's phone started ringing. He looked at the number.

"Sorry, I gotta take this." he said.

He pointed at the phone.

"Lexie's idea. The latest technology. She wanted us to be safe on the road." he said.

"Good." he said. "We'll get to know each other a little better."

They walked ahead. It was the club.

"What's up?" he asked.

"How are mama and papa Stryker?" he asked.

"I think papa wants to marry Lexie." he said.

"That okay with mama?" he asked.

"He knows better than to test those waters, believe me." he said. "What's going on?"

"I need your proxy." he said. "We're talking about doing some runs for a friend of the club. It's meth, muling, not dealing. Mainly protection. Doesn't pay like the guns, but it's safer."

"Friend of the club?" he asked. "Josh?"

"Exactly. He's good people." he said.

"I know." he said. "Take my proxy, and use it however you want. I trust you, Johnny. Mention my proxy first, you'll probably pick up some votes."

"Thanks." he said. "What's up with the new phone number?"

"It's a mobile phone. Lexie was worried about us on the road, so we picked a couple up before we left town." he said. "It's actually pretty cool."

"I think I've seen those." he said. "Aren't they those huge phones that you can take anywhere?"

"The technology has improved." he said. "It's just the size of a regular phone now."

"Listen, Erik, I want to apologize for...you know after the vote." he said. "I know you only did what you thought was best."

"There won't ever be bad blood between us, even if we throw down." he said. "You can ask Brendan about that. Still, the gesture is appreciated."

"So we're good?" he asked.

"Of course." he said.

"Be safe coming back." he said.

"I will." he said. "See you in around a week."

He caught up to Lexie and his dad.

"What time will you be over?" he asked.

"Probably around six." he said. "Will Thyra be there?"

"Everyone will, except of course, for Freyja."

"My sister." he said. "Lives in Key West."

"Nice." she said.

"Be careful on that thing." he said.

"You be careful with yours." he said, nodding towards the Jag.

"My weakness." he said. "I love my sports cars."

"It's gorgeous." she said.

"I'll take you for a ride later." he said.

"Farvel, Lexie." he said.

"Farvel, Palle." she said.

He walked back into the greenhouse.

“So everyone has old world names except you?” she said. “How did you get so lucky?”

“You ever hear of Leif Erikson?” he said. “Strangely, his father’s name was Erik. Erik the Red, in fact, who was a Viking. Technically Norwegian, but back then, all of everything in Scandinavia was the same country. I would have been happy with almost any name they gave me, but the way I see it, they named me after a Viking, Bjorn too. At least they didn’t name me Ragnar.”

“That would have been cool.” she said.

“And what about Lexie?” he asked. “Any special meaning?”

“It probably means that the year I was born, that was the most popular name for Jewish girls.” she said. “My parents weren’t so creative.”

“Well I like it.” he said.

They got on the bike and went back to the hotel.

Chapter 12

They got to the house, and the Jag was there with the top down. It was on a country road, in between two major thoroughfares. Everyone who had ever traveled it agreed that it was the worst road in Ann Arbor. It was surrounded by forest, and it wasn't uncommon to see deer and other animals.

"You ready?" he asked.

"Tell me it's going to be okay." she said.

"It's going to be okay." he said. "You won over my dad, and he's old school. What he says goes. You'll be fine."

"I hope so." she said. "Even he said she was tough."

"Don't worry about my mother." he said. "She'll love you, or rush to judgement and hate you."

She stopped.

"I'm not going in there." she said.

"Sorry." he said. "A little light hearted mom humor that obviously fell flat. Thyra will be there, and she's the sweetest person in the world. She's a good buffer, and she'll put mom in her place if necessary."

"You're lucky I love you." she said.

She started walking again.

"You're not scared, are you?" he asked. "Because we can just go back to the hotel if you are."

"Having a good time with this?" she asked.

"Frankly, yes." he said. "You can gun down terrorists in the desert, but you're scared of a 98 pound middle aged woman."

"I'm not scared." she said.

They walked in, Thyra greeted them at the door. Freesia, the yellow lab bounded up to the door to see who the new people were. Thyra was tall for a woman, but not as tall as Lexie. She had short blond hair in a style that suited her well, and big brown eyes. She gave Erik a long hug, then turned to Lexie and did the same with her.

"Thyra, Lexie. Lexie, Thyra." he said.

"It's so nice to meet you." she said. "How was your trip?"

"I've never had one like it." she said. "It was beautiful."

"I'm so glad to hear that." she said. "And you?"

"You know how much I love to ride." he said.

Freesia stood up and put her paws on Erik's chest.

“Attention starved as always, girl?” he said. “This is Freesia.”

Lexie scratched between her ears.

“You still in school?” he asked.

“Graphic design.” she said.

Just then his mom walked up. She was much shorter, and the only one in the family that was a brunette. She looked great for her age. She gave him a hug.

“It’s so good to see you.” she said. “And this must be Alexandria.”

“Lexie is fine, ma, she prefers it.” he said.

“So nice to meet you, Mrs. Stryker.” she said.

“Dorte, please.” she said.

She spoke Danish to try to exclude Lexie.

"Where did this one come from?" she asked.

He answered in Danish.

"I’ve known her for a long time." he said. "Did I mention that she speaks seven languages?"

“Really?” she asked.

“Yes.” he said.

“Welcome to our home, Lexie.” she said.

He would let his mom sweat for a few minutes.

“Dinner will be ready soon. We’re having Stegt flæsk with med persillesovs and kartofler, Æbleflæsk, Krebinetter, Mansaka, or Torsk, if you’d rather have fish, and Aeggekage and Æbleskiver for dessert.”

“When did you have time?” asked Lexie.

“Isn’t it terrible?” she asked. “He won’t even let his own mother know he’s coming, so I can make a proper meal.”

“Mom that spread you’re putting out is 3 meat dishes, cod, and a casserole that also has meat. Then two choices for dessert.” he said. “Proper meal? That’s a proper meal for sixteen grown men!”

“I just want everything to be perfect for you, honey.” she said.

“It is.” he said.

“Hello?”

It was Bjorn, coming in with his wife and three combined kids. It was his second marriage, and after meeting Samantha, Erik figured he would be looking for wife number three soon.

He gave him a hug.

“My long lost brother.” he said. “How are you?”
“Good, and you?” he asked.
“You know, livin the dream.” he said.
“Bjorn, Samantha, this is Lexie.” he said.
Lexie was looking Bjorn over. He was as tall as Erik, but he had extremely long, bushy blond hair, a goatee, and six or seven earrings in each ear. He didn’t have any ink that she could see, but she wouldn’t be surprised if he did, and probably something weird. This is the guy that’s going to help him?
“A pleasure to meet you.” he said.
Samantha just looked her up and down like she was competition.
“Likewise.” she said.
“Smoke?” asked Erik.
“Sure.” he said.
Samantha started following.
“Sorry, Sam, we need a minute.” he said. “Get to know Lexie, I’m sure you’ll like her.”
“Okay.” she said, doubtfully.
They went out on the back porch, where there was an overflowing ashtray.
“She’s beautiful.” he said. “Never thought I would say it, but she looks better than Taylor.”
“We’re very close.” he said. “Been through some shit together.”
“So what’s up?” he asked.
“I never thought I would say this.” he said. “You see, I’ve been having some problems lately. You know...?”
“No I don’t.” he said. “You need to tell me.”
“Well, it’s...I don’t know...how did you know?” he said. “With the drinking?”
“Simple, my life became unmanageable.” he said. “Does that sound like the problems you’ve been having?”
“Yes.” he said.
In spite of himself he was quietly starting to cry.
“Where are you staying?” he asked.
“Holiday Inn.” he said.
“Northside, or south?” he asked.
“North.” he said.

"Do you want help with this?" he asked.
"More than anything." he said.
"Meet me in the lobby at 11:30 tonight." he said. "We're going to a meeting."
"Are you sure that's the best way?" he asked.
"It's the only way." he said.
He moved closer and put his arm around Erik.
"You're going to be okay." he said.
"Thanks." he said.
He dried his tears.
Erik could see Lexie through the window, giving him the thumbs up/thumbs down sign. Looking for a way to escape Sam, no doubt.
He motioned for her to come out.
"How's it going out here?" she asked.
"We're going to a meeting tonight." he said.
"You can come too if you want." said Bjorn. "There's a pool table, people playing cards, other things to do."
"Is it quiet?" she asked.
"Usually during the meeting." he said. "It's totally cool if you don't want to come, just a suggestion."
"It's okay, baby, I'll be all right." he said. "I'm sure dad has some homework for you."
"That he does." she said.
Bjorn looked at her.
"She wants to learn Danish." he said.
"Good luck with that." said Bjorn.
Erik's phone started ringing.
"What's that?" he asked.
"A mobile phone." he said. "I need to take this."
"We got them at the same time, and I haven't had one call yet." she said. "Meanwhile, He's excusing himself regularly saying 'I gotta take this'."
"What's your number?" he asked.
She gave it to him.
Her phone started ringing immediately.
"What the hell." she said.
"Hello?"
"Hello, is this Lexie?" he asked.
"Yes, who is this?" she asked.

"Bjorn. Now you've had your first call." he said.

She looked up and saw Bjorn with a mobile phone in his hand.

She punched him in the arm.

"You had me going." she said.

"It's an honor to be your first." he said.

"Well, thank you, Bjorn." she said.

"Sam likes it, so she can get a hold of me while I'm driving." he said.

"Is that good or bad?" she asked.

"No comment." he said.

"That's what I thought." she said. "So, are you going to take care of my man?"

"No." he said. "We are. Me and a bunch of other drunks."

"How did you get this number?" he asked.

"Simple, I called the club." she said.

"And they gave it to you?" he asked.

"Have you forgotten who you're talking to?" she asked.

"Right, of course." he said.

"I thought you were going to call me when you got there." she said.

"Well, you know how it is, we were wiped out." he said. "We rested for a while, then went to the greenhouse, and I just forgot."

"So she is there?" she asked.

"Of course she is." he said. "But you knew that."

"Do they like her?" she asked.

"Dad loves her. Thyra, well, she loves everyone." he said. "She's out having a smoke with Bjorn, and Sam is steaming inside the house."

"Can I talk to people?" she asked.

"On one condition." he said. "You talk to her first. And pretend to like her to everyone else."

"That's two conditions." she said.

"Do you want to talk to the family?" he asked. "Because I can just hang up and pretend you never called."

She thought about just calling the house, but she didn't have the number with her. This way, they'll at least know that I'm still in communication with him.

"Okay, I'll play along." she said.
"Lexie will be on next." he said.
He walked over to Lexie and whispered the situation in her ear.
"Okay, no problem." she said.
He handed her the phone.
"Taylor! How's the Big Apple?" she said.
She was passed around the family, making sure to mention that her and Erik weren't through, they were just on a break. Most of the family played along, but Palle told her the truth.
"He's in love with that girl." he said. "I think you lost him."
Dorte, of course as discreetly as she could, told Taylor how much of a step down Lexie was, and how she had always loved her like a daughter. She passed the phone back to Erik.
"Did you talk to Bjorn?" he asked.
"Yeah, he seems to be doing okay." she said. "Not always happy with Sam, but that's been going on for years."
"Did he tell you anything else?" he asked.
"No, just asked about New York, the modeling job, you know, small talk." she said.
He was pretty sure Bjorn didn't say anything, but he had to check.
"It was a little awkward you calling while we're here, but I'm glad you talked to everyone." he said.
"Are you happy?" she asked.
"I've had a problem or two lately, but it's nothing to do with Lexie." he said.
"I want to be with you, Erik, but I'll take you being happy...for now." she said.
"Are you happy?" he asked.
"Other than missing you, I really am." she said. "We'll work it out, one way or the other."
"It might be the other." he said.
"If that's how it is, I'll learn to accept it." she said. "But I haven't given up on you."
"Thanks for calling, Taylor." he said. "I'm sure it meant a lot to Thyra, and dad too. He really likes you."
He doesn't pull any punches." she said. "He was honest with me, told me how it is. I know you're in love with her, but do me a favor? Don't forget about me?"

"I never could." he said. "Call me from Paris."

He hung up the phone.

"Dinner!" yelled Dorte.

Everyone sat down, and there was so much food that there wasn't any space left on the table. When they finished eating, Dorte packed it all up and put it in the refrigerator in the garage.

She brought out dessert, and everyone sat at the table and talked for a while.

"So where are you from, Lexie?" asked Dorte.

"Originally New York, but we moved to Jerusalem when I was very young." she said. "My father got a job offer that he couldn't pass up. After he died I moved to Tel Aviv."

"Your father died?" asked Thyra.

"He was killed, actually." she said. "By a terrorist."

"That's awful. What about your mother?" asked Dorte.

"Unfortunately, a few months later she was killed too." she said. "After that, I joined the army at a much earlier age than anyone should."

"That's horrible." she said. "I had no idea."

"Most people don't." she said. "With all of your generous hospitality, and as close as I am to Erik, I feel comfortable talking about it with you. I have no family left."

Thyra got up and embraced her.

"You do now." she said. "We'll be your family. Right?"

There were affirmations around the table.

"So how did you meet Erik?" she asked.

"We met overseas about seven years ago." she said. "Does that sound about right?"

"Yeah, about." he said.

"We've been close ever since." she said. "This is actually my first time back to the states since we moved to Israel."

"If Erik is happy, I'm happy." said Dorte. "I'm glad you're here."

"So you know seven languages?" she asked.

"How did...oh, right, the little Danish back and forth when we got here." she said. "That's true, but Danish isn't among them...yet. Palle is going to give me a book to look at."

"I almost forgot." he said.

He got up and disappeared into the back of the house.

"Parlez-vous français?" inquired Thyra.

"Oui avez-vous passé temps là-bas??" she asked.

"Un vacances inoubliable." she said. "Et toi?"

"Temps de travail." she said.

"Que faites vous?" she asked.

"I work for the Art Museum in Tel Aviv." she said. "Thyra was telling me about her trip to France, but I thought everyone would want to know what I do. I'm on sabbatical now."

Palle entered the room with 3 or 4 big books, and gave them to Lexie.

"We should be able to have a basic conversation by tomorrow." she said. "Some people are good at math, some can fix cars, but language is my thing."

"I will be impressed." said Dorte. "What do you do for the museum?"

"I find things." she said. "It involves a lot of travel, to inspect pieces, appraise them, and essentially decide if it's worth the risk for the museum. It's far easier to be objective when it's their money."

"So they trust you with hundreds of thousands of dollars of their money?" Palle asked.

"Sometimes millions." she said. "The art I look at isn't cheap."

What is this girl doing with my son?

"I met Erik at The Louvre." she said. "He has a good eye."

"You went to The Louvre?" asked Bjorn.

"Go there all the time." he said.

"I had no idea." he said.

"We fell in love immediately." she said. "Just to see him there, completely taken by art like that...I've never met a man like him."

"So romantic." said Thyra.

"I think we're going to get out of here." said Bjorn. "We have to go all the way to Saline."

"Us too." said Erik. "We had a long day."

"You'll come back and see us tomorrow?" asked Dorte. "Dinner? We could have dinner every night you're here."

"We could have leftovers every night I'm here." he said. "I'll call you tomorrow, ma."

After they got clear of the door Bjorn looked at him.

"11:30?" he said.
"I'll be in the lobby." he said.
"Lexie? You're welcome to come." he said.
"Do you see these books?" she said.
"Okay, but if you change your mind..." he said.
They got on the bike and went back to the hotel.

***

He was waiting in the lobby for his brother. He was a little nervous, he didn't know what to expect. He had heard of AA, even knew someone on the Sacramento who was in it. BM3 Roberts. He had tried several times to get Erik to go to a meeting. Apparently even back then people could see it was a problem.

A taxi pulled up under the awning. He saw a hand stick out and motion him over. It was Bjorn.

"Been a long time since I've been in a cage." he said.

"I live almost my entire life in one." he said. "If you want to ride, you can just follow me."

"No, it would be a good thing if we talk on the way." he said. "You know, you can tell me what to expect."

"There will be some people who get preachy and religious, don't pay attention if you don't want to." he said. "Your God can be anything. I use G. O. D. **G**roup **O**f **D**runks. That's all it has to be. It doesn't have to be the God who chased us around with a baseball bat when we were kids."

"I'll use yours." he said.

"It works for me." he said. "I've been doing this so long that I rarely think about drinking anymore."

"That would be something for me." he said.

"You get sober, don't worry what's ahead." he said. "One day at a time. I just tell myself I'm not going to drink today. You string those days together, it adds up."

"What about the club?" he said. "There's alcohol around all the time."

"That's something you decide for yourself." he said. "I know plenty of sober bikers. I'm sure you can do it. You just need to recognize when you're in trouble."

"I never had any problems before." he said. "I've come to realize that a certain bad behavior is directly linked to my drinking."

"Probably more than one." he said. "That's okay. It doesn't matter how you get here."

"How long?" he asked. "For you."

"Six years, three months, and seventeen days." he said. "But who's counting?"

"That's great." he said.

"How long for you?" he asked.

"Four days." he said.

"Also great." he said. "You've taken the first step."

Four days is great? He's been sober for six years!

"I know what you're thinking. Four days is nothing." he said. "You have to remember that I had four days before, and I can have it again if I'm not careful. You're taking a step to improve your life, that's all that matters."

"I appreciate you helping me." he said.

"So what about all that stuff Lexie said at the table? Is that all true?" he asked.

"The stuff about her family is." he said. "Can we pretend we're at the table? Take what I say next to your grave?"

He figured he could give Bjorn very broad strokes and be okay.

"Of course." he said.

"We didn't meet at the Louvre."

"No shit." he said. "I totally bought that."

His brother was smart. He could see back at mom and dad's that he didn't believe it.

"Because of some skills that we have, that most people don't, we were approached." he said. "I won't say it's the government, but I won't say it isn't...the way it was put to me recently is the most powerful people in the world. We go on missions, and take care of problems."

"Really?" he asked.

"Yes. I work for the Merchant Marines, but it's only so my handler can move me around. Lexie's still a soldier. Had a bit of a snag in the Middle East recently, that's why she's here. I don't know where she came up with that glorious museum story, but it was probably her cover at some point. We met on a mission about 7 years ago."

"Am I in the twilight zone?" he asked.

I probably shouldn't tell you any more than that." he said. "The stuff about her parents is true. She's had a hard life. It's also true that she doesn't have any family. Her parents were it, she was an only child."

"So when you're on deployment..." he said.

"Exactly." he said.

"But you've been stateside for a while now." he said.

"I can't talk about that." he said.

"How much do they pay you?" he asked.

"I do okay." he said.

"That much, eh?" he asked.

"Enough to make it to the Louvre now and then." he said.

They pulled into the back parking lot. Bjorn started climbing what looked like rickety wooden stairs, but they were actually quite solid. There was a porch at the top. They entered into a room with a pool table and a few card tables, and an adjacent room with doors. Bjorn hugged a good looking redhead.

"Erin, this is my brother Erik, he's new." he said.

She gave him a hug.

"Pleasure to meet you, Erik." she said.

It was 11:45. Bjorn saw a few other people who he introduced Erik to.

"Smoke?" asked Erin. "Before we get started?"

"Love to." he said.

"Washington State?" she asked, pointing to his cut.

"Bremerton. Near Seattle." he said. "You? From around here?"

"Lived in Ypsi my whole life." she said. "This is the point where I might make a clumsy pass at you. That really doesn't mean anything, I'm kind of involved with someone, and I would never do that."

She nodded towards the door.

"This is where I would normally take you up on it too." he said. "I have an old lady, but it wouldn't have stopped me. I'm trying to be a better person."

"Me too. You're in the right place." she said. "We should go in."

Erik said as much as he could at the table, and discovered that it helped to talk. His table finished first, so he went out to the lobby. A guy walked out, and Erik saw his cut. "Twisted Drifters" with Michigan on the bottom rocker.

"Seattle?" he asked.

"Yeah." said Erik.

"I know a guy from your club." he said. "Met him at Sturgis a few years ago. Brendan."

"Aye, a fine laddie." he said in his best brogue.

"Yeah, the Mick." he said. "How's he doing?"

"He's fine. Erik." he said.

"Justin." he said. "Sturgis is as far west as we ever go."

"As far east as we go. And only because it's..." he said.

"Sturgis." they replied in unison.

"We're west coast. Washington State, Oregon, and California." he said. "No charters anywhere else."

"We're not too spread out either." he said. "Michigan, Ohio, Indiana, and we just started a charter in Chicago. Smoke?"

"Sure." he said.

They went out to the porch.

"It can be difficult with our lifestyle to do this program." he said. "It helps if there's someone to talk to that you can really talk to. These people have been through some shit, but nothing like us. Say too much, you'll scare them away."

He pulled out a notepad and wrote down his number.

"Just sayin' any time, any day, a friendly ear." he said. "You can't tell me anything I haven't heard."

Erik wrote down his number.

"Same here." he said. "After being in there I found that talking helps. Problem is most of what I have to say isn't for public consumption."

"Amen, brother." he said.

Bjorn walked out.

"Hey Justin." he said.

"I was just talking to your brother." he said.

"You have at least one thing in common." he said.

"We exchanged numbers." he said.

"Do you still play? Drums?" asked Erik.

"As a matter of fact, we have a gig tomorrow night. Buhr Park, a lawn show. It's not Pine Knob, but I'll take it." he said. "You want to come? It's an AA thing."

"Sure." he said. "I'm glad it's not all doom and gloom. Can I bring Lexie?"

"Of course. We'd be offended if you didn't." he said. "Justin, you gotta see this girl to believe it. I could try to describe her, but words fail me. And his ex just got a job as a model. How do you do it, brother?"

"I don't know." he said. "Lexie says they throw themselves at me. You know that gi..." he said.

Erin burst through the door and walked past them.

"Night, boys." she said. Then she looked at Justin and held her finger and thumb to her head, and mouthed 'call me'.

He lowered his voice.

"Erin. Told me she would have hit on me if she wasn't involved." he said. "I'm guessing that's you."

Justin nodded.

"I wouldn't put it that way, we have fun every now and then." he said.

Bjorn just shook his head.

"Don't let Lexie get wind of that." he said.

"Tell me." he said. "She was on her best behavior earlier, but she can be dangerous."

"Now I have to come too, just to see her." said Justin.

"I should head back." said Erik. "She probably speaks better Danish than the old man by now."

Erik held out his hand.

"Fuck that, bring it in." said Justin.

He pulled him in for a hug.

"See you tomorrow." he said.

***

He got back to the room to see Lexie with three books open.

"Hvordan gik det?" she asked.

"It went well. I see you've been studying." he said.

"Oh, shit, I'm sorry." she said. "I didn't mean to do that. I'm studying, so I'm thinking in Danish."

"Something tells me that this is going to be way easier for you than it was for me." he said.

"So what happened?" she asked.

"Bjorn introduced me to some people, then we went inside and talked. A little touchy feely, but that's part of it." he said. "Like one at a time. There were obviously things I couldn't say, but I met this guy Justin who is with the 'Twisted Drifters' here in Michigan, and we exchanged numbers. He says it's good to have another biker to talk to because well...you know."

"I know. There's so much of my life I can't talk about to the average person." she said. "Did it help?"

"It really did." he said. "There's something I want to tell you about."

"Go ahead." she said.

He told her about when the club burned Larry to death, and even admitted (maybe for the first time to himself) that he was the one who burned his face off.

"That's dark." she said.

"I know, and we were laughing the whole time." he said. "How sick is that?"

"It's just the herd mentality." she said. "One person laughs at something that's not funny, everyone follows."

"So what do you think?" he asked.

"I wish I could say I've heard worse, but I can't think of anything." she said. "It doesn't matter. That's the past, nothing you can do about it."

"It really helped to tell you about it." he said. "I know you can keep a secret."

"What secret?" she asked.

Only the most obvious." he said. "Danielle is alive."

"She's not, Erik." he said. That's just a nasty rumor perpetuated by our employer."

"Stop." he said. "I know she's alive. She called me right after the mission."

"Okay." she said. "Murph told me that nobody can know that she's alive. For her own safety. Especially you. You can't let on that you know."

"If he finds out, I'll tell him the truth." he said. "You had nothing to do with me finding out."

"Thanks. I know we were stoned on that California weed that night, but what did I tell you?" she asked.

"You said I would sing like a canary." he said.

"Uh huh." she said.

A broad smile crossed her face.

"And what about you?" he said. "Do you need to check in with the Art Museum?"

"No." she said. "The work of art I discovered I'm keeping to myself."

"Do you want to go see a show tomorrow?" he asked. "It's an AA thing."

"Sure. What is it?" she asked.

"My brother's band. Playing a lawn show." he said.

"He's in a band?" she asked.

"He's a drummer. He may look a little weird, but there's a lot of substance there." he said.

"I wouldn't say weird. Maybe a little out of the mainstream." she said.

I bet he looks like his namesake." he said. "Maybe not as strong, but the hair, the beard, the earrings..."

"Bjorn Ironsides?" she asked. "Ragnar's son? That's his namesake?"

"Probably not, but I like to think it is." he said.

"You really love him, don't you?" she asked.

"He's my big brother." he said. "A pretty good chunk of his life he was a fuck up, but then so was I. How could I not love him?"

"You're both doing better now." she said.

***

They got to the park while it was still light out. The band was playing, a good mix of old stuff and grunge. It was a small group, maybe fifty or sixty people. Everyone was having a good time.

Justin and Erin walked up.

"Hi, how are you?" said Erin. "I'm glad you could make it."

He stood up and she hugged him. He gave Justin a hug as well.

"Justin, Erin, this is Lexie, she's my old lady." he said.

"Nice to meet you." said Justin.

"Uh unh." said Erin. "Stand up, girl!"

She stood up and Erin hugged her.

"So how's it going?" asked Justin.

"Remember what I said last night?" he said. "I get back to the hotel, and she's fluent in Danish."

"I wouldn't say that." she said.

"Really? You're going to play this down?" he asked in Danish.

"Slow it down a little, Ragnar." she said. "I'm kind of new at this."

He repeated it a little slower.

She replied in Danish.

"I've learned a little, but fluent?" she said. "You had to slow down for me. You act like I speak Danish as well as your father."

"Maybe not, but you can hold a conversation pretty easily." he said. "I rest my case. You speak Danish."

He looked at Justin and Erin.

"Am I wrong?" he asked.

"Sounded pretty fuckin' good to me." said Justin.

"Who are you kidding? You speak Danish." said Erin.

He couldn't believe it, she was turning red. With her complexion, it was hard to tell, but he knew.

"My father will be so proud." he said.

"Language is my thing." she said.

"She speaks seven languages...well I guess eight now." he said.

"Does Bjorn speak Danish?" asked Erin.

"Nope. Just me, my dad, and his father when he was alive. None of the other kids took interest." he said. "My mom too, but that's just so he can't talk about her behind her back to her face."

"Hey, there's Gillian!" said Erin. "Let's go talk to her. Come on, Lexie meet some people."

"Is that okay?" she asked.

"I don't think I could stop you if I wanted to." he said. "We'll be okay. We'll have a little biker talk."

They went to Gillian.

"Your brother's right, words fail me." he said. "How'd you land that?"

"Probably the same way you landed Erin." he said. "It's not complicated."

"She is beautiful." he said. "And your ex? A model?"

"What can I say?" he said. "Since you're the only biker I know in recovery, can I tell you a little story? Not fit for the rest?"

"Just between us. I take that shit seriously." he said. "Go ahead."

He proceeded to tell him the story about Larry. It was a good way to test the waters. He admitted to his part in it, and left nothing out.

"Where you fucked up there was letting him leave with the ink in the first place." he said.

"I know. It was discussed in church." he said. "Now we have a tattoo artist for just such occasions."

"I can tell you that if he was in my club, he would never have walked away from the jump out." he said. "Stealing from the club is a dying offense around here."

"It had never happened before." he said. "Nobody ever had the balls. A little messier, but the end result was the same. We'll have a different approach if it ever happens again."

"You did the right thing. This is the kind of shit nobody else could ever understand. You feel better?" he asked.

"I really do." he said. "I told Lexie the story last night, but it's not the same as a brother."

"You told her that?" he asked.

"I probably should have led with this, but she's done similar things." he said. "She's an Israeli soldier. She understands these things. Still not the same as a brother."

"A soldier." he said quietly. "So she really is dangerous."

"We did a little freelance mercenary work a while back." he said. "I've seen her kill. She's tougher than a lot of dudes I know. Some of my brothers back home, even."

He figured he told Johnny the same thing, but that would be as far as he would go. Mysterious mercenary work.

"She's deceptive too." he said. "Nobody would see her coming. She's taller than most chicks, that's for sure."

"I love her." he said. "The work we did brought us closer."

"I'm not going to ask about that." he said. "Let me tell you one."

He went on to describe the jumping out of a former member of his club. He didn't hold anything back either. Everyone knew that the dude wasn't walking away. Justin gave him a curb job, which killed him instantly.

"Were you sober when you did that?" he asked.

"Fuck no!" he said. "I think you and I may have come here for the same reason. The violence."

"Exactly." he said. "It started to be a problem that I was beating people within inches of their lives. I finally made the connection to alcohol. Did you lose anything? You know...your edge?"

"Don't worry about that."" he said. "I'm still the same guy. The difference is that I recognize when it's over, and I stop. Make no mistake, people are still scared of me."

That's good to know." he said.

"So what's she doing here?" he asked.

"A little trouble in the desert." he said. "Time may cure it, but it could be decades."

"Looking at her, I never would have guessed." he said.

The band started playing a Bob Seger song that was popular with the crowd. It could be any Bob Seger in Ann Arbor.

On a long and lonesome highway, east of Omaha
You can listen to the engine moanin' out its one-note song
You can think about the woman, or the girl you knew the night before

"Great song." said Justin.

"Good riding song." he said.

"Exactly." he said.

But your thoughts will soon be wandering the way they always do
When you're riding sixteen hours and there's nothing much to do
And you don't feel much like riding, you just wish the trip was through

Say, here I am, on a road again
There I am, up on the stage

Here I go, playing the star again
There I go, turn the page

"Your brother's good." he said.
"Happy?" he asked.
"He's the kind of guy who has to have a woman." he said. "Sam isn't the best, and I think he's figuring that out. Otherwise, he's happy.

Well, you walk into a restaurant, strung-out from the road
And you feel the eyes upon you as you're shaking off the cold
You pretend it doesn't bother you but you just want to explode
Most times you can't hear 'em talk, other times you can
All the same old clichés: "Is that a woman or a man?"
And you always seem outnumbered, you don't dare make a stand

"You know I love Bob Seger, but I don't think I would ever confuse him with a woman." said Justin. "As far as I can remember, he's always had that goatee."
"Great lyrics though." he said.
"True enough." he said.

Out there in the spotlight you're a million miles away
Every ounce of energy you try to give away
As the sweat pours out your body like the music that you play
Later in the evening as you lie awake in bed
With the echoes from the amplifiers ringin' in your head
You smoke the day's last cigarette, remembering what she said

Ah Here I am, on a road again

There I am, up on the stage
Here I go, playing the star again
There I go, turn the page

After that, the band took a break, and Bjorn came over. He was covered in sweat.

"Bob Seger is always a hit." he said.

"It's all about the showmanship. Give the people what they want." he said. "Where's Lexie?"

He nodded towards the girls.

"Making friends." he said. "This is progress. She's had trouble with females in the past. She's even friends with some of the old ladies back home too. Thick as thieves they are."

His phone started ringing, and he looked down.

"Sorry, I gotta take this." he said.

He walked away and answered.

"Hey Anthony." he said.

"How's Michigan?" he asked.

"Great." he said. "I'm at an AA gathering."

"Good." he said. "How's that going?"

"Good." he said. "My brother is helping me. I met a biker out here that I can talk about the more graphic stuff with. We exchanged numbers."

"Good." he said. "The first shipment went through. Because of the initial delay, they're doing another next week. The ATF will be waiting for them. You should get back there."

"Okay." he said.

"You should find a meeting when you get back home." he said. "It might surprise you who you see there."

"What does that mean?" he asked.

"Just that you never know who else is in recovery." he said. "I'm sure you didn't expect me to be a drunk."

"No, I did not see that coming." he said.

"How's Lexie doing?" he asked. "Did the family like her?"

"How could they not?" he asked.

"Indeed." he said. "Even mom?"

"When they asked her where she was from, it went seamlessly into what happened to her parents." he said. "Mom can be a hard ass, but she's human. After hearing that, and how she has no family left, she caved. She was gearing up not to like her, I could tell, but not after that."

"And dad?" he asked.

"Are you kidding? He's ready to adopt her." he said. "She virtually learned Danish overnight. He doesn't even know yet, and he loved her before that."

"That's good to hear." he said. "Call me when you get home. I want you there in 3 days, tops."

"I'll do my best," he said.

"No, you'll be there with a smile on your face." he said.

Chapter 13

He just couldn't believe it. How did this girl do that? She was a little slow, but she could really hold down her end of the conversation, and understand him too.

"So you really have to leave? Tomorrow?" asked Dorte.

"I'm afraid so, mom." he said. "The harbormaster says they want me on the Bonaventure next week. I wish I could stay longer."

"Do you want to stay, Lexie?" she asked.

What? Did my mother just ask one of my girlfriends that she barely knows to stay with her?

"I would love to, Dorte, but I'm afraid I need to go back too." she said. "My mistake was telling them where I was. They want me to look at a piece at the Seattle Art Museum by the artist Tabaimo. She's a promising young Japanese artist whose paintings have been rising in value. It's a utsushi piece, an emulation of her master's work."

Right off the top of her head, he thought. Nice touch with the Japanese artist too. Where was she when I had to come up with an excuse?

"But you're on sabbatical." she said.

"The truth is that they called me because they know I have an interest in Tabaimo." she said. "I'm looking forward to seeing her new work. And Erik is going to be gone anyway, so it will give me something to do."

"Okay." she said.

"You're an exceptional young lady." said Palle. "My son is sometimes an enigma to me, but it's no surprise that you're together."

"And here I thought I was an open book." said Erik.

"I promised you a ride in the Jaguar, Lexie, shall we?" he asked.

"I've been looking forward to it." she said.

They walked out to the car.

"This is my thing." he said. "The cars. Been buying them and selling them for years. They pay for themselves."

"It's beautiful." she said. "My dad used to have a Corvette. One of the only American cars in Jerusalem."

"That's an awful thing, losing your parents like that." he said.

"It made me grow up fast." she said. "I did some things I'm not proud of in the Army."

"We all have." he said. "That's the past. The future is what matters most."

"I try to stay in the moment." she said. "If you have one foot in the past, and one in the future, you're doing something unseemly to the present."

"I've never heard it put that way, but you're right." he said. "You've got some insight."

"Like I said, I had to grow up fast." she said.

"Did you ever think you would be where you are now?" he asked.

"I thought I would be dead a long time ago." she said.

"I'm glad that didn't happen." he said. "You're good for Erik."

"He's good for me." she replied.

They were going down Huron River Drive, and there were a lot of twists and sharp curves. He was a good driver, he knew just what to do, even though he was going a little too fast she knew that they were never in danger.

"Lexie, I'm sure you've heard the saying once a soldier, always a soldier." he said. "Probably goes double for an Israeli soldier. I know you have this great job at the museum, but I see the headlines. Do I need to worry about you?"

"No. I'm still part of the resistance, but I know what I'm doing. I'm safe." she said. "We probably shouldn't talk too much about this."

"Do me a favor? Call us every week or two, so we know you're safe?" he asked. "What Thyra said is true, like it or not, you're family now."

She was touched. It had been so long since anyone was concerned for her welfare, she forgot what it was like.

"Of course I will, Palle." she said. "And for the record, I like it. You have insight too."

"Your Danish is great." he said. "Better than Dorte."

She hadn't realized it, but they had been speaking Danish the whole time.

"It was important to me." she said, in English. "To be accepted by Erik's family. And for you to extend yourself the way you have..."

A tear was rolling down her cheek. She missed her father.

"You'll always have us." he said. "No matter what."

He put his arm around her.

"I'm sorry, I'm turning into a blubbering idiot." she said. "You...remind me of my father. I'll be fine, then it hits me. I'll be okay in a minute."

"There's nothing wrong with what you're doing, dear." he said. "I had almost 50 years with my father, and I feel the same way. If it helps, you can talk to me any time. In English or Danish."

She laughed through her tears.

"Thank you." she said.

They pulled back in the driveway,

"Thanks, that was a lot of fun." she said.

"I had just as much fun as you." he said.

They walked in the house and Erik and Thyra were sitting on the couch with Freesia between them.

"Bon soirée." said Thyra.

"Bon soirée." she replied. "Comment allez-vous?"

"Bon et vous?" she said.

"Tant mieux." she said.

"Sorry to interrupt, but we should probably go." said Erik. "We have a long trip in the morning."

"Of course." said Thyra.

"If you ever want to call and speak French, you're more than welcome." she said. "Your father has the number."

"Thanks, Lexie, I'll do that." she said. "Even if I don't want to speak French."

"Freyja will be home for Christmas, any chance you can make an appearance?" asked Dorte.

"Maybe." he said. "I'll have to play it by ear."

"You too, Lexie." she said. "Even if Erik can't make it, you're welcome to come. I know that you don't celebrate but..."

"It's fine, I've been to a few Christmas parties in my time." she said.

That was what they wanted to hear, but she had never been to one, and rarely celebrated Hanukkah. All this positive attention made her really hope it worked out with Erik. Not that she was worried, but she could get used to this, they could leave their old life behind. The only problem would be Murphy.

Would he let them go? He let Danielle go, under the condition that she stay dead, and everyone knew how that worked out.

***

They had made pretty good time. Lexie wanted to stop in Nehalem, but he told her that he wanted to get west of Skykomish because of the incident. The real reason was Danielle. She seemed pretty cool, but women as a rule were unpredictable with affairs of the heart. Better not to risk it. They stopped in Bothell, where the 522 meets the 405. They went to a little diner attached to a hotel in case they decided to spend the night.

"So, what did you think of the Stryker clan?" he asked.

"Overall they were great." she said. "You oversold how mean your mom is."

"After she heard about your parents, there was no way she could be mean to you. She's quick to judge, but she has a heart." he said. "That was some story you told about going to the art museum. Nice touch with the Japanese artist, Tabaimo. I wish I could come up with shit like that on the fly."

"I happen to be a huge fan of her work." she said. "I even saw you looking at it that day in the Louvre."

"I could take her or leave her." he said. "I'm really more of a fan of the utsushi. It does my heart good to see a young artist emulating her master."

"Never miss a beat, do you?" she said.

"Well, when you tee 'em up like that, it's I can't resist." he said.

Her phone started ringing.

She looked at the phone, then at him, then she smiled.

"I gotta take this." she said.

"Oh, sure, don't worry about me." he said. "Geez, you never put that thing down."

"Hello?" she said.

"Hey Lexie, it's Jess." she said. "How's it going?"

She had left a message on Erik's machine with her new number. Also to establish that she was there.

"Good, our trip is almost over." she said. "We're in Bothell, probably be home tonight."

"Cool." she said. "Is Friday okay for our triple date? My friend Jason's band is playing at this place called the Brass Caterpillar. It should be fun."

"Sure, that should be fine." she said.

She covered the phone.

"Friday okay for us to go out with Jess and Em and their men?" she asked.

"Sure." he said.

"It's a place called the Brass Caterpillar, probably not a biker bar." she said.

"What, you don't think I can behave in polite society?" he asked. "Brass Caterpillar, it sounds like a real classy joint. I'll try not to embarrass you."

"Yeah, that's fine Jess." she said.

"Jason put Erik's words to music." she said. "It sounds awesome. Would it be too weird if I get up there and sing it? Would Erik mind?"

"I guess we'll find out." she said.

"No, seriously, if you think it's going to be a problem..."

"It'll be fine." she said. "It takes quite a bit to upset him."

"Okay." she said. "How was the trip?"

"It was great." she said. "His family is really cool, especially his dad. He speaks Danish, so does Erik."

"Is that all he speaks?" she asked.

"No, he speaks English too. According to Stryker, that's a good thing." she said. "He says the only people who speak Danish are him, his father, and the people who live in Denmark."

"Do you speak it?" she asked.

"I didn't before we got there, but I've picked up the basics." she said. "Erik says I'm fluent, but I don't know."

"How exciting. How did you learn so fast?" she asked.

"Languages are my thing. Some people are good at math, or fixing cars, I'm good at speech." she said. "Anything good happen here while we were gone?"

"Just working out that song." she said. "I can never tell how I sound, but he recorded it and played it back for me. It's unbelievable. It sounds really good."

"It should, you have a great voice." she said. "Just that little bit you sang at the club, I can tell. I'm really looking forward to hearing it."

The waitress was on the way over with the food.

"Hey, Jess, they're bringing the food, so I'm going to let you go." she said. "We'll probably be back tonight unless we spend the night here. I'll call you tomorrow."

"Sounds good." she said.

"So what do you think?" he asked. "Do you want to stay here tonight?"

"I'll let you decide." she said. "You've been going all day, I took a nap somewhere in North Dakota."

"I know." he said. "If we don't linger here too long, we can make the last ferry. That will make the rest of the trip much shorter, and give me an opportunity to rest a little."

"It's up to you." she said. "I could go either way."

"I would really like to sleep in my own bed tonight with you and Huck." he said.

Casey had been over to look in on him since they weren't going to be gone that long. She had met Lexie, and was a little chilly, but didn't say anything inappropriate. It was understandable, Taylor and her were as close as sisters, so she didn't pretend to like Lexie. The feeling seemed to be mutual, but Lexie kept any animosity to herself. It was a shame, because under different circumstances, he was sure they would like each other. Maybe in time, but doubtful.

"Why don't we do that then?" she said. "It will be good to be home."

It wasn't lost on him that she was calling it home now. Not long ago, she went back to the hotel when she got pissed. Not long ago, it was Taylor's home. He wondered briefly if he was doing the right thing.

Those thoughts had crept in occasionally, particularly when they were in Ann Arbor. He knew that he wanted to be with Lexie, and had to admit that things hadn't been good with Taylor for a long time. It was probably natural to second guess, after all, he had been with Taylor for 15 years. Since before he met Murphy.

She had helped him with so much, that whole mess with Jenna, getting kicked out of the Navy, also dealing with the aftermath of his new life, which she knew very little about. He didn't have that problem with Lexie, she knew all about it, and could relate to and understand the things he had to deal with firsthand. She'd been doing it for longer than him.

"So why do we have to be there?" she asked. "I don't get it, isn't whatever is going to happen going to happen anyway?"

"It's not so much that we have to be there as it is that we shouldn't be absent." he said. "If something big happens and we're not around, it could look suspicious. Not so much you, but me. They already question the long deployments when I'm not around."

"But you haven't been deployed in a while." she said.

"Still. Bikers are paranoid by nature." he said. "It's best to look as normal as I can. And be here when things happen to keep them calm."

"I have a surprise for you." she said.

"Really?" he asked. "Any hints?"

"I can't think of a single one." she said.

"When should I expect it?" he asked.

"Soon." she said.

"Nothing? Really?" he asked. "You don't have any clues at all?"

"Nope." she said.

"You're very sinister." he said.

"Do you think we have time to get a room for a while?" she asked.

"I don't think they have hourly rates." he said. "But if you want to stay..."

"No, we should go home." she said. "Sometimes I get these impulses."

"Me too." he said. "But in this case we really don't have time. I'll make it worth your while if you wait til we get home."

"Works for me." she said.

She started waving at the waitress.

"Check please!" she said.

***

They were in the club with Em and Charlie waiting for Jessica and Mike.

"So how was it?" asked Em. "What was his family like?"

It was great!" she said. "His father owns this greenhouse, in the first greenhouse where the customers can but plants there's this huge rubber tree. I'm not talking about a few feet tall, it's as big as the trees outside. It's literally growing through the roof. He said someone came in there in 1967 and said it wouldn't grow. We get there, and him and his dad start speaking Danish. He always told me he didn't speak any other languages."

"I don't count Danish." said Erik. "Almost no one speaks it, so it's useless. Lexie doesn't even speak it...well she does now."

"You learned it that quick?" she asked.

"I wouldn't say I learned it." she said.

He spoke Danish to her.

"You're going to play this down again?" he said. "You speak almost as well as me, don't deny it."

she answered in Danish.

"You've been speaking Danish your whole life, and I just learned." she said. "I understand it, but I'm not fluent. I managed to get that, but you're still going a little fast for me."

"A little fast! People who have studied for years might have trouble with my pace, yet you managed to understand, even though I went 'a little fast'. I ask you, as two casual observers, does this woman speak Danish or not?" he asked.

"I have to say she does." said Charlie. "I'm with you, she shouldn't deny it. That's the only part I understood, and the part about you going too fast."

"Girl, you know that language." said Emily.

"I rest my case." he said.

"Anyway. We go to the back greenhouses, and there's plants as far as the eye can see." she said. "Then we go to the rose house. You wouldn't believe it Em, it was so beautiful. So many roses! And the way it smelled! I could really get used to that. His dad goes into this whole thing about how someday this will all be Erik's."

"Which isn't how it's going to happen." he said. "That place should go to Bjorn."

"Who's Bjorn?" she asked.

"My older brother. Worked there for years, as vice president, no less." he said. "But the old man thinks he's leaving it to me."

"Bjorn deserves it." said Lexie. "Might need to get a haircut and lose the earrings if he wants to be taken seriously, but that place should be his."

"The hair and the earrings don't matter." said Erik. "It's what's inside that counts. You should know that after meeting him, Lexie."

"He's right." said Emily. "Outward appearances mean nothing. Some of the people around here look a little weird, but they're great people."

"Of course." said Lexie. "What's inside of Bjorn is the best, I can't deny that. I was a little worried when we met though."

"But once you got to know him..." he said.

"Absolutely." she said.

Brendan walked up.

"What's this, then?" he asked. "Is there a party nobody tol' me about?"

"We're waiting for Mike and Jess." said Erik. "Going to a music club called the Brass Caterpillar."

"Aye, good luck wit' that." he said. "What're ya drinkin' lad?"

"Ginger ale." he said.

"That's a sad state of affairs, boyo." he said.

"Aye, it is." he said. "I saw a doctor back home, and he says I have early signs of Cirrhosis. Says I have to stop drinking."

"Aye, they tol' me that 3 years ago, but I'm still standing." he said. "Hasn't slowed me down a'tall, if anythin' I'm drinkin' more."

"I hate to be the one to tell you, Brendan, but you should take that shit seriously." he said. "The symptoms aren't pretty. The toxins will have nowhere to go, so they'll back up into your brain. You'll develop dementia. Your gums will bleed and you'll bleed frequently from the nose. Your skin will turn yellow, and your belly will swell. You'll lose energy and be lethargic. I could go on, but I don't have to. Between that and drinking, it's an easy choice."

"Suit yerself, laddie." he said. "T'aint much out there these days won't kill ya one way or another. At least I'll die happy."

He knew it was pointless to talk to Brendan about it. He couldn't tell him the real reason he was quitting.

Jessica and Mike breezed through the door.

"We should get going, we're going to be late." she said.

"Late?" asked Erik. "To the bar?"

"I want to be there when they start." she said. "I don't want Jason to think I don't care."

"I get it." said Lexie. "Let's go."

"Yeah, we can't disappoint the musical genius." said Mike. "I forgot Jason was involved. Lead the way, babe."

"Jason?" said Erik, under his breath. "You okay with that?"

"Yeah, it's no problem. He really is a musical genius." he said. "Jess has some musical talent, and he's helped her with it. He has a good looking old lady, nothing's going on there."

"Okay." he said. "So they're really good?"

"You won't believe how good." he said.

They got to the club, and got a table on one of the inner circles. The way it was laid out, there was a huge dance floor, then tables in a circular pattern around the dance floor getting progressively wider. The place was huge.

The name of the band was Lithium. Jess was right, they were good. They played a lot of grunge, but no covers. All the grunge songs they played were their own. They also played rock and some other genres, they were very versatile.

It sounded as good as Pearl Jam, Nirvana, and Soundgarden, some of the biggest grunge bands there were. The only difference was that no one had discovered Lithium.

"You were right, Jess, these guys are great." said Erik.

"They really are." she said. "I'm sorry if I seemed pushy earlier. I just wanted to hear all of it."

"No, Jessica, don't worry about it." he said. "I can see why. They're too good to be in this place."

"That's the music business." she said.

A long haired blonde approached the table.

"Hey, Jess." she said. "You ready?"

"Oh, hi Amber." she said. "I never am, but it's never stopped me. I'll be fine when I get up there."

"You're gonna be great." she said.

"That the old lady?" asked Erik.

"Didn't I tell you?" he said,

"Nice." he said.

Amber got Jason's attention and gave him a thumbs up.

They finished the song, and Jason stepped to the microphone.

"Here it comes." said Lexie.
"What?" he asked.
"Your surprise." she said.
"We're going to slow it down a little. I would like to welcome a very special young lady who is by far the best female voice of her generation. She's here to do something new, and I think you'll like it a lot. Jessica?"
Jessica got up and slowly walked to the stage. She stood in front of the microphone, covered in blue light. It was just Jason on guitar, a guy on the piano, and the drummer keeping a sleepy beat. As soon as the guitar and piano came in Erik recognized the chords.

For you I was a flame
Love is a losing game
Five story fire as you came
Love is a losing game

One I wish I never played
Oh what a mess we made
And now the final frame
Love is a losing game

He was stunned. It was exact. The same song, same words, same tune, everything. If Jess had some ink, it would have been a perfect match.
"How did you do this?" he asked. "It's exact."
"That's all Jason." she said. "I only gave her the words. Do you really think I know how to do that shit?"

Played out by the band
Love is a losing hand
More than I could stand
Love is a losing hand

Self professed... profound
Till the chips were down
...know you're a gambling man
Love is a losing hand

"This is really eerie." he said. "If she had some tatts, she would look just like the woman in my dream."

"Really?" she said. "It was Jess in your dream?"

"No, it was Amy Winehouse, a long haired brunette with lots of ink." he said. "Jessica's a long haired brunette."

Though I battle blind
Love is a fate resigned
Memories mar my mind
Love is a fate resigned

Over futile odds
And laughed at by the gods
And now the final frame
Love is a losing game

As she sang the last word, the blue light faded to black. The crowd was silent for a moment out of respect, then they slowly started cheering. The lights came up, and Jess was making her way back to the table.

People started shouting for an encore. She looked up to the stage, and Jason was motioning her back up. She shrugged and started walking back up there as they started cheering louder.

"They can't get enough of you Jess." he said. "One of the first rules of this business is that you never turn down the first encore. What do you want to sing?" he asked.

"Everyone here know 'Stormy Weather'?" she asked.

They all nodded.

"Let's do that." she said.

They started a slow beat behind her, and she stepped up to the microphone.

Don't know why
There's no sun up in the sky
Stormy weather
Since my man and I ain't together
Keeps raining all the time
Life is bare
Gloom and misery everywhere

Stormy weather
Just can't get my poor old self together
I'm weary all the time, the time
So weary all of the time

When he went away
The blues walked in and met me
If he stays away, old rocking chair will get me
All I do is pray
The lord above will let me
Walk in the sun once more

"I have to ask you, Mike, did you do that shit to her?" asked Charlie. "That last song, this one...she feels that. Someone hurt her bad."

"I never did anything that bad." he said. "At least I don't think I did."

"She's really good." said Em.

"She's never taken it seriously." said Mike. "If the right people ever heard her, she would be a star."

"You better hope they don't." said Charlie. "If she ever got discovered, what would she need you for?"

Mike just glared at him.

Can't go on
Everything I had is gone
Stormy weather
Since my man and I ain't together
Keeps raining all the time
Keeps raining all of the time

I walk around,
Heavy-hearted and sad
Night comes around
And I'm still feeling bad
Rain pourin' down
Blinding every hope I had
This pitter 'n patter 'n beatin' 'n spatterin' drivin' me mad
Love, love, love, love

This misery will be the end of me

"You okay?" she asked.

"It's just all too weird." he said. "Where did it all come from? I dream it, and here it is."

He was thinking about the end of the dream when Taylor got up and sang. Reminded him that she was the victim.

When he went away
The blues walked in and met me
If he stays away, old rocking chair will get me
All I do is pray
The lord above will let me
Walk in the sun once more
Can't go on
Everything I had is gone
Stormy weather
Since my man and I ain't together
Keeps raining all the time, the time
Keeps raining all the time

The lights faded out and the crowd cheered. Jess Bowed deeply left, right, and center.

"Thank you very much!" she said. "I'm going to let Lithium get back to it, it was a pleasure."

She bounced back to the table.

"Thanks for letting me use your song, Erik!" she said.

"It's not my song. It's Amy Winehouse's, whoever that is." he said. "The way you sang it, I can't take any credit."

"But the words..." she said.

"I didn't do anything but remember a dream." he said. "The woman who sang it in my dream was Amy Winehouse. I don't know if she's a real person or not. But you really nailed it. That was amazing."

"Remember a dream?" asked Mike.

"It's not important." he said. "I'm going to smoke."

He got up and out the door before anyone could object or join him.

He walked towards his bike and leaned against a nearby tree. He slid to a sitting position on the ground. He pulled out a cigarette and with shaky hands lit it and inhaled deeply. What the hell was that? He pulled out his phone and punched in the number.

"Hello?" she said.

"It's me." he said.

"Erik? What a pleasant surprise." she said. "Did you make it back home?"

"A few days ago." he said.

"What's going on?" she asked.

"I just wanted to hear your voice." he said. "Wanted to make sure you're okay."

"I'm fine." she said. "It doesn't sound like you are."

"Let me ask you something." he said. "Did I hurt you?"

"Yes." she said. "Why the sudden concern?"

"It's really weird." he said. "I had this dream."

"Those dreams." she said. "Tell me about it."

He told her about the dream, and left nothing out.

"So we go to this club tonight, with Jessica and Em." he said. "Jess knows the guy in the band. Lexie had asked me for the words to the song from the dream, so I gave them to her. She gives them to Jess to see if she knows anyone who can put them to music. The guy in the band does it, he's some kind of musical genius. Of course, I know nothing about this. He calls her up to the stage to sing. It's the song from the dream, and it's an exact match. Same words, music, if Jessica had a lot of ink, she would even look like the singer. After she came back to the table, I told them I was going for a smoke, and I called you."

"Wow. That's quite a story." she said. "What do you think it means?"

"You tell me, you're good at this kind of stuff." he said.

"I don't think you'll like what I have to say." she said.

"That's never stopped you before." he said.

"I'll just tell you what I know, Erik." she said. "We will be back together some day. I just need to let this thing play out."

"You seem pretty confident." he said.

"I am. You know about my intuition." she said. "Have you ever known it to be wrong? That's how I know."

She calls it intuition, but it's more like second sight. She's right, I've never known it to be wrong. But does she really believe that?

"I have to say that it doesn't seem too likely to me." he said. "I respect your intuition, but really? Those are some pretty long odds."

"It's okay if you don't believe me, I probably wouldn't either." she said. "I won't even say I told you so when it happens. You hurt me bad, but I'll let you make it up to me after we're together again."

He saw Lexie walking out the door looking for him. She couldn't see him the way he was sitting against the tree.

"She's out here looking for me, I should let you go." he said.

"Okay." she said. "I love you, baby."

He said it in spite of himself.

"I love you too." he said. "Call me from Paris."

Is that going to happen? Could she be right? No, it wasn't working before, and nothing's changed. What I'm feeling is probably nothing more than misplaced guilt. I love Lexie, and I'm done with her. It's over for a reason.

She spotted him and saw him put the phone back in his pocket.

He walked towards her.

"Who were you talking to?" she asked.

He didn't have the energy to lie. The whole night had taken a lot out of him.

"Taylor." he said.

"She call you?" she asked.

"No." he said. "That whole scene in there fucked me up a little. Brought me right back to the dream. Where she reminded me that she's the victim."

"I see." she said. "I can't say I like you calling her, but I'll give you a pass under the circumstances. I had no idea that was what would happen. I still can't believe it."

"It's a little scary." he said. "At least I didn't lie to you. The old Stryker would have lied out of default."

"I appreciate that, as much as I don't like hearing that you called your ex." she said. "For the record, I love the old Stryker, the new Stryker, and whatever's in between. I love you as you are, don't ever change."

She loves me. That remains to be seen, he thought. I can think of at least one thing that you would go ballistic over. But that's not going to happen, no matter what she thinks she knows.

Chapter 14

They were at the Brass Caterpillar, and Lithium was playing. Jessica was on stage, and she was singing an old Frank Sinatra song.

It's quarter to three,
There's no one in the place 'cept you and me
So set 'em' up Joe
I got a little story I think you oughtta know

We're drinking my friend
To the end of a brief episode
So make it one for my baby
And one more for the road

She sounded great. He was still amazed that he didn't know this about her before.

I know the routine
Put another nickel in that there machine
I'm feeling so bad
Won't you make the music easy and sad?

I could tell you a lot
But you gotta to be true to your code
So make it one for my baby
And one more for the road

"Can you believe this?" he asked. "She really is good! No, great!"

"That's why they asked her to join the band." she said. "They had no choice after she did that song. You made her a star."

"I didn't do anything." he said. "I just remembered a dream."

"And you know why you remembered it, right?" asked Jessica.

She had stopped singing momentarily.

"I guess." he said.

"You know why." she said. "Because of her. The sweet one. Just listen to the rest of the song."

“What are you drinking?” asked Lexie.
He looked down and saw a double rum and Coke.
“Ginger ale.” he said.

You'd never know it
But baby I'm a kind of poet
And I've got a lot of things I want to say
And when I'm gloomy, won't you listen to me
Till it's all, all talked away

Well, that's how it goes
And Joe I know you're gettin' anxious to close
So thanks for the cheer
I hope you didn't mind
My bending your ear

But this torch that I found
It's gotta be drowned
Or it soon might explode
So make it one for my baby
And one more for the road

“You know the torch I'm talking about.” she said. “You can't put it out. It's gonna explode.”

The crowd went crazy.

“She's right, you know.” said Lexie. “I might have to do something about this.”

“Don't worry about it, she doesn't know what she's talking about.” he said. “Intuition! What is that? She doesn't know anything. I'm not carrying a torch for her.”

Jason came up to the microphone.

“And now what you've all been waiting for.” he said. “All the way from New York City, I'm pleased to introduce a woman that really needs no introduction, Taylor Whitman!”

The crowd went nuts.

“Yep, I'm going to have to intervene.” she said. “She just couldn't leave it alone.”

For you I was a flame

A bullet hit her skull as she started singing, and rolled down her chest and hit the floor.

"Why did you do that?" she asked. "You know it's true. He'll be back with me. I just need to let this thing run it's course."

"He won't be back with you if you're dead." she said.

"Oh, no, you have it wrong, sister." she said. "I'm not the one who dies. In fact, you can't kill me. Isn't that right, Murph?"

"What can I say, when she's right, she's right." he said. "You know I was on your side with this fucking thing too, Lexie. You got greedy."

"What's going on?" asked Erik.

"Your ex is trying to turn the tables." she said. "And now he's helping her."

"Can they do that?" he asked.

"I don't know." she said. "It should really be up to us."

"Us? What do you think this is?" asked Taylor. "It's up to him."

"Don't leave it up to me." he said. "I'm no good at these things."

"You need to tell her." said Lexie.

"Yes. Tell me, baby." she said.

They both looked at him expectantly.

"I need to do something first." he said.

He started walking towards the stage.

"He loves me." said Lexie.

"You can't confirm that." she said. "All of the witnesses are dead."

"What are you doing, Stryker?" she said.

He looked up at her, then looked down and saw that he was pummeling Jason's head into the stage.

"I knew this was going to happen, you let him drink." she quipped. "If you can't handle something that simple, how do you expect to hold onto him?"

"Maybe I'll start by killing you." she said.

She shot her again. The bullet bounced harmlessly to the ground.

"I'm not drinking." he said. "It's ginger ale."

"Of course you're drinking you're beating the fuck out of poor Jason." said Taylor. "You never did that when you we were together."

"Aye, boyo, now yer back in form." said Brendan. "I tol' ya you can drink. Which one are ya gonna take? I'm not too proud to take yer leftovers."

"I'm not drinking." he said.

"You know who you want." said Taylor. "You just need to tell her, then we can get out of here."

I have no idea who I want, he thought.

"Someone else decide." he said. "I'm no good at these things."

"Do I need to kill her?" asked Taylor.

"No." he said. "Nobody needs to die."

He looked down and his hands were bloody, and Jason's face was a pink pulp.

"You should ease up if you don't want anyone to die." said Lexie. "Now he can't write songs anymore."

"I'm not drunk." he said. "Everyone knows that."

Lexie smiled and looked at him. She pulled out her gun and pointed it at him.

"You know nothing, Stryker!" she said.

She pulled the trigger, and it bounced off him and rolled to the floor.

"Fuck!" she yelled. "What's wrong with this thing?"

"You can't hurt us anymore." said Taylor.

"Neither can you." said Murphy. "He needs to decide this for himself. Can you please stop beating people up, Stryker? It's embarrassing."

"But I'm not drunk!" he said.

He woke with a jolt. Another classic, wonder what this one means. Probably a bit dangerous to share with Lexie...or Taylor. What's up with that? Did he really?

No. Absolutely not. My subconscious is fucking with me for some reason, but I'm not doing that. We're not compatible on that level. Lexie and I are. End of story.

He looked over at her, she looked so peaceful. She was good for him. And his family liked her, even mom. This thing with Taylor...probably misplaced guilt. That's all it is.

Murphy had mentioned that he should find a meeting around here, but he really didn't want to do it. He just didn't want to deal with it, going in there alone, meeting new people, talking about his problems, or at least trying to with the limited amount of information he could divulge. There seemed to be a drinking trend in the dream, followed by denial. Was he drinking? He didn't think so, yet he really did a number on Jason. Fuck, I guess I need to go find a meeting.

She rolled over.

"Hey, are you okay?" she asked.

"Bet you're sick of asking me that. Another weird dream." he said.

"Tell me about it." she said.

"There's no point, it was cryptic as usual." he said.

"That's what I like about them." she said. "Yours are so interesting, but I never remember mine."

"Maybe later." he said. "I'm going to try to find a meeting."

"That's good." she said. "It's important. At least until you get away from the club. They're probably as much of a trigger as the booze."

"I'm getting away from the club?" he asked. "I don't remember saying that."

"We still have to complete the mission." she said. "You can't take the club with you for that."

"But I'm still in the club." he said. "I'm coming back. That's not going to change."

"You're in the club if Murph continues to allow it." she said. "Make no mistake, he wants you out, you'll be out."

"We'll see about that." he said.

He pulled the phone book from the drawer in the bedside table, and started looking for a meeting.

"Do you mind if I move the rest of my things over from the hotel?" she asked.

"You do that, you won't have a safety valve anymore." he said. "You sure you want to do that?"

"There are hotels in Bremerton if I need to get away." she said.

Or punish me, he thought.

"Yeah, that's fine if that's what you want." he said.

"Are you okay, Stryker?" she asked.

"Still a little rattled from the other night." he said. "Give me a day or two, and I'll be right as rain."

"What does that mean, 'right as rain'?" she asked.

"I don't know." he said.

He called the number.

"Hey, I was wondering if you could tell me when the next meeting is." he said.

"Okay, thanks." he said.

"There's one at noon." he said.

"I'll go get my stuff while you're gone." she said.

"I'm going to call Justin." he said. "Or maybe Bjorn."

"Don't let me stop you." she said.

He dialed the number.

"Hello?" he asked.

"Hey, it's your brother from west of Sturgis." he said.

"How's it going, Erik?" he asked.

"I just had a fucked up dream, so I'm going to a meeting at noon." he said.

"That's good." he said. "That's what you're supposed to do."

"I just thought I'd call you and..." he said.

"I meant what I said, brother, you can call any time for any reason." he said.

"Thanks." he said. "I'm a little nervous."

"No need to be." he said. "People in AA are the same everywhere. Did you like that show we went to?"

"Yeah, it was great." he said.

"The same people who were there will be at that meeting." he said. "You'll see."

"Okay." he said. "Should I call you after to tell you how it went?"

"If you want." he said. "You're making too much of this. I remember when I was like that. You'll be among friends."

"Thanks, Justin." he said.

"How's Lexie?" he asked.

"She wants to move in." he said.

"How do you feel about that?" he asked.

"Fine, she practically lives here anyway." he said.

"If it's a problem, you need to let her know." he said. "Is it a problem?"

"Yeah, no, no problem." he said.

"I'll just tell you that this isn't something you should do early in recovery." he said. "It sounds like she's already been there for a while, so it's probably okay. They say avoid change. That change also includes her not being there. Don't complicate it. Don't let that high end tail distract you, I know I would be distracted. Do what you think is best, and don't look back."

"Okay." he said. "I should probably get going, the meeting is in Tacoma. Thanks for hearing me out, Justin."

"It's my pleasure." he said. "Call any time."

"I'm going to get going." he said. "Will you be okay here? Do you want to wait until I get back?"

"I'll be okay." she said. "You sure you're onboard with this thing?"

"I guess we'll find out." he said. "Isn't that what you said to Jess when she asked if it would be okay if she sings the song?"

"You heard that?" she asked.

"Never assume I'm not listening." he said. "Hopefully this will work out better than that did."

"I'm really sorry, Stryker." she said. "I didn't think it through. I just thought it would be cool. She loves to sing."

"She's definitely got a good set of pipes." he said. "I'll assume that you had good intentions. Normally no big deal, but in this case, it got me thinking about Taylor. I'd rather not do that."

"I would rather that you didn't either." she said. "That wasn't what I was trying to do."

"What were you trying to do?" he asked.

"I just thought that it would be something cool." she said. "Like if you hear that song, you'll be amazed. I never thought that it would be the same music, and it would give you that reaction. First of all, what are the odds that Jason uses the exact same music?"

Jason. He felt like he owed the dude an apology. For what I did in a dream? Snap out of it, Stryker!

"Maybe it was only meant for that music." he said. "Maybe every song has it's own music, and it can't be changed."

"That doesn't explain how you dreamt it." she said.

"Maybe I have a whole catalogue of unwritten music up there." he said. "Maybe in my next life I'm a rock star."

"Sure you are." she said.

He got his spare set of keys from the drawer and gave them to her.

"Does this mean we're..." she asked.

"It means you can let yourself in." he said. "Don't complicate it."

"Is the key to the bike on here too?" she asked. "Can I take it for a spin?"

"You want to ride, get your own." he said. "Nobody rides mine but me."

"Okay." she said. "That was a joke. I wasn't serious. I would never assume that...never mind. I can go back to the hotel if you want."

"Maybe you should." he said. "Why would you want to stay here? As fucked up as I am, I wouldn't blame you."

"I want to stay here so I can be with you." she said. "I want to help. I thought we were in this together."

"I'm sorry." he said. "Whether you stay here or not, we still have the mission. Going to Ireland...as newlyweds. I couldn't box you out if I wanted to."

"Are you trying to box me out?" she asked. "If you are, I can make it easy, I'll just leave. We're both professionals, the mission will be fine."

"Don't listen to me." he said. "I tend to say things I don't mean when I'm stressed, try to simplify things. I want you to be here if that's what you want."

"Am I complicating things?" she asked.

Why did I say that? Whatever you do, don't answer that question honestly.

"No, but sometimes I do." he said. "I would like to see you here when I get back."

That was the best he could do.

"If I'm pushing too hard..." she said.

"No, it's me." he said. "Please go get your stuff from the hotel. There are probably things there that you've been looking for."

She noticed that he managed not to say the words "move in". He also seemed to be a little apprehensive about it. She thought it should be exciting. A step forward in their relationship. Now she wasn't sure if he wanted to move forward or not.

"I'll wait." she said.

"Why?" he asked.
"The time isn't right." she said. "Go to your meeting."
"Okay." he said.
He thought about asking why the time wasn't right. That really wasn't his style. He was pretty sure she would be disappointed when he didn't, but he couldn't open that door. That was the door that gave her the upper hand, and he couldn't have that. Couldn't really say she gave up easily either, she pressed it more than a few times before she gave up. Maybe it was the right thing, but he needed to think about it some more.
"Will you be here when I get back?" he asked.
"Probably." she said. "You should go, you're going to be late."
"I'll see you later then." he said.

***

He got there, and the parking lot was almost full. Inside, there were a lot of people chatting, and the strong smell of coffee in the air. There was a counter that had refreshments, books, and other AA material.
It was about quarter to noon, so people were outside the meeting room talking. There was a recreation room off to the side with pool tables and video games. He went into the rec room and tried to blend in. A short haired blond walked up to him.
"I'm Melissa, what's your name?" she asked.
"Erik." he said.
"First time here?" she asked.
"What gave it away?" he asked.
"I know everyone." she said. "Welcome."
"Thank you." he said. "I've been to a meeting before, just not here."
"Where?" she asked.
"Back home." he said. "In Michigan. My brother took me. I just got back into town about a week ago."
"Why did you wait so long?" she asked.
"I don't know." he said. "It's still new to me. I talked to a friend who said I should find a meeting."

He had a hard time classifying Murphy as a friend, but what else was he gonna say?

She reached into her purse and pulled out a tiny booklet.

"This is our schedule." she said. "We have meetings every day, even at odd hours."

"Thanks." he said.

"It gets better." she said.

"Yeah, no, I had a really good experience back home." he said.

"I mean it gets better." she said. "Things might seem pretty fucked up right now, but if you keep coming back that will change. Before you know it."

"Okay." he said. "Does this really work?"

"I was a lost cause." she said. "Everyone gave up on me. Now even my family likes me again. I'm happier than I've been in years. All I've had to do is work this program."

"That's good to know." he said.

She looked at his cut.

"I think you'll find at least one person here that you already know." she said. "We should get in there."

He followed her into the room, and purposely sat at a different table from her. He liked her, he just wasn't sure if he wanted her to hear what he had to say.

A few last minute people came in, and to his surprise, Johnny was one of them. He gave him a little two finger salute. Melissa looked at him and winked.

They went around the table, and Erik brought up his situation with Lexie. He told them everything except for the things he couldn't. Most agreed that it would be okay if she stayed with him. None of them mentioned anything about moving in together either. It was probably taboo to talk about at this stage of his recovery. He listened to some of the others talk about early recovery, and it made him feel better. They closed the table, and he went out to the lobby. There was a "no smoking" sign there, so he stepped outside.

He lit a cigarette and inhaled deeply. This seems to help, he thought.

Johnny came through the door and walked towards him.

"I was wondering how long it would take you to get here." he said.

“I guess I’m the classic example.” said Erik. “My life became unmanageable. Now, when I send someone to the hospital, I would like it to be for a good reason.”

“I figured.” he said. “We all come here for different reasons. It’s not easy for us with our extracurricular activities.”

“How long?” he asked.

“Nine years.” he said. “You?”

“Week and a half.” he said. “I had no idea. I never noticed that you don’t drink.”

“Few people do.” he said. “When you’re drinking, you tend not to pay attention.”

“So what brought you here?” he asked.

“One night when I was plastered, a little kid jumped out into the road.” he said. “I didn’t notice, of course, and I hit him. Laid the bike down and everything. Do you remember that Lawrence Taylor hit on Joe Theismann?”

“When he broke his leg?” he said. “Yeah, that was gruesome. You didn’t?”

“It was worse than that. Nobody saw it, so I got back on my bike and booked. It was all over the papers the next day.” he said. “That was nine years ago. I went to try to make amends to the kid, but his father chased me away with a baseball bat. I did him the courtesy of not kicking his ass. Billy Morgan. That’s his name. The reason I got sober. That was most of the reason I wanted the gun deal. I want to anonymously give the family some money for what I did. If they know it’s from me, they won’t accept it.”

“That’s heavy, man.” he said. “I bet you think about it every day.”

“The worst part to me is that I took off.” he said. “Didn’t stick around to take responsibility. I was in AA within a week.”

“I got a number from a biker in Michigan so I can talk about the stuff that is only for friendly ears.” he said. “A member of the Twisted Drifters.”

“That’s good.” he said. “I met a couple of those guys at Sturgis last year. There’s so much I can’t talk about in there. Unfortunately, those are the things I need to talk about the most.”

“You got my number if you ever want to talk.” he said.

"Thanks." he said. "That's how this works. We help each other."
"I should probably call Lexie, we had a little dust up earlier." he said.
"I gotta go anyway." he said. "The phone works both ways, Erik. Call me if you need me too. Any time."
"Thanks, John." he said.
John got on his bike and left.
Erik punched in the numbers.
"Hello?" she asked.
"It's me." he said. "I want to apologize for earlier. I hope you can bear with me as I sort this out."
She was back at the hotel, and initially had no plans to go back. It was out of character for him to apologize so quickly. He usually let things fester until they explode. This is progress.
"Thanks." she said. "I'm sorry too. For pushing you. I don't need to do this."
"I want you to." he said. "If you weren't around, I would feel like part of me was missing."
"I'm at the hotel now." she said. "I'll just get what I need and leave the rest. I'll get your keys back to you."
"Keep them." he said. "I want you to have them. Just come back home."
Now he was calling it home, as if she lived there.
"Can I assume that the meeting went well?" she asked.
"It really did." he said. "I want to keep going, because I don't want to be the person I was earlier. I have a schedule of the meetings now. I ran into someone I know there."
"Who is she?" she asked.
"Always assume the worst don't you?" he said.
"With your reputation, I have to." she said. "Who was it?"
"It was Johnny. Oh my God, I think I may have just talked out of school." he said.
"How long has he been sober?" she asked.
"Nine years." he said.
"If he's been at it that long, it's probably okay." she said.
"It's right in the name. Anonymous." he said. "I'm not used to belonging to a secret society."
"I'm sure it's fine." she said. "Are you heading back home?"
"Yeah." he said.

"I'll meet you there." she said.

"I love you, Lexie." he said.

"And I love you." she said. "Everything's going to be fine."

She got together the things she thought she needed most. She wanted to take everything, and he said it was cool...that whole 'part of me would be missing' thing was sweet, but she still sensed a little doubt.

She knew instinctively that if she pushed this too much it would be the same as pushing him away. Playing a little hard to get would bring him closer...but maybe not with him. It's so hard when the normal rules don't apply. She figured as long as she didn't make any sudden movements, she would probably be okay. And no dramatic forced moves to go to the next level. Just be cool. We're closer than we've ever been.

***

He was in the elevator in the World Trade Center again. He finally got to the 98th floor and he got off and went through the metal detector. He went through the glass doors and was surprised to see a younger brunette behind the desk.

"Mr. Murphy for Mr. Andersen." he said.

"He's expecting you. Alicia?" she said.

Alicia materialized from behind the wall.

"Mr. Murphy. How nice to see you again." she said. "Right this way."

"Where's Janet?" he asked.

"The strangest thing, she just didn't show up one day." she said. "Nobody's heard from her. Julia was here within an hour, and she's excellent."

"I'm sure she is." he said.

He knew very well what happened. Janet said something she shouldn't have. When she "just disappeared" she really disappeared. Permanently. He couldn't even blame Leland. That's the business. No margin for error, and if you make the wrong mistake, you don't come back. Whatever she said to whoever she said it to, she should have known better. He had no doubt that whoever she talked to was gone too. An unforgiving business. He hoped that Alicia wasn't privy to anything so dangerous, she's a sweet kid.

"My apologies, Mr. Murphy, we just can't be too careful." she said.

He walked through another metal detector. The red light was on over Leland's door. He looked at his watch. 9:59 am. About 30 seconds later the light turned green.

"Go right in. Mr. Murphy." she said.

He quickly straightened himself and tried to stretch an inch or two taller. He opened the door and walked in.

"Close the door and have a seat, Anthony." he said.

"What's going on in India?" he asked.

"After Quinn got there, it went off without a hitch." he said.

"And Hartley?"

"Gone." he said.

"And Hong Kong?"

"Still on pace, but there are a lot of moving parts." he said. "I have my best team on it, and I don't expect any problems."

"You're not exactly filling me with confidence, Mr. Murphy." he said. "I don't care how many moving parts are involved, that shouldn't matter. It's your responsibility to make sure that it works perfectly. With what I pay you, I feel justified in demanding perfection."

"Yes, Mr. Andersen." he said.

"What about Paris?" he asked.

"I don't expect any problems." he said. "She'll be working with one of my best people."

"It seems that they're all your 'best' people, yet there are still problems." he said. "You need to look at these people objectively, Anthony, and recognize when their weak."

"Yes, sir." he said.

"And the Irish? They made the first run last week." he said. "When can we expect our ATF boys to pick up the MC?"

"In a few days." he said. "They accelerated the schedule since it took so long to make the first run."

"And Stryker?" he said. "I hear he's going to AA now."

"How could you know that?" he asked.

"I make it my business to know." he said. "With a phone call, I could tell you what you had for breakfast. To me a man who can't handle his liquor is weak. My generation didn't whine about our feelings, and call weakness a disease. This is a problem, Anthony. He might have to go."

"Do you remember what we talked about last time?" he asked. "The anger management issues? This fixes that. He's one of my be...he's very good. You can't just get rid of people on a whim, we won't have anyone left."

"Keep an eye on him." he said. "My solution is still in play. Short leash. I don't like this. A man should be able to drink without it causing problems. If he can't handle it, he's no good to us. When do they go to Ireland?"

"It would be best if it's not too soon after the ATF grabs up the Saints." he said. "It might look suspicious if he goes away and suddenly the Irish Kings get whacked."

"That's unacceptable." he said. "I want them dead. What does it matter, he's not going back to the club anyway."

"I may need to finesse that a little as well." he said. "I'm pretty sure Stryker is planning to go back to the club."

"I don't care what he's planning." he said. "Do you have control of your people? He doesn't get to make that decision."

"Yes, sir." he said.

"Are you set for money?" he asked.

"I wouldn't say no to another half mil." he said.

"Another half mil?" he asked. "I just gave you a million and a half not a month ago."

"Well, sir, there are 9 people involved with Hong Kong. I had to give Quinn a bonus for Hartley. I'll also have to pay the new girl. And I haven't paid Stryker and Tenenzapf, and I anticipate giving them a hefty bonus for the Irish job." he said. "It goes faster than you think."

"Give me the suitcase." he said.

He went to the vault and filled it up.

"I want everything to run smoothly from here on out." he said. "If the three remaining missions don't have any problems, the next time we speak there will be an extra quarter mil for you. You need to manage your people, Anthony. I put an extra hundred thousand in there so you can pay yourself."

"Much appreciated, sir." he said.

"Same time, two weeks from today." he said. "I expect results. That is all."

The buzzer sounded loudly, and he walked out. He would have to get Lexie to start working on Erik if he had any hope at all of getting him out of that club.

All of that talk about weakness really bothered him, but he just had to take it. Leland knew that he was in the program. They both knew it, yet they never talked about it. He said those things, almost daring him to defend himself. Leland knew he wouldn't. Murphy knew he never could. He took it because he had no choice. This was all he was good at. Too late in life to reevaluate his career choice.

Chapter 15

They were at the club talking with Jessica and Mike. He was still a little upset about the other night. He was dealing with it better. It helped to go to meetings and talk about it. Jessica was a little wary after what had happened too. She had talked to Lexie, and he had the feeling that she had told her just a little too much.

"It's really no big deal, Jess, it was just a little creepy." he said. "You sounded great. You sing with a lot of feeling, and it comes across well. You should look into doing something with that. Talk to Jason."

"Thanks, Erik." she said. "Lexie told me that you had a bad reaction to it. That's not what I was trying to do."

"It wasn't you, it was the dream." he said. "You brought me right back to it. There are some issues related to the dream that are...unpleasant. I'm glad it happened, glad you got to go up on stage. That's where you belong, even if you don't think so. We all have things we're good at, things we were born to do. You were born to sing. You told a story up there that everyone can relate to. You shared your feelings, and made it okay for the rest of us to have those feelings. How could that be a bad thing?"

"I've never heard it put that way before." she said. "Really? Did I have that effect on you?"

"Absolutely." he said. "Not only that, you had the same effect on everyone else who was there. You have that gift, to make people forget about life and get lost in your song. Am I wrong?"

He looked at Mike and Lexie.

"I've always loved your singing." said Mike. "It's what attracted me to you from the start. Every time you sing I feel it."

"No, I was amazed." said Lexie. "I felt it to. You brought me back to that other guy...that I mentioned when I was telling you the story of me and Stryker's adventure. With him, it was a losing game. I hurt the same way you did while you were singing that song."

"Herschel." he said.

"Yes." she said. "There's only been him and you that I felt that way about. We won't get into yours."

"If I was at the Trevi Fountain today..." he said.

"I said we're not talking about it." she said.
"The girl in France." said Jessica.
"Yes." she said.
"Well, no matter what we know, officially she's dead." said Erik. "I thought we had this worked out. You're as bad as Taylor."
"But you still have this." she said.
She picked up his keys and looked at the cameo.
"You think it looks just like her, but I don't see it." she said. "She told you that to get in your head. This thing could look like almost anyone."
He took the keys from her.
"This is all I have left." he said. "It's been lucky for me. I've had it for fifteen years now. Taylor wanted me to get rid of it too. I hope you don't start reminding me of her again."
"I'm sorry." she said. "This isn't about you. It's Herschel. Some of the things he did. Hearing that song brought it back. It's definitely not about Danielle."
"It's okay, but you're making me worry a little. How long has she been out of my life?" he said. "Taylor was the same way, and she didn't even know she's alive. I'll try to forget what you said today, and give you a do over."
"I'll take the do over, I'm sorry Erik. It really is more about the shit Herschel put me through, and I'm taking it out on you. I'm really sorry, that was inappropriate. Just so you know, Jess, this isn't a negative reflection of your singing, or the song." she said. "You brought back feelings I haven't had in years. It's incredibly powerful for you to be able to do that. Stryker was right, you made me feel it. There aren't many people who can do that."
"Thanks." she said.
"The best musicians always make people feel things." said Erik. "It's not always a happy song. We need to feel that too, if for no other reason than to remind us of how good things are."
He winked at Lexie.
"How do you always know what to say?" she asked.
He shrugged his shoulders.
"Miggy, turn that up." he said.
He turned up the volume.

“In a daring early morning sting operation, ATF agents intercepted a large scale arms shipment from a local motorcycle gang. The ‘Satan’s Saints’ were detained just outside of Waterville with the weapons. We now go live to Tonya Crawford with the latest. Tonya?”

She was standing with a guy in a suit and sunglasses in front of two large trucks, and several large folding tables covered with various weapons including rocket launchers, submachine guns, grenade launchers, and AK-47s.

“That’s right, Ken, I’m here with Special Agent Jack Morrison of the ATF, who tells me that this is one of the largest shipments of Illegal weapons he’s ever seen.” she said.

“Agent Morrison, is this something you were expecting?” she asked.

“We acted on a tip from another agency which has always been reliable in the past. We’re just glad to get these weapons off the street.” he said.

“What agency?” she asked.

“I’m not at liberty to divulge that information, Ms. Crawford, we’re just grateful that we were able to stop them.” he said.

“Do you have any idea how much these weapons are worth?” she asked.

He looked over the tables.

“I can’t say for sure, Ms. Crawford, but if I had to guess, probably at least $425,000 on the street.” he said.

“That’s a lot of weapons.” she said. “I’m sure we’ll all feel safer tonight knowing that these weapons didn’t make it to the street. Thank you, Agent Morrison.”

“You’re welcome, Ms. Crawford.” he said.

He walked away.

“There isn’t any information on who’s behind this, Ken, but the speculation is that the weapons may have come from the Middle East. That’s all from here, back to you, Ken.”

“You were right.” said Mike.

“It would seem that we both were.” he said. “The vote caused a little bad blood, but this should definitely make people reevaluate things. Did you get that, babe? Their blaming the sand people.”

"The sand people would have been on the receiving end." said Lexie. "They need all the weapons that they can get so they can keep killing Jews."

"I'm just glad we didn't do it." he said. "That could be us. And that's way more guns than I thought we were going to try to move."

"Well it's over now." he said. "We move forward from here."

Just then John walked in. Erik went up to him.

"Hey, prez, did you hear?" he asked.

"Hear what?" he asked.

"It was just on the news." he said. "ATF picked up the Saints while they were making the run."

"Well, I'll be damned." he said. "I guess I should be thanking you."

"I only did what was best for the club." he said. "I always will."

"I know, son." he said. "Can we talk in the back for a few minutes?"

"Sure." he said.

He caught Lexie's attention and pantomimed that he was going to the back. She nodded.

"I made a bad decision." he said. "I could have cost all of us our freedom."

"You did what you thought was best." he said.

"After talking to you the other day, I'm glad to know it wasn't just greed." he said.

"Greed or no, it was a selfish decision." he said. "The context means nothing. I wanted to do something that would ease my guilt. I think this might not be the best thing for me anymore."

"What? Step down?" he asked. "Because of this? I think that's a bit of an overreaction."

"It's not just this." he said. "I've known for a while now. Kirk has no interest, he barely wants to be VP. You made the best decision on the guns. The men respect you. You're the logical choice."

He wants me to take over as president? Really? I'm sure Kirk wants it, he just won't say so.

"I don't know, John, I don't think it would be a good fit." he said. "My drifter lifestyle doesn't line up too well with responsibility. I'm still with the Merchants. I'm going away in the next week or two. I never know when I'll be back. You need someone more stable to run things. I do the two rides per month to stay active, but you shouldn't expect more than that. I'm Sergeant-at-Arms, but there are people who can step in while I'm gone."

"I want to pass this fucking thing down to someone I can trust." he said. "We've got great guys, but none who can fill these shoes...except for you."

"I'll talk to Kirk." he said.

"Already have." he said. "Try if you want, but he doesn't want it."

"Neither do I." he said.

"Do you think I wanted it?" he asked.

"After the old man was killed I was funneled pretty roughly into this chair. Nobody asked if I wanted it, it was assumed." he said. "I did what was best for the club, even though I was grieving."

"That's a lot different than this situation." he said. "You have time. If it's over for you, that's fine, but I would make a bad president. Find a good one."

"Promise me you'll think about it?" he asked.

"I will." he said. "But I'll tell you, I'm less likely than Kirk to do it. I appreciate the offer, and the vote of confidence, but this isn't for me."

"Okay." he said. "How's everything else going?"

"Ups and downs." he said. "I've been going to meetings, which seems to help. A few problems with Lexie, but nothing I can't handle."

"Don't take that shit lightly." he said. "You're putting on a great show, but I can tell what's really going on. You need to come to peace with that."

He can probably tell from all that AA, he thought.

"I know." he said. "At least she's easy to talk to."

"Then do that." he said. "Secrets get us in trouble."

"Thanks, John." he said.

"You'll think about it?" he asked.

"Sure." he said. "But it's not going to happen. I might have what it takes, but there are others who would be better with the commitment. I'm leaving in the next week or two. I already have my orders, their just waiting on the repairs. Do what's best for the club again, find someone who won't be gone for months at a time."

"I hate to say it, but you might be right again, kid." he said. "I talked myself into the club being okay while you're gone. That's no way to start. Whoever does it will need to be here so they can adapt to the job. Just do me a favor? Think about my replacement? Your opinion carries a lot of weight."

"I'll do that, John." he said. "We'll figure it out before I leave."

***

Her phone started ringing.

"Hello?" she said.

"Hey, Lexie, I need your help with something, can you talk?" he asked.

"Sure, just give me a minute, I'll go outside." she said.

"Sorry guys, I have to take this." she said.

"Is that?" Jessica whispered.

Without thinking, she nodded.

She walked out to the parking lot.

"What's going on, Anthony?" she asked.

"It's Mr. Big. My boss. When this is over, he wants Erik out of the club." he said.

"Geez, Murph, why don't you give me something tough?" she asked. "Do you have any idea how deep he is in this thing?"

"I'm well aware of the situation." he said. "The alternative is worse. As a matter of fact, it's as bad as it gets."

"Really?" she said. "He would do that?"

"If you think I'm heartless, you have no idea what heartless is." he said. "He has people killed for sport. Like ordering a cup of coffee."

"I'll start today." she said. "How much time do we have?"

"I think he's safe at least until the end of the mission." he said. "He doesn't like the idea of him going to AA either. Thinks a guy who can't handle his liquor is weak. He wanted to whack him just for that."

"So now I have to worry about keeping him alive, too?" she asked. "There's no way around this? Nobody above him?"

"The President answers to him." he said. "I think if we make a good showing with the Irish, he might forget about it. More likely, he'll always have it in the back of his mind, and Stryker will have to be as close to perfect as possible."

"You've killed people without killing them, is that an option?" she asked.

"I know you think I know everything, and I do know most things." he said. "This guy knows more than me. Erik would have to die for real for him to forget about it. There's no way we could keep it from him."

"Is there anything we can do?" she asked.

She was feeling hopeless.

"Get him out of that club." she said. "If we need to we can kill him and make it look good to them, but he can't go back there."

"I'll make sure it happens." she said. "One way or another."

She wasn't going to let that bastard kill Erik. She would kill him first. Just when things are going good.

"Maybe let him keep it until you leave for Ireland, but start steering him in that direction." he said. "It will be easier when he's away from it. Tell him the truth if you need to. Getting him away from the club will go a long way to making things right with Mr. Big, the AA thing he can probably live with. He's known about me for years."

"Why is AA such a problem?" she asked.

"He's from a different generation." he said. "When people bottled up their feelings. He sees it as a weakness disguised as a disease. Do well in Ireland, get him away from the club, and hopefully we can get back to normal. He had someone clipped just a couple weeks ago in India because the target made them. He doesn't know Erik like we do. We're lucky we have a chance to talk to him before he gets killed, and he might kill him anyway."

"Okay, Murph." she said. "I'm on it. Probably don't need to tell you that they picked up the Saints?"

"Yeah, I know all about it." he said.

"They blame it on the Arabs to make the Irish feel safe?" she asked.

"Yes." he said. "That was us. No need to send you over there and let them know you're coming, is there?"

"I guess not." she said.

"Don't worry too much about this." he said. "As long as we can get him away from the club, and you do a good job over there, he'll be safe. But those things need to happen. Tell him what's going on, I'll leave it up to you whether you tell him about Mr. Big. That should probably be a last resort."

"Okay." she said.

The line went dead.

She went back into the club.

"So that was him?" she asked. "Mr. Big?"

"Don't call him that." she said.

She couldn't believe that she let her guard down and tipped Jessica that it was Murphy.

"Sorry." she said.

"It's okay." she said. "That's what he calls his boss, who isn't a very nice person. He just wanted to brief me on what's going on in the desert."

"So you're not going on another adventure?" she asked.

Lexie laughed convincingly enough to make it seem real.

"I'm afraid that my life isn't anywhere near as exciting as you think it is." she said. "The last such adventure I've been on was the one I told you about, and that was seven years ago."

"But if he needed you to go..." she said.

"A lot of the work I do for him is pretty close to home." she said. "Well, what used to be home. I guess I'm homeless now."

"No you're not, you live with Erik." she said.

"I guess you're right." she said. "But he's going to be deployed in the next week or two, and I'm going to visit my uncle in New York. Who knows what will happen after that?"

"You'll come back when he gets back, of course." she said.

Neither one of us is coming back, she thought.

"I hope you're right." she said.

"Of course I am." she said. "He loves you."

She looked at Mike.

"It's true, he does." he said. "Talks about you all the time."

"We should hang out a lot over the next couple of weeks just in case." she said. "Me, you, Em, and Allie."

"You'll be back when he comes home." she said. "But I still want to spend some time with you before you leave."

"That sounds good." she said.

Erik came back to the table.

"Hey, how's it going?" he asked.

"Good." she said. "Did you still have that thing later on?"

"That...oh, yeah I almost forgot about it." he said. "We should get going."

"I'll call you later Jess. Mike." she said. "You guys have a good afternoon."

"Thanks, I'll talk to you later." she said.

***

"So what was that about?" she asked. "You and John?"

"You're not going to believe this." he said. "He's stepping down, and he wants me to be president."

"You?" she asked. "The president?"

"That's exactly the reaction I had." he said. "He says Kirk doesn't want it, and there's nobody else he trusts. I pointed out my transient lifestyle, and at first he acted like it doesn't matter."

"So where did you leave it?" she asked.

"By the time we finished talking, he had accepted the fact that I shouldn't do it." he said. "Wants me to help with recommendations, vetting, and such. I told him we'll work it out before I leave."

"That's good." she said. "You have any ideas?"

"As crazy as it sounds, Brendan." he said. "He's got the experience, he's already in on most of the major decisions, and he loves the club."

"Of the choices besides Kirk, I would tend to agree." she said.

"I'm still going to talk to Kirk, see how solidly he's against this." he said.

"I talked to Murphy." she said.

"Really? What's going on?" he asked.

"He says you have to go in the other direction." she said.

"What does that mean?" he said.

"When this is over, you have to leave the club." she said.

No point in beating around the bush, she thought. The stakes are too high.

"I'm not leaving the club." he said. "I don't care what Murphy thinks."

"I'll explain it to you the way he explained it to me." she said.

"I don't care how you explain it, I'm not leaving the Centurions." he said. "End of story."

"Just hear me out." she said. "I would never ask you to do something you don't want to do, except under these circumstances."

"Say what you have to say." he said.

"Okay, but you have to listen." she said.

She could tell that at this point it didn't matter what she said, his mind was made up. He needed to hear the situation, and actually understand it.

"Why are you telling me?" he asked. "Doesn't he have the balls?"

"It's better coming from me, believe me." she said. "He's scared."

He let out a big sigh, and prepared to argue some more.

"Go ahead." he said.

"His boss wants this. Wants probably isn't the right word, he demands it." she said. "This is a guy that doesn't answer to anybody. He looks at killing people as a business decision. He had a guy killed in India recently because the target made him. He wants to kill you."

"It sounds like the decision has already been made." he said.

"Maybe we can change his mind if we do well in Ireland, and you leave the club." she said. "Those are our options. Anthony was scared. And he wasn't afraid to admit it. Have you ever known him to be anything but a cocky bastard?"

He hadn't. Murph always acted like he was above it all. Erik always believed he was. Was he really scared? Or was Lexie projecting her feelings on to him? The Murphy he knew was too smart for that. He had never seen him the least bit rattled. From that first day he met him in Dubai seven years ago. Always smug. Like he knew a secret that you didn't, and the worst part of it was that he did.

"I'll have to think about this." he said. "How could I do that? These are my brothers."

"Trust me, they'll be better off if you don't come back." she said. "It could be more than just you getting killed. This guy doesn't like outlaws. They could go away for a long time."

She didn't actually know this, but it sounded good. Something he could understand, and something awful that could happen if he didn't leave the club. She was going to make this happen by any means necessary.

"I take your point." he said. "I still have to think about it. I wouldn't want them to think I just left them."

"You know as well as I do that your death could be easily arranged. Something they would believe." she said. "The alternative is you really getting killed, and I'm not going to let that happen."

"We'll talk about this later." he said. "We'll have plenty of time in Ireland."

"But we're newlyweds!" she said.

"I'll make sure that the nuptials are my number one priority." he said. "I thought you knew me better than that."

"Just protecting my interests." she said.

His phone started ringing.

"Hello?" he said.

"Erik, we need to talk." he said.

"I've already been talking to Lexie." he said. "You couldn't tell me yourself?"

"We should get together." he said. "Any of your guys live in Bremerton?"

"No." he said.

"Any of them have business there?" he asked. "I don't want to be seen."

"Nobody ever makes it to this side of the sound, Anthony, you know that." he said.

"I know, but sometimes things change." he said. "It's not like I'm inside the clubhouse."

"If we meet here, we won't be seen." he said.

"Good. It will be 10 minutes tops. How 'bout the Boat Shed?" he said. "You and Lexie can have a nice steak after we talk."

"Okay." he said.

"I'll be there when you get there." he said.

The line went dead.

Maybe this fucking thing is serious, he thought. Why else would he be in Bremerton? He always has several missions going on all over the world.

"Let's go, he wants to meet." he said.

"Okay." she said. "Is he here?"

"He's meeting us at that little restaurant on Shore Dr." he said. "We're only meeting for a few minutes, then he has to go. We'll get a steak after we talk to him."

"Sounds good, I'm starved." she said.

They got to the restaurant and Anthony was in the corner with his back to the wall.

"It's good to see you two." he said.

"Is there no way around this, Anthony?" he asked.

"The obvious answer is yes, you could be dead." he said.

"Still cocky as ever." he said. "Lexie said you're scared."

The waitress came over with menus.

"Can I get you anything to drink while you're looking at the menu?" she asked.

"Nothing now, but could you give us about 10 minutes?" he said.

"Sure thing." she said.

"If my jest makes you think I'm not scared, then it worked." he said. "The truth is yes, Erik, I am scared. Whether I say it often enough or not, I love you...both of you. This job is hard enough without losing my best people. Although we don't socialize, I consider both of you my friends."

"In context, I would say the same thing." he said.

"Me too." said Lexie.

"Good. Now that we've established that we all like each other, we can get down to business. You ship out next Friday on the Plantagenet. You'll take it as far as San Diego, then you'll get on the Mauritius to go through the Panama Canal bound for New York City. It will take a total of 6 days. We can fly you, Lexie, after all you're going to New York to visit your uncle." he said. "In two weeks, you're getting on the Norwegian Breakaway, a very touristy cruise ship that makes a stop in Cork, Ireland. There will be a car waiting for you when you get to Cork, talk to the harbormaster. You'll drive to Belfast. It's 421 kilometers, or if you still claim that tiny percentage of the world who hasn't gone metric, 261 miles."

"That never did catch on here." said Erik.

"Should be about a 4 or 5 hour trip. We put you two lovebirds on a cruise ship since it's your honeymoon." he said. "Erik, we're going to have you killed 4 days after you leave. It will look good, there will be no doubt. We'll send a package with pictures to the club, since you've listed them as an emergency contact, and you'll be buried at sea, according to your wishes. You'll be dead to everyone. Your family, Taylor, everyone."

"I didn't say I was doing it." he said.

"You didn't have to." he said. "The alternative is you die for real.

"But my family? Taylor? Is that really necessary?" he said.

"What if the club calls your parents?" he asked. "Forget that, what if Taylor calls the club? It has to be this way. That's the only way you get to live. This guy will have you killed, make no mistake. You'll never see it coming."

I'll find a way to tell mom and dad, he thought. Probably better Taylor thinks I'm really dead.

"Okay, if that's how it has to be." he said.

"I'll still know you're alive." said Lexie.

"What? They're not taking you away too?" he asked. "How nice of them."

"I'm just trying to keep you alive." said Murphy.

"Me too." said Lexie.

"This is a lot to take in." he said. "What did I do to piss this guy off?"

"I mentioned to him that you don't want to leave the club, and he went off." he said. "This is a guy with old fashioned values. And he's paying us a lot of money. It's business to him. Doling out money or having someone killed, it's all in a day's work. It doesn't affect him at all. That's why this is such a dangerous situation. And speaking of money..."

He handed each of them a satchel filled with cash.

"I'm almost over my 10 minutes, so I'm gonna get out of here." he said.

He handed them each a piece of paper.

"This is your list." he said. "I know it's long, but there should be a hefty bonus if it goes well. You'll be staying at the Malmaison, it's a really swanky hotel in Belfast, but you're newlyweds after all. It's all on me, charge whatever you want, hell, you can even eat the macadamia nuts, which are like four bucks each. When you get to Belfast, call me. I'll have more details about the targets."

He got up and walked away.

The waitress came back as soon as he was gone.

"Have you decided?" she asked.

He hadn't looked at the menu, but this place was famous for their steaks.

"We haven't had a chance to look, but I would love a good ribeye. Not bloody, but rare." he said.

"It's the house specialty." she said.

"Good, I'll have the same." said Lexie. "And bring me a Coke please, and a ginger ale for him."

"I'll put in the order for your steaks, and be right back with your drinks." she said.

"Thanks." he said.

"So has anyone ever revealed that they weren't really dead?" he asked.

"I'll pretend that you didn't just ask me that." she said.

"Oh, right, Danielle." he said. "But that was extenuating circumstances."

"How in the fuck was that extenuating circumstances?" she asked. "She was under strict orders not to contact you. She went out to the cottage that night trying to see you, then actually had the nerve to call you after you got home. I guess you probably think it was because she loved you so much."

"If I thought that, would I be wrong?" he asked.

"How the hell do I know?" she said.

The waitress came back with the drinks. As soon as she left she started again.

"You know, you're lucky." she said. "You got to live out your little lost love dream without having to watch her get killed. For all I know, she contacted you to spite me. She knew that we were together. Whatever fantasy you had going in your head, I can assure you that it isn't true."

She was obviously talking about Herschel. That had to be tough. But he could see how Danielle would have wanted to make contact. Particularly after the way it ended. There would be no settling this with Lexie, she still held a grudge.

"We really shouldn't be talking about this." he said.

"I'm sorry." she said. "There I go again. There are some things between me and her that you don't know about. I shouldn't have said what I said to you. It's not your fault. You're just like catnip to most women, and that doesn't help."

"There's only one woman that I want to nip me." he said. "And it's not Danielle."

"Erik Stryker, a one woman man? That seems pretty unlikely. Nevertheless, I might give you a little nip later on." she said. "In fact, you can count on it."

The waitress brought their steaks. They looked great. He was hungry too.

"Thank you." he said.

Lexie cut a piece off and stuffed it in her mouth.

"I like this Lexie better than vegetarian Lexie." he said.

"So do I." she said.

"We should go to the club later." he said.

"I was thinking the same thing." she said. "I really have made some friends here."

"I wish we could come back." he said.

"Me too." she said. "Where do you want to go when it's all over?"

"It really sucks that Washington State is out." he said. "I really love it here."

"Me too." she said.

"Maybe California, but we'd have to go too far south." he said.

"We?" she said.

"Unless you don't want to come with me." he said. "You might want to get back to the desert."

"Too soon for that." she said. "I would like to stay with you...if that's what you want."

"If it's California, I probably wouldn't want to. If we're too far north, our paths could cross with the club, and Southern California sucks." he said. "People are pretty snotty on the East Coast, but then, Seattle has its moments too. Michigan would be cool, but again, we might be too close to people who think I'm dead. That leaves the South. New Orleans would be okay, but not in the city. Maybe Metairie or Kenner, or even somewhere in the bayou like Lafayette. Or maybe Mobile, Alabama. Very cosmopolitan. Or Europe if that's okay with Murph. You'd have a head start on me with all of the languages you know. What do you think?"

"Unless it's Denmark." she said.

"Since the Viking age, Denmark is one of the most peaceful places on earth." he said. "I don't foresee any missions coming up around there."

"That's okay, we don't need to be close to the action." she said.

"I probably have to stay with the merchants." he said.

"Maybe. There are dozens of things you could do for cover. You seem to have a lot of ideas." she said. "Almost like you've already been planning this. How do you know about all of those places?"

"Honey, I've been rolling around this country for years. I see places I like, I make a note. And you know I don't forget anything." he said. "If we were talking about Israel, you would have some ideas too. Do you want to talk about Israel?"

"No." she said. "I don't want to go back there."

"Are you sure you want to stay with me?" he asked. "I'm bound to do some shit you don't like. You've only been around for a few weeks, so you don't know, but I'm hard to live with."

"I've taken that into account." she said. "I'll just have to keep you on a short leash."

"Then you're asking for trouble." he said. "I don't even like a long leash, in fact, I can't have one at all."

"You don't need to be on one, you just need to respect me." she said.

"I'll do my best." he said.

She looked at him, and he cracked the faintest of smiles. She couldn't tell if he was serious or not. This will probably come back to me someday, the first time he screws up, and he'll say "I told you I'd do my best," she thought.

"What does that mean?" she asked.

"I love you, Lexie, that's all you need to know." he said. "I may not always be perfect, in fact, I can guarantee you that I won't. Neither will you. We will have trials and tribulations, and we'll get through them, or we won't. That's what that means."

"Okay." she said. "Breaking out the Catholic shit on me, the 'trials and tribulations'?"

"Don't be so serious, it's just life." he said. "Do you think my parents have had a perfect life? No. I won't tell you the problems they have had, but you can probably guess, he's a

Stryker. They got through it. If it's important enough, so will we."

"Okay." she said.

He had an annoying habit of always making sense, and making her feel like she was making too much of things.

"In any case, we have some time to decide." he said. "We don't have to figure it out today. That's if we even have a choice."

"Do you want to be with me?" she asked, suddenly feeling insecure.

"I would like that very much." he said. "As long as you can let me be me."

"I'm not trying to change you, Erik." she said. "That would be asking for trouble."

"Good." he said. "We still have time to think this through. Murphy might actually tell us where we have to live, so we may not have to think about it at all. If you can take me as I am, I don't see any major problems."

The whole "take me as I am" thing bothered her. She didn't know what to make of it. It could mean "whoops, I just banged the girl down the street, I said I'd do my best. Take me as I am."

But he did come across with an unsolicited "I love you." He was probably right, she was making too much of this.

She had really developed feelings for him, stronger that Herschel even, which was more than she had ever felt for anyone. She wanted him to feel the same way, and she wanted to know it.

He always played it so close to the vest. Always left an escape route. It was like he was laying out the framework to explain virtually anything he did wrong. Was she expecting him to do something wrong? Was she not giving him a chance to be good? She wasn't going to give up, which meant she had no choice but to trust him.

"I can do that." she said. "But you need to take me as I am too."

"Now you're talking." he said. "We need to be understanding of each other. That doesn't mean that we do things to hurt each other without consequences, it just means that we can make mistakes and learn from them. I love you, Lexie, and I want to be with you. There's no need to complicate it. If you love me and want to be with me, that's all we'll ever need."

"I can live with that." she said. "It seemed like you were setting up your defense for the next time you cheat on me. I'm sure it's just my overactive imagination. You'll have to bear with me, I have trust issues. Mostly with Herschel, but with the way women look at you..."

"I don't want to sleep with anyone but you." he said. "I can't help it if women notice me. Personally, I think that your idea of that is grossly exaggerated, but I'm yours."

"Thank you." she said.

Chapter 16

They got to the club, and it was crowded and lively. Lexie saw Jess, Allie, and Emily at a table. They waved and she headed over there. Erik went to the bar to talk to John.

"I ship out next Friday." he said. "About that thing we talked about, I think it should be Brendan."

"Why him?" he asked.

He shrugged his shoulders.

"Kirk doesn't want it. We have some great guys in the club, but no one I see taking the gavel." he said. "Brendan is already in on most of the important decisions, he's been around forever, and he loves the club. He's the best choice."

"No, you are." he said.

He thought about it. What if he just told Murphy and his boss to fuck off? Would they really get rid of him? This wasn't the kind of job you can just quit. It's like the mob, you don't get to walk away. He really didn't want to leave the club, hell, he didn't even want to go on this mission. "He'll kill you, and you'll never see it coming." Murphy's voice in his head. To leave here forever though, dying was almost preferable.

"I can't." he said.

"Say what you want, Erik, but I just saw your wheels spinning up there." he said. "You're still thinking about it."

"Whether I am or not, I can't." he said. "It's no good for the club."

He knew that argument sounded weak, and he could tell that John thought so too. Under different circumstances, he would love to take the gavel. He couldn't very well tell John that some executive maniac would kill him if he stayed.

"You made a mistake, son, you let me know you're still thinking about it." he said. "It's not too late. Lexie loves it here, and so do you. You could settle down, maybe start a family."

That was something he wanted to do. He had always wanted to be a dad. And here would be the perfect place to do it. But you can't. It's unlikely you'll ever have a family. What kind of dad goes away for months at a time on killing sprees?"

"I'll admit that I've thought more about it. If nothing else, this isn't the right time. Let's revisit this in a year." he said. "I'm going to be gone for a while this time. Southeast Asia, then across the Indian Ocean to Africa. Probably with unscheduled stops at other places if they don't have what we need in P.I. or Mombasa. If you want to do this now, it needs to be someone else. If you still have the gavel when I get back, I would probably be more receptive."

"I can do that." he said. "I'm willing to wait if it means you'll take the gavel. We'll talk about it in a year. I'll still be around."

After you get the package from my boss, you'll rethink that, he thought.

"Sounds good." he said. "I'm still no good with rules."

"Neither am I." he said. "So what's Lexie going to do while you're gone?"

"She's going to New York to visit her uncle." he said. "She hasn't seen him in forever. She moved to the desert pretty early on."

"The desert?" he asked.

"Not really. Israel. That's what she calls it." he said. "I'm sure it's a lot like here, but she's a soldier, so she spends most of the time in the desert."

"You doing any soldiering this time around?" he asked.

"Why would you think that?" he asked.

"Your mercenary work." he said. "Since you told me that, I have to wonder what you're up to when you go away."

"Oh, Johnny, that was years ago." he said. "That guy hasn't been in touch since the last time I saw Lexie. I'm just a sailor."

John looked at him for a few seconds.

"I'm not telling you what it is, son, but you have a tell." he said. "If you don't want to tell me about it, that's cool, but I know you've talked to this guy, and pretty recently too."

I have a tell? Really? Nobody wants to hear that. Tells were never good. Unless you can figure out what your own is and use it as a misdirection.

"I can't tell you how disappointing it is to learn that I have a tell." he said. "I'm telling you everything I can, Johnny, and that's the truth, regardless of any tell I have. If I could say more, I would."

"And Lexie?" he asked.

"Going to visit her uncle in New York." he said.

"Right." he said. "That's probably all you can tell me, right?"

"You don't want to get involved in this, trust me, Johnny." he said. "If there was a way to make you forget all that shit I told you, I would do it. It could be dangerous. If word gets out that you know anything, I'll probably get clipped."

"Your secret's safe with me, kid." he said. "It would be counterproductive if you got killed. Just be careful over there, wherever it is."

"P.I. and Mombasa." he said.

"Dangerous places." he said.

***

"So next Friday?" asked Allie. "That's so sad."

"It will be okay." she said. "I'm going to visit my uncle in New York. If he's gone a long time, I'll probably get back before him. I have a few other things to do on the East Coast."

"Do you trust him?" asked Jess. "I've heard about those sailors."

"Completely." she said. "I can't tell you anything now, but we have plans when he gets back."

"How mysterious." she said. "Wedding bells?"

They all started giggling.

"Not exactly." she said. "He's not really the marrying type. I'm not really supposed to talk about it. He knows, but I can't say anything for the next three months."

"Do you think we're stupid?" asked Em. "The first three months means the first trimester. You're pregnant."

How could I be so stupid? *They're women, they know these things*. The cat's out of the bag now.

"Remember what I just said about Stryker knowing?" she said. "He doesn't. That part was a lie, and I need you to not tell him before I have a chance to. I can't believe I thought I would get that past you."

"Honestly, I could tell just looking at you." said Jess. "It's true, you know. There's such thing as that glow you always hear about. I knew something was up."

"I'll tell him tonight, but until then you have to keep my secret." she said. "I'm pretty sure he'll react well to it, but you never know."

"Yes you do." said Emily. "The time I got pregnant, I knew the guy was going to be a prick. He wanted to get rid of it, but I wanted to keep it. I made the decision that I thought would be right from the child. It's father didn't want it, so I had an abortion. It was the toughest decision of my life."

"I'm sorry to hear that." she said.

Erik walked up to the table.

"There are certain words in the English language that a guy can't help but hear no matter how far away he is." he said. "One of those words is pregnant. Who's going to be a mom?"

Jessica, Allie, and Emily all shrugged their shoulders and acted innocent. Lexie had no reaction except...nobody else in the club saw it, but he did. Her complexion was dark enough that you could hardly tell, but she was blushing.

"Why Ms. Tenenzapf, I do believe you're blushing." he said. "Is the stork coming to visit you?"

She covered her face with her hands and wished she could disappear.

He lifted up her face and gave her a kiss.

"Really? I'm going to be a dad?" he said.

She nodded.

"Miggy! Drinks for everyone in the house, on me!" he said. "The Stryker name lives on!"

He took her in his arms and kissed her some more. They broke apart, but he was still looking deep into her eyes.

"I love you, baby." he said. "You're going to make a great mom."

"See that's the reaction I was looking for." said Em. "You're so sweet, Erik."

"I'm really happy that we're here to share this moment with all of you." he said. "You're my family, and I love all of you. And I'm going to be a dad."

This was beyond any reaction Lexie could have dreamed of. She didn't know what she was expecting, but it wasn't this. And how did he hear that? She wanted to tell him when they were alone, at home. It seemed that he wanted this as much as she did, more even. She had no idea, they had never talked about it.

She wrapped her arms around him and kissed him.

"Erik Stryker, you're unbelievable." she said. "I love you so much!"

John walked up.

"Seems like we were just talking about you settling down and starting a family." he said. "Congratulations."

"Thanks, Johnny." he said.

"It really sucks that you're leaving." he said.

"It will all work out." he said. "You have no idea how much I wanted this."

"Neither did I." said Lexie.

"We never talked about it." he said.

I didn't dare bring it up." she said. "This isn't the reaction I was expecting. Not complaining, of course, but you surprised me."

"What did you expect?" he asked.

Probably something more like Em's guy, she thought.

"I don't know." she said. "But it couldn't have been better. I'm so happy. We're going to have a baby. I'm going to be a mom."

Bet she never expected to say *that*, he thought.

"We'll have to talk about the next logical step when I get back." he said.

"Don't even say it, I don't want to jinx it." she said.

"I think we both know what I'm talking about though, eh?" he asked.

She just nodded. She was blushing again.

Brendan walked up.

"What's all this then?" he asked. "Did ya win th' lottery, son?"

"In a way." he said. "Lexie's going to have a baby."

"Aye, fath'rhood's rearin' it's ugly head, eh? Seems like it suits ya. Congrats." he said. "Lemme go getcha a proper drink!"

"No, that's okay, Bren." he said. "I'm enjoying it all the same sober."

"Nonsense. How many times are ya goin' ta get this kinda news?" he said. "Hopefully not as oft'n as me da'. I'm not takin' no fer an answer."

He walked away.

Maybe he's right. Just this once. I'm in such a good mood, how could it turn violent?

He looked at Lexie. She shrugged her shoulders.

"You've been doing so good." she said. "Do you really want to open Pandora's Box?"

"I'll do whatever you think." he said. "I don't see how one could hurt. But it's up to you."

"Oh no." she said. "You're not putting this on me. You need to make the decision."

Brendan came back with a rum and Coke with about an inch of Coke just the way he liked it. He looked at Lexie again.

"Don't look at me." she said. "It's up to you. I'm not going to give you permission, cause then it's *my* fault."

"Ya askin' yer ol' lady fer permission, Rikky boy?" he asked. "I never thought I'd see the day."

"I guess just *one* wouldn't hurt." he said.

"Now yer talkin'." he said.

He gave Erik the drink.

Lexie spoke to him in Danish.

"I'm armed." she said. "Please don't make me show these people who I really am. I *will* stop you if you get out of hand. If you're going to do this, just the one. And I would advise against that."

Where the hell did that come from? He couldn't very well say no after what Brendan said.

He took the drink and downed about half of it in one gulp. He felt that familiar sting in his throat, and it seemed that it was instantly swimming in his head.

Lexie was staring daggers at him.

"Come on! I'm going to be a father!" he said. "Let's celebrate!"

He spoke to her in Danish.

"There was no way I could say no after what he said." he said. "There are certain things I can't do. I'll just have this one, then that will be the end of it."

She replied in Danish.

"Standing up for yourself is the opposite of being a pussy." she said. "Just because he's a drunk doesn't mean you have to be."

Everyone at the table looked back and forth to them wondering what they were saying. It was pretty evident that it wasn't pleasant.

He finished the drink. He couldn't believe how she was acting. He used to drink all the time, and it *never* bothered her. He really wanted another one.

"Aye, let me getcha a refill, boyo." he said. "'Nuther just like that one?"

"I'm good, Bren." he said.

"Ya can't stop at jus' one!" he said. "We're celebratin'! Have all th' conversations ya like in a foreign tongue, but don't be a wuss!"

"I've never known anyone who can stop at one." said John.

He looked at Johnny. He looked like someone had just shot his dog.

"You know, Brendan, I get violent when I drink. Part of the reason I stopped." he said. "But I don't need to tell you that, hell, I put *you* in the hospital. The funny thing about it is, I can get violent when I'm sober too. I guess I'm just a violent guy. When people piss me off enough, I'm liable to do just about anything. I humored you and had one drink. Now my humor is about to take an ugly turn. I'll take a ginger ale."

Brendan turned white as a sheet.

"All ya had t' do is say so." he said. "I'm jus' tryin' ta spread good cheer wit' yer happy news an' all. A ginger ale?"

"If ya please, laddie." he said.

He scuttled away quickly.

"You handled that well." said Lexie.

"I look forward to handling something else later." he said, in Danish.

She smiled.

"Oh, sorry, I reverted to Danish." he said. "I was just telling her...that I appreciate her support. Yeah, that's it, *I appreciate her support.*"

She started laughing.

"Yeah you do. This is fun." she said with a knowing look.

She answered in Danish.

"I look forward to fucking you later too." she said, and started laughing some more.

"I don't guess we need a translation to get the jist of *that.*" said Jess.

"I guess some things you can figure it out by the tone." he said.

"I didn't know the word I really wanted to use there." she said.

"I believe the word you're looking for is fuck." he said. "They don't have a separate word for it."

"Good to know." she said.

She started laughing some more.

The problem was that he really wanted another drink, in fact it seemed like he needed it. He had never felt this before. Probably because in the past when he needed a drink, he just took it.

Johnny wrapped his arm around his neck.

"Step into my office." he said.

They went to the back.

"I know you really want another drink right now." he said.

"How?" he asked.

"I've been right where you're at. The difference is that I took another drink and never looked back. Well, obviously I looked back and fixed it, but not that night. It might be best if you go home." he said. "Not that I don't want you around, but this environment...you're asking for trouble. You're starting a family. You don't want your son...or daughter seeing the kind of example that you *were*."

"You're right." he said. "Did I ruin her girl time with her friends by drinking? You know, sharing the news?"

"Not yet." he said.

"You're right, we should get out of here." he said. "I'll go home, I don't have any booze there."

"Get to a meeting tomorrow." he said. "Talk about what you did. And don't let Brendan talk you into stupid shit. If you need to get all dark like you did earlier, that seemed to work pretty good, hell, even *I* was scared."

"Okay." he said.

"You're about to take on the biggest responsibility of your life, and you're no good to anyone drunk." he said.

"Thanks, Johnny." he said.

"You still think Bren is the best choice?" he asked.

"Nothing's changed." he said. "It's not like he just started drinking. He's...Irish. It doesn't seem to cause problems for him."

"You don't know much about his home life." he said.

"I know he bickers with Deirdre quite a bit." he said. "He seems to spend a lot of time in the crib, but he's been that way since I've known him. She just doesn't want to take his shit, that's all. They seem to make it work. I don't know her well, but she seems okay. She must love him, or they would have split years ago."

"Aye, laddie, but she's from the old country too. Alcoholism isn't gender specific. Believe it or not, years past, she's done more damage to him than you did. She nearly beat him to death with a shovel. Then there was the time he shot her. Mind you, neither one of them has ever pressed charges." he said. "Have you ever seen him happy? Besides the fleeting moments of pleasure he may find now and again? He leads a miserable life, moving from one drink to the next. He has no family life, his only kid has disowned them both. You want me to leave my club to that? Is that what you want? For your family?"

Johnny was the very definition of buzzkill right now.

"I never thought I would have a family." he said. "The life I lead..."

"I promise you, son, we'll get back to that someday." he said. "Against all odds, you have a family now. You're going to be a father. Think about what kind of father you want to be."

"Okay, Johnny." he said. "Thanks for this."

"Do you think I can just watch my brother relapse and say nothing?" he said. "If you find yourself in trouble later on, use my number *before* you take a drink. It doesn't matter what time."

"Okay." he said. "I'll see if Lexie wants to go, and if she doesn't, I'll meet up with her later at home."

"No." he said. "Right now, you can't be alone. You leave alone, I'm coming with you. It's simply too dangerous. There are package stores en route. I'm sure she'll come along. She probably wants nothing more than to be with you."

I hope you're right." he said.

***

"Are you sure?" he asked.

"I was right there when she said it." she said. "Erik was thrilled. He even had a drink."

"He had a drink?" he asked.

"Yeah, but it was no big deal, just to celebrate." she said.

Sounds like no big deal to you, but you don't know what I know, he thought.

"How far along is she?" he asked.

"No more than a few weeks." she said. "It might sound funny, but I could tell. There was something different about her."

"Anything else I should know about?" he asked.

"They had a little back and forth in Danish." she said.

"In Danish?" he asked.

"Yeah." she said. "She said his father prefers it. She learned some while they were in Ann Arbor."

"She speaks a lot of languages, but Danish wasn't one of them." he said. "Did it sound like she understood it?"

"When they first got back, he said something, but she said he was going a little fast for her, but she got it anyway." she said. "Last night, she didn't miss a beat. She wanted to learn so she could impress his father."

"I'm sure that's not the only reason." he said. "What else?"

"There was a bit of a tense moment between Erik and Brendan involving a second drink." she said. "Brendan tried to get him to take another drink, then Erik got all serious and scary and Bren backed right down."

"You told me that John is trying to step down last time." he said. "Any news on that?"

"Believe it or not, Erik is going to suggest Brendan." she said. "I can already tell you that John won't like that. He doesn't drink."

"Really?" he asked. "Something I didn't know."

"But I thought you knew everything." she said. "That's what Lexie says."

"That's why I have people like you, Jess." he said.

"I'm happy to help, Mr. Murphy." she said.

"You've done well, Jessica." he said. "This information is good. Meet me at Ivar's tomorrow at 3, and I'll have another envelope for you."

"Thanks, Mr. Murphy. Is it true that you're the mysterious boss who sent Lexie and Erik on that trip down the Nile?"

Someone's been talking out of school. Don't make me think about killing you, Jess.

"I don't know what she told you, Jess, but it was nowhere near that exciting." he said. "Lexie has a vivid imagination, and often fantasizes about being a secret agent. Tomorrow at 3 at Ivar's."

The line went dead.

***

"She's pregnant." he said. "It shouldn't change our plans, she can still do this. It's early on."

"That isn't good news, Anthony." he said. "Not only does it jeopardize her, it also jeopardizes Stryker. They'll both be distracted. This is unacceptable."

Probably considers unplanned pregnancies weakness too, he thought.

"Mr. Andersen, I can assure you that this won't be a problem." he said. "She is one of the strongest people I know, and so is he." he said. "When they get over there, their primary focus will be on the mission. Has there ever been a problem with either of them?"

"That's not the point. This is an unprecedented situation. There's no telling how *either* of them will react." he said. "He's already on thin ice. Her temper got her in trouble with her people, and there's no fixing that. How soon can you have someone else ready?"

He knew what this meant. If he replaced them, they wouldn't be of any use to Leland. And he knew what happened to people who were no longer of use to him.

"Months. I'm spread thin as it is. *They can do this.*" he said. "You need to trust me."

"I don't need to do anything of the sort." he said. "What about the girl in France?"

"She's never done that type of work." he said. "This is a job that requires experience. These two have it in spades. I wouldn't feel comfortable sending anyone else in at this point."

“It’s a good thing that your comfort is of no consequence to me.” he said. “What about Quinn? He did a good job in India.”

“He’s in Australia. Remember? The guns?” he asked. “Besides, this is a two person job, you’ve seen the list.”

“Can you take anyone off Hong Kong?” he asked.

“That situation needs everyone it can get.” he said. “I could even use a couple more, but we’ll manage. We need to stay the course. I know what I’m doing.”

“You know what happens later, don’t you?” he said. “If I let you have your way?”

Probably the same thing that happens if I don’t get my way, so what does it matter? He shouldn’t have told Leland that she was pregnant. But if he didn’t, and he found out some other way, *that* would be worse. He wouldn’t put it past Leland to have someone from the club watching them. Hell, *he* did.

Now he had to try to keep her alive too. If only she wouldn’t have gotten pregnant. Maybe in a week or two he could say she lost it. The problem is that I’m sure they both want it, Jess said as much. It would be hell trying to get them to play along. Maybe not, they’re both smart, they probably have some idea of what’s coming. The sad fact was that even if she did lose the baby, there was a strong possibility that Leland would have her killed anyway. The way he sounded it was a foregone conclusion no matter what happens.

“That’s not necessary.” he said. “And it would ruin him.”

“The way I see it, he’s already ruined.” he said. “And what’s she going to be, mercenary mom? You know what has to happen, Anthony, don’t make me say it.”

“Promise me you’ll at least think about it.” he said. “Losing her...them would be a devastating blow.”

“I’ll reevaluate, but my mind is pretty much made up.” he said. “If you can’t do it, I will. And then you could be next. I would have to question your commitment.”

“See how the mission goes before you make any rash decisions.” he said. “I think you’ll be pleasantly surprised.”

“I admire your commitment to your people, Mr. Murphy.” he said. “At the same time I question your commitment to the greater good. Don’t make me sorry.”

"If you're sorry, it's bad for me too." he said. "I'm giving them my trust because they deserve it. You'll see. If they don't deliver, you can do what you want."

"I don't need your permission to do what I want, Anthony." he said. "Send them on the mission, but if I don't get results, you might not survive either. Think about that the next time you go to bat against me."

The line went dead.

Now I have to worry about *both* of them, he thought. It's unlikely that Lexie will survive this. Having a kid has no place in this world. Particularly with Leland. All I can do at this point is let it play out. *Maybe* the miscarriage idea, but that would be a tough sell. He knew that they could handle the mission, but the rest was out of his hands.

***

"Do we tell Murphy?" he asked.

"No. You're in trouble for going to AA, how do you think his boss will react to this?" she asked. "I wouldn't be surprised if he already knows, anyway."

"How could he?" he asked.

"Are you forgetting who we're talking about?" she asked. "There were a lot of people there last night. It wouldn't be like him not to have someone watching us. Like I said in the beginning, it's best to just assume he knows everything, because he probably does."

He knew it too. He knew what she was going to say before she said it. He hoped they were wrong. Nothing was private with him. Her being pregnant could be a problem. Within a few months there would be no hiding it anyway. He worried about her going on the mission, but he had enough sense not to go down that road. She would go, and take any risks she deemed fit regardless of what he thought. It was best to just accept it. He couldn't stop her from being her, and he wouldn't want her to change. It was part of what he loved about her.

"You ever been on a ship before?" he asked.

"Once or twice." she said.

"I'll hold your hair back if you get seasick." he said. "You can do it right over the side."

"I don't plan to get seasick." she said.

"Nobody does." he said. "There are two kinds of people in the world. People who get seasick every time, and people who never do. We don't know which you are yet."

"What about you?" she asked.

"An old salt like me?" he asked. "I've never been seasick, not once."

"Well if it happens in the morning, I guess I'll have an excuse." she said, patting her belly.

"Of course. Knowing what I know, I think I would put you in the category that doesn't." he said.

"But the morning sickness skews the data." she said. "If we really want to know, you'll have to take me on a cruise after junior is born."

"You think it's going to be a boy?" he asked.

"Women know these things." she said. "We'll try to help him avoid some of the pitfalls that dogged his dad when he was younger."

"What do you mean when I was younger?" he asked. "I still have my share of pitfalls."

"Who are you kidding?" she said. "You've lived a charmed life ever since girls started noticing you."

"Some of those girls *were* the pitfalls." he said. "I haven't done bad lately though."

"Nice save." she said. "So we're going to be newlyweds on a cruise ship. Wonder if anyone will know that the bride's knocked up."

"When will you start showing?" he asked.

"According to what I've read, first time moms don't start showing for 12-16 weeks." she said. "So you have 3 or 4 months to see my body this way. Maybe a little less, I've been pregnant for a while."

"It doesn't matter what your body looks like when you're pregnant, because you're carrying my kid." he said. "You'll be beautiful to me no matter what."

"You can make that call when I start showing." she said. "There's no way I can hold you to that."

"I mean it." he said quietly. "That's a part of me growing inside you. I've never talked about it, but I've wanted this for a long time. Me and Taylor tried. She couldn't get pregnant. I told her that I could pay for whatever treatments she needed. She was so frustrated that she didn't even want to try. Then she talked about adoption, and we weren't even married. It's a great thing, and it's helped a lot of people, but that's not for me. If I can't have my own kid, I don't want one. Does that make sense?"

"More than you know." she said. "I've been told I couldn't have babies. I've never tried, hell, I wasn't trying this time. I just figured that I would never have kids. I've never been with a guy I wanted to have one with until now."

"Have you seen a doctor?" he asked.

"I have an appointment tomorrow." she said. "I'm just going to tell him that I'm going abroad for a while, so he can set me up with what I need for a few weeks."

"Make sure you do that." he said. "I'm doing my best not to play the overbearing dad. We should knock this thing in Ireland out as quickly as possible, though."

"Overbearing is too much, but you can be concerned." she said. "I might not like you telling me what to do, but if you need to you should. I could be bitchy anyway. I'm carrying him, but this is as much you as it is me."

"Thanks." he said. "I think I know by now what I can get away with...even if you're bitchy."

"The baby is the most important thing, don't worry about my feelings." she said. "To a point, of course."

"I probably know when to stop, but if I go too far, just let me know." he said. "I just want you and the baby healthy."

"Me too." she said.

***

She was waiting for him at Ivar's. She had been there since 2:30 and it was getting close to three. She wasn't sure how to approach it, but she was going to ask him today. She had done a good job for him; he said so himself.

And she wasn't really betraying Lexie, the things she told him weren't that important. The Danish thing, the fight with

Bren, the drink...but what about the pregnancy? Maybe she shouldn't have told him that. How could that get her in trouble? He would have found out anyway, according to Lexie he always does. I'm sure it's nothing to worry about.

At exactly 3 PM he walked through the door and headed for her table.

"Ms. Silfin. How are you today?" he asked.

"Doing fine, and yourself?" she asked.

"Good. I really appreciate your help with this." he said. "I would have gotten the information anyway, but it was easier with your help."

"I'm sure you would have." she said. "Should I feel bad about this? Did I get her in trouble?"

"The information that you gave me was necessary so I can keep her *out* of trouble." he said. "You shouldn't feel bad. You only told me what she couldn't, and I would have known anyway. The money helps you, the information keeps Lexie out of trouble. It's a win/win."

"I feel better now." she said.

"Don't tell her we've met." he said "She'll never know we've talked. You should be happy, you did your friend a favor. Sometimes she's not forthcoming with things that aren't a problem until it's too late. You stopped that from happening. This is for you."

He handed her an envelope with several hundred dollar bills.

"Thank you, Mr. Murphy." she said. "I was wondering, how do you decide who works for you?"

"I usually surveil someone for several years before I approach them. It's a long process. I evaluate their strengths and weaknesses. I make sure they can handle the job." he said. "I make sure they have experience with what I want them to do. There are certain things that can't be taught. It's usually years of watching."

"I see." she said.

After hearing all of Lexie's stories, she really wanted to do it. She would love to do it. It was something she was counting on, yet he made it seem like it took years.

"Have you ever been approached by someone who wanted to work for you?" she asked.

Here we go, he thought.

"Someone would need to know what I do to approach me." he said.

"Well, I know what you do." she said.

"No, you don't." he said. "No doubt Lexie told you a lot of glamourous tales of her adventures with Erik. Like I said on the phone, she has a vivid imagination. She tends to exaggerate. I watched her for years before I approached her, Erik too. They both have...skills that the average person doesn't have."

"I could learn those skills." she said.

"Remember when I told you that certain things can't be taught?" he said. "Those are the things I'm looking for. Those are the things I watched Erik and Lexie do for years before I took a chance on them. Things most people simply can't do. *They're* not even working now, and I'm not looking for anyone new."

"I want to try." she said. "It's not just the adventure, it's the money."

"Jess, you have a beautiful voice. If you ever wanted to, you could make more than they ever could singing." he said. "You don't have what it takes to work with me, I know that's blunt, but that's how it is. I can't even find work for Erik and Lexie, and they're my best."

He pulled out a notepad and scribbled a number.

"Take this number, it's Phillip Brooks." he said. "He's a music promoter and manager out of Los Angeles, and he's the best. I know a lot of people. By the time you talk to him, I will have talked to him. He owes me a favor, but after he hears you, he'll owe me another. If you tell him I sent you, he'll be on the next flight to Seattle. All you need to do is sing for him. I'm giving him your number in case you chicken out. When he hears you, you'll probably literally see dollar signs in his eyes. He's going to make you a star. Do you know what this money I gave you is for?"

"For me helping you?" she asked.

"No." he said. "It's for you to forget we ever met. It would be much better for you if you did. Call Phillip when you get home. You're by far the best singer he has."

He got up and walked out.

She looked at the number. It made sense that Lexie and Erik weren't working, they hadn't left Seattle for weeks, except for those few days they went to his parents. What was he talking about? Certain things that can't be taught? Things most people simply can't do?

She tucked the number away. She had no doubt whatsoever that he meant what he said about that guy. If she didn't call him, she could expect a call.

Chapter 17

They were in a bar, it was a small venue, but Tom Petty and the Heartbreakers were playing there. He was sitting at a table with Lexie, Taylor, Jessica, Mike, and Murphy. He really liked Tom Petty, it was the music of his generation.

Well, she was an American girl
Raised on promises
She couldn't help thinkin'
That there was a little more to life somewhere else
After all it was a great big world
With lots of places to run to
And if she had to die tryin'
She had one little promise she was gonna keep

"I really am an American girl." said Taylor. "Not like *some* people."

"Me too." said Jessica. "These guys are opening for me in L.A. next month."

"That's right, you got the contract." said Lexie. "How's that working out?"

"Couldn't be better." she said. "You were right, Anthony, I just needed a little exposure. Thanks for the hookup."

He held his finger to his lips and nodded towards Erik and Lexie.

"After I heard you, I thought it would be a sin if the rest of the world couldn't." he said.

"Wait, when did you hear her?" asked Erik.

"At the Brass Caterpillar, of course." he said.

"You were there?" he asked.

Erik and Lexie looked at him confused.

O yeah, all right
Take it easy, baby
Make it last all night
She was an American girl

"You may be an American girl, but that's the only part of this song that relates to you." said Lexie. "By the way, I was born in New York."

"I don't know, I've always wanted to see the 'great big world with lots of places to run to'." said Taylor. "And now I have my chance."

"Because you're a model?" she said. "What a weak way to see the world. You're not living, you're just walking on a stage. Spend a day in my shoes."

"I will." she said.

Anthony held his finger to his lips again and nodded towards Erik and Lexie.

"The two of you need to learn to keep a secret." he said.

"What secret?" asked Erik.

"Don't pay any attention to them." he said. "They have delusions of grandeur. Even after she becomes a star, this one still wants to get shot at."

Well it was kind of cold that night,
She stood alone on her balcony
Yeah, she could hear the cars roll by,
Out on 441 like waves crashin' on the beach
And for one desperate moment
There he crept back in her memory
God it's so painful when something that's so close
Is still so far out of reach

"I'm giving him something you never could." said Lexie. "We're going to have a baby."

"Don't count your humans before they're hatched." said Taylor. "You were never supposed to have a baby, and you know it. It's unlikely someone with Polycystic Ovarian Syndrome will make it to full term. That's good news for the baby, if nothing else."

Lexie's hand, which was already resting on the butt of her gun quickly withdrew it from the holster and aimed it before Erik stopped her.

"Nobody has to die here." he said. "It's a simple difference of opinion."

Lexie looked to the floor and swore under her breath.

"What do you know about PCOS?" she asked.

"What's PCOS?" he asked.

"Did you hear what she just said?" she asked. "And you're defending her? Are you drinking again?"

He looked down and saw a double rum and Coke in front of him and several empty glasses.

"No, just ginger ale." he said. "I'm not defending anyone."

"You should be defending me!" she said. "Your baby's growing in my belly!"

How did I get myself in this mess? She was right, of course, it did appear that he had taken Taylor's side.

"We both know that baby ain't making it nine months." she said. "Be lucky to live three."

"That's it." said Lexie.

She shot her seven times, the bullets forming a smiley face on Taylor's face. She looked down.

"I was trying for a frowny face." she said. "Oh well. Aesthetics aside, the results are the same."

"Thanks, Lexie, she was getting on my nerves." said Jess. "She's probably right, though. You'll lose the baby."

O yeah, all right
Take it easy, baby
Make it last all night
She was an American girl

"These guys really are great." said Jessica.

They finished the song. Tom was looking at Jessica.

"I'd like to bring someone up here who is the best voice of her generation." he said. "We love this girl. Put your hands together for Jessica Silfin!"

Jess got up there, and they bathed her in her signature blue light.

"I'd like to dedicate this one to one of my best friends, Taylor Whitman." she said. "She's over there at my table with a smiley face."

He woke in a cold sweat. Why is it always in a bar? He got up and went to the bathroom. He looked in the toilet, and there was a lot of blood in there. He went downstairs to find Lexie crying on the couch.

"What's wrong, hon?" he asked.

"I lost the baby." she said.

***

They were at the club, and the girls were fawning over Lexie. She was distraught, but ready to move on. It wasn't meant to be.

She had Polycystic Ovarian Syndrome, and doctors in the past had told her that she would probably never get pregnant. They also told her that if she did, the risk of a miscarriage early on was likely. She hadn't had a chance to tell Erik about it.

When she did, he made her repeat it twice. Then he got quiet. He comforted her, but he was in another world. She asked him about it, and he said he had another crazy dream. He didn't want to talk about it. Then asked her again to repeat what she said. She told him and he got quiet again. When she demanded to know what it was about, he told her. In the dream, Taylor had mentioned Polycystic Ovarian Syndrome specifically, and told her she would lose the baby. So now he's having detailed prophetic dreams. No wonder he got quiet.

Now she was sitting with the girls at the club trying not to talk about it.

"Let's talk about something else." she said. "We'll try again when he gets back from deployment."

She hadn't told them about the PCOS. It wasn't easy to talk about. She wished that she never got that shred of hope for a few days, only to get it bitterly crushed.

"There's a promoter from L.A. coming up to listen to me sing. Says he has to hear me." said Jessica. "Apparently someone saw me that night at the Brass Caterpillar and told him about it."

"What's his name?" asked Lexie.

"Phillip Brooks." she said.

She let out a low whistle.

"He's one of the biggest guys on the West Coast." she said. "My cousin is a music producer, and he's mentioned this guy. He's supposed to be the best. I wonder who told him about it. Must be someone big to be able to talk to him."

"Who knows?" she said. "He called me and said he has to hear me. Out of the blue."

"This is your chance, girl." she said. "Phillip Brooks can make you a star."

"Do you really think so?" she asked. "Do you think I'm good enough?"

"The man is flying up from L.A. because *he has to hear you.*" she said. "A guy that big doesn't just get on a plane to check out someone who isn't good. Besides, you *are* good."

"I hope so." she said.

"You're lucky your stage presence is better than the person I'm talking to now." she said. "A little confidence. You got this."

"Okay." she said.

"I give up." she said. "Just get up there and sing. The rest will take care of itself."

Erik walked over.

"Guess what?" she said. "Some big shot L.A. promoter is coming up to hear Jess sing. She's going to be a star!"

"Uh huh." he said.

"Don't be so excited." she said. "A little enthusiasm."

"No, that's okay." said Jess. "He's broken up about..."

"The dream." he said.

"What?" she asked.

"Jess was in it too." he said. "She was talking about going on tour...Tom Petty and the Heartbreakers were going to open for her. It was all arranged by..."

He couldn't say it. Murphy. Had he been talking to Jess?

"That's ridiculous." she said. "Tom Petty opening for me. You dreamed this?"

"I have to go." he said.

He walked out the exit into the parking lot. He lit a cigarette and inhaled deeply. There was an explanation to this, and he knew it, but he didn't want to think about it. He pulled out his phone and dialed the number.

"Mr. Stryker." he said. "To what do I owe the pleasure?"

"She lost the baby." he said.

He was quiet for a moment.

"Are you still there?" he asked.

"I don't know what's more shocking, her losing the baby or you knowing that I knew." he said.

"You found out from Jess." he said.

Another brief moment of silence.

"I don't know what she told you, but I can assure you..." he said.

"Stop." he said. "I know. Maybe when you were scrambling my brains when I was young, you connected a few wires that should have stayed separate. You hooked her up with a promoter from L.A.? He's coming up here to listen to her?"

"Whatever she told you..." he said.

"I dreamed it." he said. "Just like I dreamed about Lexie's Polycystic Ovarian Syndrome, and that she was going to lose the baby. I've never heard of that before. Yet I dreamt it. Then Lexie tells me about it when I wake up after she loses the baby. Jess wants to become a spy, but she doesn't have what it takes, so you pull some strings and get her an audition with a hotshot promoter hoping she'll go away. How am I doing? Sound about right? Do you see what's happening here?"

"It would appear that your dreams..." he said. "Do you know what this means?"

"It means a lot of things." he said.

"I want you to see someone when you get back from Ireland." he said. "There's always been the possibility that one of you..."

"You want me to see someone?" he said. "So you can fuck with my brain some more?"

"So I can help you." he said.

"I don't need your kind of help." he said.

"This is something you're going to have to deal with." he said. "I have the best people. I'm not trying to hurt you. I want to help you control it."

Lexie was walking up to him.

"Do you want to talk to her?" he asked.

"Yes, but we need to work this out." he said. "When you get back."

"Okay, here she is." he said.

She covered the phone.

"Are you okay?" she asked.

He just nodded.

"Hello?" she said.

"Erik already told me." he said. "I'm sorry for your loss."

But at the same time it keeps you alive, which is a good thing, he thought.

"Thank you." she said. "What's going on with him?"

"Something that was always a possibility, but we never expected." he said. "I should say *I* never expected it, the doctors have believed it for years. The good news is that it will keep him alive. Don't let on, he still has to quit that club."

"Seems like things have changed. He might even be able to do whatever the fuck he wants." she said. "So is he psychic or something now?"

"Or something. Smarter people than me know about it. Please try to get him to come in after you get back. This is groundbreaking. The club is still a problem with the boss. Also logistically." he said. "The Irish Kings get whacked, and he's back a week later? If you think that his condition gives him liberty to call the shots, you're sadly mistaken. It's not just me you have to worry about."

"I'll do my best." she said.

"Are you okay?" he asked. "Are we still on for the mission?"

"Relax, Anthony, I'm still in." she said. "What happened wasn't totally unexpected. We'll leave at the end of the week."

"Good." he said. "Do your best with Erik."

The line went dead.

"He says whatever's going on with you buys us some time at least." she said.

"Whatever's going on with me is the result of them tinkering with my brain when I was a kid." he said. "You should have heard him. He could hardly contain himself. He's looking at this as a scientific breakthrough. I'm looking at it as more damage from that fucking camp I went to."

"My guess is that it could be worse." she said.

"He says 'there's always been the possibility that one of you...'" he said. "Like we were a bunch of lab rats. I'm the experiment that worked, I guess. Makes me wonder what happens next."

"You need to let them have a look at you when we get back." she said. "Whatever it is, you can't self-diagnose it. There's no telling what could happen."

"Does he have you working on me now too?" he asked. "I expect it from him, but you? Whose side are you on?"

"I'm on your side." she said. "This shit scares me. Maybe they can give you something."

"Give me something?" he asked. "I wouldn't take baby aspirin from *them*. They're the ones who fucked me up in the first place."

"And they're the only ones who can help you." she said. "Has it been so bad? The only side effect I see is photographic memory, and most of us would kill for that."

"It's convenient that you failed to mention the mind control." he said. "By the way, the photographic memory isn't for me. They isolated a section of my brain so I can catalog my memories so they can use me to carry messages to other people. I'm essentially a walking tape recorder, whose orders are to self-destruct if they catch me. I could see these people keeping me in a tiny room in hopes that I can forecast the future. *That's* exactly the way their minds work. Me being fed by tubes, induced to sleep, so that they can see the future."

"Is that really true?" she said. "About the memory? I think you're making too much of this."

"You weren't there." he said. "They didn't send you to a camp and brainwash you. From the research I've seen, it *is* true. Not that there's much of that, the CIA destroyed almost all o9f the information on MKUltra. Of course, I don't remember ever being sent on a mission like that, but why would I? I'm sure they would find a way to make sure I *don't* remember that!"

"But you don't remember anything about that camp!" she said.

"And that's supposed to make it *better*?" he said. "Let someone take two weeks out of your life, and see how you feel."

"You're right. They didn't do that to me." she said. "But it could get worse if you don't get checked out."

"It could get worse if I *do* get checked out." he said. "I don't trust these people. He worked extensively with the MK program. And it went on long after they said it was over. Don't think that it can't happen to you. I'm sure Murphy has people working on *that* right now."

This is going nowhere, she thought. I can't really blame him either. I might be thinking the same thing. She had heard of MKUltra, but only what everyone else had heard. The LSD, sensory deprivation, hypnosis, verbal abuse, and other forms of psychological torture. It was officially supposed to force confessions through mind control. It was also officially over in 1973, but that never happened. From what she could understand, Erik's experience was one of several offshoot programs designed to create the perfect soldier. In 1973 the CIA destroyed all traces of the original MKUltra program. Before that happened, they started several other projects, including the one Erik was involved in. He had told her as much as he knew about it, which wasn't much. The problem was that he couldn't find any information about it. The CIA destroyed any evidence of any projects immediately. They had learned their lesson.

"Look, I just want you to be sane. And happy." she said. "I worry if you go it alone, you're not going to get the help you need. *I'm on your side.*"

"If you're on my side, then at least recognize the danger." he said. "I don't want to become a prophetic vegetable, which is a distinct possibility if they get their hands on me again. Let me think about this."

"Okay." she said. "I love you, and I won't let them do that to you."

"Like you can stop them." he said.

"We should go home." she said. "It's been a tough day...for both of us."

"I'm really sorry if it sounded like I think you're abandoning me, especially after what happened to you...us." he said. "I just don't trust those people, and if Murph has his way, he's going to send me right back to them. Are you okay? I don't want my thing to overshadow what happened to you."

"I'm fine." she said. "This wasn't totally unexpected. The Po..."

"The Polycystic Ovarian Syndrome." he said. "I know. Yesterday I didn't know what that was. When I woke up, I knew it before you told me. Are you sure you're okay?"

"If you want to take me home and try to make another one I wouldn't argue." she said.

"We better get going then." he said.

***

It was a small venue again. Amy Winehouse was on stage, and she looked a little drunk. She was still beautiful, and her singing was spectacular. She had really big black hair, and lots of tattoos. She was really skinny.

"This one's off of Back to Black." she said. "It's a pleasure playing to a small crowd like this. You might think we all love mobs of adoring fans, and all, but I prefer a more intimate setting. This goes out to my Blake, wherever he is. I take my part of the blame, baby."

The British accent definitely didn't match up to her singing voice.

Meet you downstairs in the bar and hurt,
Your rolled-up sleeves in your skull t-shirt,
You say, "What did you do with him today?"
And sniffed me out like I was Tanqueray,
'Cause you're my fella, my guy,
Hand me your Stella and fly,
By the time I'm out the door,
You tear me down like Roger Moore,
I cheated myself,
Like I knew I would,
I told you I was trouble,
You know that I'm no good,

The waiter came up and asked what people wanted.

"This is going to sound like a weird question, but what year is it?" asked Erik.

"2006." he said. "Isn't this amazing? She's on a U.S. tour, and she stops in here. This place is known for that, you know. The Red Hot Chili Peppers played here once. Just showed up and got up on stage, no shit."

"What will you have?" he asked.

"Ginger ale." he said.

"Good, rum and Coke comin' right up." he said.

"I said ginger ale." he said.

The waiter was gone. He looked down and saw several empty drinks that looked a lot like rum and Cokes.

Upstairs in bed, with my ex-boy,
He's in a place, but I can't get joy,
Thinking on you in the final throes,
This is when my buzzer goes,

Run out to meet you, chips and pitta,
You say, "When we're married,"
'Cause you're not bitter,
"There'll be none of him no more,"
I cried for you on the kitchen floor,

I cheated myself,
Like I knew I would,
I told you I was trouble,
You know that I'm no good,

"I would never do that to you, you know." said Taylor. "You rolled out the red carpet, but I never cheated. Not even once. She says she cheated herself, because she feels guilty. I did nothing wrong. I just need to wait this thing out. Didn't I tell you she would lose the baby? Damaged goods."

"You never even got that far." said Lexie. "Couldn't even get pregnant. That's what he's always wanted, you know. You ask me, there's something wrong with *your* shit. Young healthy girl like you? You should be popping out babies left and right. At least I have an excuse."

"Can you two please stop fighting?" he asked. "I'm trying to listen to the song."

"She started it." said Lexie. "Don't you want to be free?"

"Of course I do." he said. "No one has ever stopped me from doing that."

"I hate to keep flip-flopping Erik, but I need to side with Taylor on this one. Chances are..."

Sweet reunion, Jamaica and Spain,
We're like how we were again,

I'm in the tub, you on the seat,
Lick your lips as I soak my feet,
Then you notice little carpet burn,
My stomach drop and my guts churn,
You shrug and it's the worst,
Who truly stuck the knife in first?

I cheated myself,
Like I knew I would
I told you I was trouble,
You know that I'm no good,

"Chances are what?" he asked.

"What do I know?" he asked. "This is the future. You're the only one who knows *that*. Amy Winehouse is here, she was a teenager in 1997. She just came out with 'Back to Black', it's an incredibly successful album. I really need to get you in to see Dr. Heisenberg. He'll straighten you out."

"I'm not seeing any of your 'doctors'." he said. "They're the ones who screwed me up in the first place."

"Screwed you up?" he asked. "They made you better than you could ever hope to be. I know you feel it."

"I feel nothing." he said. "I just want to be normal."

The crowd went wild. As the cheering dissipated, she started speaking again.

"You know you did Taylor wrong, Erik, admit it." she said. "It wasn't as bad as Blake did me, but you're not innocent."

"What the fuck are you doing here, anyway?" asked Lexie. "Don't you have a runway to walk down?"

"You know nothing, Lex." she said. "I'm waiting for him to be through with you."

"Could be a while." she said.

"Not as long as you think." she said. "When it's over, he's going to need someone to help him pick up the pieces, and I'll be right there. And you'll be gone."

"That's it." she said.

She pulled out her gun and took aim.

"I have to stop you there, Lexie." said Murphy. "This isn't how it happens. Ask Erik, he knows. He can see the future."

"Is this true, Erik?" she asked.

"I don't have that information yet." he said.

"Sure you do, Erik, it's 2006, and Lexie isn't here." said Murphy.

"She's right there." he said.

He looked over, and Lexie faded away to nothing.

He woke with a jolt. What the fuck was that? Does this mean that she has less than nine years left? Maybe it isn't always true, he thought. But he believed that Amy Winehouse was a real person, and she comes out with a hit album in 2006. He would have to tell Jess to stop using that song. But how would he explain it?

He looked over at Lexie. She was asleep with a slight grin on her face, like she knew something he didn't. Sorry, babe, it's the other way around.

Chapter 18

He got up, went downstairs and made some coffee. Huck was doing circles around him, rubbing his face on his legs.

"You're going to stay with Aunt Casey." he said. "I'm leaving end of the week. If you're good, I'll bring something back for you."

He could hear Huck purring loudly.

Lexie made her way downstairs.

"Coffee?" he asked.

"Sure." she said. "You cooking breakfast too?"

"Yeah." he said. "Bacon and eggs?"

"Sounds great." she said. "What are you doing up so early?"

"Another weird dream." he said.

"Did you see anything from the future?" she asked.

"Amy Winehouse is real." he said. "Probably a fourteen or fifteen year old girl in London right now, but she's real. That song gets released in 2006."

"I guess we should tell Jess, but how?" she said.

"Diplomatically." he said. "But she shouldn't use it anymore. Amy would probably come to Seattle and kick her ass. 9 years from now, of course."

"You think she would do that?" she asked. "After all, if Jess makes it a hit now, isn't it hers?"

"I'm not up on the time traveling rules, after all, I didn't exactly know I was in the future the first time." he said. "But Amy Winehouse owns that song. It has more meaning for her than it ever will for Jess."

Wait. Lexie didn't fade away in the first dream, and that was obviously at least 2006. Maybe she'll be okay. I have no idea what the rules are.

"Anything else happen?" she asked.

"You and Taylor were both there, bickering as always." he said. "Amy sang another song from the album 'Back to Black', it gets released in 2006."

"You know I've only met her once, right?" she said. "And I behaved myself, it was very cordial."

"It was a dream." he said.

"What was the new song about?" she asked.

“Her cheating on her boyfriend. Blake.” he said. “Probably a two way street, or maybe not. She sang about how she cheated on him and how he didn’t care. Of course Taylor reminded me that she never cheated on me, even though I gave her permission.”

“See to me, that’s self-serving.” she said. “It’s great that she was an angel while you were gone, but to bring it up in that context defeats the purpose. Or she’s trying to make you feel guilty for taking advantage of the deal.”

“Trust me, I don’t need her to make me feel guilty.” he said. “I wanted to be good, I just couldn’t. Probably another side effect of the alcohol. They meant nothing. I felt guilty every time.”

“Would you ever do that to me?” she asked.

“I don’t know if I would ever get the chance.” he said. “I think we’re a team now. We work well together, you can’t go back home...I don’t see us going separate ways after this is all over.”

“That wasn’t what I was looking for, but I’ll take it.” she said.

“I didn’t mean it like it sounded.” he said. “Who knows what the future holds?”

“You do.” she said.

“I don’t get to pick and choose what I find out.” he said. “That‘s if this thing is even real.”

“You believe in Amy Winehouse, don’t you?” she asked. “How crazy does that sound?”

“You’re right.” he said. “But it’s possible that I just have weird dreams.”

“Come on!” she said. “Polycystic Ovarian Syndrome. I know if you knew what it was, you would remember. But you only saw it in a dream. Maybe all that programming when you were a kid triggered something. You’re seeing things in your dreams.”

“I don’t know what’s going on, but Murphy seems to think he does.” he said. “That’s what scares me.”

“We’ll get through this, baby.” she said. “I’m right here with you.”

“Okay.” he said.

He brought her the bacon and eggs.

"Going out to smoke." he said.
He walked out on the balcony and stared at the sound. He lit a cigarette. He pulled out his phone and dialed the number.
"Hello?" she said.
"It's me." he said. "I was just wondering how you were."
"I'm fine, Erik, how are you?" she said. "You don't sound too good."
"More weird dreams." he said.
"You and those dreams." she said. "What was it about?"
"That's not important." he said. "I'm starting to get bits and pieces of the future in them."
"Oh." she said. "Anything I should know?"
"Amy Winehouse is real." he said.
"What makes you say that?" she asked.
"I saw her last night...in my dream. It was 2006." he said. "The album that that song was on had just been released, it's called 'Back to Black.'"
"I was there?" she asked.
"Of course, you're in almost all of these." he said. "After I figured out that I was seeing stuff from the future, I asked someone what year it was. They said 2006."
"Do you believe it?" she asked.
"From another dream." he said. "Lexie has a condition. Polycystic Ovarian Syndrome. She was pregnant. She had a miscarriage. I came up with the name of her condition from a dream, before she even told me about it. You know me. How could I dream it if I didn't already know what it is? I didn't have any idea what it was before the dream. When I woke up, she had lost the baby, and explained this condition to me...but I already knew. And there's some other stuff that I knew about Jes...never mind, it's not important."
"She was pregnant?" she asked.
"Do you even hear what I'm saying, Taylor?" he asked.
"Sorry." she said.
"You could always figure this stuff out." he said. "Any ideas?"
"Dream up the lottery numbers." she said. "I don't know, Erik."
Where are you?" he asked.
"Monte Carlo." she said. "We did a bikini shoot yesterday."

"Sorry I missed that." he said.
"Are you okay, Erik?" she asked.
"I think so." he said. "I just wanted to hear your voice."
"Me too." she said. "I'm glad you called. Please accept my condolences for your loss, and express them to Lexi as well. Whether she believes me or not, I am sorry for her. That's gotta be tough."
"She's doing okay with it." he said. "Of course I didn't know ahead of time, but with her condition, this wasn't an unlikely outcome."
"When are you going to Ireland?" she asked.
"End of the week." he said. "There was something else."
"In the dream?" she asked.
Yeah." he said. "Murphy was there. Lexie was about to shoot you, but he stops her. Said 'This isn't how it happens.' Tells her to ask me, because I can see the future. I don't know anything, of course. He says 'Sure you do, Erik, it's 2006, and Lexie isn't here.' I look over at her, and she fades away to nothing. I don't know what that means."
She was quiet for a moment.
"It might not mean anything." she said. "Probably everything you see doesn't necessarily come true."
"The part that bothers me is that *he* pointed it out." he said. "Like he knows something."
"You're probably overthinking this." she said. "I'm sure she'll be fine."
"I hope you're right." he said.
"I'm taking Huck to stay with Casey." he said.
"Say hi to her for me, and of course, little miss Dee." she said.
"Dee will be happy to have Huck around for a while." he said.
"I'm sure he'll be happy to be there too." she said. "I gotta go, they're calling me for a shoot. I love you, Erik. Be safe."
"I love you too." he said.
"That's nice to hear." she said.
"You chewed me out in a dream for how long it took me." he said. "Just making up for lost time."
"Call me if you ever want to talk...or even if you don't." she said.

"Phone works both ways." he said.
"I can't." she said. "Not with *her* around."
"What? Are you the other woman now?" he asked.
"So it would seem." she said. "I don't want to get you in trouble."
"It would be nice to hear from you." he said. "But if you don't want to call, I guess it will be up to me."
"That's not too much pressure, is it?" she asked.
"You're funny, Whitman." he said. "Be safe."
"You too." she said.
He hung up.
Lexi walked out to the balcony and lit a cigarette.
"Who was that?" she asked.
"What?" he asked.
"I know you don't think you're that slick." she said. "You were on the phone, I saw you."
"Oh, that." he said. "It was Taylor."
"She called you?" she asked.
"No...she always had a way of figuring out my dreams." he said. "I thought I should run this latest development by her."
"Really?" she asked.
"Yeah, you know, another perspective." he said.
He was trying to make it sound as innocent as possible, but it wasn't working. There weren't any overt gestures of anger, but he could see the bubbles rising to a boil inside of her.
"So what did she have to say?" she asked, calmly.
"I think she believes me." he said. "I told her what happened...with the baby, she sends her condolences, by the way. Thinks not necessarily everything I see will come true. Did I tell you about Jess?"
"What about Jess?" she asked.
"She was working for Murphy. I'm not going to let on that I know, and neither should you." he said. "Nothing serious, just getting information about us. That's how he knew about the pregnancy. After your wild tales, she wants to do what we do. Murph knows she doesn't have the right stuff, so he pulls some strings to get her an audition with the hotshot from L.A. I knew it all before I talked to him, and after a little feigned shock, he admitted to everything."
"Huh." she said. "Really? Jess?"

"Don't be too hard on her." he said. "Anthony approached her. You know how he is."
"Yeah, I know." she said. "We couldn't bring it up even if we wanted to."
She felt betrayed. She thought Jess was her friend. Still, Anthony probably flashed some cash, not much, but a lot to Jess. Hell, *she* would probably do it under the same circumstances.
"Yeah, that wouldn't be a good idea." he said.
"So what did your ex think of that?" she asked.
"I didn't tell her *that* part." he said.
I just told her the part about you dying.
"At least some things are sacred." she said.
"I'm sorry I called her." he said. "She's just good at this stuff."
"Did it help?" she asked.
Not for the reasons you're thinking, he thought. It did help to talk to her...hear her voice, know that she's okay. He wasn't sure what that meant, but it was a little disturbing that he turned to his ex to help with something instead of her. And now there's a secret. He couldn't very well tell her that she might die. But she didn't give him anything he didn't already know. It just felt good to talk to her.
"It usually does." he said.
"I don't like you calling her, but if it's helping you with your shit, that's not a bad outcome." she said. "I know you love me."
"I do." he said. "And you have nothing to worry about."
"Okay." she said, doubtfully.
"I love you." he said. "That's not going to change."
"Okay." she said. "But you know me, if there's a way to fuck this up, I probably will."
"Me too." he said quietly.

***

"She lost the baby." he said. "So there's no need for the final solution."
"That remains to be seen." he said. "If it happened once, it can happen again. Best to nip these things in the bud."

"I'll make sure she doesn't." he said. "It will never happen again. There's something else."

"What would that be, Mr. Murphy?" he asked.

"You know all about the MK program." he said. "Stryker was one of the seventeen. He's starting to exhibit precognitive abilities." he said. "This is what we've been waiting for. By the time he returns from Ireland, he should be ready for the next stage."

"Very interesting." he said. "This is excellent news. I had given up on the seventeen. How many years has it been? Has there been any developments with the others?"

"Nine of them are dead," he said. "Six are in mental institutions, and Stryker and Jacobs are with us."

"What of Jacobs?" he asked.

"Well, I *say* he's with us, but that's not quite accurate." he said. "I can't have him do anything important. He has all of his faculties, but he's plagued by nightmares to the point that he avoids sleep. He's good in the field, but he has trouble focusing. I have doctors working with him, but they don't predict any change."

"Why haven't you kil...ah, right, he's one of *them*." he said. "Still there comes a time to cut losses. I'm going to look into this. So Stryker..."

"Exactly." he said. "It finally happened. I'll bring him in as soon as the mission is over. He needs a little time to adjust before we start the next stage, and if they handle this thing in Ireland like they should, he'll be ready when it's over."

Leland knew that he couldn't kill Stryker now, even if he wanted to. After all these years! He had doubted quite a bit of what those MK spooks said, but it was finally producing results. There had been so many other programs since then that he had all but forgot about the seventeen. He didn't even know that Stryker was one of them. Could it really work? The precognition was the first sign. One out of seventeen wasn't a great percentage, unless you don't care about the other sixteen. And he didn't give a shit about the others.

"This is good news, Anthony." he said. "Keep me apprised. What else is going on?"

"Hong Kong will go next week. Quinn is in the outback running guns with the Aborigines. It's all set up for delivery to Iraq." he said.

"Good." he said. "Give the Arabs guns, and they'll kill each other...maybe a few Jews. Either way, it keeps them out of our back yard. The Hong Kong thing has to happen. Before next week."

"I'll make sure that it does, Mr. Andersen." he said.

"And what of the girl in France?" he asked.

"She's coming along nicely." he said. "There's been another development with her. The doctors have sworn me to secrecy until they've done more tests. You'll know as soon as they give the okay. I'm not sure if she's ready yet, but soon."

He never liked it when Murphy knew something that he didn't. He would find out within the hour.

"That's not what I want to hear, Anthony." he said. "See that she *is* ready. At a moment's notice. That's why she's there."

"Yes, Mr. Andersen. I'll just sat that...never mind sir." he said. "Those doctors take these things seriously. I'll just say that this development is good news."

"Excellent. Let me know of any developments with Stryker." he said.

"Yes sir." he said.

The line went dead.

I guess that went as well as expected, he thought. A stay of execution for both of them, but he was still worried about Lexie. The whole 'nip these things at the bud' comment. The thing that could save her would be her relationship with Erik. He definitely doesn't want to take any chances with him now. But he's a heartless bastard. He might not see the value of keeping her around. He needed to set up his contingency plan now. If worse came to worse, he would do it his way. He picked up the phone and made the call.

***

They were back at the club for one more night before they left. It was somewhat of an impromptu party, Lexie was at a table with the girls, and Erik was talking to John.

"So, Southeast Asia? Africa?" he asked.

"I wouldn't rule out an unscheduled stop somewhere else, but yeah." he said. "Asia is always fun."

"Probably a girl in every port, eh?" he asked.

"That's really not necessary." he said. "Pussy finds you whether you're looking or not."

"Will you be looking?" he asked. "Or are you going to try to stay true to her?"

"I'm going to try." he said. "It will be tough, the way they hound you over there. I was never faithful to Taylor, but I think the alcohol had a lot to do with that."

"How's that going?" he asked.

"Okay." he said. "I have a few other things going on. It helps to talk."

"They have meetings everywhere." he said. "Even in P.I. if you can get past the main drag. I've been stateside since I've been sober, so I never had to try it. I made a list for you of where you can find meetings. If they aren't where they're supposed to be, all you need to do is pick up a phone. AA is everywhere, because people are fucked up everywhere."

"Thanks, John." he said.

"What about Africa?" he asked. "Anything going on there?"

"It's the place where I first met Lexie. If I have time, I'm going to visit this place we went to the first night. Called 'Yul's' on the beach.' Right on the Indian Ocean. We discovered a sandbar out there that I suspect she already knew about. She acted all cold when we first met, but after we eat, she says she's going for a swim, and would I like to join her?" he said. "She just gets up and starts walking towards the beach. I follow, and discover a trail of her clothes as I'm going. We get in the water, I swim past her, and there I am treading water and I see her getting taller. She's walking up this sandbar, until she's standing there naked. She gives me a look, and I get up there too. I don't need to tell you the rest."

He started shaking his head.

"That whole philosophy you told me about earlier? Treat 'em like shit and act like you don't care?" he asked. "Is that how you make it happen with women?"

"Not so much treat 'em like shit, as much as don't take any shit from them. You have to understand in *that* situation, she was trying to act like a badass. We had just met, and if I didn't stand up for myself, it would have sent the wrong message." he said. "You can probably tell just looking at her that she doesn't meet too many guys that don't do literally anything she wants. I had to let her know that it wasn't going to be that way with me. I think she respected that, and that's why she gave it up."

"So what were you doing in Africa with her?" he said.

"Mostly traveling." he said.

"Ah, one of those things you can't talk about." he said.

"Unfortunately." he said. "It's too bad, because it's a great story."

"I bet it is." he said. "You doing anything you can't talk about this time out?"

"Nope. Just a run to the far reaches for goods they don't have here." he said.

"But you wouldn't tell me if you were anyway." he said.

"John that part of my life has been over for a long time." he said. "It was exciting while it was going on, but that's not me anymore. I'm just a sailor and a biker now, I seem to find enough trouble with that."

"Okay." he said. "If you ever want to tell me, you know I can keep a secret."

"If they ever tell me I can, you'll be the first to know." he said. "If you knew who it was, you'd probably leave me alone. These are people that even guys like us wouldn't want to cross."

"Fair enough." he said. "But on my deathbed when it doesn't matter anymore, I want to know."

"It's entirely likely that you'll outlive me, John." he said. "I'm serious about that. All the shit I've done, the people I've associated with...and that doesn't even include the club."

"Something tells me you'll be fine." he said.

Wait until you get that envelope in a few days, he thought.

"Whatever happens, you'll always be my brother." he said.

"Goes without saying, but I appreciate you saying it." he said. "You'll always be part of this family."

***

It was just her and Jess, everyone else had said their goodbyes.

"So you're going to New York City?" she asked.

"To see my uncle." she said. "I haven't seen him since I was a little kid. He's Ari's father. Remember I told you about my cousin? The music producer?"

"Right." she said. "The guy who knows Phillip."

"Yeah." she said. "I have a little bad news for you. That song? 'Love is a Losing Game'? Erik's aunt Debbie wrote it. She made a single out of it in the seventies, it was actually pretty big on the East Coast for a while. So you probably shouldn't use it anymore."

"Well, that's disappointing." she said. "It shouldn't matter. Jason's been writing for me. Phillip hired him to deal with the music. I have a couple that I wrote words for."

"It sounds like things are going well." she said. "This could be big."

"He wants an album by the end of the month." she said. "He's going to promote the shit out of it, and I should be on tour within a year."

"Look at you!" she said. "My little Jessica a star! Didn't I tell you?"

"I'm a little nervous about it." she said. "It's all happening so fast. Jason has me booked at the Caterpillar the next four weeks straight. Just on the weekends, Lithium will be playing behind me. He says I should get my own band, based on my sound. They're mostly grunge. He knows some people."

"Wow. This is really happening." she said.

Wonder who Murphy knows.

"I guess." she said.

"Confidence, Jess." she said. "You need to work on that. You'll be calling the shots. You can't be indecisive. They'll take advantage of you if you're not strong."

"It's so easy for you." she said. "I doubt anyone's ever pushed you around. How do you do it?"

She thought about Herschel...and Stryker. Those were the only ones she had ever been submissive to. She just learned from an early age not to take any shit.

"Some people are born with it, I guess. But you were born with something better. An amazing musical talent. You can learn to be confident. One word, it's simple. No." she said. "Say it and mean it when someone's trying to get over on you. Once you've said it you can't change your mind. *You* made the decision, they'll have to live with it. They want you, not the other way around."

"Okay, thanks Lexie." she said. "There's something I have to tell you."

"Okay." she said.

"This guy came to see me..." she said.

Lexie put her finger on Jessica's lips.

"A good spy never reveals her secrets." she said. "I haven't told you everything, and I don't expect you to."

"But..." she said.

"This is a good time to practice." she said. "You're trying to tell me something you shouldn't. Use your confidence and self-control and keep it to yourself. I won't be offended."

She knows.

"Shit, you know. I'm sorry, Lexie." she said.

"I know nothing." she said. "I only want to hear confidence from you. You're going to be a star. Don't forget about me when you're rich and famous."

She definitely knows about Murphy, but she's letting me off the hook. And I was spying on *her*...for money. And he thinks I'm so unfit to be a spy that he pulled some strings to give me an awesome music career.

"I would never." she said. "Anytime we're in the same town, all-inclusive backstage passes, and we're going out to dinner so I can tell you about my adventures."

"You're sounding better already." she said.

Erik walked up.

"Sounding better?" he asked.

"Our little Jess *used to* have a confidence problem." she said. "She's working through it. I told her about your aunt Debbie."

"My aunt Debbie?" he asked.

"Yeah, the song." she said. "You didn't remember it because...well, you didn't remember. Jason has been writing for her, though, so she'll have her own songs."

"Right." he said. "I'm sorry, Jess. I remember everything, except for things that happened before I went through this...training when I was younger. I totally forgot that it was aunt Deb's song. It actually had a little run back in the seventies."

"That's what I hear." she said. "I actually have a few of my own now, and I wouldn't want to take anyone else's song."

"At the time, she had just been through a bad breakup." he said. "It still has a lot of sentimental meaning for her."

"When I'm a big star, I want both of you to see me." she said. "Like I told Lexie, all-inclusive backstage passes...but I'm afraid you're not invited to dinner, Erik. I'm sorry, it's girl time."

"That was great, Jess! You're going to be fine." she said.

"I hate to say it...but it's an early morning for both of us." he said.

"I know." she said.

She pulled Jess in close and kissed her.

"I love you." she said.

"I love you too, Lexie." she said. "When will you be back?"

"Whenever he gets back." she said. "Maybe a little before. I need to do some things on the East Coast. You'll be so busy, you'll hardly notice."

"I'll never be that busy." she said. "Be safe."

"You too." she said.

They walked out and got on the bike.

***

"It really sucks that I can't come back here." he said. "These people are like family to me."

"You still have your own family." she said.

"Did you forget already?" he asked. "I'm going to be dead to *everyone*. Even my mom and dad."

"Sorry. I guess I never really thought about it." she said. "My list would be pretty short. Maybe you can parlay this latest development into letting your mom and dad know or something. You never know, I've never seen Murphy so giddy before. But I'm sure the club is still out of the question."

"They go hand and hand." he said. "The club gets that envelope, my folks will be the first people they call. It would go the other way if mom and dad heard first. They don't like the club, but they respect my choice to be there. The phone lines will be burning between Michigan and Seattle next week."

"But after that." she said. "Everything's settled, you're buried at sea, there's no more reason for mom and dad to be communicating with the club, suddenly a phone call. Probably not from you, but from someone who can delicately explain the situation."

"Do you really think he'll let that happen?" he asked.

"I think he would if it was up to him." she said. "Both him and his boss know that you're in too deep with the club, why do you think they want you out so bad? He would have to be heartless to keep you from your parents."

"Have you forgotten who we're talking about? And he's not the only one. He has a tougher, meaner, less understanding boss." he said. "From what Murph says, this guy's still living in the thirties. Hell, he was probably alive then, and made his first million during the great depression while everyone else starved."

"Just keep an open mind, and if it's supposed to happen, it will." she said. "There's nothing we can do about it now."

"Look at you. I'm supposed to be the calm, cool, collected one who makes sense." he said. "Are you okay? With what happened? Will you be okay for the mission?"

"The mission is what I really need right now." she said. "Nothing will be better for me than to get in the field."

"Good." he said. "I'll talk to Murphy and see if he's willing to perform a miracle."

"You need to be prepared for the worst." she said.

"I know." he said. "But you met them. My dad...this would kill him. And my mom. Everyone."

"People have done it before." she said. "I've only known one who didn't keep the secret."

"Danielle." he said.

"Yep." she said.

"Do you ever wonder why she did that?" he asked. "Why she would risk her life to talk to me?"

She shrugged her shoulders.

"She must have loved you." she said.

"But what if it was more than that?" he asked. "What if she..."

"What if she what?" she asked.

"Never mind." he said. "It just seems strange to me that she would break the rules just for me. Like she had something important to tell me."

"Well, she never broke the rules, but she was bad in the field." she said. "Almost got me killed one time."

"How did that happen?" he asked.

"She was working intelligence. I was meeting with a target in Italy, little coastal town called Terracina, between Naples and Rome." she said. "She sends me in there with the wrong name. She had done this research, finding out everything about the guy, and got so focused on his enemy that she gave me *that* name instead of the guy's real name. I do my best to not think the worst that she did this on purpose, but I had to think about it. The target gets really pissed, but with a little quick sidestepping, I smooth it over. Since then, he knows I don't want to work with her."

"It seems like an honest mistake." he said.

"Are you really defending her on this?" she asked.

"I wouldn't say defending, but everyone makes mistakes." he said. "I doubt she did it on purpose. How did he get you to work with her that time in Monte Carlo?"

"Guess." she said.

"Mel Singer." he said.

"Yep." she said. "The only good thing about *that* getting out is that he doesn't have it to hang over my head anymore."

She thought about that situation. She was pretty unstable back then.

She remembered the warehouse going up in a huge cloud of smoke. She started running towards it as fast as she could. She felt the wind blowing, and as she got closer she could feel the heat from the blast. She saw a small figure running towards her. As it got closer she recognized it.

"UN-fucking-believable!" she cried.

It was Mel.

She was covered in ashes, and bleeding from the shoulder. She grabbed her by the collar and pushed her against a tree.

"Where is he?!" she screamed. "Where the fuck is Hershel?"

"He was inside!" she panted. "We held them off for about 10 minutes, and then it was too much. Me and Adam were covering him when Adam got hit. He didn't make it. Hershel got inside. That was the plan all along after their reinforcements arrived." she said.

Lexie gritted her teeth.

"What do you mean 'then it was too much'? He didn't have to die." she said. "If you had done your job and held them off for a few more minutes, he could have got out! He would have lived! Instead you ran away like a little bitch!"

"Fuck you! Adam's dead, and I was hit! You see this?!" she said pointing frantically at her shoulder.

"That's your left shoulder! You could have kept fighting! You let him die! You're a coward!" she cried. "Admit it! The shit got heavy and you ran away!"

"You weren't there! You were back at camp with the rest of them!" she screamed. "If I didn't run I'd be dead too!"

"You should be dead." she said.

She had made her decision. Hershel was 10 times the soldier Mel ever was. She pulled the gun from the back of her waistband and pointed it at Mel.

"Get on your knees, bitch."

"Think this through, Lexie, you don't want to do this!" she said, her voice wavering with panic. "Hershel wouldn't want this!"

"*I SAID ON YOUR KNEES!*" she screamed.

Mel slowly dropped to her knees. Lexie moved behind her and pressed the muzzle against her skull. She started out at almost a whisper, getting progressively louder.

"You ran away. From your position, it was obvious that you ran before the building blew up." she said. "You left him to die. You're a coward. Admit it and I might let you live."

"You really don't want to do this Lexie! Think about the unit, think about the cause!" she cried. "These things happen, people die! There was nothing I could do!"

"Quit sniveling and admit what you've done!" she screamed. "At least have an ounce of dignity! Have a little respect for

HIM! I swear I'll kill you, you dumb bitch! *ADMIT YOU'RE A COWARD!!*"

Mel looked back and saw Lexie standing behind her with a maniacal grin on her face, tears streaming down. That was the moment she knew she was dead.

"Ok, anything, I admit it! I'm a coward!" she cried. "You don't need to do this Lexie! Hershel wou..."

Lexie squeezed the trigger. She couldn't stand to hear that cunt speculate on what Hershel would want again. She draped Mel over her shoulder and headed towards the building. There was a gas pump about 300 yards from the wreckage. Lexie doused Mel liberally from the pump and then dragged her a safe distance away. She lit a cigarette and tossed her Zippo onto the body. It burst into flames and started crackling. She stayed there a long time watching Mel burn, then she started back to camp. The sun was going down as she got there.

And I left the bullet in her skull. That's how Murph got over on me. I'll never let that happen again

Chapter 19

"It's the best I can do, Anthony." he said. "We both get something, and neither of us loses too much."

"That's not how it's done, Erik." he said.

"I know you can force me to do your thing, there's no disputing that." he said. "But I'm smart enough to know that if I come in willingly, things will go better for you. Trust me, I can be a real pain in the ass about this."

"What difference does it make?" he asked. "You'll still be gone."

"I'm willing to give up the club, but not my family." he said. "Your boss doesn't have a problem with my family, does he?"

"That's not the point." he said. "A decision has been made that you'll be dead. You don't get to choose how."

"I have to disagree with you." he said. "Things have changed since that decision was made. I became more important. Whatever the fuck is happening to me is more important. You've been waiting years for this, and so has your boss. I'm lost at sea. That's the only way I go willingly."

"So man overboard, eh?" he said.

"Yeah, it happens all the time. After all this blows over, and any suspicion from the Irish is gone, I'm found on a deserted Island. Make the phone call Anthony. Tell the Plantagenet I'm staying aboard." he said. "I'll go to the Mauritius as Jack Samuelson, so make that happen too. The Plantagenet is only in San Diego for a couple of hours. I'll sneak off with the commissary people. There shouldn't be another muster until tomorrow morning, they're not letting anyone off the ship."

"You drive a hard bargain, Stryker." he said. "Under the circumstances, I might be able to sell it to the boss."

"You have to, because this is happening." he said. "What happened to the other people who were at camp with me?"

"That's classified." he said.

"Sure, if you want to play it that way." he said. "You forget, I can probably find out just about *anything* without your help now."

"Do you have that much control?" he asked.

"Not yet, but soon." he said.

"I'll do this for you, but you need to promise me that you'll see..."

"Dr. Heisenberg, I know." he said.

"Where did you get that name?" he asked.

"Three guesses, and the first two don't count." he said.

"How long has this been going on, Erik?" he asked.

"I didn't recognize it until Lexie lost the baby." he said. "Polycystic Ovarian Syndrome. That was the moment. Who knows? I've been having whacky dreams for years."

They had always said that the precognition would be the first sign, and it would almost certainly appear in dreams. The supernatural mental abilities would grow stronger, and supernatural physical abilities would surely follow. That was what they were really after. The perfect soldier. He had no idea how it worked, a cocktail of gene splicing, LSD, sensory deprivation, and some other things that Anthony knew nothing about. He still couldn't believe it was happening. He only half believed the things the MK people told him, because they were so far out. This was one of the extreme things that almost nobody believed, yet it was happening. He had kept a close eye on Antoine over the years too. Even Leland didn't know about *that*. It was the main reason he was still in touch with Danielle. He didn't say so, but he was sure that Leland wasn't aware that Erik was one of the seventeen.

"Okay, Erik. You don't make muster one morning, they look for you, and can't find you." he said. "It's assumed that you fell overboard and drowned. If there's no island in the area for us to find you on, we'll make one. But you're done with the club."

"Taylor needs to know too." he said. "I'll make sure she doesn't tell anyone in the club."

"That's a lot of moving parts." he said. "Are you sure you can trust her?"

"Can you trust me if you don't do what I want?" he asked.

"This isn't going to last forever, you know." he said. "I'm still the guy calling the shots."

"And I'll still let you." he said. "As long as you're reasonable. In the grand scheme of things, I'm not asking for much."

"You're asking me to have an uncomfortable conversation with my boss." he said. "He makes me uncomfortable, I make you uncomfortable. That's how it works."

"There's no need for that." he said. "I'm lost at sea. The club will never know they found me. The Plantagenet is leaving in 15 minutes, Anthony, I have to let you go. Lost at sea. Right? No gory pictures of my corpse, just an unsettling feeling that I *might* be dead."

"You're right, it will be better if you don't resist." he said. "And if I put you in motion, it can be unpredictable. Call me when you're in New York."

He hung up the phone. Lexie had left early that morning, and he spent the day putting things in order, and dropping his bike, his cut, and other important items at storage. He did the best he could to erase any trace of himself from the world. He didn't leave things that his brothers could find. Bikers were suspicious by nature, and when they heard he was lost at sea, they would try to piece things together. If there was no trace, they would give up. They would still be looking out for a while, but with time, they would let it go. He still toyed with the thought of coming back someday. Probably no good way to get away with it, but it was something to think about.

"Stryker, the bridge." he said.

"You know where Ops. Quarters are?" he asked.

"Yeah." he said.

"Find a spot there." he said. "Check the duty roster once you get settled."

"Okay." he said.

He wouldn't be on this tub for long. Just to San Diego, then the Mauritius through the Caribbean to the Atlantic. Then New York to meet Lexie.

Anthony would make all the arrangements for him to disappear from the Plantagenet, probably have the whole crew believing it too. It'll give them a good story to tell when they get home, he thought.

He found a bunk and unpacked the sea bag. He had already made arrangements to have his real sea bag sent to the Mauritius. It would be there when he got there, as Jack Samuelson. He knew that under the circumstances that Anthony would have to let him do it his way, so he made the arrangements in advance. The crew would find all of his stuff unpacked into the bunk, reinforcing the idea that he was lost at sea. All he needed to do was get off the ship unnoticed in San Diego and get over to the Mauritius. He had plans for that too.

He went up to the Signal Bridge. He always loved it up here on top of the ship. There was nobody around, and he figured it would be best to lay low anyway. Show up for at least one muster to prove that he was on the ship, then disappear.

His phone started ringing.

"Hello?" he said.

"Hey, it's me." she said. "Are you on the ship?"

"What kind of sailor would I be if I wasn't?" he asked.

"Good." she said. "I'm staying at the Plaza. Room 1312."

"Seeing how the other half lives?" he asked.

"I think we both know how the other half lives." she said. "It's on Murphy's dime, so of course I'm staying here. I'm even eating the macadamia nuts. Just waiting for my fiancé to show up."

"Well, your intended is taking a less conventional route." he said. "I'm sure he looks forward to spending a night or two at the Plaza. The two most recent women in his life have been staying there, and he's never been. Never even been to New York City."

"You've never been to the Big Apple?" she said. "What a sheltered life you've lived."

"I recall saying the same thing to you when we were in Cairo." he said. "You didn't even know how to make a pipe for weed out of an empty can before you met me."

"But now I know." she said. "I can even open a bottle with a Bic lighter."

"Valuable skills." he said.

"You've really never been to New York?" she asked.

"Never had any interest." he said. "From all I've heard, it's not my kind of place."

"What?" she asked. "There's something for everyone here."

"Sure." he said. "Everything's overpriced and dirty. Shitty weather too. Seattle is overpriced, but at least it's clean, and the weather is nice."

“What about the culture?” she said. “New York is very cosmopolitan.”

“There are plenty of words I would use to describe New York, cosmopolitan isn’t one of them.” he said. “Just because millions of people live there, doesn’t mean it’s good, or classy, or nice. People living on top of each other and paying $2000 per month for the privilege. No thanks.”

“And Seattle is so much better?” she asked.

“Seattle is the birthplace of grunge.” he said. “You have the mountains, the water, and the green. It’s overcast a lot of the time, but that overcast is water. The overcast in New York is smog.”

“Okay, you make a good point.” she said. “I’ll show you around when you get here, and then tell me what you think.”

“I don’t plan on leaving the room before the Norwegian Breakaway leaves.” he said. “They probably have decent room service, right?”

“You’re impossible.” she said.

“So they tell me.” he said. “There is one slight change of plans.”

“Oh?” she asked.

“I’m not getting killed.” he said. “I talked Anthony into being lost at sea. You know? Like I fell overboard?”

“That’s good.” she said. “How did you manage that?”

“I used the only bargaining chip I had.” he said. “I guessed, as it turns out correctly, that things will go smoother if I go in to see the spooks voluntarily. He’s a little nervous about how things are going to go when we get back, so he’s being careful with me. I still can’t go back to the club, but my family...after it’s safe, they’ll ‘discover’ me on an island somewhere in the Pacific.”

“That’s great, Erik!” she said. “I know how important that is to you.”

“Muster on the bridge, 10 minutes!” shouted The OOD.

“Okay.” he said.

“I gotta go, Lexie.” he said. “I have to show up to at least one muster before I disappear.”

“Okay.” she said. “Call me from the Mauritius.”

“Sure.” he said. “I love you.”

“Love you too.” she said.

***

When they got to San Diego, he stood on the bridge looking down at the pier. As he expected the commissary people arrived, all wearing yellow shirts with the letters "DHS" on the back of them.

"Muster, Stryker, let's go." he said. "Starboard side, main bridge."

"Aye, on my way." he said.

He would have to hope that there wasn't a muster after they got underway. If they did, Murphy would have to work it out. He went down there.

They took roll call. After it was over, the Ops Officer walked up to him.

"Erik, long time no see." he said. "How the hell are ya?"

"Hey Ernie." he said. "I didn't know you were on this tub."

"Been here 4 months now." he said. "Finally got that promotion."

"I can see that." he said. "Congratulations."

"Where have you been?" he asked.

"I had some shit to deal with stateside." he said. "My brother has been having some health problems."

"Sorry to hear that." he said.

"Yeah, no, he's going to be fine." he said. "Made me think a little about how I'm living though."

"Something we should all think about." he said.

"So how's Katie?" he asked. "Did you finally..."

"Last month." he said. "She had to plan it for a whole year. I would have been fine with having the skipper do it right here, but you know women. You ever been married?"

"In another life." he said. "If it makes you feel any better, I actually talked that one into doing it on the ship. It was the Chaplain, not the skipper."

"So what happened?" he asked.

"Another life, Ernie." he said.

"Okay." he said. "How long you with us?"

"Until the end." he said. "It'll be good to get away for a while."

"I know what you mean." he said.

"Oh, Ernie, not already?" he asked.

“No, not her, I just feel better when I’m out here.” he said. “What about you? Did you ever make it legal with Taylor?”

“Well, Ernie, you know I’m an outlaw, no need to make anything legal.” he said. “I actually went the other way, we split.”

“I have no doubt you’ll land on your feet.” he said.

“I already have.” he said. “Hey, can I ask you a favor?”

“Sure, anything.” he said.

“I was up all night last night, and I have the midwatch tonight.” he said. “I was hoping to get a little rack time. Can you cover me for the muster after we get underway?”

He actually *did* have the midwatch, he had checked the duty roster. Midnight would be the time they discovered him missing. They would be about halfway to Hawaii.

“Sure, in fact since you have the midwatch, I can excuse you from it all together.” he said.

“Thanks, Ernie.” he said. “I’m going to head down there right now, but we’ll catch up later. It’s good to see you.”

“You too, Erik.” he said. “Go get some sleep.”

He headed down to Ops. Quarters and opened his bunk. He took out a razor and went into the head and shaved his beard off. He had been growing it for the past few weeks, and he didn’t know why until now. Most of the guys in the club had beards, but Erik normally didn’t. Never liked facial hair, he could never get past the itchy phase. He stuffed a shirt into a smaller bag, then he put on a pair of jeans and a yellow shirt with the letters “DHS” on the back of it. To complete the outfit, he put on some mirrored sunglasses.

He hoped that Ernie wouldn’t see him, even in this get up, he might be recognized. He felt a little bad, because he knew that Ernie would be upset after he they discovered him missing. Unfortunately, there were things more important than Ernie’s feelings.

He walked up to the quarterdeck and nodded at the OOD who nodded back and extended his arm towards the gangway. He calmly walked off the ship, and didn’t look back.

The Mauritius wasn’t leaving for another two hours, so he changed his shirt and went into a bar near the pier. It was a place that he’d never been, with little chance that he would be recognized. If only I had a little more time, I could go to Tijuana, he thought.

He ordered a ginger ale. The barmaid raised an eyebrow and looked at him.

"Nothing stronger?" she asked.

"I'm driving." he said.

"Where?" she asked.

"New York." he said.

He did his best to seem disinterested, but she wasn't taking the hint.

"Long trip." she said.

"I have six days to do it." he said.

"What's in New York?" she asked.

"My fiancé." he said.

"Why so far away?" she asked.

"That's just where she is." he said.

"Okay...let me go get your ginger ale." she said.

"Thanks." he said.

She came back with his drink.

"Did you at least have a good bachelor party?" she asked.

"We went to Tijuana for a few days." he said.

"Oh. I hope you didn't get in any trouble." she said.

"I'm pretty used to trouble." he said. "I flew out here, I'm driving back so I can visit all of my old girlfriends on the way. I have quite a few on the gulf coast."

"I see." she said.

He wasn't sure if that was going to get rid of her, or make her more interested.

"I'll be right back." she said. "I gotta check the other side of the bar."

More interested. I did my best to sound like an asshole, but it didn't work. Maybe there's something to that, like I was telling Johnny.

He looked out the window and saw the Plantagenet tossing off her lines and easing out into the harbor. He took out his wallet and got a fifty dollar bill and covered it with his drink. She was talking to someone else on the other side of the bar. He walked out, and went back to the pier. He found the Mauritius and walked up the gangway.

"Samuelson, the bridge." he said.

The OOD looked over the manifest. He looked at Erik.
"Did you have your stuff shipped here?" he asked.
"Yeah, sorry about that." he said. "I had a family emergency, and I was pressed for time. Honestly, I'm lucky to have made it here at all."
"Pick up your stuff with the storekeeper." he said. "You'll be in Ops. Quarters. Welcome aboard."
"Thanks." he said.

***

Sweat was running down his forehead and through his sweatband, threatening to drip into his eyes. It had been a long game, and he had been in there almost the entire time.
He played for the Saint-Germain-en-Laye High School, the most renowned international high school in France. He was by far their best player, and there were rumors that there were scouts at the game from the Paris Saint Germain, one of the best teams in the French League. He was only fifteen, but there were others his age that were able to join the big team with parental permission.
Eighty-eight minutes and thirty-seven seconds. He was roving near midfield, looking for an opportunity to advance. It was a bitterly contested game, tied 1-1 for the last seventy-five minutes, and tempers had flared more than once. Antoine tried to focus on the game and not get involved with the extracurriculars. It wasn't always easy. There was at least one kid out there that he wanted to smash his face. Number 13. He had taken out one of Antoine's friends with a cheap shot and broke his ankle. He never came near Antoine, he didn't have the balls. Antoine was 6'1" and still growing.
Eighty-eight minutes and fifty-nine seconds. The ball was deep in Montreuil's territory. Now or never, he thought. Even though the ball was to his right, Antoine ran left. He was all alone. One of the defenders kicked the ball towards Saint-Germain-en-Laye's zone, as soon as it was parallel to Antoine, he tilted his head to the left and the ball took a sharp right turn and landed on his foot. He was just outside of the penalty area, looking at the startled goalie who was trying to figure out what happened. He kicked the ball into the upper right corner

of the goal as the goalie dove for it. He watched the net puff out as the ball caught it.

Eighty-nine minutes thirty-one seconds. His side was cheering in disbelief, the rest of the crowd couldn't figure out what had happened. They brought the ball out to the centre mark as the rest of the time elapsed.

Montreuil's number 13 was heading straight for him. Look who grew a pair of balls, he thought.

"You cheated!" he said. "I don't know how you did it, but that ball was headed for your zone."

"You're just pissed because your team sucks." he said. "There are scouts from Paris Saint Germain in the seats, but they're not looking for goons. Even if they were, you're the worst kind of goon, you only go after smaller players."

The kid was about 6 feet, so he was almost as big as Antoine. He hoped his comments would be enough for the kid to get stupid. He came up to Antoine and got in a fighting stance.

"Yeah? So?" he said. "That's cute, you just going to stand there? Were you actually going to try to do something?"

Some of the adults were starting to walk in their direction. Number 13 took a swing at him that he easily blocked, then he countered with an uppercut that sent him flying onto his back. Antoine jumped on top of him.

"This is for Paul." he said.

He unleashed a flurry of punches to his face that sent a mist of blood into the air. It was only about 15 seconds before the coach pulled him off, but the damage was done. He would be explaining to people for at least a few weeks what happened to his face.

The coach pulled him aside to talk.

"You really fucked this whole thing up, kid." he said. "You know that right?"

"He had it coming." he said.

"That doesn't matter." he said. "I was talking to those scouts. You had a shot."

"Really?" he asked.

"Well not anymore. They know you're young and impulsive, but you're good enough that they might have looked the other way on that. But you took the bait." he said.

"You got in a fight after the game was over. You were the hero. But doing what you did, showed them that you're not ready to play on their team."

"That guy's a pussy." he said. "You saw what he did to Paul. Then he fought a guy his own size, and you saw what happened."

"How did you do it, Antoine?" he asked. "The ball. Their player kicked it towards our zone. Hard, really hard. Next thing anyone knows, it takes a sharp turn and lands on your foot."

He didn't do it very often. Eighty-eight minutes and fifty-nine seconds. What else could he do?

"It must have hit a rock or something." he said. "I dunno."

"Hit a rock? Is that what you're going with?" he asked.

He had walked the field before the game, and he knew there weren't any rocks out there. He couldn't explain it, and it was beyond logic to think that Antoine had anything to do with it. But what happened?

"What else could it have been, coach?" he asked.

"I don't know, but I've seen a few weird things happen when you're out there." he said.

"I guess I'm just lucky." he said.

"I'm suspending you for the next two games for this." he said.

"Oh, come on coach!" he said. "He started it! You need me. I promise it won't happen again."

"The only way it won't happen again is if you have consequences." he said. "Two games."

"Hey coach." she said. "Our boy scored both goals, eh?"

"I'm more concerned with what happened after the game." he said. "I'm suspending him for two games."

"As much as I love to see him play, I agree with you." she said. "He needs to have consequences."

"Listen to your mother, boy." he said. "I appreciate you backing me up on this Danielle. You can still practice, but you're out for the next two games."

"Okay, coach." he said. "I guess."

He might have tried again if it wasn't for his mom. If she agreed, there was nothing he could do.

He walked off. It really didn't matter. He didn't like doing it, but he could have made the entire crowd that was there believe whatever he wanted. He could have them all swear that he stole the ball, split the defense, and did a back flip into a bicycle kick goal like Pelé. And there would be no two game suspension either. He probably should have, but who knows if someone taped the game?

A crowd that big, it would have taken a lot out of him too. There was always a price to pay. He would need to sleep for several hours to recover. A little thing like bringing the ball to him barely affected him at all. Whenever he used that option he tried to make it a little more believable, but the team needed the win this time.

"So what was that?" she asked. "The ball came right to you."

"Not you too! I don't know, ma, sometimes I just get lucky." he said.

"Like your father." she said.

"Tell me about him again?" he said.

"He was an American." she said. "Very handsome, but not as handsome as you. He was a bit of a rebel. We had a torrid love affair, which produced the most beautiful boy in the world. He got in some trouble and he had to go, but he's coming back. If he knew about you, he would already be here. He's coming back, I have no doubt about that."

Every time she told him he *really* wanted to meet this guy. In her eyes, he could do no wrong. He couldn't understand the losers she brought home. They were all abusive. He had tried to help her, but usually just got humiliated. Was his father really better than that?

"What makes you so sure?" he asked.

"His character." she said. "He said he was coming back, so he will. There are other things that you don't know about that are preventing him from coming back for the time being, but he'll be here...or maybe we'll go to him."

"To America?" he asked.

"Yes." she said. "We just need to get a few of the obstacles out of the way. When you meet him, I'm sure you'll love him. After all, I gave you his name."

"You have to admit that Stryker sounds better that Babineaux." he said.

"I don't know about that, but it suits you." she said. "You're just like him."

"So he was lucky too?" he asked. "He could make a soccer ball come to him at a crucial moment?"

"I believe that if that was what was required, he would find a way to make it happen." she said. "Your father is a remarkable man."

"Is it okay if Angeline comes over for dinner?" he asked.

"Are you two getting serious?" she asked.

"I dunno." he said. "I like her a lot. I'm pretty sure she likes me."

"How could she not?" she asked. "You're the cutest boy in school."

He started blushing.

"It's good that you say that even if it's not true." he said. "You've always been there for me, mom. No matter what happens."

"And I always will." she said.

***

The phone was ringing and she answered it.

"Hello?"

"Ms. Babineaux." he said. "How are things?"

"They could always be better, Anthony." she said. "To what do I owe the pleasure?"

"I was just curious about your boy." he said. "How is young Antoine?"

"He's fine, looks more like his dad every day." she said. "Speaking of him, when are you going to let me talk to him? At this rate, Antoine will be an old man."

"I'm working on it." he said. "Certain people need to be convinced. Have you taught Antoine English?""

"He speaks decent English. Better than your French." she said. "How is Erik?"

"He's on assignment. With Lexie." he said.

"Why do you have to do that?" she asked. "You know as well as I do that she's no good for him."

"I have to disagree, Danielle." he said. "She centers him. He has the same effect on her. It's kismet."

"If he knew..." she said. "Never mind. What do you want?"

"Your money's still coming isn't it?" he said. "I would think that buys less interference."

"Interference?" she asked. "When have I had the opportunity to interfere? He doesn't know I'm alive."

"Yes he does, and you know it." he said. "Remember that time about 25 fuck ups ago? When you called him?"

"And he would have called me back if you didn't set him in motion." she said.

"You're lucky he didn't." he said. "If he did, I would have been forced to tell him about what you did. That would have gotten him off your scent forever. What's going on with the boy?"

She knew he was right. She did what she did back then because she thought she had no choice. Looking back, if she knew this was how it was going to be, she never would have done it. She didn't know that she only did exactly what Anthony programmed her to do. The guilt was all part of it, and it gave him even more leverage.

"He's a great soccer player." she said. "There were scouts from the Paris Saint Germain at his last game. According to the coach he fucked it up by getting in a fight at the end of the game. Something a little weird happened before that though."

"Really?" he asked. "What?"

"The ball was headed for his team's zone, and he tilted his head to the left, and it turned sharply and came right to him. He scored the winning goal." she said. "I've never seen anything like it."

He was stunned. It was happening. Antoine was the only offspring of any of the seventeen that survived, and it was happening. They told him that the genes of the seventeen played a significant role in the children. Antoine was the only one. A few of the others had children, but they all came out horribly deformed and died within weeks. *He made that soccer ball come to him.* How long has he been able to do this?

"I want you to bring him to the states." he said. "There are people he needs to see."

"Are you kidding?" she said. "You want me to uproot my life here and go to America? Why?"

"There's something in Erik's genes. Something he passed along to Antoine." he said. "He needs to see a specialist to figure out what's going on. I'm only asking out of courtesy, if you won't come willingly, we'll have to do it the other way."

"Which other way?" she asked. "With you it could literally be anything."

"Use your imagination." he said. "It won't go well for you Danielle, and in the end he's still coming."

She knew he was serious. It really could be almost anything, and none of it was good.

"When?" she asked.

"I'll check the flights out of Paris and get you on the first one." he said. "A courier will come with the tickets. Go pack. I'll see you soon."

The line went dead.

She went out to the living room. Antoine and Angeline were sitting on the couch. They looked like they were making out, and she interrupted.

"I'm really sorry." she said. "I'm afraid I need to talk to my son, dear."

"Okay, no problem Ms. Babineaux." she said. "It's getting late anyway."

"I'm really sorry." she said.

Sorry that I'm taking him away, she thought.

Angeline gave him a kiss on the cheek.

"I'll talk to you soon." she said.

"Bye." he said.

She walked out the door.

"So what is it now?" he asked.

"Remember when I said maybe we'll go to him? Your father?" she asked.

"Yeah, to America." he said.

"Well, we're going." she said.

"When?" he asked.

"Probably tomorrow." she said.

Chapter 20

He was on the Mauritius, in the Atlantic going north towards New York. Somewhere around Jacksonville, he thought. He thought back to that fateful cross country trip from Jacksonville to Bremerton fifteen years ago.

Getting pulled over and being given a pass by the cops. He didn't know it at the time, but it was all Murphy. He literally got away with murder. That guy he killed at Wild Bill's who was only trying to back up his buddy. He didn't have a choice on that one, if he didn't kill that guy, he would be dead.

Ross Goodwin in Reno was a different story though. He really didn't need to die. His problem was that he didn't know when to shut up. If he did, he would still be alive, talking shit with his dark glasses and that stupid fucking derby hat.

Then there was that massacre at Jenna's place. He had changed his thinking on that over the years. After all, she had sold him out to Robinette, no matter how innocent he tried to make it sound.

He realized that he was giving her a pass because she wasn't in the life, and he shouldn't. After all she took the money. No matter how naïve she was, she had to know that people don't just give you $50,000 if they don't have serious plans for the person they're looking for. And they generally don't give you that much if it's something good. Hell, maybe she didn't know. In the end she paid with her life.

Not that he thought she deserved to die, she wasn't evil, just stupid and naïve. But if he never got involved with DuBois, it never would have happened. After he killed three of his men and sent one home crippled, he figured DuBois got the message. Of course, he told the lone survivor to tell Dubois that he was dead.

The guy kept his word too. The next time he saw DuBois, he was shocked. Erik figured he was talking shit saying that Danielle was still alive before he killed him. Turned out that she really was alive. Not that it would have mattered. Nothing would have stopped him from killing DuBois. Whether he knew Danielle was alive or not, he still had to answer for Jenna.

After that trip he joined the merchant marines just to get out of Bremerton for a while as the cops tried to figure out what happened at Jenna's. Right after he met Taylor. Even after everything that happened, it took Murphy eight years to contact him. And his first assignment was to kill DuBois.

The captain strolled up to the signal bridge.

"How we doing, skipper?" he asked.

"Beautiful night." he said.

"It sure is." he said. "What time do you think we'll get there tomorrow?" he asked.

"Probably around noonish." he said. "You got a hot date?"

"You could say that." he said. "I'm getting married."

"Congratulations, son." he said.

"Thank you." he said. "We're getting on another ship for the honeymoon."

"You don't say?" he said.

"A cruise ship." he said. "At least I don't have to work."

"Her idea?" he asked.

"Yeah, but I don't mind." he said. "For her it's worth it."

"Well that's great." he said. "You see anything out here tonight?"

"You're looking at it." he said. "Probably see more the closer we get to New York."

"Don't I know it." he said. "Keep an eye out, son, and congratulations again."

"Thank you, sir." he said.

He made his way back down to the bridge.

Against his better judgement Erik pulled out his phone. He didn't know why he kept doing it, but he couldn't stop himself. They had been together for the past fifteen years.He wanted to be with Lexie, but he still felt the need to call her. He dialed the number.

"Hello?" she said.

"Hi, it's me." he said.

"How are you, Erik?" she asked.

"I'm fine." he said. "On a ship headed to New York."

"What for?" she asked.

"Meeting Lexie, from there we go to Ireland." he said.

"Why didn't you just go from Seattle?" she asked.

"Cover." he said. "We're posing as newlyweds. Taking a fucking cruise ship over."

"Newlyweds, eh?" she asked.

"If we went as ourselves they would see us coming." he said. "We're killing Brendan's father, uncle, and probably some of his friends."

"That sucks. So they think it will be better if you're newlyweds?" she asked.

"I don't make those decisions." he said. "Murphy figures all that out."

"Hmm." she said. "How do you feel about that?"

"Honestly I really don't know." he said. "I *thought* I did, but now I'm not so sure. I'll do it for the mission."

"Why are you hesitating?" she asked.

"I don't know." he said. "I wish I did. I feel like something unexpected is going to happen, and it's going to change my life. In a good way. I think I'm starting to get your intuitions, but they're hazy."

"Really?" she asked.

"I don't know what the fuck is happening to me Taylor." he said. "Murphy wants me to go and see his spooks when we get back."

Saying that reminded him why he shouldn't be talking to Taylor at all. He was supposed to be dead...or at least missing. Too late now, he thought.

"Are you going to do it?" she asked.

"It's the only way...I need to tell you something, Taylor, and you can't tell anyone." he said.

"Okay." she said.

Obviously she hadn't got the news that he was missing yet. At this point, there was no way she could hear it and believe it anyway.

"Murphy wanted to kill me. Not really kill me, but stage my death for the sake of the club." he said. "I talked him into just making it appear that I fell overboard on the Plantagenet. That way I can still see my family. I told him that I would see his doctors if he did it that way. You'll probably get word soon that I'm missing. Nobody in the club can know that I'm alive, that's part of the deal. I did it for my parents...and you."

"Well, I'm glad you called then." she said. "I would hate to think you're dead."

"I realized that I shouldn't have called after it was too late." he said. "You need to do the best acting job of your life, I'm sorry."

"I'll be interested to see what your life changing event is." she said. "The next time you have a premonition, try to stay as still and quiet as you can. That's how it works for me."

"Now I'm getting psychic advice from the other woman." he said.

"The other woman knows what she's talking about." she said.

"Where are you?" he asked.

"Still in Monte Carlo." she said.

"You know that's where..." he said.

"I know." she said. "That's where you met Danielle. The irony isn't lost on me."

"Irony?" he asked.

"Yeah." she said. "You pop up in Monte Carlo on a topless beach, you would be putty in my hands just like you were in hers. That kind of irony."

"Do you really think so?" he said.

"Reroute and come here, and we'll see." she said.

"Tempting, but I'm dead." he said. "I might not be able to call for a while."

"You'll find a way." she said.

"You sound pretty confident, Whitman." he said.

"I *am* pretty confident." she said. "Call me from Ireland...or sooner."

"I'll try to find a way." he said.

"Ciao, baby." she said. "I love you."

"Ciao baby? What the hell is that?" he said. "I love you too."

He hung up the phone. He wondered how Lexie was, but he didn't want to call her right after talking to Taylor. It was strange that he wanted to talk to Taylor so much, but he didn't see the problem. He decided to try to get some shuteye.

***

He was at the Blind Pig in downtown Ann Arbor. It was a relatively small bar, but they packed in a big crowd most nights. This night was no exception, The Who was onstage playing.

Big acts tended to come to the Blind Pig unannounced. There was a rumor that the Rolling Stones played there one night after a show in Detroit. It was believable because all of the rock stars knew about the Blind Pig. Pearl Jam, Nirvana, Soundgarden and many other groups had played at the Blind Pig as well.

The weird part was that all of the members of the band looked like they did when they were young. They had to be in their mid fifties by now. Wait a minute. Keith Moon is playing drums, but he died in 1978. He remembered it, it was shortly after he was done with his MK Ultra camp. He had died of an overdose of Heminevrin, a drug he was taking to help with his alcohol withdrawals.

I must be dreaming, he thought. Good, maybe I can get some answers. It had been a long time since his last lucid dream.

One, two, three, four, five, six, seven, eight...

I've got my clipboard, text books
Lead me to the station
Yeah, I'm off to the civil war
I've got my kit bag, my heavy boots
I'm runnin' in the rain
Gonna run till my feet are raw

Slip kid, slip kid, second generation
And I'm a soldier at thirteen
Slip kid, slip kid, realization
There's no easy way to be free
No easy way to be free
It's a hard, hard world

Lexie and Taylor were sitting with him, getting along remarkably well. They weren't chatting or behaving like Lexie did with her friends back home, but they weren't bitching at each other either. I'll take it, he thought. Back home. Could he even call it that anymore?

The waitress came up and asked what people wanted.

"What the fuck, I know I'm dreaming, give me a rum and Coke." he said.

She leaned over and gave him a good look at her cleavage.

"What kind of dream is it, baby?" she asked.

Both Lexie and Taylor shot daggers at her.

"To early to tell, I'll let you know." he said.

He saw Danielle and a kid who looked to be a teenager sitting at a table nearby. Is he even old enough to be in here?

I left my doctor's prescription bungalow behind me
I left the door ajar
I left my vacuum flask
Full of hot tea and sugar
Left the keys right in my car

Slip kid, slip kid, second generation
Only half way up the tree
Slip kid, slip kid, I'm a relation
I'm a soldier at sixty-three
No easy way to be free
Slip kid, slip kid

He had to know. Who is that kid with Danielle? He looked at Lexie and Taylor who seemed to be paying no attention to him. He walked over to the table.

"Hi Danielle." he said. "Who's the kid?"

"Vous êtes mon père?" the kid asked.

"English, dear." said Danielle.

"Je ne me souviens pas que maintenant, maman." he said. "Pourquoi ne me souviens plus?"

"I don't know, Antoine." she said. "Maybe you're not ready to talk to him yet."

"So who's the kid?" Erik asked again.

He really wished he knew French. He didn't know why, but it seemed important for him to talk to this kid.

"He's your..." she said.
"I have to stop you there, Danielle." he said.
It was Murphy.
"It's not him, it's Erik that isn't ready." he said. "Remember what we talked about?"

Keep away old man, you won't fool me
You and your history won't rule me
You might have been a fighter, but admit you failed
I'm not affected by your blackmail
You won't blackmail me

I've got my clipboard, text books
Lead me to the station
Yeah, I'm off to the civil war
I've got my kit bag, my heavy boots
I'm runnin' in the rain
Gonna run till my feet are raw

"I was just going to tell him that Antoine is the slip kid." she said. "You have to admit that he fits the bill. He's a little older than 13, but he's going off to be a soldier."
"Not right away." he said. "You still have so much to learn, Danielle. Most of all how to keep your mouth shut."
"What's going on?" asked Erik. "I know I'm dreaming."
The waitress walked up to him, handed him his drink and seductively rubbed against him.
"That's it." said Lexie. "First he goes over and talks to that tramp, and now the waitress wants to fuck him."
"Allow me." said Taylor.
She produced a large handgun and shot the waitress in the head. Her brains splattered all over the kid.
"You should have stayed away too bitch." she said. "If you don't want to be next, I suggest you take that kid and get the fuck out of here."
"We should go get you cleaned up." she said. "I'm sorry, Antoine, some people don't know how to behave in polite society."
She looked longingly at Erik.

“I’ll see you soon, baby.” she said.
“See me soon?” he asked.
“*You best move NOW*!” said Taylor.
She brought the hammer back on the gun and pulled the trigger, nearly hitting Danielle.
She wrapped her arms around Antoine and moved quickly to the door.

Slip kid, slip kid, slip out of trouble
Slip over here and set me free
Slip kid, slip kid, second generation
You're slidin down the hill like me
No easy way to be free

He went back to his table and sat down.
“What were you doing over there with that skank?” asked Lexie.
“Nothing. I just wanted to know who the kid was.” he said. “He spoke French, what did he say?”
“I don’t speak French.” she said.
“Bullshit, you speak 8 languages.” he said. “What did he say?”
“I must not have heard him, the music is really loud.” she said. “Probably nothing important, he’s just a kid.”
“Why are you two so chummy?” he asked.
“Common enemy.” said Lexie.
Good, now *both* of them are paranoid about Danielle.
“When Lexie’s gone, I’ll be there, baby.” said Taylor.
“You’ll be gone before me, bitch.” she said.
She pulled out her gun at the same time as Taylor.

“Sir? You awake? We’ll be in New York in a half hour.” he said.
It was the messenger. Come to wake him up so he would be ready to disembark. So much for answers, I’m more confused than ever. Who was that kid?
He got up and got dressed and went up to the signal bridge. I better do it now, who knows when I’ll get another chance? He dialed the number.
“Hello?” she asked.

"It's me." he said. "We're going to be in New York soon."

"Good. You'll get to see Lexie." she said.

"Yeah, then it's back to work." he said.

"Are you okay?" she asked.

"Yeah, no, I'm fine." he said. "Just another weird dream."

"Tell me about it." she said.

He told her, and she acted shocked when he told her what she did to the waitress.

"The worst part is that I don't remember what he said." he said. "I tried to go back there, but it doesn't always work with dreams. Him speaking French didn't help either."

"The Blind Pig, eh?" she said. "That's a strange name for a bar."

"And the Brass Caterpillar isn't?" he asked. "Blind Pig was a slang term used to describe cops who were bribed to ignore illegal speakeasys during prohibition. I think it's clever."

"Still the master of triviality, eh?" she asked. "Isn't Lexie usually the bad guy?"

"Lately, nobody has been good." he said. "Any ideas on who the kid might be?"

She had a thought, the math worked, but she wasn't about to share it.

"Sometimes a dream is just a dream." she said.

"Not for me." he said.

"Who knows? It was a dream." she said. "The kid could be you, or your dad, or your brother, or virtually anyone. Dreams use a lot of symbolism. Maybe he represents young Erik, like while you were at that camp. Who knows? How old were you in 1978?"

"Sixteen." he said.

"Maybe the kid was you." she said. "He was the right age if it was 1978. Everything else was the same, but you were 16 when Keith Moon died. Maybe your dream was trying to tell you it was you by having Keith Moon there."

"Okay. It's me, but I speak French? Like I never have in my life?" he said. "Thanks for splattering the waitress's brains all over me, by the way, if it even is me which I'm starting to doubt."

"I didn't have the right angle." she said. "I was trying to get them on Danielle. It might still be you. Speaking French doesn't rule that out. It was a dream."

"You need to get to the range then." he said. "Looked like a clear shot to me."

"You probably don't know this about me, but I can shoot. I'm sure I was aiming at the waitress if I hit her. Didn't hit you, did I?" she said.

"Which me?" he asked.

"Either." she said. "Do you really think me and Lexie could ever be friends?"

"Probably not." he said. "Under different circumstances I think you would get along though. She became great friends with the girls at the club."

"You're probably right." she said. "But the circumstances are that she stole my man."

"I don't know about that." he said. "Things were pretty rough before she showed up."

"I know." she said. "But I'm different now. I hope you call me when it's over with her."

"I don't know if that's going to happen." he said.

He said it, but it didn't carry the same weight as it used to. Maybe it was just this time apart. Maybe the time apart from Taylor was why he kept calling.

"It will." she said. "And when it does, I want you to come back to me."

"We'll see." he said. "We're in the harbor now, I should go."

"Okay." she said. "I'll be expecting a call when you get to Ireland...or whenever you want to call."

"I'll do what I can." he said.

"I love you, Erik." she said.

"Me too." he said.

He hung up the phone. He had to get out of the habit of telling her that he loved her, even if it was true. It sent the wrong message. She definitely had delusions that they would be together again. Were they delusions?

As they approached the pier he saw her. She looked spectacular. He noticed that she had a fan club of all the guys out on deck. Just like that time in Mombasa, he thought. She locked eyes with him on the signal bridge and started waving.

For a hot second the guys on the bridge thought she was waving at them, then they looked up and saw him waving back.

"Fucking Samuelson!" he said. "How did you get so lucky?"

"You see, you say I'm lucky, but you don't know her." he said. "I'm actually the luckiest guy in the world."

He looked up and shook his head.

As he walked down the gangway with his sea bag on his shoulder, she was walking towards him. He met her on the pier and gave her a big hug and kiss.

"I missed you." he said.

"Me too." she said. "You shaved. I like it."

"So do I." he said. "I'm not really a beard guy, but it helped me get off the Plantagenet without getting noticed."

"I like you with or without...maybe a little better without." she said.

"I definitely like it better without." he said. "I can't get past that itchy part."

"If you don't want to see New York, maybe we can go to AC. They have casinos there, and we have a couple of days."

"I haven't gambled in years." he said. "I realized a while back that I'm not anywhere near as good as I think I am."

He thought back to those times he went to the poker rooms in California and got his ass handed to him. It took a long time and a lot of money before he admitted to himself that he was better off not playing.

"Maybe we can just go to the boardwalk and look around then." she said.

"The most expensive property on the board." he said.

"As it turns out, it's the most expensive property in Atlantic City too." she said. "But I'm sure you know that."

"I played a lot of Monopoly as a kid." he said. "That sounds fun. I have a pressing matter to attend to back at the hotel, though. We'll go to AC tomorrow."

"Sounds good." she said. "Wait til you see this fucking room. I feel like royalty."

"Lexie Tenenzapf. Queen of Atlantic City." he said. "Shall I arrange a litter to carry you to your room?"

"No, I'll just hop on your back." she said.

"That in itself is worth the price of admission." he said. "Never mind the show we're about to put on in our luxury suite."

She jumped into his arms and laid her head on his shoulder.

"I love you Erik." she said.

***

It was against his better judgement to involve Leland, but he had no choice. He might already be in trouble for not telling him sooner. There was no way he could keep this to himself. If only Leland wasn't so rigid...and more human.

He had managed to get a VHS copy of the game she was talking about, when Antoine made the ball come to him. It was amazing. He saw Antoine move his head a little, then the ball made a sharp turn and landed on his foot.

This was the real deal, and if he did it intentionally, he would be invaluable to the MK program, even if he didn't (which was unlikely), he still possessed an ability that was supernatural. He was further along than Erik...further along than anyone in history. He had no choice, he just hoped that Leland wouldn't interfere too much. They would be here at four o'clock today.

He got off of the elevator and went through the metal detector. The glass doors opened in front of him and he went up to the desk.

"Hello Julia." he said. "Anthony Murphy, here to see Mr. Andersen."

"Yes, he's expecting you." she said. "Jeanette?"

A blond with short hair appeared from behind the wall.

"Mr. Murphy, right this way." she said.

"What happened to Alicia?" he asked.

"From what I hear, she was offered a better job." she said. "I've been here for about a week and a half."

"I see." he said.

What could she have known? He was hoping that what he was thinking wasn't true, but in this line of work it happened all the time.

"I'm sorry, Mr. Murphy, you can't be too careful." she said.

"No apology necessary, Jeanette, I know the routine." he said.

She smiled at him.

He walked through the metal detector.

They got to Leland's office and both watched the light above his door. At exactly eleven A.M. it turned from red to green.

"Go right in, Mr. Murphy." she said.

"Thank you." he said.

He tried to straighten himself up and stretch so he would be a little taller when he entered.

"Close the door and have a seat, Anthony." he said.

"There's been a development." he said. "Very exciting news. Erik Stryker's son has developed abilities."

"He has a son?" he asked.

"He's fifteen years old now." he said. "The product of a liaison between him and Danielle. You remember, the French girl? The one who wants to come in from the cold? We still have her under control."

"That may be helpful as we move forward. Why wasn't I informed of this?" he said. "He was one of the seventeen! He has a child that survived?"

"I've been keeping an eye on him." he said. "I've asked you about her several times, and your answer has always been that she needs to stay in the dark. There have been no signs until recently, but this sign was a big one."

The French girl. She's always been a pain in the ass. He had mostly forgotten about her except that Anthony had brought her up from time to time. Why wouldn't he tell me that she had a kid? With one of the seventeen no less.

"You need to be much more transparent with me, Mr. Murphy." he said. "It's disappointing that I'm just hearing about this now."

"I apologize, sir, but nothing was happening." he said. "I didn't think you would want to be bothered with something that was essentially meaningless, and frankly, you never want to talk about her. But I've been watching. Do you have a VHS player?"

He pulled out a remote and pressed the button and two wooden doors silently separated to reveal a large TV. He turned it on.

"It's right below the TV on the shelf." he said.

"May I?" he asked.

"Please." he said.

"It's of a soccer match that Antoine...Danielle's son was playing in." he said. "Antoine is number 9 on the blue team. Watch what happens when the other team tries to clear the zone."

He watched as the red team kicked the ball towards the blue end of the field. Suddenly the ball took a hard right turn and landed on Antoine's foot, which was already in motion waiting for the ball. He put it in the upper right corner of the net.

His jaw dropped.

"Play that again." he said.

He played it again and Leland shook his head. It was true. All that crazy shit that the spooks had been talking about for all these years was real.

"They're on their way here now, I'm picking them up at the airport at 4." he said. "We need to let the MK people figure this out. I have him set up for a two week analysis. Something like what Stryker and the others went through back in the seventies. We'll need to fragment him."

"I'm willing to defer and let them do their work." he said. "God knows I don't know anything about it."

"Good." he said. "We should talk about Stryker. I think he should know about this. Not now, but after he gets back from Ireland."

"I'll have to think about that." he said. "Does he know about this boy?"

"No. That's why Danielle has been trying to come in from the cold." he said. "It's been tough on her, but she's always cooperated. Not without a certain amount of bitching sometimes, but she hasn't contacted him. He thinks she's dead."

"Is there any reason he should think otherwise?" he asked.

"Apart from the fact that he's never met his kid, and doesn't even know about him? With our plans for Antoine,

Stryker could be a valuable asset." he said. "He's been through a lot of the same stuff, and even though Antoine is showing stronger signs than him now, it's possible that in a short time Erik will be just as strong."

Bet you're glad you didn't kill him now, he thought.

"I'll have to talk to the experts and see what they think." he said. "I'm for anything that will help us get to the next level."

"That's good to hear." he said. "These are amazing times. It turns out all that whacky shit the spooks have been saying all these years is true."

"Protect this kid with your life, Anthony." he said. "We're too close for any fuck ups."

"He's going straight to the institute." he said. "There's more security there than Fort Knox. He'll be fine."

He went back to the vault and filled up a suitcase.

"Give this to the girl." he said. "It's $250,000. That's more than enough to buy any cooperation that we need. Let me know if she's going to be a problem."

"I don't expect that she will, sir." he said. "After all, she's under our control."

"Call me after they're settled." he said. "That is all."

He picked up the suitcase and departed the office.

***

"How long do we have to stay, mom?" he asked.

"Don't you want to meet your father?" she asked.

"Of course. But what about Angeline?" he asked. "She wasn't happy when I told her I was leaving."

"She'll be fine." she said. "Young love rarely lasts. Besides, we're going to America, the most beautiful girls in the world live there."

"But I want Angeline." he said.

"We're going on an adventure." she said. "Your father is away on business, so you're going to spend a couple of weeks at a very special place that is going to help you develop your abilities. But we can see him as soon as he gets back."

"I don't have any abilities." he said.

"You don't need to lie to me, son." she said. "I know what's going on. You get them from your father."

"What abilities?" he asked.

"Are you trying to embarrass yourself?" she asked. "I know what you did when the ball came to you at the end of the game. I've seen other signs too. Maybe you just think it's magic, but it's in your genes. You can do things that nobody else can. That's why you're going to that place. So they can help you understand it."

"When will my father be back?" he asked.

"Probably before you're done at the institute." she said. "He has some business in Ireland."

"So he's a businessman?" he asked.

She started laughing.

"No, no, dear." she said. "But it's better if we call it a business trip. Look down there! There it is, New York City."

He looked down and saw the Statue of Liberty on an island in New York Harbor, and a massive metropolis behind it.

"Is it true that we gave that to them?" he asked.

"Yes. It was a gift from the French people commemorating the alliance of France and the United States during the American Revolution." she said. "They put it in New York Harbor in 1886 because back then almost all immigrants came here through New York. They wanted everyone to know that this is a free country."

"Have you ever been here?" he asked.

"Nope, so it will be new for both of us. When you get out of the institute, you can call Angeline if you like." she said. "But I doubt you'll still be thinking about her. There will be more important things."

He doubted that, but he knew it was pointless to protest. When his mother made up her mind on something, there was no talking to her. He would see her when they got back to France.

"Are we going back to France when this is over?" he asked.

"That will depend on some things that we have no control over." she said. "But a lot of that depends on you."

The plane was landing. As they entered the airport, a man that was probably an inch or two shorter than Antoine greeted them.

"How was your flight?" he asked.

"It was fine." she said. "It was the first time for Antoine."

"Antoine, Anthony Murphy." he said.

He extended his hand, which Antoine shook.

"Do you know why you're here?" he asked.

"My mom tells me that I'm going to some institute." he said.

"That's right." he said. "These strange things that you've been able to do? They're going to help you with that. They'll explain it to you so you can understand, work with you so you can harness it for the greater good."

"How do you know about that?" he asked.

"Your mom and I are old friends." he said. "She told me about it, and I have the right connections to figure this thing out."

They got in a black limousine that had to be at least 20 feet long.

"Would you like something to drink, Antoine?" he asked.

"If you two don't mind, I think I'll take a nap." he said.

"That's fine, Antoine." he said. "We'll be there in a little over an hour. Your English is great, by the way."

"My mom taught me when I was young." he said.

A few minutes later he was asleep.

"Are we going to be able to see him?" she asked.

"I'm working on that." he said. "As long as the doctors can convince my boss, I think so."

"Good." she said. "What's this place you're taking him to?"

"There will be a lot of doctors and specialists checking him out." he said. "This is unprecedented. Some of the others in Erik's group had kids, but none survived. Not only did Antoine survive, he's thriving. And we're seeing something that most of us had given up on."

"Was his like mine?" she asked. "His camp?"

"It was a little more intense." he said. "You didn't think you bumped into him by accident on that beach in Monte Carlo, did you?"

"What do you mean?" she asked.

"Never mind." he said. "It was just fortunate for us that you did."

She was, programmed to meet him, of course. One of the four personalities of hers that they controlled, the Beta. It was by far the strongest. The fragmentation worked okay on her, but they weren't able to develop a memory center in her. It wasn't unusual. She wasn't as dissociative as others.

Erik on the other hand was a perfect candidate. Due to severe trauma early in his life, he already had a dissociative personality. They had fragmented his brain when he was at the MK camp. Did tests on him, exposed him to a lot of dark shit, and made sure he didn't remember any of it. They didn't know it at the time, but his experiences at the camp attached to his DNA. Back then, they had only hoped that *he* would develop supernatural abilities.

Later they figured out that any offspring that the seventeen had would have a good chance of developing abilities, after they discovered that parents can pass trauma and dissociation through epigenetic memory. Literally his DNA. Him procreating with Danielle helped too, since she had dissociative alters as well. That wasn't a mistake, they made sure that they got together. Her Beta personality, the sexual one. It was the strongest one she had. Erik never stood a chance. It was what controlled his feelings for her to this day. That and periodic reminders from Murphy to his Beta alter.

He knew that the same thing that happened to Erik was going to happen to Antoine at the institute. Maybe worse. But they had to do it. They had never been this close, whatever the price, there was no stopping now. He had steeled himself against any feelings about what he was doing to Antoine.

They were on the outskirts of Princeton, New Jersey. Danielle had fallen asleep too. He nudged her.

"We're here." he said.

Chapter 21

It was a tall shimmering building, at least 20 stories high. The glass had mirrors on the outside so you couldn't see in. They went through the entrance, which was a large entryway of clear glass. Above the entrance were big block letters that said "The Monarch Institute".

"Is this a government building?" she asked.

"No." he said. "Officially it doesn't even exist."

"Doesn't look like they're trying to hide it." she said.

"If we tried to hide it, they'd find it." he said. "The Monarch Institute is nothing more than a large research facility. Privately owned, doing research to try to make people's lives better. Some of the funding is from Princeton University."

"Officially." she said.

"We're getting into an area that I can't talk about." he said. "Antoine will be fine. They just want to check him out and run some tests."

"Like they did with Erik?" she asked.

"Exactly." he said. "And you know as well as I do that he's fine. And you turned out okay, didn't you? Antoine will fine."

They went up to the desk and checked in. Before they had a chance to sit down the receptionist called them up.

"Good afternoon, Mr. Murphy." she said. "And you must be Antoine."

"Yeah." he said.

"You're going to the 17th floor to see Dr. Heisenberg." she said. "The elevators are right this way."

She escorted them over there.

"You're going to be just fine." she told Antoine.

Why wouldn't I be? He wondered.

They got on the elevator and it sped up to the 17th floor. They got off and went down a bright mostly white hall. About halfway down, they turned into an office where a balding man with a goatee and glasses greeted them.

"How are you, Antoine?" he asked.

"Okay I guess." he said.

"You're going to be staying with us for a couple of weeks I understand." he said. "We're sorry that your mom can't stay, but there are plenty of pretty nurses."

"Okay." he said.

"If I could just ask you some preliminary questions." he said. "Have you ever felt like you're someone else? Like you do things that might be out of character for you?"

"I don't know." he said. "Is this about the fight? Because that kid had it coming."

"I don't know anything about a fight, Antoine." he said. "Is it out of character for you to fight?"

"It depends on the...circumstances? Is that the right word?" he asked

"Very good Antoine!" he said. "That's exactly the word. Under what circumstances would you fight?"

"When I'm out on the soccer field, I try to stay away from that kind of thing." he said. "I try to focus on the game. When I fought that kid, I was hoping he would try to throw the first punch. He hurt my friend."

"What if he didn't throw the first punch?" he asked. "Would you still have fought him?"

"Every now and then I don't worry so much about the rules." he said. "In that case, I might have. Probably would have. He broke Paul's ankle."

"But he approached you first?" he asked.

"Yeah." he said. "He accused me of cheating. I figured if I insulted his team maybe he would take it to the next level. I hoped he would. He started it, and I finished it."

"So you manipulated the situation to make him do what you wanted?" he asked.

"Manipulated?" he asked.

"You tricked him into doing what you wanted him to do." he said. I think the French word is *manipuler les."*

"Yeah." he said. "I was pretty sure it was going to work. The only thing I thought might stop him was that I'm a little taller than him. He likes to pick fights he knows he can win."

"There's no shame in beating up bullies, Antoine." he said. "That's just another side of you. The protector. I think you'll find that you have many sides."

"I guess." he said.

"I think we have something to build on." he said. "Mr. Murphy and I will give you a few minutes alone with your mother to say goodbye. You'll see her again before you know it."

They walked out of the office.

"Did you see the tape?" he asked.

"Amazing." he said. "Just that little discussion in there about the fight is enough for me to know that he'll be receptive. He's already splitting on his own. What kind of trauma has he been through in the past?"

"He's never known his father. He fought one of his mother's boyfriends when he was beating on her." he said. "The guy kicked his ass pretty good, then turned back to Danielle."

"That's good. Anything else?" he said.

"His mother has never been in a good relationship. With the exception of Erik." he said. "She picks a lot of losers who abuse her. He's tries to intervene when he can, but it tends not to go well for him...or her. She hasn't had a boyfriend for almost a year now though."

"Good, we can work with that." he said. "She's the one with the overactive Beta, right? It's no wonder she can't pick'em. Those types attract abusers, because they're so submissive."

"Yeah, she's a primary Beta. It's why Erik still thinks about her. With a little help from me of course." he said.

"How is his relationship with his mother?" he asked.

"Antoine loves her unconditionally, and she loves him more than anything." he said. "She still pines for his father, and I'd like to bring him back after the work here is done. You calling Leland would go a long way in making that happen."

"I think that's a good idea too." he said. "I remember Erik. He could reinforce what we do here. Of course, he'll have no idea he's doing it. I'll give Leland a call.""

"We can bring the mother in when he's ready. She's still under our control." he said.

"That's good." he said. "Having someone he loves is important. I'll still be his primary savior, but he'll think his mother is too. When she comes in as the bitch, that will probably be all it takes. With a little luck, this won't take long at all. If we could delay the reintroduction to Erik for a while, that would be best. At least a few weeks from now, but not longer. They won't remember anything of course, but I remember Erik. If he sees them in peril it won't be good, even if he's still under control."

"He is." he said. "By the time he gets here, they will look normal. There won't be a way he'll know what really happened to his son."

"That's always best." he said.

"Erik may be carrying some baggage, but I could make that go away easily enough." he said. "She knows about it."

"Very good, Anthony." he said. "We'll start right away."

***

"Are you sure about this, mom?" he asked. "This place is creepy."

"You have nothing to worry about, baby." she said. "Anthony has done this many times. He works with a lot of people with your abilities. They're just going to help you make the most of your gifts."

My gifts, he thought. How long had she known? He thought he was doing a good job of hiding it. She said he got it from his dad. The whole situation was just weird to him.

"Okay, mom, I trust you." he said. "You wouldn't let anything bad happen to me."

She gave him a hug.

"I love you." she said. "We're going to see your dad really soon."

"I hope he's everything you make him out to be." he said.

"He's all that and more." she said.

The doctor came back in.

"I'm going to take you to your room, Antoine." he said. "A pleasure to meet you, Ms. Babineaux. We'll take good care of your boy."

"Thank you, doctor." she said.

They headed the opposite direction down the hall. Antoine turned to look just as his mother was getting on the elevator. She slipped in without noticing him.

They came to a room at the end of the hall. He hadn't seen any other people in this place besides the doctor. That's strange, he thought.

He opened the door and entered the room. It was all white just like the rest of the floor. There was a bed in the corner, a white leather easy chair, a white couch, a coffee table and a TV.

"Would you like to watch some American TV Antoine?" he asked.

"Sure." he said. "I'm a little hungry, when do we eat?"

"I'll send someone right up." he said. "It's not the Ritz, but it's better than hospital food. What would you like to drink?"

"Coke would be great." he said.

He turned on the TV. It was one of those shows that have predator animals hunting down weaker animals. He watched for a while and changed the channel. The other channel was wrestling.

There was a knock on his door.

"Mr. Stryker?" she asked.

"Come in." he said.

A very attractive girl in a uniform with a short skirt came in.

"I'm Vanessa. Sorry, all they had was chicken tonight." she said.

"I'm Antoine. Chicken is fine." he said.

She sat down next to him on the couch.

"Oh, I just love him! Hollywood Hulk Hogan!" she said. "They got you hooked up with pay per view, you must be special."

"I just turned it on." he said.

She put her hand on his knee.

He wanted to change it again, but he didn't want to upset Vanessa.

A quiet dull bell sounded in the room.

"Oh shit! That's me, I gotta go." she said. "I'll look forward to seeing you again, Antoine."

"Me too, Vanessa." he said.

As soon as she was gone he started eating and changed the channel again. It was that scene from Scarface at a run-down hotel in Miami shortly after Tony got there. The bad guys (Tony was also a bad guy of course), had chained him to the shower curtain rod. The other guy has a chainsaw in his hands.

"Yeah, okay, you gonna give me the cash or am I gonna kill your brother first? 'Fore I kill you?" he asks.

"Try sticking your head up your ass. See if it fits." says Tony.

After carving up his brother, the guy turns back to Tony.

"Frog face, you just fucked up. You steal from me, you're dead." says Tony.

"Okay, my 'caracortada', you can die too. Makes no difference to me." he says. "Last chance, carajo?"

"Fuck you!" says Tony.

He spits in his face.

Then Tony's guys come in and kill everyone except the original guy, who somehow makes it out to the street, the chainsaw still in his hands. Tony follows him out and in front of several witnesses shoots him in the head. He changed the channel again. It was a scene from The Godfather. He had only seen the French version. It was the scene where Michael is in the church becoming Godfather to his sister's son, with the audio from the church playing in the background while Michael is having all of his enemies killed. Settling all family business. They made it in the seventies, and considered graphic back then. Antoine had seen worse in the nineties, but nothing as cold as Michaels face while he's in the church renouncing Satan. He was suddenly very sleepy. He tried to turn the TV off, but dropped the remote before he could press the button.

"Okay, he's out." said Heisenberg. "Get a crew down there now. He's going to wake up in a different place."

***

"I guess that's it." he said.

They were staring at a piece of land off in the distance.

"How does it feel to be on a ship and not working?" she asked.

"Pretty weird." he said. "I almost volunteered for a watch."

"You can stand watch whether it's official or not, you know." she said.

"Don't think I haven't." he said.

"You ever been there? To Ireland?" she asked.

"Almost everywhere but." he said. "You?"
"I had an assignment in Belfast." she said.
"Where you picked up the brogue, no doubt." he said.
"You could do it too." she said. "It's easier than Danish."
"If I did, I would feel fake." he said. "Like I'm trying to impress someone and I don't know I look like a fool."
"You'd love it there." she said. "All they do is drink and fuck...sorry."
"Don't apologize." he said. "I'm down for the fucking."
"You okay with bombing a church?" she asked.
He had thought about that. He wasn't sure how he felt. He had been raised Catholic, but that ship sailed long ago. It was likely that it would be the best place. They met at churches for just that reason, because people might think twice about causing trouble at a church.
Not that it mattered much in Northern Ireland, virtually everyone was on their side.
"If that's what we have to do, we'll do it." he said. "We could probably get most of them at once."
"I'd rather not." she said.
"But you're..." he said.
"Just because I'm Jewish doesn't mean I'm not human." she said. "It's a place where people go to practice their religion."
"What if it was a mosque?" he asked.
"Bombs away." she said.
"That seems a little..." he said.
"Shut up. That doesn't mean I won't do it, I might just have a brief pang of guilt." she said.
"We *both* will." he said. "I'll have to remember it's not Father Leary back home. I went to Catholic school for eight years."
"I can guarantee it won't be Father Leary." she said.
They got to Cork and collected their luggage. They both traveled light. They went to the harbormaster who was expecting them and had the car. They were going as Mr. and Mrs. Jensen.
"Do you want me to drive?" she asked.

"Maybe you better, it's been a long time for me." he said. "Besides, the whole left side of the road thing might mess me up."

It had been since that trip through Africa since he had driven a car. It wasn't that he didn't know how, he was an excellent driver, he just didn't want to. He barely wanted to ride in one.

"No problem." she said.

"Of course, if you get tired, I'd be happy to take over." he said.

"I'll be okay." she said. "I know where the Malmaison is."

"How long ago were you here?" he asked.

"A few years after we went to France." she said. "If we could live overseas after this is all over, this would be a great place."

"Have you ever thought about...you know...leaving?" he asked. "I think we might be able to get away with it."

"Yeah, sure." she said, rolling her eyes. "Are you forgetting about that little prick watching us? He has every intelligence agency in the United States at his disposal, and probably others in every major country. I've thought about it, but I know how it ends. We don't get to say we're sorry and come back. You shouldn't be thinking about that. Like it or not, this is our life."

He hadn't told her about that dream. The one with the kid in it. Yet he had spilled everything to Taylor. Why was that?

"I had another dream." he said.

There. That fixes it, now I'm telling her.

"Tell me about it." she said.

He told her.

"You know, I don't dislike her." she said. "It's just the situation."

"I know." he said. "I told her the same thing. That under different circumstances you would probably like each other."

"When did you talk to her?" she asked.

"I don't know, I just told her the last time I talked to her." he said. "She thinks the kid might be me. You know? Because Keith Moon was there, and I was sixteen when he died."

"So you talked to her since having this dream?" she asked. "The one you had just before you got to New York?"

He was just digging himself deeper. Time to just confess and hope for the best.

"Yes, I talked to her from the Mauritius." he said. "She's really good at these things."

Inside her head was exploding, but her exterior remained calm.

"She's probably right." she said, as calmly as she could.

She was thinking the same thing that Taylor was thinking and she didn't even know it. She had never heard of Danielle having a kid, but the timing was right.

They kept everything about Danielle quiet since she was put out in the cold. Even past information wasn't available. It made sense though, and the way he was seeing things in his dreams. How had he not figured this out? She didn't know, but she damned sure wasn't going to tell him.

"Why was he speaking French?" he asked. "And why would you tell me that you don't speak French?"

Because he lives in France, she thought.

"I don't know, Stryker." she said. "I'm sure I know a lot less about dreams than Taylor."

"Listen, I don't know why I called her." he said. "I just did. It's nothing for you to worry about. She's a long way away."

"Not as far as she used to be." she said.

"She's in Monte Carlo, not Ireland." he said. "I'm here. With you, Mrs. Jensen. On our honeymoon."

She cracked the faintest of smiles.

"It's annoying how hard it is to stay mad at you." she said. "You're going to do whatever you do. If you want to call her, you'll call her. Not saying it's cool, but I can't stop you. I'll let you make it up to me when we get to the hotel."

"I promise you won't be disappointed." he said.

"I better not be." she said.

They came to a checkpoint going into Northern Ireland and they asked them what their business was.

"Aye, I'm just a lass from Derry on me honeymoon taking me beloved to meet me folks." she said. "He's a Danish fella I met in the states. So nice t' be back home."

The guard looked her over, and she couldn't have looked more innocent. Her story seemed legitimate.

"How do ya like Ireland, sir?" he asked.

"Det er et dejligt land, du har her...oh, undskyld..." he said. "It...is a...lovely...country du har here."

"Still learnin' the language." she said.

"You two have a wonderful night." he said.

They pulled away.

"Nice touch." she said. "Couldn't even make it through the sentence without reverting. 'Du har'. like 'you have' was so hard to figure out."

"Well, you said I was a Danish fella, I had to make it look real." he said.

They arrived in Belfast and checked in to the Malmaison. It was everything Murphy said it was. She knew a restaurant near the water called Holohan's, so they went there.

"So who did you come here with before?" he asked.

"Doesn't matter, I'm here with you now, Mr. Jensen." she said. "And we're on our honeymoon."

"It really doesn't matter." he said. "I'm right where I want to be. Have you ever thought about it? Being married?"

"Is that your clumsy way of proposing to me?" she asked.

"I was just wondering." he said. "I don't suppose either of our lifestyles would permit it."

"Unless we found someone who shared that lifestyle." she said.

"Hmm...I don't know anyone like that." he said.

"Smart ass." she said. "I've thought about it. It's not something I don't want to do. But it would have to be someone I knew I could spend the rest of my life with. Someone I could trust."

"Don't know anyone like that either." he said.

"Stop." she said. "If you're testing the waters, I could have that discussion...*if* that's what you're doing. Because if it's not, I take back everything I just said."

"I might be persuaded to have that discussion too." he said. "But if you're not up for it, I take back everything I just said."

"Let's not worry about it." she said. "We could break our ankles from so much backpedaling. Let's just enjoy our honeymoon. And do that other thing we came here for."

"We should get back to the hotel." he said. "After we consummate our marriage, we can make plans for tomorrow."

"I'm glad you have your priorities straight." she said. "Let's go.

***

He woke up in the dark on the concrete floor. Where was he? The last thing he remembered he was on his way to his room at the institute.

He felt...funny. Like his mind wasn't completely there. He noticed a faint light in the distance. He saw a barely visible shadow on the wall. It started moving. It wasn't a shadow of anything, just a slight variation in the dark. It slowly took the shape of a huge dragon. He could see flames shooting out of its nose of a slightly lighter color. It's eyes turned red.

He suddenly realized that he was naked. He felt his head and discovered that he was also bald. The dragon was slowly walking towards him. Is that a real dragon? He heard a loud roar, and real flames shot out as it got closer. Suddenly it turned into a pig, and started snorting. It's eyes were still red, and it looked angry. He could tell that it was sniffing the air trying to find him.

"What are you doing here, Antoine?" it asked. "If you're here to fight, I can promise I'll throw the first punch."

The pig had turned into that kid from Montreuil that he beat up. The problem was that he was about 9 feet tall now.

"Fuck that, I don't care if you want to fight or not, I'm kicking your ass!" he said.

Antoine held his arms over his head before the kid rained down several vicious blows on him. Nothing happened for a few minutes, so he peeked through his arms to see if he was still there. He was and his face was huge. He was inches away with his arm cocked back.

"Come on, Louis." she said. "This kid is a loser. I hung out with him for a while, but he's a pussy. It took him a month to try to kiss me. You and I fucked on the first night. That's what a *real man* does."

It was Angeline. She came over and kicked him in the face.

"What's the matter, boy?" she said. "Did I hurt your feelings? I bet you can't even get it up. I'm done with you, you were a waste of time. A waste of oxygen, really. I'm going to suck Louis's dick. Maybe he'll let you go next."

Louis came back and hammered him in the face some more.

"I'll be right with you babe, feel free to start without me." he said. "I just have to remind this idiot one more time why you're with me."

"I'll be ready for you, baby." she said. "Don't waste too much time on that little boy. I want to feel you inside me."

She came back and started laughing.

"Look at his little pecker!" she said. "My cat has a bigger dick."

She kicked him again and spat on him.

She grabbed Louis's cock.

"This is what I need." she said.

She got on her knees and started sucking.

He couldn't believe this was happening. Where was he? Was Angeline really with *him*? How could she?

"It was easy, junior, he's a man, and you aren't." she said. "You're barely a boy."

He wanted to defend himself, but he couldn't speak. He was also deathly afraid of Louis.

The last thing he remembered he was going to his room with Dr. Heisenberg. Now it came back to him. The white room. The TV. The girl...Vanessa?

"She's right, you know." she said. "You are a waste of breath. Nobody wants your tiny pecker. Move over, Angeline, I want some!"

Vanessa. She got on her knees and looked into his eyes.

"I've been waiting all day for this." she said.

Suddenly it was pitch black again. It stayed that way for several hours. He couldn't even sleep, he was wide awake. He was scared that Louis would come back...or worse, Angeline. He crawled around, he couldn't even find a wall. Just cold hard concrete. And he was naked.

Suddenly a wolf appeared. It was growling, showing its sharp, yellow teeth, which were dripping with blood. It paused to howl, then its mouth snapped shut again. Its eyes were bright green with pupils the color of blood. Other wolves started to appear. They were all growling, barking, and snapping their teeth. One of them grabbed his arm, and another his leg. They started viciously pulling. He tried to fight back but he couldn't reach them. As they pulled, they ripped his skin. His arm came off, which only brought more wolves with the smell of blood. He tried to scream, but no sound came out.

Suddenly he was underwater. The strange part was that he was still breathing. He adjusted his eyes just in time to see a huge shark coming at him. He reflexively lifted his arm to defend himself, and realized that his arm was gone from the wolves. The shark had cold, dark eyes. He tried to swim away, but without the use of his left arm, he couldnt. He looked back. The shark was at least 30 or 40 feet long. The dead eyes were riveted to him. In an instant it caught up to him and snapped his leg off like a twig. It was too big for the shark to swallow whole, and it broke in half. It gulped down the part that was still in its mouth, then quickly turned around and inhaled the other part.

Now it was looking at Antoine again. As it sped towards him, he felt something lifting him from below.

An island had appeared beneath him, and now he was on dry land. He tried to sit up, but he couldn't, because his arm was missing. He just laid there, bleeding profusely from where his arm and leg used to be attached to his body. If only I could sleep...or die. He heard another growl. He did his best to straighten himself and look up. Out of the corner of his eye he saw a large bear approaching. It was at least 30 feet tall. When it saw him, it ran to him and took a chunk out of his belly.

***

"What's he thinking?" he asked.

"Of course, there's no way to know for sure, but an educated guess says it's his deepest fears. Humiliation is a big part of it, powerlessness to do anything about it. We need to break him down to properly fragment his brain. This one should be easy. He already has a start. Most have to suffer severe trauma to become pliable." he said. "Antoine is lucky...in context. He has intergenerational trauma passed down from his father through epigenetic memory. The trauma and dissociation is literally in his DNA."

He was glad that the kid couldn't see what was really going on in Antoine's head. He knew what they were doing, and he had the clearance to be in here, something that was rare and meant a lot.

The CIA's best and brightest. He knew that they were working with mind control, but he didn't have any idea on what level.

People had become squeamish in the past and tried to talk, but few listened. Once it was evident that they were talking, they "committed suicide". During the vetting process for virtually everyone, unbeknownst to them, an alter was created. A suicide alter.

All they needed to was to set them in motion. The subject did the rest, suicide note and all. Then the police would discover evidence of mental instability and suicidal tendencies so nobody would look into it any further.

"I've read about that, but it seems so unreal." he said.

"This is the place where the unreal is possible." he said.

"How long has he been in there?" he asked.

"About an hour." he said. "But it's been much longer than that for him."

He looked at the monitor of Antoine. He was in a sensory deprivation chamber. Floating in saltwater with opaque black goggles on, earplugs, a nose plug, and a mouthpiece to prevent him from talking.

He knew that none of these items stopped the terror. There were intravenous tubes running from his arms, which was how they administered the LSD. Now they were alternating amphetamines and barbiturates from one arm to the other. They discovered in the seventies that this method kept the subject disoriented and speeded up the process of dispensing with the conscious mind. The unconscious mind would take over, and that was where the fragmentation occurred.

"How long do we leave him like that?" he asked.

"It needs to run its course." he said. "At least 6 hours, more would be better. Unfortunately for him, time isn't the same where he is. You can generally multiply it by at least 5. His vitals will tell us when he's ready, then we put him to sleep. 12 hours later, we start again."

"How many times?" he asked. "When do we work with him physically?"

"After the second time we let him wake up." he said. "He won't be in a happy place. You've seen the cells in the basement?"

"Yeah." he said.

"Not a pleasant place. It will all be real down there too." he said. "It seems harsh, but he won't remember any of this. If anything he'll be grateful that his life is going so well. You'll be with me for the whole process, you'll see."

"He looks so peaceful." he said.

"That's a good way to look at it." he said. "Working here isn't for the meek. It gets dark sometimes. The thing to focus on is the end result."

"Can I see that tape again?" he said. "From the soccer field?"

"Sure." he said.

Dr. Heisenberg had the whole tape. Including the fight. While the movement of the ball was amazing, he was more interested in the fight. It was an early example of one of Antoine's alters.

Chapter 22

They were outside of a St. Patrick's Church in Belfast. Erik had come the previous night to rig the C-4. It was all set up for a remote detonator.

They just needed to see who was in attendance. It would probably be most of them, but they would have to take care of any stragglers quickly. After the bombing, any element of surprise would be lost. If they left anyone live they would be on guard. Liam and Brendan's father Aidan were there. Almost everyone was, with the exception of Marcus O'Neil and Ryan Bailey. She looked over the list carefully. He was looking through the binoculars, announcing who he saw to Lexie.

"Nope." he said "Rowan Kelly isn't here either."

"Is anyone else missing?" she asked. "I've looked through it 3 times. Give me those, you take a look."

He handed her the binoculars.

He looked it over and saw that she was making check marks next to the ones that they confirmed.

"Put a check mark next to O'Neil, he just showed up." she said. "They're shutting the doors. We'll have to deal with Bailey and Kelly later."

"We should make that happen tonight at the latest." he said.

He knew he was stating the obvious, but it felt better saying it out loud.

"We will." she said. "Bailey should be easy, he has that cailín on the south side. Kelly likes to gamble, we should find him at that game in the Gaeltacht Quarter."

"Do you know where that is?" he asked.

"You know how I like to gamble. Don't worry, I had some business in the Gaeltacht Quarter last time I was here, I can find it. It's on Falls Road. It's in the western section near Dunville Park." she said. "Bailey's moll lives on Fitzroy. We should probably do him first. Unless you want to split up."

We should stay together." he said. "You know this place, but I don't."

"Okay." she said. "You ready to get this part over?"

He had to put it out of his mind that he was about to blow up a church. Psychologically it was tough. But while it might be a good church...with questionable leadership, the men they were killing were bad. He took one last look.

"You okay?" she asked.

"No, yeah, I'm fine." he said. "It's just the church thing. But this takes care of most of the list."

He pulled out the remote and pressed the button. The church exploded, leaving a trail of fire and smoke much higher than he had anticipated. It was a bigger than the explosion of the warehouse in Cairo, but then it was smaller. There was nothing left except for the smoldering remains of the foundation.

"I guess they're dead." he said.

Lexie didn't respond. He looked over and saw her lying motionless on the ground. There was a surgically neat bullet hole in the middle of her forehead. Blood spurted out and her eyes were still open, in a lifeless stare.

"No!" he said.

He cradled her in his arms and looked around. There was no one in sight. He stayed there for a moment until he realized that he might be next. He never heard a shot. They must have timed it to be silenced by the blast. He didn't want to leave her like this, but there was nothing he could do. He closed her eyes and headed for the car.

He got in the car and headed for Fitzroy Street. He read the same intelligence that she did, so he knew the address. When he got there, he looked at house. It was a private residence, grey with a red door. There was a blue Renault parked out front. Bailey's car. He went up and tried the handle. It was locked.

He pulled out an eyeglass screwdriver and pushed it into the keyhole as far as he could. He jiggled it, twisted it, and turned it until it caught the groove and clicked open.

He silently entered and drew his gun. He went straight upstairs, assuming that Bailey would be in the bedroom with the girl. The door was ajar, and he heard the sounds of lovemaking. He quietly pushed the door the rest of the way open and saw Bailey behind her facing the wall, neither one aware of his presence. A bullet hit the back of his head after a low whoosh from the silencer. He fell on top of the girl who still didn't know what had happened. She looked back and put one in her eye.

He left the house, relocking the door from the inside, got in the car and headed for the hotel.

He would have to wait to do Kelly. The game would start in a few hours. Fortunately, the game wasn't run by the Irish Kings, so as long as he hadn't found out about the bombing he would be none the wiser. Kelly was a low level member who wasn't included in everything, but he was still on the list.

Back at the hotel he turned on the news. They were talking about the bombing, but there was no mention of the IRA. They were also talking about the mysterious woman found dead of a gunshot wound about a quarter mile away. He had to hope that Kelly didn't see the news. It had been a few hours since the explosion. He decided to call Murphy.

"Mr. Stryker." he said.

"Hey." he said. "We bombed the church. Bailey wasn't there but I took care of him. The only other one that wasn't there was Kelly, but I'll take care of him tonight. There's something else..."

"I know, Lexie's dead." he said.

He knew that Murphy found a way to know everything, but how could he know about this?

"How do you know?" he asked.

"I have feeds from the same news agency you're watching in Belfast, Erik." he said. "Mysterious woman shot near the scene? I knew it was her. I'm sorry for your loss."

"Thank you." he said. "I never heard the shot. It was like they timed it so it would get lost in the explosion. Do you know anything about this?"

The line went silent for a moment.

"Hello?" he asked.

"No. I wish it never happened." he said. "Whether you know it or not I cared a great deal for her, and you too. Most of my agents don't get that, but you and Lexie...I guess you're different. I never want to lose an agent, but when it's someone I care about...well I care about all of you but..." he said.

"I get what you're saying, Anthony." he said. "It will be tough for both of us. I assume that you'll take care of the body?"

"One of my people has already claimed it, and it will be on its way to Israel tonight." he said. "She'll be buried with her parents. Mount Olivet cemetery if you want to visit."

"Thank you." he said "I hope Kelly hasn't seen the news."

"Doubtful." he said. "He's been out of town all day."

"Right, the grandmother." he said.

Kelly went to visit his grandmother in Ballymoney every Wednesday, and went straight from there to the game.

"There's something else." he said. "Liam Gallagher survived. Maybe the first time a cigarette saved a life. He's at Mater Infirmorum Hospital. I'm sending someone to help you. She'll be there by morning."

"She?" he asked.

"She'll be a nurse at the hospital." he said. "We can't send you because he knows you."

"Who is she?" he asked. "Is she any good?"

"You'll see soon enough." he said. "I have the utmost confidence in her. Take care of Kelly tonight and you'll meet her in the morning."

The line went dead.

Another female agent. He knew that Anthony had the best, but there weren't any better than Lexie. None even as good.

It seemed odd that they shot her and left him alone. He had to wonder if it was the Irish Kings or someone closer to home.

It dawned on him for the first time that he had a premonition of her death in his dream. She was lying next to him when he woke. It was eerie. Whether he liked it or not, he was seeing the future.

He decided to look through the pay-per-view movies. May as well, it's on Murphy's dime, and he needed to kill a couple of hours. He also need something to take his mind off Lexie if that was even possible. He found something on the first page, "Pulp Fiction." He had never seen it, but the guys from the club raved about it. It was a few years old, but he wasn't much for going out to movies. He wasn't a huge Travolta fan, but Samuel L. Jackson, Bruce Willis, and Uma Thurman were in it too. He was cool with almost anything with Samuel L.

Jackson. After he finished watching it, he had to admit that John Travolta did a pretty good job. The whole story was good. Quentin Tarantino even made an appearance.

He left the room and got something to eat at the restaurant that in the hotel.

He really missed her. There was nobody to share his goofy insights with.

He didn't like her when they first met. She was bossy, and assumed that he didn't know what he was doing. The fact was that she was right, it was his first mission.

But he would be damned if he was going to let her know that. After a few hours she changed her tune. Then that wild ride down the Nile into Egypt. He knew she was falling in love with him, but he didn't feel as strong about it. Towards the end, it was starting to get annoying, particularly after they got to France.

He didn't know it at the time, but Danielle was in the mix in Monte Carlo. At that point he still thought she was dead. And of course, there was bad blood between Lexie and Danielle, which he didn't know about either. It was a situation that understandably made Lexie a little crazy.

He didn't exactly see her best side while they were in Monte Carlo, really from Cairo on, after she screwed up the timers on the C-4 at the warehouse. He didn't give her as much shit as he could have about *that*.

He figured that when they talked to Murphy after the warehouse, he told her that Danielle would be waiting for them on the other side of the Med. That was why she was so fucked up.

That day she appeared out of nowhere at the club she was different. It was great to see her, he had thought about her quite a bit since their mission.

It didn't take long for him to see that she had changed. She was always confident, but now she acted stronger, less needy. When they first met, he would have never guess that she could fall so hard for him.

She was acting like *that* Lexie, the one he met on the pier in Mombasa without the bossiness. It was very appealing. He tried not to be superficial, and most of the time he didn't think he was, but there was no denying how beautiful she was. That was always a big part of it. A man will put up with a lot of shit for a beautiful girl.

He paid the check and went out to the car. He had the address, Falls Road went right through Belfast, so he got on it and headed west looking for Dunville Park. There were address numbers painted on the curb and he found the right address. It was just a doorway with a stairwell going up. Great, one way in, one way out, he thought. He had his Glock, with a 19 round magazine and an extra clip. Let's hope it doesn't come to that. He knew that it was likely that he would have to kill them all, and some of them would be armed. He had an eye for picking out the most dangerous people first.

He came to a door with light creeping out of the bottom. There were sounds coming from the room of gambling and chips splashing the pot. The other door was dark. Here goes nothing, he thought.

He burst in and shot the two people facing him with their backs to the wall. He swiveled around and got one more as another tried to flee. He shot the runner in the back and looked back at the table. The sole survivor was Kelly, whose back was to the wall, and his hands were up.

"I'm really sorry, Mr. Kelly, but you're the one I'm here for." he said. "The rest of these guys were just unlucky."

"Why?" he asked.

"It's nothing personal." he said. "It's just a job."

He put a bullet in his forehead. There wasn't a huge rush to get out of there, he used his silencer.

He picked up Kelly's cards. He had had to look, they were playing draw. Aces and eights. Dead man's hand, how appropriate. He absently thought that it might not have made a difference if Wild Bill Hickok had his back to the wall or not. That bastard McCall might have killed him anyway.

He decided to take a drive. It was weird at first driving on the left, but he was getting used to it. He found a diner at the edge of town.

He walked in and it looked the same as an American joint. He didn't know what he was expecting, but he thought it would be different. The waitress even looked like a typical American diner waitress. She walked over to him. She had a nametag that said "Colleen." She had dark red hair, and a lot of freckles. It worked well for her, she was a good looking woman.

"What can I getcha, luv?" she asked.

"How 'bout a cup of coffee?" he said.

He didn't have much interest in sleeping tonight, he doubted that he could anyway.

"Aye, cuppa Joe. Any afters wit' that?" she asked.

"I'm sorry, I used to have someone to help me with this. She...never mind." he said. "What are afters?"

"Ya know? Somethin' t' go wit' yer coffee." she said. "Like a donut er a piece o' pie?"

"Oh, thanks." he said. "What kind of pie do you have?"

"All kinds, and they're all lovely, but I'd steer ya towards th' Brioche Bread and Butter Puddin'." she said. "It's a taste of the old country made right here at Conner's by the owners ma. The recipe goes back 400 years."

"How could I say no?" he said.

"Savage, fine thing." she said. "Just so I don't leave ya wonderin' savage is a good...so is fine thing."

"I think fine thing is universal, but thanks for the translation on the other, Colleen." he said. "Savage means something entirely different in the United States."

"Yer American?" she asked.

"Like you didn't know." he said. "Is it that obvious?"

"I had my suspicions." she said. "Welcome to the Emerald Isle. Business or pleasure?"

"A little of both." he said.

"Don't be put off by the news." she said. "I know our reputation, but things really don't blow up too often around here." she said.

"A church though?" he asked.

"Aye. Some of the boys were meetin' there. Ya know, the Sinn Féin?" she said. "They think it's an inside job, a couple o' the lads didn't show. It won't go well for those maggots."

I think they'll figure out that it's not them, he thought.

A little ironic the IRA getting bombed, no?" he said.

"I suppose." she said. "I'll go get your coffee."

She turned and walked away quickly.

What happened? We were having a good back and forth there. Was it the crack about the IRA?

She came back with his coffee.

"You know, I didn't mean any offense by that IRA comment." he said. "Sometimes I speak without thinking."

"Thanks fer tha apology." she said. "It's just that I'm close to the cause. Anything negative sets me off."

"Honestly, if I lived here I would probably be a member." he said.

"Okay, we'll start anew..." she said.

"Erik. Pleased to meet you." he said. "I might be here for a while, Colleen. I'll tip you well, if American money is okay. I feel bad tying up you're table."

She looked around. There was only one other customer, an old man struggling to stay awake at the bar.

"American money is fine lad, I bring it to the bank an' they exchange it." she said. "Worth more than Irish Pounds. As for taking up space, I don't think that's a problem. I'd rather you stay, otherwise I have to try to make conversation with Rip Van Winkle over there."

"Okay." he said.

"Order up!" said the cook.

I'll be right back wit' yer brioche." she said.

I killed seven people today, and a bombed a dozen more. And it doesn't bother me. Who am I? And the woman I love...he couldn't say *that* didn't bother him. In fact, her getting killed probably cancelled out the guilt for the others. To live through this...without her. He wished it would have been him. Well, maybe not. People always said that, but few really thought about the ramifications. He only knew that he wished it didn't happen.

He pulled out his phone and called Taylor. It went to voicemail. What he had to say couldn't be left as a message.

Colleen came back with his food. She looked at the phone.

"Fancy!" she said. "What are ya a secret agent?"

He cracked a thin smile.

"No, my boss just needs to get a hold of me at any time." he said. "*He* pays for the phone."

"What do you do?" she asked.

"Global marketing." he said. "That's what brings me to Belfast."

"Yer gonna love this, Erik." she said. "I'll leave ya to it."

He looked at the plate. It was an enormous amount of food. He'd never seen anything like it before, but it smelled good. He started eating and he was hungrier than he thought, he ate the whole thing. At least I won't offend Colleen, he thought. Suddenly he was very tired.

She came back.

"Can I assume ya liked it?" she asked.

"It was great, thanks for the suggestion." he said.

"I knew ya'd like it." she said. "Can I get ya another cuppa?"

"You know, Colleen, I'm actually more tired than I thought." he said. "I hate to leave you with Skippy over there, but I have a client early in the morning."

"Aye, the Brioche an' Puddin'll do that to ya." she said.

"Let me give you this." he said.

He pulled out a hundred dollar bill.

"Aye, but it's too much!" she said. "I can't take 'tis from ya."

"Global marketing has been good to me, Colleen." he said. "I can afford it."

"Ya sure?" she asked. "Lemme get ya some change."

He held up his hand.

"I've given more to less deserving people." he said. "Buy yourself something nice."

"Aye." she said. "Sorry we got off on th' wrong foot."

"But we made up for it nicely, didn't we?" he asked.

"That we did." she said. "Can I expect to see ya again?"

"If not on this trip, next time I'm in Belfast." he said.

"Aye. Have a lovely evenin'." she said.

He got back in the car and went back to the hotel. When he got in, he laid down on the bed fully clothed and fell asleep.

***

He was back at the club. Pink Floyd was playing on the jukebox. Lexie was there and so was Taylor. Danielle and the kid from before were at a separate table.

"You know I'm not really here, don't you?" asked Lexie.

"I know." he said.

"I never disliked you, it was just what you did." said Taylor.

"I know." she said. "But you can't deny you were trying to get him back."

"It doesn't matter now, does it?" she asked.
"No." she said quietly.

Hello,
Is there anybody in there?
Just nod if you can hear me.
Is there anyone at home?
Come on now
I hear you're feeling down
Well, I can ease your pain
And get you on your feet again

An appropriate song, he thought.
The kid started walking up to him, but Danielle stopped him. Lexie was as sad as he had ever seen her. Taylor tried to look understanding.
"I'm here for you, baby." she said. "We'll be together soon."
Lexie remained silent.
"You just going to let that go?" he asked.
"There's nothing I can do." she said. "I'm gone."

Relax
I'll need some information first
Just the basic facts
Can you show me where it hurts?

The kid got up again, this time he was undeterred by Danielle. He walked over.
"Leland Andersen." he said. "He's the one responsible for this."
"Who are you?" he asked.
Danielle was at the table now.
"Never mind that." she said. "But what he says is true."

There is no pain, you are receding
A distant ship smoke on the horizon
You are only coming through in waves
Your lips move but I can't hear what you're saying

When I was a child I had a fever
My hands felt just like two balloons
Now I've got that feeling once again
I can't explain, you would not understand
This is not how I am

"I want to know who the kid is." he said.

"You'll know soon enough." she said. "We have to go."

"Yeah you do." said Taylor. "This is a hard time for Erik, I wouldn't want to make it worse with violence."

O.K.
Just a little pin prick
There'll be no more aaaaaaaah!
But you may feel a little sick
Can you stand up?
I do believe it's working, good
That'll keep you going through the show
Come on, it's time to go.

"He's right, it's time to go." said Danielle. "I'll see you soon."

"See me soon?" he asked

"Not if I can help it." said Taylor. "You want to weigh in on this, Lexie?"

"I can't, I'm gone." she said.

Danielle and the kid made their way to the exit.

There is no pain you are receding
A distant ship smoke on the horizon
You are only coming through in waves
Your lips move but I can't hear what you're saying
When I was a child
I caught a fleeting glimpse
Out of the corner of my eye
I turned to look but it was gone
I cannot put my finger on it now
The child is grown
The dream is gone

I have become comfortably numb.

He heard a loud knocking. He woke up, someone was knocking on the door. Must be the new girl. He looked at the clock. It was 10:14 A.M.

More knocking.

"Coming." he said.

He got to the door and opened it.

"What are you doing here?" he asked. "You should probably go, I'm expecting Lexie's replacement. We can catch up later."

"It's me." she said.

"I know it's you, I don't even know how you found me." he said. "But really. Spy stuff. You should go."

"No, it's me." she said. "I'm her replacement."

"How?" he asked.

"I would have thought you figured it out." she said. "AMM? Anthony Murphy Modeling? That time in New York? Monte Carlo? All training. I'm here to kill Liam Gallagher."

Chapter 23

He woke up in a jail cell. He was grateful to be away from the horrors he suffered with all of the animals, sharks...and Louis. It had been months. He didn't know it was a dream, every moment seemed as real as this one in the cell.

He missed his mother. He never thought he would say that, as much as she tried to control him, but now he just wanted someone he knew loved him.

All of the unsavory characters and animals he had encountered all that time had taken a toll on him. It wasn't just Louis, although he was by far the most scary. He had seen several of his mother's loser boyfriends, and he was powerless to defend her or himself. He was always powerless, no matter what the situation.

He had so many fatal wounds he wondered why he didn't die. It was just one after the other, taking another piece of him. Arms and legs grew back from time to time, but they were immediately removed again. Now he sat in a cell, completely whole but he felt battered.

He was grateful to be out of that place, whatever it was. He almost felt human. He hadn't seen another human being in at least 8 hours. Honestly, he didn't want to. He didn't care if he ever saw anyone ever again...except for his mother. He needed to know that there was still someone who loved him.

He heard the door at the end of the hall creak open. He heard footsteps approaching.

"Good morning Antoine." he said.

It was Dr. Heisenberg. He hadn't seen him since he showed him to his room what seemed like two months ago.

"D-Dr. Heisenberg." he said. "W-What's happening to me?"

"I'm afraid there was a mistake, Antoine." he said. "One of my interns mixed up the medication, and caused you to have a bad dream. He's been fired."

A bad dream? That lasted months? What the fuck is going on?

"Why am I in a jail cell?" he asked.

"Strictly for your own protection, I can assure you." he said. "*I'm on your side.* I want to help you through this. You'll see, things will be better. I'm bringing your mother in to see you. I had to do some things for my bosses, but I talked them into letting me do it. It's something that's never been done, but your welfare is my chief concern. I would do anything for you."

"Really?" he asked, unsure.

Could it be true? Is he really bringing mom here?

"Of course." he said. "You're very important. Not only that, I feel horrible for what you've been through. These kind of mistakes should never be made."

Mistakes? It was months! Is he really going to help me?

"It wasn't just a bad dream, doctor, I was tormented for months." he said.

"Sometimes in dreams time isn't exactly fluid." he said. "It may seem like months, but I can assure you that you were only asleep for 9 hours. I feel just horrible about this. There's someone here who wants to see you."

"Really?" he said. "Is it my mom?"

"She'll be here later. Probably tomorrow." he said. "This is someone special who came from a long ways away."

"My father?" he asked.

"He's away on business, but you'll see him soon." he said. "Come with me."

"Okay." he said.

He took him to a bright room that was all white.

"Sit down, Antoine, she'll be here in a moment." he said. "I think you'll be pleased. I had to call in some favors to make this happen too. I have to go to New York for a meeting, but I want you to let me know if there are any problems when I get back."

"Okay, thanks Doc." he said.

He waited after the doctor left for whoever was coming. He wondered who it could be. He said "she." Vanessa? He didn't want to see her. He'd seen enough of her in what was apparently a dream.

The door opened quietly and she walked in.

"Antoine?" she asked. "They brought me here to see you. They said you're not doing well, so I came right away."

He couldn't believe it. Was it really her? The Doc really did this for him?

"Angeline?" he asked.

"I missed you so much." she said. "Don't ever leave me again."

It was her. And not the bad her, but Angeline, the girl he left in France. No sign of Louis, no Vanessa, just his love and it was *her* not that bitch from his dream. She came over and kissed him. She held him tight.

"I was lost without you, I love you so much, baby." she said. "Dr. Heisenberg had to pull some strings to get me here, and I'm so glad he did. He really understands."

"You were in some of my dreams. I say they were dreams, but they were nightmares. It felt like I was awake." he said. "I'm glad it's you...*really you.* I love you."

"What happened in the dreams?" she asked.

"N-Never mind." he said. "T-Things I never want to see again."

"You're shaking." she said. "What happened?"

He started crying softly.

"I'm just really grateful for Dr. Heisenberg." he said. "He made all this possible. He brought me one of the things I love most in the world."

"Oh, baby. I'm here now, it's all going to be okay." she said. "I won't let anyone hurt you."

"That's what I should be saying to you." he said. "Instead I turn into a blubbering idiot."

"That's not what I think, baby, I know you're strong." she said. "You've been through a lot."

A man entered the room.

"I'm sorry, Miss Devereaux." he said. "That's all for now. He needs his rest, Doctor's orders."

"A few more minutes?" she asked. "He needs me."

"I'm sorry, Miss Devereaux." he said. "You'll see him again soon enough. Next time he'll be stronger, and you'll have more time. Please, this way."

She kissed him and hugged him tight like she wasn't going to let go.

"I'll see you soon." she said. "Only good dreams about me from now on. You know what I'm talking about."

He smiled.

"I do." he said. "Hopefully in real life soon."

"I can't wait." she said.

She walked out the door.

Dr. Heisenberg really came through. He never expected to see Angeline...possibly ever again, but he made it happen. A different man entered the room.

"There's one more person that Dr. Heisenberg would like you to see." he said.

She slowly walked in. It was Vanessa. She sat down next to him, very close.

"Hello, Antoine." she said. "Who was that? The girl?"

He looked at her. There was no sign of the person he saw in his dream...if it was a dream. It must have been, Dr. Heisenberg said so. She was very attractive...even prettier than Angeline. He knew that he should tell her everything about Angeline, but the part of him that wanted to get to know Vanessa stopped him from doing that.

"A friend from back home in France." he said.

"She's pretty." she said. "Is she your girlfriend?"

"I wouldn't say that." he said. "She's more like...an acquaintance? Is that the right word?"

"Your English is better than my French." she said. "If you're trying to say that she's just a friend, acquaintance is the right word."

"Parlez-vous français?" he asked.

"We're probably better off not going down that road." she said. "Just the basics. If you want to talk about food or colors, I'd probably be okay, but nothing beyond that. So she's not your girlfriend?"

Why is she asking this? It's rather direct. He would rather not talk about Angeline, his mother had always told him that he was a terrible liar. But half of him was his father, and he intuitively knew that his father had no trouble in these situations. In fact, his father knew how to handle women better than most people.

"We're close, but no." he said. "Her mother is good friends with mine, so we spent a lot of time together when we were younger. She's more like a sister to me."

There, that was good. He said something he knew was a lie, but he said it convincingly. He knew without asking her that she believed him.

“That’s just another side of you. The lady’s man. There’s no shame in a little white lie to win a woman’s heart.”

It was Dr. Heisenberg’s voice in his head. He was right. He was sure that his father would agree.

“That’s good to hear.” she said. “The way it looked, I thought you were together. That would be a shame when you and I are just getting to know each other.”

He thought about telling her about the dream, then another voice in his head said no. Talking about that dream made him appear weak. You want this girl to think you’re strong.

“I’m glad we are.” he said. “I like you, Vanessa.”

“I like you too, Antoine.” she said. “That first night we met, I brought you your food. It probably looked like I work here. I’m actually just like you. I’m here as a patient. They noticed something about me and they wanted to evaluate it. I told them that I wanted to meet you.”

“When did you see me?” he asked.

He didn’t remember seeing anyone else except the doctor.

“I was in another room as you passed by.” she said.

She put one hand on his leg, and the other around his neck. She kissed him deeply.

“I’ve been waiting all day to do that.” she said.

It was almost the exact thing she said in the dream...to Louis. Don’t focus on that! The pretty girl just kissed you, and you want to think about that nightmare?

He leaned in and kissed her back. He had never done anything like this before. It always took him forever to work up the nerve to make a move on a girl. Today, something inside of him made it happen. It was like he was a different person, someone who knew exactly how to handle the situation. Could it be my father? He didn’t know anything about Erik except for what his mother told him, but he instinctively knew that this daring man kissing Vanessa was him.

***

"Would I be correct in assuming that this is all for your benefit, Doctor?" he asked. "This little reunion is designed to build trust between him and you? The other girl?"

They were watching through the two way mirror.

"Yes, Anthony. And for your benefit too eventually. Trust is everything. He needs to know that I'm his friend, possibly the only one. That's how this works. I do nice things for him, and only nice things. Amid the rest of the horror, he looks to me as a savior. I'm the one who doesn't hurt him. He can trust me. I'll handle him initially, then I'll hand him off to you. The girl has done her part, she'll be on a flight back to Paris tomorrow. If she protests, I'll tell her he took a turn for the worse, and he needs rest. I'll tell her that we'll send for her when he's better. Why wouldn't she believe me? After all, we flew her out here on a whim. The truth is he'll never see her again." he said. "The other girl, Vanessa...she's a different story. She's here specifically for this reason. She's a Beta, and a good one. We may let him sleep with her before it's all over. We may not. It doesn't matter. When it's over, he'll be able to seduce any woman he wants. Did you see how quickly he denied the relationship with Angeline? That's another alter. The male version of a Beta. Very strong in his father. I would love to take credit, but it's the epigenetic memory. It's literally in his DNA. It's extraordinary how he switched gears between the two girls."

"So Stryker? His success with women?" he asked. "All a part of the conditioning?"

"I'm afraid he was born with it. Something like that is difficult to replicate. All it took was Vanessa to bring it out in Antoine. He *does* get it directly from Erik, passed down through the genes. If you asked either of them to explain it, they wouldn't be able to. It's just there. Can you have the mother ready tomorrow? I have the feeling that he'll depart from his conscious mind quickly and completely after what happens with her. He's already exhibiting dissociative behavior. That's where the magic happens. His conscious mind leaves and I can get in there and do my thing."

"She'll be ready." he said. "Will you be able to generate the usual alters?"

"And then some." he said. "I have theories on his abilities, but I can't completely explain it. I will, however, find a way to control it, which means that you will too. We won't be able to control it the way *he* does...yet. It may take decades of research to figure out how to do *that.*"

"I'm just amazed that it's happening at all." he said.

"I knew it would someday." he said. "I wouldn't say I'm amazed, since it was expected. If I'm amazed about anything, it's that it took so long."

"We'll have to make things rough for him again before his mother returns." he said. "We'll use the standard LSD, amphetamines and barbiturates formula to keep him disoriented. He'll have horrible dreams. I wish we didn't have to send him where he's going, but he'll never remember any of this. That's what I tell myself whenever it tugs at my conscience."

"How does that work out for you?" he asked. "I ask, because contrary to popular belief, I also have a conscience."

"I've heard that rumor." he said. "I try to focus on outcomes. How is this going to help my country? That kind of thing. This type of work has been my dream job for all of my adult life, and part of my childhood. I've known about the moral issues for a long time. It's easier to think of what we do here as helping them become something more than they ever could on their own."

"I see." he said. "What about controlling them? Is that ever a problem? Any guilt there?"

"I go back to what I just said." he said. "Who would this person be if they never came here? What would their life be? I don't think anyone can deny that our operatives lead very fulfilling lives. You've probably met people who would give anything to do what they do."

He thought of Jessica. She didn't know how lucky she was.

He was onboard with everything that was happening, everything he did, but sometimes he regretted knowing the nuts and bolts. It would be much easier if he could explain it away as magic.

Maybe Levi was right, they were becoming more than human. The work here made them stronger, less vulnerable. He didn't like to think about the fact that if push came to shove, they had no free will. That's why he did his best to convince his people to do what they had to *without* using that option. That's what it's there for though.

"Yes, I can name more than a few." he said. "Nobody knows what they're giving up though."

"The return on that sacrifice is more than worth it, don't kid yourself, Anthony." he said. "Who wouldn't want to be Erik Stryker?"

He couldn't argue with *that*. There were a lot of times that he would love to be Stryker.

"What time should I bring Danielle over tomorrow?" he asked.

"Around 3." he said. "Antoine will be well prepared to give it up. You know what we need, right?"

"She should be as mean and nasty as possible. I'll get her to disparage the girl, Angeline too." he said. "Maybe tell him that they went out on the town and the girl disappeared with a couple of guys, something like that."

"That's all good, we can use that. The most important thing for him to believe is that Danielle no longer loves him." he said. "After that happens, he should let me in to do my work. He'll be a new man within a week."

***

"Yes, we're going to see him, but we need to talk first." he said. "He's doing great. Nothing to worry about."

"So let's get it over with. Talk." she said. "I want to see my son."

"How far back in your training do you remember?" he asked.

"I don't know, I remember when it was over." she said. "I remember how happy my father was."

"Do you know why he was happy?" he asked.

"He told me that I was serving my country." she said. "But I don't think France ever had anything to do with this."

"He was talking about *his* country. America." he said. "I can almost guarantee if Erik knew about this he would be proud. So try to remember that."

Actually the opposite was true. If Erik knew about any of this he would be unhappy. This program was designed to make the subject forever grateful to the handler, but that part never took hold with Erik. The best he could figure, Erik was too smart for that. There was something in his mind that had managed to escape Heisenberg. Levi even admitted it. It was rare, but then so was Erik. It was good that they wouldn't remember anything.

"I'll ask him myself when I see him." she said. "When will that be?"

"Probably a week or two." he said. "There were complications with his mission. Lexie didn't make it."

"Didn't make it?" she asked.

"She was killed in action." he said. "Her replacement should be there by now."

"Who is it?" she asked.

"Try to temper your grief for Lexie...and Erik." he said.

"I thought I was." she said. "I wasn't aware that I exhibited any emotion either way. Of course I feel bad for him, but that bitch deserved it. Who is her replacement?"

"I don't think you've ever met, but I'm sure you've spoken on the phone." he said. "Remember that call you *didn't* make 15 years ago? Someone answered and gave him the phone."

"Taylor." she said.

"That's right." he said.

"But she's not an agent." she said. "What's going on?"

"She *is* an agent." he said. "As of last week. She showed me some initiative with another situation, so I approached her. Him getting together with Lexie was the tipping point. She figures if she becomes an agent, she can give him what Lexie does. And now Lexie is gone."

"Not *everything.*" she said. "Lexie is...was a stone cold killer. Taylor can't do that."

"What do you think she's going to Ireland for?" he asked. "One of the IRA guys wasn't killed. She's taking care of that. Erik can't, because he knows too many of them, particularly this one."

"Are you doing this to spite me?" she asked. "Throwing all these beautiful women in his face?"

"You forget, he still loves you." he said. "Recent history between him and Taylor hasn't been good. Lexie is dead. You may never have a better opportunity."

He might be right. Then there was Antoine. What man wouldn't come back to the mother of his son? A son he didn't even know he had?

"Time will tell." she said. "What else do you need to tell me? I want to see Antoine."

"I want you to listen very carefully to me now, Danielle." he said. "The Red Queen came to a fork in the road. The last time she chose the left path and there were monsters there. As she recalled, the Black Queen was to the right. She unsheathed her sword and went to the left. Now Danielle I need you to do something for me."

"Yes, Mr. Murphy." she said.

"We're going to see Antoine." he said. "You need to make him believe that you don't love him anymore. You'll also say some bad things about Angeline. Use your imagination, the worse it sounds the better. Then we're going to come back here. After I bring you back, all you'll remember is having a great time with Antoine, and you'll be grateful to the institute for taking such good care of him. Do you understand?"

"Yes, Mr. Murphy." she said.

"Repeat it back to me." he said.

"We're going to see Antoine. I'll make him believe I don't love him. I'll talk about Angeline in an unflattering way. We'll come back here, and after you wake me, I'll only remember is what a great time I had with my son, and I'll be grateful to the institute." she said.

"Very good, Danielle." he said. "We should go. I have a car waiting."

***

He was back in the same place as before. It was still dark, but there was more light than before. He couldn't tell if anyone or anything was approaching him. He was naked and bald again. The strange thing was that when he was in the cell, when he saw Angeline and Vanessa, he had all of his hair.

Now he wondered which reality was real. He felt his head again. It was smooth and bare.

Suddenly he heard something snorting. It was a pig sniffing the air, trying to find him. As it got closer, it morphed into Louis.

"What's the matter, boy?" he asked. "You just hanging out with all of your friends?"

He came over and started beating on him. This time Angeline wasn't there, and neither was Vanessa. He did his best to curl up in a ball and block the blows, since he was unable to fight back. Louis tossed a few more insults at him, then gave up trying to talk to him and continued the beating.

Antoine couldn't answer if he wanted to. He steadily beat him for quite a while, but Antoine discovered that if he didn't think about it, it wasn't so bad. He had found a way to...depart his mind, mentally go somewhere else. He left his conscious mind to deal with the abuse. When it was all over, he could come back. He had already tested it and it worked. The problem was that when his conscious mind returned, he could feel the pain much worse. Best to just stay away. Louis finally gave up, and he uncurled and looked around. He saw two glowing eyes headed his way. As it got closer, a loud roar. He had seen TV shows about wildlife, and as near as he could tell it was a tiger. He went back into the fetal position and left his mind again. His conscious mind was safe, but the tiger was eating the unconscious mind.

He felt the pain, it just didn't matter. He wasn't there. He was somewhere else. A place he could go when it got to be too much. He wished he had known about this the last time he was in this predicament.

The tiger walked away full. He looked down, and his left leg and right arm were missing. Good thing I'm a lefty, he thought. Not that he could have done anything to resist anyway. In this world, he was always powerless, no matter the situation. Except now he had discovered a way to go away. What did it matter? He couldn't stop it from happening even when he was fully there, why stick around?

Now he was in the water, and five barracudas were screaming towards him. The saltwater made his injuries hurt even more. He shrugged and left his mind again. Until this is over, there's no reason to stay.

***

He was excitedly looking at the gauges and dials. This was an extraordinary development. He couldn't say he was surprised. The kid was smart. Smart enough to get out of the way when things went south. He had figured out how to separate his conscious mind from the ugliness. He was literally going away when something bad happened.

Of course he had no idea, but he was playing right into his hands. This was where he needed to be for the fragmentation. And he had discovered it on his own. He was sure that this would be exactly what he would do after or during his mother's visit, and he could start right away after that. He needed to at least be in communication with the subconscious mind for it to work, and it looked like Antoine would be more than willing to let that happen.

"Did you see the readings?" he asked.

"It's amazing. His defense mechanism kicked right in. He's in another world." said the intern. "Does it always happen this way?"

"It's rare, but then Antoine is a rare subject. This is where the intergenerational trauma and the epigenetic memory come into play." he said. "Some people are tough to crack no matter how much you terrorize them. The problem is that if you tell them, it rarely works. It has to occur...naturally so to speak. With most people it's the only way."

"So we'll work on the fragmentation tomorrow?" he asked.

"That's the plan." he said. "I'm just going to let this play out for a couple more hours to make sure it sticks. Then I'll put him to sleep. We should have an easy day tomorrow. Maybe you should skip the part with the mother. It can be graphic."

"In for a penny, in for a pound." he said. "I want to see the whole process."

"Well, if it gets too disturbing, you can always leave, no one will think any less of you." he said.

"I want to be here." he said.

“When it comes time to fragment, I’m afraid you’ll have to stay on the sidelines.” he said. “That will just be me. You can observe from the monitor.”

“I figured that’s how it will be.” he said. “I still want to observe. Maybe someday someone will be observing me.”

“That’s the hope, son.” he said. “I won’t live forever. Be here tomorrow around noon, you can help me prepare him.”

“Yes, sir.” he said.

***

“Mother?” he asked.

She was screaming like a lunatic. He had never seen her this way before.

“There he is! The freak who ruined my life!” she said. “What is it now? You’ve already taken the best years of my life. My best years! Waiting on you hand and foot, and for what? Couldn’t find a decent man, because you were always around. Next thing I know the ball comes to you, and we’re in America! I figured it was a good chance to get rid of you. I hate you!”

“But this was your idea.” he said. “*You* were the one who insisted that we come here. I wanted to stay in France.”

“To be with that tramp Angeline? Her and I went out on the town last night, and she hooked up with a couple of guys early on. They were all over her, practically fucked her right there in the bar. They got a room at the hotel next door. I was jealous. I never get to have the men I want because you’re chained to me like an anchor. We came here because I wanted to get rid of you.” she said. “I figured they would want to keep you. But no, they’re giving you back to me. I should have abandoned you as an infant. I should have killed you! It’s not too late for that, you know. Just let me get my hands on you, I hate you!”

He was shocked. Was it true about Angeline? Visions of that dream came back to him in a rush. What was wrong with her? Why was she talking to him like this? She said she hated him.

“Why are you acting this way?” he asked. “What’s wrong with you? What happened?”

"What happened is that I'm letting you know how it really is." she said. "I wish you were never born. I hate you! I've never loved you. You're an anchor. Holding me down. If I can't kill you, I'll kill myself. I hate you!"

A blank look washed over his face.

"Get her out of there." he said.

Two men came in and wrestled her away.

"I'll kill you, I swear to God I will if it's the last thing I do." she screamed, as they dragged her out.

He quickly went into the room.

"I'm sorry you had to see that Antoine." he said. "Let me show you something."

It was Dr. Heisenberg. He started to bring his conscious mind back, then he heard her screaming again.

"Best to stay where you are for the moment, Antoine." he said. "She's unstable, and sometimes when people are like that they get crazy strong. Strong enough to take out guards. Your conscious mind is safe where it is, and it should stay there. Close your eyes. I want to take you somewhere. Let your conscious mind go while I show you some things."

"Okay." he said.

They went down a long white hallway that led to a large white room. They went inside, and it appeared to be empty except for countless filing cabinets.

"Do you know where we are, Antoine?" he asked.

"No. Some kind of warehouse?" he said.

"Something like that." he said. "We're in your memory center. The filing cabinets are empty now, but as soon as we're done...examining you, they'll start filling up. Every memory you ever have will be at your fingertips. Just like your father. It's a great gift."

"I don't understand." he said. "I already remember things."

"Do you?" he asked. "Who was that woman who was screaming at you earlier?"

"Uh..." he said.

He thought about it. He didn't know. Why didn't he know?

"That's not important." he said. "Either your past memories will come back to you or they won't. The important part is moving forward. Have you noticed that you see much clearer in this state? In your memory center?"

“Now that you mention it I do.” he said. “I feel stronger too.”

This would be his front alter. The one the world sees the most of. It ran alongside the Delta alter which gave him 40 times visual acuity and 5 times the strength of the average man.

“These things are a gift from your father. With these abilities you can become the perfect spy. Your memory will start populating again as soon as we’re done here, don’t worry.” he said. “You’ll never forget anything again, your memories will be organized here so you can get them at a moment’s notice. Let’s go somewhere else.”

They left the memory center and entered another room. One of the walls displayed an image of him beating the shit out of Louis that day at the game. It felt good to see that. He knew that this guy was a punk, it was just a nightmare.

It switched to a scene from a bar where a blond man was helping a good looking redhead line up a pool shot. Suddenly a dark haired man clocked him in the face with a pool cue. The blond guy gets up, hits the guy with another cue, grabs the cue from the dark haired guy, breaks it in half and starts beating him with both pieces. Then the blond guy reaches down and snaps his neck. He gets up and walks out of the bar, gets on a motorcycle and tears off.

“Do you know where you are now, Antoine?” he asked.

“The place where I kick Louis’s ass.” he said.

“That’s right, this is your aggression center.” he said. “That man you saw was your father. He knows how to take care of business. Perhaps he went a little far that time, but after all, he had quite a bit to drink. You get your guts from your father too. You can actually thank your father for almost everything.”

“What about my mother?” he asked.

“She has good qualities too, but the important stuff you get from your dad.” he said. “Let’s move on.”

They went to another room. He saw Angeline and Vanessa. They both looked like they were longing for him.

“Come back to me.” said Angeline. “We belong together.”

“I’ve been waiting for you all day.” said Vanessa. “You know what you want, just take it.”

He leaned in and kissed her.

The next thing he saw was his mother. She was on a beach, and she wasn't wearing a top. She looked young, not much older than him. She approached a man that he now knew was his father. He looked young too. They started talking, and soon his father's arms were around his mother and he was kissing her. That would have taken me forever, he thought.

"That would have taken the old Antoine forever." he said. "You're connecting to your father's genes now. You intuitively know how to handle women, and you're always successful. Another gift from your father. Do you know where you are now?"

He was starting to catch on.

"I'm in my sex center." he said.

"Exactly. We call it Beta." he said. "And your father is right here to tell you what to do. You'll never have a problem with a woman again. As fun as this is, we need to move along."

They went to another room. There was a blackboard with a problem written on it.

We need a magic word to open a certain box. A secret code assigns each letter of the alphabet to a unique number. The code for the magic word is
9 23 14 14 18 5
What's the magic word?

"Well, Antoine, what's the magic word?" he asked.

He quickly scanned the numbers.

"Winner." he said. "The magic word is winner."

"Very good, Antoine!" he said. "This is your intelligence center. Let's try another."

The first problem disappeared from the board and another appeared.

What is the last digit of?
1x3x5x7x9x11x13?

"Well?" he asked.

"The last digit of that product is 5." he said.

"Excellent!" he said. "How did you figure it out so quickly?"

"I isolated the 5 factor and noted that the problem is times an odd number (there is no 2 factor). 5 times any odd number will always produce a number that ends in 5. Hence the product here must end with 5." he said.

"Very good." he said. "You get your intelligence from both of your parents. Let's move on."

They went into another room. There were the laughing and crying masks on the wall. They watched a short video of him breaking down while he was with Angeline. Next they watched a video of what happened moments later with Vanessa.

"Do you know where we are, Antoine?"

"From the art on the wall, I'd say we're backstage." he said.

"In a way we are, Antoine. We're in the theatric center of your brain. Everyone has to put on a show now and then. You put on a doozy earlier. First you gave Angeline just what she needed. You broke down so she could take care of you. That's what she does." he said. "When Vanessa came around, not two minutes later, you instinctively knew that she needed to be dominated. That's what she likes. You knew that because of what your father passed down to you."

"Really?" he asked. "I've always had trouble figuring women out."

"Not anymore." he said. "That's part of the reason we wanted you to come in. So you could get some genetic guidance from your father."

He realized how ridiculous this sounded, but to Antoine in his fragile state, anything anyone said with authority sounded true.

"Wow, thank you." he said.

"My goal is to help you become everything you can be, Antoine." he said. "I only hope I'm doing you justice. Let's move on."

The next room they went had military stuff on the walls. There were guns, bombs, grenades, and other weapons.

"Do you know where we are now, Antoine?" he asked.

"Some kind of military base?" he asked.

"Not quite. We're in the part of your mind where the super soldier lives. We call it Delta. Your father is a very strong soldier." he said. "In this world you'll have 40 times visual acuity, and 5 times the strength of a normal man. How do you like that?"

"That sounds great." he said.

"Let's move on." he said.

They entered another room. All that was in it was a noose hanging from a beam in the middle of the room.

"Where are we now?" he asked.

"I'm only showing you this room so you know it's here. Sometimes, through no fault of their own, soldiers and spies are captured. Unfortunately, a person of your standing is incredibly valuable to the enemy." he said. "If you are ever captured, you will take your own life. This is your suicide center. It happens rarely, but when it does you will kill yourself. There's no other way."

He had created 7 distinct alters, each with a specific job.

He set up a code phrase to activate each one. There used to be one phrase for all, but over the years they discovered that it was more precise to have a different phrase for each.

Antoine was so fascinated with the process that it never occurred to him to return to his conscious mind. When it was over, he put Antoine to sleep. When he returned and woke him, he tested each distinct phrase to make sure it worked. He had done a good job. More testing was necessary, but he was confident that the framework was in place.

"Bring the mother back tomorrow." he said. "I want to make sure that neither one remembers what happened today."

"Sure, Levi." he said. "How did it go?"

"Very well." he said. "I expected as much. It was nice having the mother come in. I hate being the bad guy. Genetics did most of the work for us today. We'll need to test his primary functions. I have expendable subjects available. It's important to know that he can do it."

"Probably more my end than yours, but I admire your dedication, doctor." he said.

"Make no mistake, this is also my end." he said. "If he can't kill, it reflects poorly on me."

Chapter 24

"You're here to kill Liam Gallagher?" he asked.

"Yeah, what's the problem?" she asked.

What's the problem? You're the sweetest person in the world and you're not a killer!

"Tell me about it." he said. "How did he get you to do it?"

"It really didn't take much." she said. "You dumped me for Lexie, he approached me, and I said yes."

"She's dead, you know." he said. "Don't think it can't happen to you."

"I heard. I'm sorry for your loss." she said. "I'm just here to do a job."

Just here to do a job.

"All those times I called you." he said. "You were in training, how could you answer?"

"I don't really remember a lot of the calls. Anthony knew that you would call." she said. "When you did, he made sure I answered. He made sure that I had my phone with me at all times. He told me to encourage you to call. He didn't need to do that, I wanted to hear from you. I'm sure my training was like yours, just better accommodations."

So Murphy was in on this all along. He had to wonder if he knew anything about what happened to Lexie. He was almost certain that he knew who Leland Andersen was.

"I can't remember mine." he said. "Maybe we were on the 16th floor of the Plaza too. I got the voicemail a few times."

"And you didn't leave a message?" she asked.

"I'm not a message guy." he said. "I don't remember anything about my training, but if I had to guess, I was isolated most of the time. Yet you were able to take calls."

"If it makes you feel better I don't remember talking to you." she said. "At least not until you were on the Mauritius, I remember both of those. My training was over by then. Oh, I remember calling you on my cell phone. You were my first call."

"It doesn't make me feel better." he said. "Doesn't that bother you? Not remembering?"

“I did what I had to do.” she said. “You were off with Lexie, the only thing I figured she had that I didn’t was that she was a spy. So I became a spy.”

“You became an assassin.” he said. “Let’s not dress it up too much.”

“Why do you always say spy then?” she said. “The point is that I’ve changed. Whether you want me back or not, at least give me that. I’m not going to pressure you. I can only imagine what you’re going through with Lexie.”

That was another difference. Lexie would seize the opportunity under these circumstances. He wasn’t sure which he liked better, but in spite of everything he was glad that Taylor was here. She could help with how he was feeling about Lexie. How fucked up is that?

“I say spy for the same reason you did. I’m not ready for anything like that yet. She was killed yesterday.” he said. “They say you’re going to be a nurse. Are you sure you’re ready for this? I’m sure he can send someone else.”

“I’m ready.” she said. “He made sure of it.”

“What does that mean?” he asked.

“Take it however you like.” she said. “This isn’t going to be a problem. Do you want to see? The outfit? I’m sorry, apparently the sexy nurse hasn’t made it to Ireland yet.”

I’m sure you’d make almost anything look good, he thought. That’s probably why the whole “modeling” thing was so believable.

“I’m a little concerned with you going in there.” he said. “Not only will there be cops, but there will probably be plenty of IRA around.”

“I’ll be fine.” she said. “You worry too much. I know exactly what to do. I’ve even done it before.”

She started getting undressed. She wasn’t wearing a bra, yet her breasts held perfectly in place, with just the right amount of jiggle. She really looked good.

“Done it before?” he asked.

“Anthony shared your concerns.” she said. “He gave me the name of someone at a hospital in Paris. Told me it didn’t matter, the guy was going to die whether I did it or not. He gave me a nurse outfit, much better than this one by the way, and I went in there and did it. He's dead now, so you see, you have nothing to worry about."

She finished putting the outfit on, and she was right. It was grey with a white collar that went halfway up her neck. It looked good on her, but on the average woman it would have been a good form of birth control.

"You still have the French one?" he asked.

"There's the Erik I know." she said. "Sorry, I got rid of it after the job. I might have something in here you'd like though."

Got rid of it after the job. She even sounded like an assassin. She sounded a little like...like Lexie.

"We probably shouldn't do that." he said. "After all, I'm still grieving. At least give me a few days."

"I can't tell if you're joking." she said. "A problem I've often had with you."

"You look great, but I'm not going to have sex with you." he said. "I don't know how long I'll be this way. I don't know if it will ever happen. Whether you want to believe it or not, losing her was a big deal. I'm not ready to jump into anything else. That's the best I can do."

"That's fine." she said. "When you're ready to talk about it, let me know."

"When were you planning on doing the job?" he asked.

"As soon as possible." she said.

"Mater Infirmorum Hospital." he said. "It's on the north side of town. How did you get here?"

"They flew me in." she said. "Since it's my first mission, I guess they thought it would be okay."

"Your first mission was in Paris." he said. "Did he pay you for that?"

"He said we'll settle up after I take care of Gallagher." she said. "I'm not worried about it. Everything I've done since the last time you saw me has been paid for."

Even your programming. He didn't like this at all.

"We'll take a drive up there later so you can get the lay of the land." he said.

"I know everything I need to know." she said. "I even know what room he's in. They gave me a dossier. All of the intelligence I need."

"We're still going to check it out before you run off halfcocked." he said. "Excuse me."

He grabbed his phone and went out on the balcony. He had trouble dialing the number he was so pissed.

"What can I do for you, Mr. Stryker?" he said.

"Really? Taylor?" he said.

"Erik...." he said. "I take it Lexie's replacement has arrived."

"Yes. How long have you been planning this?" he asked.

"I don't know that I planned it at all." he said. "Taylor wanted to become a field agent. She showed promise in another area, so I decided to give her a chance. It was when she tried to put you in motion. The whole *'Red Knave'* thing."

"What does that have to do with this?" he asked.

"She tried to put you in motion. Doing something like that caught my attention." he said. "I thought if she can do that, she might do other things. So we did a little sleight of hand and made you believe that she became a model. After all, she has the goods. She went through training, and now she's like you."

"You know I'm grieving the loss of Lexie right now, don't you?" he asked. "It's fucked up you sending my ex at a time like this."

"We're both grieving." he said. "But we still have a job to do. Taylor was the best choice for this mission. Did she tell you about Paris?"

"Who is Leland Andersen?" he asked.

"Where did you hear that name?" he asked.

He hit on something there. Murph was almost always cool, but he let on that he was concerned with his tone of voice. Andersen must be his boss.

"Did I touch a nerve? Sorry about that." he said. "Where do you think I heard it? He's your boss, isn't he?"

"You're getting into a very dangerous area Erik." he said. "Whatever you're thinking, forget about it. You'll lose. There will be no way to connect him to it. It doesn't matter what we know. It only matters what he *thinks* we know. If he even suspects that you're looking into this, you die. That's as plain as I can put it."

"So it's true?" he asked.

"I strongly suspect it. Since he would never let any evidence slip through the cracks, that's as good as it gets. You need to leave this alone. We *both* need to leave this alone." he said. "This is not a man who loses. Ever. I'm sorry to spring this thing with Taylor on you now, but you can handle it. Liam Gallagher needs to die. She's the most efficient way of making that happen."

"I don't like it." he said. "Did she really take care of that guy in Paris? Was it actually someone who needed to die? Or did you look through a list of patients and randomly decide who was unlucky?"

"The man she killed had it coming, that's all you need to know. I was proud. It went off without a hitch." he said. "She'll be done with Gallagher before you know it."

"Okay. I still don't like this." he said. "You took the sweetest girl in the world and turned her into a killer."

"No, I turned her into something better than she could ever be on her own." he said. "Just like you. You like to act like some terrible injustice has been done to you, but most guys would kill to be you."

"They would have to, that's how I got on your radar." he said. "I was a normal guy before all this started."

"You were never a normal guy." he said. "For your information, I was watching you long before you killed. And you know that. Did I *know* you would kill? Of course, but that's not the point. Try to stay out of her way, she knows what she's doing. There will be tickets for you at the front desk. You're flying out. Under the circumstances, a quick getaway is best. I almost hate to say it, but you have another surprise coming. Call me when it's over."

The line went dead.

Another surprise? What the fuck is he talking about? Is he going to dig up a girlfriend from high school?

He lit a cigarette. There was a good view of the Lagan River from the balcony. It really was a pretty town, there was a good mix of modern architecture and old buildings. Lexie was right. This would be a great place if they...he was ever allowed to live overseas.

He was still thinking like she was still around. He knew it would take some time. And now Taylor was here. The thing was, he knew she was sincere when she said she was sorry about Lexie. He knew that even though she might have hopes of getting back together, she would never wish for Lexie's death as a means to an end. He wondered if she still even had that part of herself.

"You got another one of those?" she asked.

He hadn't even heard her come out.

"I don't know Lex...Taylor." he said. "First you're killing people, now you're smoking. What's next?"

"Most things are okay in moderation." she said.

He handed her a cigarette and lit it.

"So you moderately killed that guy in Paris?" he asked.

"That was just a job." she said. "Maybe I'm letting my hair down a little. You've been smoking for years, and it doesn't seem to affect you."

"Just a job?" he said. "Do you even hear yourself? You killed a guy."

"I try not to think about it." she said. "It doesn't feel as bad if I call it 'just a job'. How do you handle it?"

"That's a good question." he said. "I stopped thinking about it morally a long time ago. I don't want that for you."

"But it was okay for Lexie?" she asked.

"Please. She was a stone cold killer long before we met." he said. "I'll never look at you the same way I did her."

As he was finishing that sentence, he realized that he was also a stone cold killer before they met. Was there any hope left for Taylor?

"I wouldn't expect you to." she said. "You two had a lot of history. A lot of stuff that I never had with you. Maybe that's why it was so easy for me to say yes to Murphy. *I wanted that.*"

This was getting them nowhere. Maybe she can help with the dream.

"I had a hell of a dream just before you started pounding on the door." he said.

"Really?" she said. "Tell me about it."

He told her about how Lexie didn't do anything since she was dead, How Danielle tried to stop the kid before he got there, the name the kid gave him, Leland Andersen.

"And I was mean? To Danielle?" she said.

"What's so hard to believe?" he said. "She was your number one enemy not too long ago. Hell, she might still be."

"I've decided to let that go." she said. "There's nothing I can do about it."

"At least the kid talked to me this time." he said. "I still want to know who he is. Something tells me he's important."

How in the fuck do you not know who he is? It's your son, you dope! I may be sweet, but I'm not sweet enough to tell you that.

"Who knows?" she said.

Any idea who Leland Andersen is?" he asked.

"Nope, I just got here." she said. "If you don't know, how should I?"

"Murphy tensed up when I mentioned it." he said. "It's his boss. He said I shouldn't pursue it. Said it's a good way to die."

"I would think he knows." she said. "After all, he knows everything."

She even sounds like us.

"He says I have another surprise when this is all over." he said. "It'll be hard to top you showing up at my door."

Another surprise? Those dreams...they're coming true. Is it possible that she's still around with that fucking kid? Just when I'm trying to get things back to normal.

"I wouldn't hazard a guess as to what it could be." she said. "With him it could be anything."

"I don't know why, but I think it involves this kid." he said. "I guess I'll find out when the time comes."

Is he *fucking* with me? Or does he have such a huge blind spot about this kid that he's in denial? It doesn't make sense that he hasn't figured it out yet.

"Take me for a drive?" she asked. "We can do a little recon on the hospital?"

"Sure, just let me take a quick shower." he said.

They went to the car. He headed for Crumlin Road. They drove past it once and it didn't look too well guarded. The second pass they saw a couple of cop cars.

"I'm coming with you." he said.

"Not inside." she said. "Some of these guys know you."

"Gallagher knows me. He's actually the only one left." he said. "That's Brendan's uncle you know."

"I know." she said quietly. "It was all in my package."

"There will probably be some Sinn Féin hanging around." he said. "Not as many as there were yesterday, of course."

"Sinn Féin?" she said.

"It's what the locals call the IRA." he said. "Strange that it wasn't in your dossier of crack intel."

"But now I know." she said.

"Let's get something to eat." he said. "I know a good place."

"You do?" she said. "How long have you been here?"

"A few days." he said. "You'll love this place."

"Okay." she said.

They pulled into the diner and walked in. Colleen was waiting tables and there were a few more people there this time. They sat down.

"Who's this then?" she asked. "Your interpreter?"

"No, she's...indisposed. This is a business associate." he said. "The people I'm pitching tomorrow tend to do a bit better with a woman in the room. Taylor, this is Colleen."

"Pleas'd ta meetcha." she said. "Any friend o' Erik's is a friend to me. Can I startcha off with somthin' ta drink?"

"Coffee." said Erik.

She looked at Taylor.

"Same." she said.

"I'll be right back with that." she said.

"You make friends fast." she said.

"I always have." he said. "I came here in the middle of the night, and it was just me, her, and an old guy who was trying to stay awake. So we talked. We're in global marketing, by the way."

"Global marketing?" she said. "That's what you came up with?"

"It's best to be as vague as possible when you talk to civilians." he said. "If you tell them something too specific, they'll remember you."

"Be as vague as you like, but that woman is going to remember you regardless." she said. "It's that Stryker charm."

"Well, I can't help that." he said. "Hopefully we'll be gone before anyone starts asking questions. I would hope that

Murphy could help us in Ireland if it comes to it, but this is heavy IRA territory. By the way, don't say anything negative to Colleen about them. We almost got into it the other night before I smoothed it over."

"I'm sure you can bail me out if I get in trouble." she said.

"Don't count on it. She's a tough cookie." he said.

She came back with the coffee.

"How are ya likin' our fine country, Taylor?" she asked.

"Oh, I love it." she said. "I try to get here at least once a year. That client Erik was talking about almost guarantees it."

"Which company is that?" she asked.

Erik's heart leapt.

"Allen & Overy. They're a parent company to over 40 companies in Northern Ireland." she said. "They employ 12,000 people. I would be willing to bet that you know at least one person who works for them in one form or another."

"Aye. My uncle Seamus." she said. "He works at St. Mary's University College. Allen & Overy contract out the work he does. So ya get here often?"

"Not as often as I would like." she said. "A lot of my business can be conducted over the phone. They needed a face to face this time and they asked for me."

"And poor Erik just wouldn't do?" she asked.

"What can I say?" she said. "I think the CEO has a little crush on me."

"Aye. I can see why. Yer gorgeous." she said. "But I'm sure Erik has 'is qualities too."

"I don't think any of the CEOs have crushes on me, if that's what you're getting at." he said.

"Must not be any female CEOs." she said. "Did ya know what ya wanted, or do ya need a minute?"

"Maybe just a few minutes." said Taylor.

"Aye, I'll come back then." she said.

She winked at Erik.

He waited for her to get a safe distance away.

"*Where in the hell did that come from*?" he whispered.

"Vague is okay, but sometimes it's good to have a few details. A bit of a backstory." she said. "There was an article about them in the inflight magazine. She likes you."

"Really?" he asked. "I can't tell anymore. But that was amazing, Taylor."

"She winked at you." she said.

"She probably thought that crack about the female CEOs was cute. I'm sure that's all it was." he said. "After all, I'm here with you."

"Your business associate." she said. "She laid the groundwork last time, and she'll be waving you in for a landing later. All I am is a coworker."

"You sound like..." he said. "Never mind. I think you're wrong. She's just friendly."

"Friendlier to you than me." she said. "I can promise you that wink wasn't meant for me."

"You had a great back and forth going there." he said. "Talking about your ovaries. I wasn't included in that."

"Allen & Overy. A multinational company. Overy spelled with an 'e' not an 'a'." she said. "I promise I wasn't talking about my ovaries."

"Whatever. You know every girl we come in contact with doesn't want to sleep with me." he said. "You and Lex...*you* get a little melodramatic about these imaginary women who just can't seem to live without me."

"I think it's cute." she said. "I'm going to get an omelet. What do you like?"

"She talked me into the Brioche Bread and Butter Puddin' last time." he said. "It was great, but a ton of food. That's called an after by the way. Something to go with your coffee like a donut or a slice of pie. I'll do an omelet too, I guess."

They put their menus aside and Colleen came over.

"A bacon and cheese omelet for me." said Taylor.

"I'll do the same." said Erik.

"Aye. No Brioche?" she said.

"It was great, I'm just not that hungry today." he said.

"Aye, it is a bit much." she said.

"I'll get the cook workin' on those omelets then." she said.

She started giggling to herself.

"Why Mr. Stryker, I do believe that you're blushing." she said.

"I'm sure it's an optical illusion." he said. "I stopped blushing after my first trip to the Philippines."

"Okay." she said. "Then you're turning red for another reason entirely."

He knew he was. He could feel the heat on his cheeks. It really was something he never did.

"You're funny, Whitman." he said. "If you only knew how often you blush."

"But I'm allowed." she said. "I'm a girl."

"You're all about the equal rights, yet you still hold on to blushing." he said. "Way to fight the tough fights."

"I never said you're not allowed." she said. "It's just unusual to see a man do it."

"So what do you think?" he asked. "Tomorrow?"

"That sounds good." she said. "There really isn't anything for you to worry about. I'll be fine."

"That's cool, I'm just going to make sure." he said. "I'm doing it whether you like it or not. I've already lost...well, I'm not losing you on this trip."

"That's fine, just stay out of sight." she said. "I'll be in and out, I swear."

He was being very protective. It felt good. She wasn't sure where this would lead, only that she wanted to be with him. She realized that it could be a long time before he showed any interest...but it *is* Erik.

"You know I have that thing you have now." she said. "With my memory?"

"Really?" he asked. "Why do you think that is?"

"I don't know, part of the training I guess." she said.

"They didn't do that for you...or me. It's the result of them fracturing your brain. When people hear about it, they think it's great, but they don't ever do anything that's not going to benefit them. After they've fractured your brain, they isolate your memory center. They make sure that you can recall anything that you hear, read, see, whatever." he said. "You don't forget anything. Then they can use you as a messenger to relay information to another party. They know you'll never forget, because you're programmed not to. I've even heard of agents killing themselves if they get caught, simply because they've been programmed to self-destruct. You may think all of this is really cool, but it isn't. That's why I was pissed that he got you involved. It's too late now."

"I had no idea, but it makes sense." she said. "Have they ever done that to you? Used you as a messenger?"

"If they did, chances are I would never know." he said. "See they can make it so you remember everything, but they can also make you forget. They still have that control. All they need to do is put you in motion. Like you tried to do to me."

How does he know about that? It didn't work. I always thought I just did it wrong. Does he know? About the Red Knave?

"I can hear your gears grinding." he said. "Murphy told me."

"How did he know?" she asked.

He rolled his eyes.

"You have a lot to learn, Whitman." he said. "It was Lexie. I told her about what you did, she had a reaction, and the next thing I know, she's calling Anthony. The next time I talked to him, I confronted him with my suspicions and he confirmed it. She only told him because she was concerned about me."

"I'll admit that at the time I did it to try to stop you from leaving me." she said. "You were talking all that crazy stuff about how the club was a job, and I needed to get away from you for my own safety. But it was okay for Lexie. I didn't know what else to do."

"It's okay." he said. "I would have never brought it up if you didn't get in so deep. There are things you should know. Things I wish someone would have told me in the beginning."

Colleen came back with the omelets.

"You two are as thick as thieves." she said. "What ar' ya plannin'?"

"Just an animated discussion about a mutual friend." he said. "Global marketing can be a mean business."

"Aye, but you two have a past." she said. "Somethin' that 'as nothin' t' do wit' global marketing."

"I suppose we do." he said.

"Aye, an' more than jus' an interoffice romance I reckon." she said.

"You'll have to keep that under your hat, I'm married." he said. "And not to her."

"And what about you, lassie?" she said. "What do you have to say fer yerself?"

"He's charming, what can I say?" she said. "I'm a sucker for big brown eyes."

"Me too." she said. "How does it feel ta have all these women pinin' fer ya, Erik?"

"It's a blessing and a curse." he said. "Something I've been dealing with since I was 13. But seriously, Taylor and I are purely platonic. She's great friends with my wife."

Her eyes shifted back and forth between them several times. She smiled.

"Yer secret's safe wit' me." she said. "If I had to guess, I'd say *you're* the wife. I'll let ya get back to yer platonicness."

She walked away.

"I told you she likes you." she said. "She was jealous."

"It was just friendly banter." he said. "She works for tips."

"How much did you give her last time?" she asked.

"That's not fair, you know how I am." he said.

"How much?" she asked.

"Not more than she deserved." he said. "What time do you think you want to do this thing tomorrow?"

"We can play it by ear." she said. "We should have some kind of exit strategy."

"Murphy's sending us some tickets." he said. "We're flying out tomorrow night, the tickets are going to be at the front desk."

"I think I can get in and out undetected." she said.

"Always plan for the worst." he said. "If it works out like you hope, it doesn't cost anything extra to be prepared."

"I have my own room...but I can stay with you if you like." she said. "If you don't want to be alone. But if you do, I totally understand."

"Maybe we could go back and watch a movie." he said. "I don't think I want you to stay with me. Nothing personal, it's too soon. I wasn't expecting you. It caught me by surprise. I think I'm getting used to the idea of what happened...with you at least. Lexie's another story."

"I completely understand." she said. "I would love to watch a movie with you though, if you want to do that."

"Do you think we can agree on one?" he asked.

"I don't know if I mentioned it, but I've changed." she said. "I'm willing to explore other genres besides romantic comedies."

"Okay." he said.

He waved at Colleen.

She came over.

"It was a pleasure to see you again Colleen." he said. "We need to get out of here, do you have the check?"

"Aye." she said.

She pulled it off of her pad.

"I really shouldn't take anythin' from ya after las' night." she said.

"Allow me." said Taylor. "After all, I'm landing that big account tomorrow."

She pulled out a hundred dollar bill and handed it to her.

"I hope American is okay." she said. "I haven't had a chance to exchange it yet."

"I'll get yer change." she said.

"No, darlin' that's for you." she said. "I can't be outdone by Erik, now can I?"

"You yanks!" she said. "Yer a little loony, but I'm grateful! Don't never see such generous folks around here."

"So you'll keep our secret?" she asked.

Colleen pantomimed locking her lips and throwing away the key.

"Have a great night." said Erik.

They went back to the hotel. Back in his room they looked for a movie they could both agree on. She had brought a small bag with her, and changed into a skimpy nighty before they started looking for a movie.

As they were going through the choices, one stood out to here. *Strangers on a Train.*

"You'll love it, it's Alfred Hitchcock." she said. "It was based on a novel by Patricia Highsmith. She also wrote 'The Talented Mr. Ripley and four sequels to it. She was a great writer. Probably not any skin in this thing, since it was made in 1951, but it's a great movie."

I have the feeling if I'm looking for skin, I won't have to look for it on the screen, he thought.

"Who's the master of triviality now?" he asked.

“What, because she’s a woman?” she asked.

“It has less to do with her being a woman, and more to do with me...and almost anyone else besides you, knowing anything about her.” he said. “Go ahead, I’m sure I’m a huge Patricia Highsmith fan, I just don’t know it yet.”

“Thanks, you’re gonna love this movie.” she said. “If for no other reason than Alfred Hitchcock.”

She was right, he was a huge Hitchcock fan. The movie was actually pretty good.

Taylor, of course, falls asleep when it’s halfway through. So much for separate rooms, he thought.

He didn’t want to admit it, but he really *did* want her to stay with him. He was trying to do all the things he was supposed to do after losing her. It wouldn’t look too great if he was banging his ex a day later. Unfortunately, that was what he really wanted to do. He didn’t know why, he just did. He wasn’t about to let *that* happen though. He turned off the TV, and rolled over away from her. About an hour later, she had herself wrapped around him. He turned around and looked at her. She’s wide awake.

“You’re not making this easy, you know.” he said.

“We don’t have to do anything, I just want to be close to you.” she said.

“But when you’re *this* close to me, I start thinking of other things.” he said. “I’m only human.”

“Do you want me to leave?” she asked.

She knew the answer to that as well as he did. He didn’t even know why she asked. She was probably just trying to say the right things, even though she had ulterior motives.

“I’m trying to do the right thing here.” he said.

“Who’s to say what’s right or wrong? We don’t have to live with what we *should do*, or what *people expect us to* do. I know you just lost Lexie. But what if us getting together is exactly what you need right now?” she said. “I would never say that this is what she would have wanted, but at the same time, I think she would want you to be happy. That’s what I take from what I know about her. She was a person who lived life to the fullest. She wouldn’t want you to waste time being depressed.”

"What, did you practice that in the mirror on the way over?" he asked. "I'm not a guy who says no too often, I feel like maybe I should right now. It would be easier if you didn't make such good points."

"Just let me snuggle with you." she said. "What's the harm in that?"

He turned and faced her, and she eased herself around facing the other way, got everything lined up and pushed back against him. She grabbed his arm and pulled it around her, placing his hand on her chest.

"I love you." she said.

She squeezed his hand and pulled him in tighter.

"I love you too." he said.

I may as well do it, there's no way I can keep this up, he thought. No, I have to stay strong. For Christ's sake, at least make it two days, Stryker! That shit about Lexie living life to the fullest really made sense though. She wouldn't want him moping around. Maybe not, but there's no way anyone could say she would want him banging Taylor, probably before she was even in the ground!

How did this happen? Murphy. Somehow thought it would be a good idea to send Taylor to him the day after Lexie was killed. What could possibly go wrong? After all, it's the most natural thing in the world for him to find comfort with his ex less than two days after his woman was brutally murdered. Nothing wrong with *that.*

And now he had to worry about keeping her alive on this mission. Of course he couldn't be there with her, that would be too easy. She had to go in on her own. But she already whacked someone in Paris so it's all cool.

She started slowly rubbing against him.

"If you want to do it, baby, it's okay." she whispered. "I won't tell anyone."

There's no way I'm going to make it through the night, he thought.

***

He dropped her off at the emergency entrance. He picked a spot not far from the exit. They had agreed to meet there after it was over.

Taylor was wearing the nurse's outfit, but she had taken a bag with her so she could change after she killed Gallagher. It was likely that they would be looking for a nurse.

He wanted her to bring a wig along too, but she wouldn't agree. She thought if she got caught before she did the deed, it would be hard to explain the wig. She had her hair pinned back, and it would be a significant difference when she let it out. She was confident that it would go off without a hitch, yet he worried. It was a new role for him, he was usually the one who took too many chances.

He followed her, and was watching her from a safe distance. There was a guy sitting in a chair outside Liam's room. She flashed him a pretty smile and acted like a nurse. He let her pass. He watched as she entered his room.

She got inside and Liam was awake. She didn't remember if the guy in Paris was or not. That's a little strange, she thought.

"Good mornin', Mr. Gallagher, how are ya feelin' today?" she asked.

"Where's the other girl?" he asked.

"A bit o' a tragedy from what I hear." she said. "Poor Moira woke ta find 'er cat, Pebbles dead. She begged off ta see t' the arrangements. I can tell her ya asked about her."

She had remembered his regular nurse's name from the dossier. She prayed that it was right.

"Who the hell names a cat Pebbles?" he asked.

"I think it's cute." she said.

She went to check the tubes running from his arm.

"Aye, most cailíns would, I reckon." he said. "Where ya from?"

"Originally Maghery, but I came here wit' me' da after me' mother passed." she said. "Name's Shannon."

Her brogue was by no means perfect, but it was passable. It mattered very little anyway, because she had the hypodermic needle out and was inserting it into his tube.

"Aye, on Lough Neagh." he said. "Like livin' on the water didja?"

"My apologies Mr. Gallagher." she said. "It's nothing personal, just a job."

He tried to speak but nothing came out. He started choking and coughing. His color changed to a much paler shade. Then he stopped breathing. She put everything back in her bag, she quickly checked his pulse and found nothing. She walked out.

"You should probably leave him alone for a bit." she said. "New medication, he may have an adverse reaction. Something may happen that neither of us wants to deal with, luv."

She winked at him.

She fascinated him so much he barely understood what she was saying.

"Aye." he said. "I'll give the lad some time."

"Name's Shannon, have them find me should anythin' go wrong." she said. "Unless he messes himself, in that case I'd be grateful if ya called someone else."

"Aye, yer far too pretty to be dealin' wit' that type o' thing." he said.

"Aye, and so are you, luv." she said. "I'll be seein' ya in about an hour."

"Aye, thanks Shannon." he said.

She ducked into the ladies room and changed. She walked towards the exit. After she got outside she took a deep breath. She saw the car on the other side of the parking lot. As she got close, she saw someone walking towards her. It was Colleen from the diner. She was smiling at her as she waved. Suddenly a dark red spot appeared on her forehead and she fell. A gun fell out of her hand and rattled to the ground. Erik was beside her now.

"Just keep walking." he said. "I used a silencer, nobody heard. She was going to kill you. Let's get to the car."

She was in shock. How did he see it and I didn't? While she was waving with her left hand, she had withdrawn the gun from her overcoat with her right. And I had no idea.

They got in the car. He very calmly exited the parking lot and got on the road.

"How did you know?" she asked.

"I didn't get overconfident." he said. "And I looked for things that were out of place. She got out of a car near where I parked. And she didn't just get here, she was waiting for us to come out. Maybe she was even here before we got here. And why would the pro-IRA waitress be here just as we're leaving? These are the things you need to pay attention to."

"You saved my life." she said.

"I'm sure you would have done the same for me." he said. "Maybe not the same way, exactly, but you would have found a way."

"We should get out of here." she said.

"No shit. We'll head back to the hotel, get our things, and stop by the front desk and pick up the tickets." he said. "We'll take a cab to the airport, people have seen way too much of this car."

"Okay." she said.

"How did it go?" he asked. "With Gallagher?"

"It's done." she said. "The guy at the door ought to be checking on him in about ten minutes."

"You shouldn't have interacted with him as much as you did." he said. "It's best to keep it as simple as possible. It would be optimal to not talk to anyone at all."

"I talked to him." she said. "Gallagher. Just enough to put him at ease."

"Overall you did a great job." he said. "Right until the point that Colleen almost killed you."

"I should have known." she said.

"Should have known?" he said. "No, you shouldn't have known, you shouldn't even be here. He's turned you into something you should never have been."

"Yet here we are." she said. "I can't take back what's happened Erik, but the fact is that I am what I am now for better or worse. This is what I am. I accepted you after you signed on with Murphy."

She was right and he knew it. He would have resented it if she tried to talk him out of it back then too.

"I'm sorry." he said. "I just didn't want any of this for you. You were the nicest person I'd ever met. But now you're a killer. I'm trying to understand."

"Okay." she said.

They were at the hotel.

"Meet me back here in ten minutes." he said.

They went upstairs and got their things. They picked up the tickets, didn't bother to check out, and they got in a cab from the stand in front of the hotel.

Chapter 25

They had run a battery of tests on him, most with good outcomes, but some were inconclusive.

Did they have his heart as well as his mind? Was he willing to do what was required of him regardless of any feelings he might have. Most of the time he would be dealing with strangers, but there was also the possibility that he would need to deal with someone he knew. Even a friend. They needed to know that they could count on him no matter the circumstances.

For example, there were things that they had trouble with his father on. There were times that they weren't sure if his mind control would work. He was naturally rebellious. In the end, they always got what they wanted, but occasionally it was more work than was normally required. It was part of the reason Heisenberg wanted to get him back in there.

They had set everything up earlier for Antoine, made sure he knew which one was the right one, and he knew what to do. He didn't know it consciously, of course. In the field, it would be easier, he would know who the bad guy was before he went in.

This was more a test of...loyalty. They were sending him into a room with several people, knowing one of them was an anti-American agitator. It was up to him to figure out which one it was. Of course, he had been instructed subconsciously which one it was, but he didn't know that.

They had allowed him to sleep with Vanessa. He had forgotten about Angeline long ago. Things were definitely better for him now than they were after he first arrived. He was something of a celebrity. People had seen the soccer tape, and everyone was amazed. He got to see his mother every day, and there was no return of the crazy one that screamed at him. Of course, he didn't remember that either.

"Are you ready, Antoine?" he asked.

"Sure, another test?" he asked.

"A very important one." he said. "We're very close to being done with your training, and your father should be here in the next few days."

"Okay." he said. "I'm looking forward to meeting him."

"I'm sure he's looking forward to meeting you too." he said. "He doesn't even know about you."

"That's what mom says." he said. "She said if he knew, he would have already come. She says there are things preventing him from coming that we don't know about."

"Your father is a very special man." he said. "You're just like him. What your mother says is true. There are reasons that he couldn't know about you until now."

"Okay." he said.

He gave Antoine a gun.

"This is important, Antoine." he said. "You're going into a room with several people. One of them is an enemy of the state. An anti-American. This is your country now, Antoine. We're allies with France, but your number one concern will always be America."

"Okay." he said. "France was great, but after spending some time here, I like it. It feels like my home."

"Very good Antoine." he said. "You're a smart guy. You should be able to figure out who the bad guy is just by talking with them for a few minutes. Once you know, eliminate them. After you do that, depart the room immediately. I have confidence that you'll be able to tell right away. Ms. James will take you there."

He nodded at the nurse.

"Right this way, Mr. Stryker." she said.

She held out her hand towards the door and nodded. He walked in and closed the door.

"They got you in here too, eh?" she said.

It was Vanessa. She looked great.

"Yeah, you too?" he said.

"I had a great time the other night." she said. "I'm looking forward to the next time we can get together."

"Me too." he said.

There was a guy who looked to be in his late thirties. He was looking at Antoine.

"Hey, you're the kid from the video." he said. "How did you do that?"

"That's what they're trying to figure out." he said.

“I played football growing up.” he said. “I know some people call soccer football, but to me the only football is that kind. You know? Where there’s actually physical contact.”

“American football?” he said. “I’ve seen it on TV. You know there’s plenty of physical contact in soccer.”

“I guess.” he said.

“I met your mom.” she said. “She seemed pretty cool. From France, eh?”

It was a woman who looked about his mom’s age. His mom looked a lot younger than she was. He suspected that it was the same for this woman. She looked like she was in her twenties, but actually probably in her thirties.

“Yeah.” he said. “I lived there my whole life until now.”

“Your English is great.” she said. “Someone taught you early on.”

“My mom.” he said. “My dad is American, so she thought it was important.”

“There might be a few people around here that speak Spanish, but French would be hard to find.” she said.

“Je parle français. Pas aussi bon que votre anglais, mais j’ai pouvons probablement limp à travers elle.” she said.

It was Vanessa.

“Oh, Vanessa, that’s not necessary, I can speak English.” he said.

“You two know each other?” asked the woman.

“Intimately.” said Vanessa.

“Nice.” said the man. “Do it all you can now, son, because someday it won’t be so easy.”

There were a few other people in the room talking, but none of them stood out. He knew who it was. He calmly walked over and shot Vanessa in the head, kept walking and left the room.

***

He was watching on the monitor. He was glad that a couple other people interacted with him, the others weren’t so important.

The key was that he picked the right one. Not only that, he didn’t hesitate at all. He could actually see it in his face the moment that he figured it out. Once that recognition registered, he went immediately over there and put one in her head and left the room. And it was someone he cared about. That was big.

Vanessa was expendable, obviously. She was a good Beta, but she tended to say too much at inappropriate times. More than once, she said things that could have put other agents in jeopardy. You didn't get second chances in this line of work. And it was good practice for Antoine.

"Let's bring him in here for a moment." he said. "There are other things we should try to figure out before his father gets here. If he sees that we're poking and prodding, the outcome could be unpredictable. Best to have as much of it over with as possible before Erik sees him."

Nurse James corralled him back towards the examination room.

It would be interesting to hear him try to explain why he thought it was Vanessa. He knew it was her because they programmed him to pick her. He would be certain that he picked the right one, but may have a hard time explaining why.

"Antoine!" he said. "Very good. How did you know it was Vanessa?"

He looked confused for a moment, then confident again.

"It was the way she was acting." he said. "Like she was trying too hard. I could see that underneath she was nervous. Everyone else was acting natural, but Vanessa...I knew it was her."

"You really are smart, Antoine." he said. "It might have taken others hours to figure it out, but you knew within minutes."

"She was the one who told me." he said. "She practically screamed it."

"How did you feel about what you had to do to her?" he asked.

"I knew what I had to do for my country." he said. "America is my priority. We had some fun together, but that doesn't give her a pass. I had to do what I did."

"Of course you did." he said. "I'm very proud of you. Can you do something for me?"

"Sure, what?" he asked.
"Bend this spoon?" he said.
He handed him a spoon. Antoine looked at it. It looked like an ordinary spoon.
"Sure." he said.
He started bending it with his hands.
"No, Antoine." he said. "Give me the spoon."
He handed it over. Dr. Heisenberg placed it on the table.
"I want you to bend it without touching it." he said.
"I don't understand." he said.
"I think you do, Antoine." he said. "Something tells me that it would be nothing for you to bend that spoon with your mind. Like when you brought the soccer ball to you. Go on."
He was right, it wouldn't take much. Something that simple wouldn't even phase him. He hadn't used his...abilities since he'd been here.
He tried so hard when he was in that horrible place. Nothing worked there. He wasn't sure if he could even still do it. He looked at the spoon and closed his eyes. So this is what it comes to? You want me to perform magic tricks? He opened his eyes and gazed at the spoon. It slowly started vibrating on the table. He levitated it with his mind, and it started to stretch. It was 3 times its original length, and was starting to bend. It looped around itself, and started to tie itself into a bow. Once it was finished, he lifted it about an inch towards Dr. Heisenberg, and slowly lowered it onto the table in front of him.
"How's that?" he asked.
"Spectacular." he said. "Do you know how you did that?"
"You're the doctor, you tell me." he said.
"I can only guess it's your father's genes." he said. "We've been watching you for years, Antoine. We thought it might be possible that you would possess these abilities, but we weren't sure. Then we saw the tape of the soccer game. How long have you been able to do this, son?"
"I don't know." he said. "Maybe my whole life. I only noticed it in the last few years. There have always been things I can't explain. Whenever I do it on purpose...like I did in that game, I try to make it more believable. I didn't have any choice in that game though, you see a tie would have done us no good. We needed a win to make the playoffs."

"Well, I'm glad you did, Antoine." he said. "When we saw the tape, we knew we were dealing with something special. Your father will be here soon. He's on his way back from Ireland."

"When will he be here?" he asked.

"Soon." he said. "He needs to come in for a few tests before he can see you, but we'll go as quickly as we can."

***

"So what happened last night..." she said.

"I don't remember anything." he said. "I just remember waking up and taking you to the hospital."

"Fine, we don't have to talk about it." she said. "Do you wish we hadn't?"

"I only wish *I* hadn't." he said. "I didn't want to shame her memory that way. Why didn't I have the decency to stop?"

"It was emotional for both of us." she said. "I hadn't seen you in a month, and all I wanted was to get you back. To find a way to make up for all of my bad behavior."

"And you thought sleeping with me the day after *she* was killed was the way to do that?" he asked. "If you only knew the guilt I'm feeling right now. If only I could have held off."

"But you couldn't." she said. "I don't find any fault with you for that. *We were together for more than 15 years*. It's natural for you to want to connect again after your loss. At least it was *me*, and not some one night stand."

"I'll pretend I didn't hear that." he said.

"You know what I mean." she said. "You needed to be comforted. I was there for you as always. If you think about it, it was probably going to happen eventually anyway. You didn't shame her memory. You did exactly what she probably would have expected."

Maybe she was right. *But it was only a little more than a day!*

He should have known he was doomed when they got back to his room and started watching that movie. Taylor was making a good point here and there too. She was thinking a little like a dude.

"So where do we go from here?" he asked.

"I hope you're willing to give us another try." she said. "There's nothing to lose."

"Let's play it by ear." he said. "You caught me at a weak time, I'm not sure there's going to be a second act."

"I understand." she said. "You know you're not the only one who feels guilty. I'm not exactly proud of myself."

"We'll figure it out." he said. "I'm not making you the bad guy, if anyone is, it's me."

"I don't see it that way." she said. "We were two people who needed something, and we helped each other. And I for one had a great time."

"So did I." he said. "That was never our problem. Where do you want to go? When we get back? I promised Anthony that I would let his spooks look at me, but what about after?"

"Do you want to be with me?" she asked.

"Does it have to be like that?" he asked. "Whatever happens, I think I want you around. Whether that means we're together or not, who knows? I just don't want to lose you."

"You won't lose me." she said. "I want to have you around too...whatever happens. I guess we can't go back home, can we?"

"Nope. I'm dead." he said. "That still pisses me off. It's mostly Murphy's boss. He doesn't want me in the club anymore."

"What do you think?" she said.

"It would probably have to be on a coast wherever it is." he said. "You know? The merchants?"

"Right." she said.

"California would be okay." she said.

He started shaking his head.

"The only way I would agree to that is if we were in the north." he said. "Northern Cali has too much overlap with the Centurions. I'm not too thrilled about the east coast either. Maybe somewhere down south."

"Maybe." she said.

The seatbelt light came on. She pulled up the shade and looked out the window. There was New York Harbor with the Statue of Liberty.

"We'll be landing soon." she said. "Murphy's meeting us at the gate?"

"Unfortunately." he said. "With everything that's happened, he's the last person I want to see."

"Why?" she asked. "Maybe you could get some answers."

"You have a lot to learn, Whitman." he said. "The only thing he'll give up is something he might *want* me to know, so I can do something for him. Or maybe he'll tell me everything I want to know, only to erase the conversation. I really wish I hadn't agreed to come in and see the spooks."

"Yeah, but it was the only way." she said. "If you're lost at sea, you can come back. See your family."

"I know. I'm going to try to find a way to see the club too." he said.

"You know that won't go well for you." she said. "You need to let those guys go. Start over."

Now she was sounding like the old Taylor. He wondered how long that was going to take.

"Do what you want." she said. "I'm not trying to tell you what to do. No good came of that before. But we both know what you're up against."

"Are you sure?" he asked. "You're not trying to influence me, make me do what you want? Because that's not going to work. It never did. If you want a chance, that's how it has to be. I might want to give this thing a try, but not with *that* Taylor."

"That's the last you'll hear from her." she said. "I don't know what I was thinking. I've changed. I don't want to change you. I'm onboard with whatever you want to do."

"Okay." he said. "Let's just go one step at a time. I've been through a lot in the last few days."

"You certainly have." she said. "I only want to help you get through this."

"That might mean staying out of the way." he said. "I really haven't had any time to think about her. Not the way I should. Everything just happened so fast. I don't even know what I'm doing here with you. It's the last thing I would have expected."

"I know." she said. "But you remember those dreams, don't you? I was always saying she would be gone, and I would be back. There's probably something to that."

He hadn't thought about that, but she was right.

"What in the fuck is up with me?" he asked. "This is too weird. You're right, of course. I don't know if I like this or not. Does anyone really want to know the future?"

"We'll figure it out, baby." she said. "Everything is going to be fine."

They landed, and Anthony was there waiting for them at the gate. A woman who looked nervous was with him. Maybe an intern, he thought.

"How was your flight?" he asked.

"Long." he said. "What's the word from Belfast?"

"They're still calling it an inside job, even though the guys they're blaming it on were dead before Gallagher got it." he said. "I guess the theory is that someone on the inside eliminated Kelly and Bailey. The only problem is that there was no one left on the inside after the explosion. You did a good job. All of you. What was up with the waitress?"

"She was waiting for us when we left the hospital. Probably overheard us talking the night before. Big IRA supporter. I'm sure you know about the gun." he said. "So the job won't be traced back to anyone back here? The club?"

"I don't think they have any idea who did it." he said. "That works for us, the club, everybody. Now there's a danger out there that they don't know about, and apparently no way to stop it. That's just where we wanted them."

"Well, at least one thing went right." he said.

"I'm having your luggage sent to your apartment. It's only temporary while we're here." he said. "Two bedrooms...should that be required. We'll figure out something more permanent after the doctors check you out."

He knows. How could he? We literally just stepped off the plane. Does he just assume that I would just automatically sleep with her? *Well, if he does, he's right. Couldn't even wait two days.*

"Okay." he said.

"Taylor, you'll be riding back with Ms. Adams so she can debrief you." he said. "It'll give me and Erik a chance to catch up."

"We're going to the same place, right?" she asked.

"Of course." he said. "There are just a few things Erik and I need to talk about. And you need to be debriefed."

"Okay." she said.

They were at the curb, and there were two identical Limousines waiting for them.

"We're in this one." said Ms. Adams.

She guided Taylor towards the door. She looked back at Erik nervously.

"It'll be fine, babe, just go with her." he said. "I'll see you in a little while."

"Okay." she said.

She looked back at him one more time.

"Really, you'll be fine." he said. "I just need to talk to him. Call it a debriefing. I'll see you in a little while."

"Okay." she said.

She got in the limo and he got in his.

"First of all, I just want to express my condolences once again." he said. "We both loved her. She was a wonderful person. Not too many knew her like you and I."

"Leland Andersen." he said. "Is he the one who did this?"

"Getting straight to business, I like that." he said. "And you bring up the first thing on my list. We just need to get one thing out of the way first. Listen carefully. The Blue Queen loves Knights and Knaves. The only man she won't sleep with is the King. Now Erik, I need to know where you heard that name. Leland Andersen."

"I heard it in a dream, Mr. Murphy." he said. "That young kid told me."

"Good." he said. "Based on the latest developments with you, nobody knows if this is going to work, but we need to try. From this moment forward, you won't remember anything about Leland Andersen. Is that understood?"

"Yes, Mr. Murphy." he said.

"My apologies, we've sent you on a bit of a ride here lately, Mr. Stryker." he said. "The drinking. As an experiment, we programmed you to get violent when you drank. We figured...correctly, I might add, that you would put it together and stop. We wanted to see how you would behave if you weren't drinking. As far as we could tell, it had no effect until you started having these dreams. Then when Antoine accidentally showed us what he could do, we knew we were getting somewhere. That thing at 'The Blackout Saloon' was a bit unfortunate. You see redheads are a trigger for you. Remember Emily in Reno? And what you did to Ross Goodwin that night? It wouldn't have mattered if Brenda's boyfriend attacked you that night or not. Just that short association with a redhead, combined with how much you were drinking was enough. Someone was going to die. I'll be the first to say that Jimmy deserved it. He should have remembered how Brenda was, and he should have seen the signs in you. But that's all over now. Can I assume that you slept with Taylor?"

"Yes, Mr. Murphy." he said.

He thought about telling him that he did the same thing a few times while he had her under. He couldn't trust Stryker though. He had a bad habit of remembering things he wasn't supposed to, like this conversation.

He only hoped that information about what he did to Taylor wouldn't make it to him in a dream. He was confident that Taylor didn't know anything about it. Even if he did get the information from a dream, there would be no way to prove it. If he asked Taylor, she wouldn't remember.

"Do you have any plans to get back together with her?" he asked.

"Yes, Mr. Murphy." he said.

"What about Lexie?" he asked.

"Yes, Mr. Murphy." he said.

Good, we're stuck on a loop. This happened sometimes when they were under for too long. With Erik's personality, it usually didn't take much. Something inside him rebelled, and most answers were useless after a minute or two. He went a little long with the story about 'The Blackout Saloon' too. If you talk too much, it can cause them to zone out.

"Okay, Erik. This is the important part." he said. "You will not remember this conversation. For you, we just had a pleasant talk on the way back to Princeton. I release you now."

"Yeah, nobody really knew her like us." he said. "She loved you too. It was strange, I never heard a shot."

"Well, it was probably drowned out by the blast." he said. "She's back home now, buried with her parents."

"Where are we going?" he asked.

"Princeton, New Jersey." he said. "That's where the institute is now. It's a state of the art facility. They've made a lot of advances since they've seen you."

"I'll let them have a look at me, but that's going to be it." he said. "Just a quick in and out."

"That's all I'm asking for." he said. "They want to figure out what's going on with these dreams."

"I can't figure out if I like them or not." he said. "It's nice to have inside information, but there are plenty of things I don't want to know...like Tay...just things are sometimes better if you don't know them I guess."

"They'll figure all of that out." he said. "God knows I don't know anything about it."

"They think this has something to do with that?" he said. "The camp all those years ago?"

"I think a lot of things in your life are tied to that." he said.

Like virtually everything. We control every almost every aspect of your life.

"So how did things go with Taylor?" he asked. "I'm really sorry to do that to you, but it was the only way. She was next in line."

"I can't believe you actually recruited her." he said. "I've known a lot of people, and she is by far the nicest. I would be willing to bet that she's never even had a bad thought....well she probably has, everyone has. But you took a sweetheart and turned her into a killer."

"Believe it or not, Erik, She was far more willing than you might think." he said. "From the time she tried to put you in motion, I knew. She was very receptive. She looked forward to her first experience in the field."

"But she didn't know what she was getting into, and you know it." he said. "She's not one of us."

"She is now." he said. "I'm sure you thought you knew Lexie too. There were some things about her that I think would surprise you."

"Like what?" he asked.

"I'm not going to sully her name when she's not around to defend herself." he said. "If it makes any difference, everything she did in the end was for you. She really loved you."

"For whatever reason, she loved you too." he said. "Sure she bitched, but she couldn't hide her true feelings. In many ways, you were a surrogate parent to her. She lost them so young. She had to look after herself from an early age. You helped with that. Not that a parent would ever blackmail her to get her to cooperate. And in the end, you told them anyway."

There's the old Erik, he thought. Everyone's favorite crusader.

"Nobody knows how the Israelis found out about Mel Singer." he said.

"You forgetting who you're talking to?" he asked. "I know you did it, and so did she. Neither of us could figure out the why."

"I have to make tough decisions every day." he said. "I didn't do this, but no one would fault me if I did. She was in a downward spiral in the desert. You were just what she needed."

He hoped that this was believable, but Erik had an annoying habit of knowing when he was lying.

"You can keep this up if you like, but we both know the truth." he said. "The only thing there that I agree with is that she was better off in Bremerton than the desert."

Let's change the subject. Can I put you under again?

"So anything going on with Taylor?" he asked. "I know it was strange, her turning up at your door in Belfast."

"Yeah. And do you remember the part about it happening the day after Lexie was killed?" he said. "I guess it could be said that after what happened to Lexie, Taylor showing up could have been what I needed as strange as that sounds."

He was pretty sure it was, but it was nice to hear it from Erik. From the time he recruited Taylor, he had planned for this eventuality.

He didn't want Lexie to die, but he knew she was in danger. Probably since she left Israel. He had to plan for her death, as morbid as that was. Taylor was a good solution. Erik was always a little more pliable when he had a woman around. Not that he was ever easy to work with. Having Taylor around would take that edge right off...or maybe Danielle. He needed to decide on that soon. There was a good reason to give him back to Danielle. He could virtually make him do whatever he wanted, and more importantly, he would think it was his own decision.

"People like us, Erik, sometimes do things differently than the average person." he said. "It may seem a little crass to most, but we understand better than anyone that life has to go on."

"Don't do that." he said. "Lump yourself in with me. You wouldn't last a day. But you're right, life must go on."

They were pulling into the apartment complex.

"I need to ask you one more thing before I let you go, Erik." he said. "Have you ever heard the name Leland Andersen?"

"No, should I have?" he asked. "Is it from one of my dreams?"

"It's nothing." he said. "They'll figure out what's going on with your dreams at the institute."

He had thought quite a bit about his dreams. There really was something to that. Maybe he really *did belong with* Taylor. There was no denying that the dreams were coming true. Could she be the one he was supposed to be with all along?

They got to the apartment, and somehow their luggage was already there. It looked like a decent place, even if it was temporary. Erik was almost sure that neither of them wanted to live in Princeton, New Jersey. He knew he didn't.

"I'll let you two settle in." he said. "First thing tomorrow, Erik. I'll be here at 8 am."

"Okay." he said.

"So what did you and him talk about?" she asked.

"Just the mission. Lexie. You. The usual stuff." he said.

"I'm the usual stuff?" she asked.

"You are now." he said. "I always get the feeling that he's fucking with me. Like he knows everything, and I'm clueless."

"I think everyone feels that way with him." she said. "It's his personality. I was worried that he was going to take you off somewhere else and leave me alone."

"I could see that. You were nervous." he said. "He'll do a lot of things, but there are things he won't do. Abandoning you is one of those things he won't do. He would probably kill you first."

"That's comforting." she said.

"Your comfort will never be his concern." he said. "His concern is getting the most he can out of you until you're no longer useful."

Lexie became more of a problem than she was worth, so she was killed. Not by Murphy, he was sure of that, but there was someone else...why couldn't he remember?

"What does that mean?" she asked.

"It means that as long as you serve a purpose, he'll look out for you." he said. "It's not really him that you need to worry about, it's...I don't know. Why don't I know?"

Neither of them knew it, Ms. Adams made sure that Taylor forgot all about Leland Andersen too.

"It's been a long day." she said. "I'm sure it will come back to you. It looks like there's a VHS player here, and some movies. Maybe we can have another movie night."

"That sounds good." he said. "There's something I need to tell you."

"Anything, babe." she said.

"I've thought a lot about this." he said. "There's obviously something to these dreams. I think it's possible that we really are supposed to be together. Maybe forever. I haven't had a chance to get to the jeweler yet but...what the hell am I doing? What...?"

"Keep going! You were doing great!" she said. "What is it?"

"I think I went a little too far." he said. "The dreams. I think maybe we should give it a try."

"I would love to try again." she said.

He sounded like he was about to ask her to marry him. As much as she wanted to make a big deal of it, she knew it would be best if she didn't.

"Great. I love you, baby." he said.

He went over and took her in his arms. She held him as tight as she could.

"I love you too." she said. "Always."

They watched "The Godfather". It was a movie that they had both seen, but it was obviously it was worth watching again. Taylor picked it out. She was careful not to pick a romantic comedy. About halfway through there was a knock at the door.

"Who could that be?" she asked. "No one even knows we're here."

He got up and went to the door. He opened it and couldn't believe his eyes. It was her. She still looked the same after all these years. A little older, but then they both were. She still looked like she was in her twenties.

"Hello." she said. "Is it really you?"

"Hi...it's really me. Is it really you?" he said. "This must be my next surprise."

"Next surprise?" she asked.

"Yeah, no, the first one was Tayl...never mind." he said. "Anthony said I could expect a surprise. If you're not it, I can't imagine what it could be."

"Who is it, baby?" asked Taylor.

"Won't you come in?" he said.

She came in and they went to the living room.

"Danielle, this is my girlfriend Taylor." he said. "Taylor, this is Danielle."

Chapter 26

"I guess this must be your next surprise." she said. "I think we can both say you're completely unexpected, Danielle."

She was going to get through this without getting nasty. Those fucking dreams, she *knew* this was coming. The kid comes next. To top it all off, she's beautiful. And that fucking French accent!

"I honestly never expected to see Erik again." she said. "We have a mutual friend who's been keeping us apart. It's been so long, I thought it was never going to happen. I heard about Lexie, I'm sorry for your loss, Erik."

You didn't wait too long to bounce back, she thought. It was probably Murphy's plan all along, anybody but me.

"Thank you." he said. "How long have you been in the states?"

"Not long." she said.

"How did you hear about Lexie?" asked Taylor.

"Our mutual friend." she said.

"Murphy." she said.

"You know about him?" she asked.

"Better than I used to." she said. "I recently started working for him. Erik and I were together in Belfast. After Lexie was killed."

"I see." she said. "You seem like a nice person. A little friendly advice. Be careful with Anthony. He's a snake. Don't trust anything he says."

"I knew about him before I started working for him." she said. "Can we assume you're still working for him?"

"Yes." she said. "I'm sure in a much more limited capacity than the two of you. There's something else I need to tell you, Erik."

Here it comes, she thought. The fucking kid.

"Okay." he said.

He still couldn't believe she was here. Whatever this is, it has to be advancing Murphy's agenda somehow.

"Maybe I should tell you in private." she said.

"Whatever it is, Taylor can hear it." he said. "We don't keep secrets."

"Okay." she said. "It's probably more of a surprise than seeing me. I've been wanting to tell you this for years...you have a son."

"Excuse me?" he said. "Did you just say I have a son?"

"It's true." she said. "His name is Antoine. He's fifteen. Almost sixteen. He's the reason we're here."

"Why didn't you tell me?" he asked.

"It's...complicated." she said. "Anthony stopped me. There's something in my past that...well, something that I couldn't let get out. He's been holding it over my head for years. You have to know I wanted to tell you. I tried a thousand times. I was there that night at the cottage in Monte Carlo. When you killed DuBois. I ran away because of what Anthony has on me. I went there in hopes of seeing you, then when I did, I ran away. But I wanted to stay, I wanted to see you, to talk to you, tell you about Antoine. When I called you a week later, I wanted to tell you then. I've wanted to see you ever since you left me. I'm almost constantly in trouble with Murphy. I have to be very careful."

"That time you called." he said. "Taylor answered the phone. Why didn't you tell me then?"

"I couldn't. I've always wanted you to know, but he's been preventing it. He doesn't see a boy with no father, he sees a distracted agent." she said. "Of course I wasn't supposed to call you either. But after seeing you...I wanted you to know. I've wanted you to know all along."

"So why are you here? In the states?" he asked. "What does it have to do with my son?"

"Antoine has developed...abilities. Supernatural abilities." she said. "He was the only offspring from your group who survived. You know? The people you went to camp with as a teenager? They think that these abilities are the result of the experiments you went through at camp. Something about your DNA. He's at the institute now."

"How could you agree to send him *there*?" he asked. "Don't you know what they do to people there? Don't you know what they did to me? To you?"

"I didn't have a choice." she said. "He told me that either we could come willingly, or it could go the other way. I thought it would be less traumatic for Antoine if he wasn't forced to go. You know as well as I do that he would have done whatever it took to get him in there. There are a lot of ugly ways it could have happened. I thought if we went willingly, it would seem better. And I was right. He's doing great."

"What did he do to make them take notice?" he asked.

"He plays soccer." she said. "He's really good. There was a game where he made the ball come to him when it was going in the other direction. I've been noticing strange things for years with him, but I kept it to myself. When Anthony got a hold of a tape of the game, it was over. We were on the next flight here."

There's no way I'm telling him that I'm the one who told him about what happened with Antoine in the first place. This is already going shitty enough.

"Wow. So I have a son." he said.

It was a lot to take in. Now his son, who he didn't even know about, was at the institute. He could only imagine what they were putting him through. He would see this kid before he let them do anything to him.

"What's your secret?" he asked. "The thing he has on you?"

"I can never tell you that, Erik." she said. "Especially after all I've been through trying to keep it from getting out. You can't know."

"It's the only way to take the power back." he said. "Lexie's secret got out, and after it did she never felt more free. There's nothing you can say to make me think less of you."

"Mine is more personal than killing a comrade over a man." she said. "You may as well stop trying. I'm not giving it up."

How did she know about Mel Singer's death? What else did she know?

"How long have you been working for Murphy?" asked Taylor.

"Longer than Erik. You could say our meeting wasn't by mistake. They had their eye on him since the MK camp. And they wanted us to make a baby." she said.

"And of course, that's what happened." she said.

"I should really go. I'm interrupting. Antoine is at the institute." she said. "He would love to see you. Sorry to blow up your night and walk away like this."

We'll clean up the mess, just walk away, thought Taylor. You've caused enough damage for one night.

"This isn't over." he said. "We have a lot to sort out."

"Yes." she said.

She looked at his keys on the coffee table.

"You still have it." she said. "The cameo."

"I've been holding onto that for a long time." he said. "It's all I have left of you."

"Not anymore." she said.

She looked at Taylor.

"I'm not a threat." she said. "But we *do* have a child together. So we'll always have that connection. I'll stay out of the way as much as possible."

"Thank you." she said.

"We'll talk again tomorrow." he said.

He walked her to the door.

He came back into the living room and she was crying. She tried to hide it, but he could tell. Or maybe she was pretending to try to hide it, who knows?

"It's okay, baby." he said. "Things just got a little more complicated. Do you remember how I introduced you? I said you were my girlfriend."

She started shaking her head violently.

"That doesn't matter. You have a kid with her." she said. "How am I supposed to compete with that? The kid changes everything."

"It changes a lot of things for me...for us." he said. "I have a kid. He's already a teenager. Probably the one from my dreams."

Really? You're just putting that together now? I figured it out the first time you told me about it. I'm sure Lexie did too.

"I don't want to hold you back." she said. "Go be with her. Go be with your son. I guess we weren't meant to be."

"You're talking crazy." he said. "Do you remember what we talked about earlier? Getting back together? Hell, I almost went all the way. You know what I'm talking about. Does it sound like I'm trying to leave you?"

"No." she said. "But now she has everything. And I have nothing."

"You have me." he said. "And she doesn't. Does anything else matter?"

"She's gorgeous." she said. "And she has your kid. What do I have?"

"Snap out of it, Whitman! You were a model. Doing bikini shoots on the French Riviera. What? Is she Miss Soccer Mom? Does she get a tiara for that? As far as Antoine goes, I want him to be a big part of your life too." he said. "It'll be great! I've always said if I have a kid, it would be better after the potty training and so forth are over. I can get him a motorcycle. We can go riding together."

"I guess." she said. "Do you really want me to be a part of his life? Wouldn't I be like a 3rd wheel?"

"We'll get you a bike too." he said. "If I'm a part of his life, you'll be a part of his life."

"Okay." she said. "You're not going back to her?"

"I'll tell you like I told Lexie. That part of my life was over a long time ago." he said. "It was a shock to see her, and yeah, it was interesting, but I'm with you."

"What about the cameo?" she asked. "You've held onto it for so long, and now the real person is here. How you going to deal with that?"

"I'll always have a connection to her. She was my first real love." he said. "But I've had many other loves since then, including you. I'm keeping the cameo, sorry. I've been carrying it around for most of my adult life. You'll have to find a way to deal with that."

"Maybe you should think about this." she said. "I know you're trying to tell me what I want to hear, but this is serious. You have a kid."

She was right. But he would be have to be insane to let her know he thought so too. There was nothing he could say right now that would be acceptable except that he wanted to be with her.

It didn't matter that Danielle looked great, and he was very interested in reconnecting with her, he was on dangerous ground. He had to ride this out with Taylor before he figured out what he was going to do.

It was shitty timing that he had just told her that he wanted to get back together, but how was he to know that Danielle was going to show up at his door?

"My plans for the future include you." he said. "I wasn't expecting this either. How could I? How could you? We? It would have been nice if Anthony gave us a little warning."

"That's not his style." she said. "The only thing that would make this better for him is if he could see us now. Even though he can't, I'm sure he's laughing his head off."

"He's not that sadistic." he said. "This has always been a job for him. It allows him to occasionally play God and mess with people's lives, I won't deny that's part of what he likes about it. But he's been there for me...and Lexie, against some dangerous people. Who knows why he didn't tell us she was coming? He's kept Antoine a secret for years. There must be a reason that it's okay for me to know now."

"Who knows?" she said. "Still, I'm letting you off the hook. You don't have to honor any promises you made to me. You should think about this, and figure out what's best for you...and Antoine. I may not like it, but I'm not going to stand in the way."

He could try to pacify her again, but there would be no point. There was no good comeback to what she was saying. Especially if he eventually went the other way. If he got back together with Danielle, she would have to tell him what Murphy has on her. He really wondered what could be so bad. She had never been anything but a sweetheart. Nicer than Taylor, even.

"This isn't something we need to worry about right now." he said. "Tomorrow we'll meet Antoine. I'm sure Danielle will be reasonable about this."

Not something we need to worry about now? If not now, when? She knew he was still trying to tell her what she wanted to hear. Hell, it was worse than that. He was trying to soften the blow. Talking about how reasonable she'll be.

"Okay." she said. "Shall we finish the movie?"

"Sure." he said.

Epilogue
Santa Cruz, California 1999

He was on his bike on the P.C.H. down near Monterey. He had been seeing a girl down there, Emma, and it was getting a little serious. He wasn't down there to see her that day; he was just enjoying the freedom. He wasn't wearing a helmet, and the wind blew freely through his hair.

It seemed to him that he had a girlfriend in France, but he couldn't remember. It was strange; after he was in the institute he remembered literally everything. It was like there was an elaborate filing system and he could pull up information from his memory instantly...as long as it happened after he went to the institute. Things before that were a little fuzzy. He knew he was from France, but he didn't remember ever being there. He still understood French, but he didn't remember learning it. He didn't remember learning English either for that matter.

He started heading back north. He would call Emma later.

The institute had been paying him...very well, to fill out surveys. The questions were strange. They told him that these were psychological surveys to help them with other candidates. He didn't care either way. At $1000 per survey, he would fill out just about anything. Life was good. His mother and him had a beautiful house, with a private beach on the Pacific Ocean. His father was there too; they had gotten back together about a year and a half ago. They both seemed happy, and he loved his dad. He knew it was probably time for him to get his own place, but the arrangement here was pretty good.

He pulled into the driveway and cut the motor. There was another bike there, a little bigger than his. It was a '97 Harley Davidson Road King. His Dad's bike. He had a '97 Harley Sportster 883. He wanted the 1200, but his mom vetoed that idea. She thought it was too big for him, even though he was almost as big as his dad now.

He walked inside.

"Hey, there he is." said Erik. "You down with Emma?"

"No, just out for a ride, dad." he said. "Beautiful day."

"It sure is." he said. "I'm shipping out in a couple of weeks."

"Where to this time?" he asked.

"Officially Asia." he said. "But probably Europe. I'm making that trip up north before I go."

"Are you sure about that, babe?" she said. "You know who isn't going to like that."

"What he doesn't know won't hurt him." he said. "It's been two years. Don't worry, I'll be careful."

"Famous last words." she said. "Why don't you take Antoine with you?"

He looked at him.

"Yeah, no, I don't think so, dad." he said. "I have too much going on here."

"Probably better off anyway." he said. "In the remote possibility that someone knows."

"Do you have to?" asked Danielle. "If he finds out, it can be unpredictable what will happen."

"No one's going to know." he said. "It's not like I'm staying up there. I just want to reconnect."

He knew who they were talking about. Uncle Anthony. Or Murphy as they sometimes called him. Anthony had been in communication with him a lot more lately. He had always said that he would work for him someday. Lately, he had been saying that the time would be soon. He was old enough now. His mother and father had been working for him for years. From what he could tell, they made pretty good money too. He couldn't figure out why he didn't want his dad to go visit his friends.

"For the record, I'm against it." she said. "There's no reason to tempt fate."

"I'll be fine." he said. "You're paranoid. Besides, I can get away with a lot more than you can."

"Sure, golden boy." she said. "Your father and I represent the top and the bottom rungs of Anthony's ladder, Antoine. A word of advice. Be more like your father."

"That shouldn't be too difficult." he said. "He's already there."

She looked at them. They looked like a pair of twins but one was older than the other. It was the best way to describe it. He got virtually zero from me as far as the looks go. Erik's genes rolled over hers and molded that boy in his image. Not that she minded.

She was still amazed that this was how it all worked out. She was sure that he was going to stay with Taylor. He tried. He fought it with everything he had. In the end he couldn't deny it. His destiny was with her.

He told her that his wish from the Trevi Fountain came true. Then they moved out here, and things couldn't be better. Antoine had his dad now, she had Erik, and they were happy. He was a little worried about Northern Cali, because of the proximity to the club, but in the end he couldn't think of anywhere he'd rather be. Neither could she.

"I'm going to call Emma, I think we're going to see a movie tonight." he said.

"Don't do anything I wouldn't do." he said. "Leaves you..."

"Yeah, it leaves me open to almost anything." he said. "Never gets old, does it, dad?"

"I guess maybe it just did." he said.

"I'll be in my room." he said.

"Dinner in a half hour." said Danielle.

"Okay, ma." he said.

He went in his room and closed the door.

He dialed the number.

"Hello?" he said.

"He's making the trip north." he said. "Tomorrow. He'll probably leave here around 10 or 11."

"Thanks." he said. "You're sure?"

"Yeah." he said. "He said he's shipping out in a couple of weeks too. Can I assume that's for you?"

"Yeah." he said. "I appreciate you doing this Antoine. It's really in your father's best interest. Now that I know what he's doing, I can protect him. You'll learn more about that when you're older."

"Well, you asked me to keep my ears open, and that's what I heard." he said.

"You did good, kid." he said. "I need to make a few calls. I'll be in touch."

The line went dead.

He really didn't think he was doing anything wrong. It was Uncle Anthony after all. He called Emma.

***

He took the P.C.H. until he got to San Francisco. The 5 was arguably faster, but it was California after all, and that almost always meant traffic. The Pacific Coast Highway was also beautiful. It was a pleasant ride no matter what the circumstances.

He would head east to the 5 after he got to San Francisco and take it all the way to Seattle. The traffic was relatively light through Oregon, but started to get a little thicker when he got close to Seattle.

He almost got off on the 101 to Bremerton out of force of habit. He wondered how things were there. He had heard that Taylor moved back there.

He pulled into the lot, and there was only one bike. It was a little newer than the ones most bikers had. He walked up and tried the door.

It opened and he went inside.

"Hello?" he said.

He heard footsteps. Johnny appeared from the back.

"You shouldn't have come here, Erik." he said. "You're dead."

"Where is everyone?" he asked.

"I made sure we would have the place to ourselves." he said. "Your buddy Murphy is a complicated guy."

"You talked to him?" he asked.

"Been talking to him for a long time." he said. "For what it's worth, you passed all the tests. No matter how I pressed you for classified information you shut me out."

"Why?" he asked. "Does he have something on you?"

"Just the money." he said. "Billy Morgan was a grade school buddy of mine. Murphy told me the devil was in the details. A good back story works wonders, and he was right. You ate that shit up. So I didn't get sober for some poor kid I hit with my bike. I didn't get sober at all."

"So that was an act?" he asked.

"Where you're concerned, quite a bit has been an act, my friend." he said. "Didn't you think I went a little overboard with those guns? Have you ever seen me so passionate about anything? I just carried my guys to make sure it seemed close. Murphy never wanted the deal to go through, and neither did I."

"So what now?" he asked.

"I need you to listen to me very carefully now, Erik." he said. "The Blue Queen loves Knights and Knaves. The only man she won't sleep with is the King. Now Erik, I need you to do some things for me. First, you need to get rid of any club ink. You're not a Centurion anymore. Murphy has a guy for that, it will be like you never had them. I need the cut too. When you leave here, go to the place you used to live. Wait there for 30 minutes. Don't go inside, wait outside on your bike. After that, you'll go back to Santa Cruz. When you get home, you won't remember any of this. Do you understand?"

"Yes, John." he said.

He took off the cut and gave it to him.

"Repeat it back to me." he said.

"I'll have my club ink removed. I'm not a Centurion anymore. Then I'll go to Spyglass Hill and wait there for 30 minutes. I won't go in, I'll wait on my bike." he said. "Then I'll go home, and I won't remember any of this."

"Very good, Erik." he said. "One more thing. You can never come back here again."

"I can never come back here again." he said.

"Good. You should head over to Spyglass Hill now." he said.

"I'll go to Spyglass Hill now." he said.

Erik left, and John went to the phone.

"He's on his way to Bremerton." he said.

"Good." he said. "Wait there. I'll bring your final installment by 5 pm. You're not expecting anyone else to show up, are you?"

"No, nobody will try to come here until tomorrow." he said. "I made sure that the place will be empty all day. Everyone knows."

"Good, I'll see you in a while." he said.

The line went dead.

When He got to Spyglass Hill, he started to go up to the apartment. Then he remembered that he was to wait outside. He got back on his bike and waited.

***

She was about 300 yards away, high in a building across the street, aiming her .338 Lapua Magnum Sniper rifle at him. The crosshairs perfectly split with his forehead.

This alter was unexpected. Discovered by accident really. She had found a friend in training, and she wanted to come out to the range with her. Her friend asked her if she wanted to give it a try. She agreed, and proceeded to match the course record. The instructor was flabbergasted. He hadn't ever seen anything like it. He figured with just a little training, she would be better than him. She was truly a natural. They had decided to make this her Alpha personality. She didn't remember any of the people, places, or things from before when she occupied this alter, she was strictly business. She didn't even remember her current target, which was a testament to how good her programming was. Never mind the girl she killed in Ireland, someone else she should have known. He told the Beta alter that she killed a guy in the hospital in Paris.

She gently squeezed the trigger. A large maroon spot appeared on his forehead. He tumbled to the left but stayed on the bike for a brief moment before he fell off and hit the pavement.. She was satisfied that he was dead. She knew it before she pulled the trigger. She disassembled the weapon and put it in its case.

She looked down at the victim. He laid motionless a few feet away from the bike. She had used a silencer, so no one had heard. There was no activity on the street. She picked up the case and headed for her car. Sha paused to look at him one more time. She couldn't remember where she knew him from. She thought she knew him, but wasn't sure. Doesn't matter now, she thought. A job well done. She put the weapon in the trunk. She got in the car and sat down. She picked up the phone and dialed the number.

"Hello?" he said.

"It's done." she said.

"Good." he said. "Thank you, Taylor. I need you to go take care of the guy in Seattle we talked about."

"Okay." she said.

“After you’re done, call me.” he said.
“Yes, Mr. Murphy.” she said.
The line went dead.
She went to the trunk and pulled out a small bag. There was a red wig in there and she put it on. This one was a little more public, so there was a chance someone might see her. With what she was doing, the police would surely be looking for the culprit.
She got to the building, and the lot was empty except for one late model motorcycle. Again, this place looked familiar, but she couldn’t figure out from when. She shrugged her shoulders. She reached into her overcoat and withdrew her pistol. She went to the door and opened it. Footsteps came from the back of the building.
“I wasn’t expecting you for a while.” he said. “You made it soo…Taylor? You can’t be here. What’s with the hai…”
A red spot appeared on his forehead as he tumbled to the ground.
Hmm, this one seems to know me. He said my name. She noticed these things from time to time, but they programmed her not to investigate them any further.
She walked over and put a couple of fingers on the carotid artery on his neck. Nothing. Satisfied, she went back to the car and got a 5-gallon can of gasoline. She spread it liberally throughout the club, using a little extra on the target.
She wasn’t worried about the bullet, the gun was unregistered. She had heard that Murphy looked for these kinds of things to use as leverage against his agents. There was no way for her to know it, but he would never need such things where she was concerned. Her front alter never made mistakes.
The final bit of gasoline made a trail to the door. She tossed the can back into the club. She lit a match and dropped it in the gasoline. It quickly spread throughout the building. As she was leaving the parking lot, one of the front windows burst out from the pressure, and a big flame escaped and licked the side of the building on its way up.
She picked up the phone.
“It’s done.” she said.

"Good. Your next assignment is in Morocco." he said. "Meet me at Ivar's, I'll give you a dossier and your pay."

"Okay, Mr. Murphy." she said.

"Anthony." he said. "Call me Anthony."

"Yes, Mr. Murphy." she said.

Her alter was far too severe to ever call her handler by his first name.

The line went dead.

The phone started ringing.

"Hello?" she said.

"Uh huh." she said.

"Yes." she said.

"Okay, I'll take care of it." she said.

She got to Ivar's, and Murphy was sitting in the back. She looked at the terrace, and it was empty. It was a little cold.

"Hello, Taylor." he said. "I like you as a redhead. This is your dossier for Morocco. You'll be leaving tonight."

He handed her a large envelope.

"Yes, Mr. Murphy." she said.

He shook his head.

"You know..." he said. "Never mind. Read it over. Here's your pay. There's $200,000 there. You're getting a bonus for efficiency."

He handed her a large briefcase.

Can we go out on the terrace Anthony?" she asked.

She used my first name. Maybe I'm getting through. All those times we make love while she's under, I can never get her to do that. He said made love, but it was of course, rape. It appeared that she did it willingly, but in the end, she was just following her programming. She actually had no idea it was even happening. He had a way of blocking that part out.

"Sure, Taylor." he said. "I'm glad you feel comfortable using my first name."

She didn't feel comfortable, she needed him on that terrace and using his first name was a way of making that happen.

When they got out there, she went to the far corner near the water. There was still a small line of sight from the interior of the restaurant, but it was better than doing it inside. She doubted that anyone would notice, they were a long way away from the door.

He was leaning over the railing looking over the water. She withdrew her pistol and put one in the back of his head. He started to slump, but she caught him with one hand and lifted him over the railing and into the water. This alter, her main one, had 5 times the strength that she normally would have.

She looked back at the restaurant, and it appeared that nobody had seen her. She picked up the briefcase and the envelope and calmly walked back to the car.

As she was leaving the parking lot, she took off the wig and tossed it out the window. She picked up the phone.

"It's done." she said.

"Good." he said. "Did you get the dossier?"

"Yes, Mr. Andersen." she said.

"You're still going to Morocco." he said. "You'll leave out of Sea-Tac airport tonight at 7 pm. Your tickets will be waiting for you at the gate. Park in long term parking, and leave the weapons in the car. There will be a Lapua and a couple of handguns waiting in your room. You'll be staying at the Riad Kheirredine. You'll have a new handler, and he'll be checking in with you shortly after you arrive. His name is Mr. Nolan. The password will be Red King."

"Yes, Mr. Andersen." she said. "The password is Red King."

The line went dead.

She started heading for Sea-Tac.

Made in the USA
Monee, IL
04 November 2026

67383939R00236